THE POWER
OF THE PAST

THE POWER OF THE PAST

History and Statecraft

HAL BRANDS AND JEREMI SURI

EDITORS

BROOKINGS INSTITUTION PRESS
Washington, D.C.

The Brookings Institution is a private nonprofit organization devoted to research, education, and publication on important issues of domestic and foreign policy. Its principal purpose is to bring the highest quality independent research and analysis to bear on current and emerging policy problems. Interpretations or conclusions in Brookings publications should be understood to be solely those of the authors.

Library of Congress Cataloging-in-Publication data

The power of the past : history and statecraft / Hal Brands and Jeremi Suri, editors.
     pages   cm
  Includes index.
    ISBN 978-0-8157-2712-5 (pbk. : alk. paper) — ISBN 978-0-8157-2713-2 (e-pub) — ISBN 978-0-8157-2714-9 (pdf)   1. United States—Foreign relations—Case studies. 2. United States—History. I. Brands, Hal, 1983– II. Suri, Jeremi.
  E183.7.P685 2015
  973—dc23   2015025598

9 8 7 6 5 4 3 2 1

Typeset in Minion

Composition by Westchester Publishing Services

Contents

HAL BRANDS AND JEREMI SURI

1

Introduction: Thinking about History and Foreign Policy

During the summer and fall of 2009, the U.S. policymaking community engaged in what one observer called an "official binge of historical consciousness."[1] Amid intense debate over U.S. strategy in Afghanistan, policymakers sought insights from two books that seemed to be locked in a duel over the history of America's earlier conflict in Vietnam. White House officials skeptical of expanded intervention, including President Barack Obama, devoured Gordon M. Goldstein's *Lessons in Disaster,* a book that chronicled the folly of incremental escalation in Southeast Asia in the mid-1960s and argued implicitly against a similar approach in Afghanistan. Inside the Pentagon, however, the favored historical work was Lewis Sorley's *A Better War,* which argued that the U.S. military had developed an effective counterinsurgency strategy during the late 1960s and early 1970s, and asserted that the United States might have salvaged a favorable result in Vietnam if not for the collapse of public support and political will at home. The "moral" of Sorley's book, and one that military leaders deemed applicable to the Afghanistan debate, was that the U.S. military could master counterinsurgency if given the requisite time, backing, and resources. In 2009, as in other periods of policy transition, arguments about history were central to both sides of the debate about American national security.[2]

1

The Presence of History in Policy

Examining the course of American statecraft over the last century, one cannot escape the conclusion that history—historical knowledge, insights, lessons, analogies, and narratives—permeates the ways in which the United States interacts with the world. From World War I to the Cold War to the war on terror, American officials have frequently drawn on their perceptions and understandings of what came before as reference points in seeking to deal with the dilemmas of the here and now. They have used history to gain perspective on the world and its challenges; to impose familiarity on novel and perplexing issues; to channel the perceived verities of the past in grappling with the uncertainties of the future; or simply to frame and market their policies in an appealing fashion. Sometimes, as in the Sorley-Goldstein debate, these uses of history are explicit and deliberate; most often they are implicit, even unconscious. "Even when people think they are striking out in new directions," observes Margaret MacMillan, "their models often come from the past." Either way, history—an understanding, whether accurate or inaccurate, of the past—is omnipresent in foreign policy.[3]

This is not to say that policymakers use history as historians might like them to use it. Numerous scholars have noted that policymakers are often selective, uncritical, one-dimensional, and biased in their thinking about the past. Facile historical analogies litter the documentary record of U.S. foreign policy; misrepresentations, misunderstandings, and oversimplifications of the past are legion. Indeed, some of the most frequently used historical reference points for U.S. foreign policy—the Munich analogy, for instance—tend to obscure more than they clarify.[4] And for every case in which policymakers seem genuinely interested in learning from history, there is another in which history appears to be used more as an ex post facto justification for a policy already decided upon.[5] It is small wonder that even as historians encourage policymakers to use history in official deliberations, they often cringe when it is actually done. History and policy have an intimate, but frequently dysfunctional, relationship.

The purpose of this book is to work toward a more fruitful interaction between the production of historical knowledge and the making of U.S. foreign policy. The volume aims to explore the dynamics and intricacies of that relationship and to offer insights on how the study of the past can more usefully serve the present. The chapters in this book bring together a distinguished group of thinkers: historians and policymakers who have long grappled with these issues in their research and professional endeavors. In the essays that follow, the contributors explore a series of interrelated questions: How and why do policymakers use history? How has policy benefited or suffered as a result? What are the potential avenues for using history more successfully, and what light can history shine on the dilemmas confronted by contemporary policymakers? How can scholars and policymakers improve the relationship between knowledge and practice? What are the limits of historical utility for policymaking? As a whole, this volume aims to shed light on the complex nexus of history and policy, and to engage policymakers and historians alike in thinking through the requirements for creating and deploying a more usable past.

This is not, of course, an original endeavor. The effort to use history to elucidate lessons of leadership traces back to Herodotus, Thucydides, Sallust, Petrarch, Niccolò Machiavelli, Edward Gibbon, and many other writers who came long before us. A more recent scholarly literature on the history-policy nexus is anchored in influential volumes written by Ernest May and Richard Neustadt in the 1970s and 1980s, and supplemented with additional, and often more specialized, works in the years since.[6] This scholarship is still quite valuable—it offers useful frameworks for thinking about the history-policy relationship, shows just how pervasive the links between history and policy can be, and illustrates many of the pathologies that commonly afflict the relationship between the two through a spectrum of historical cases and examples. Nonetheless, and without slighting the contributions of these earlier works, we believe that there are at least five key reasons why renewed attention to this subject is necessary.

First, notwithstanding more recent contributions, discussions of the history-policy relationship are still dominated by the books written by May and Neustadt decades ago. This is not inherently a bad thing; the fact that these books have few peers today demonstrates the continuing validity of some of their insights about how history is used and how policymakers might use it better. But it also indicates that there is a need for a fresh look at the long-standing questions—questions whose relevance has only increased in the context of the recent wars in Afghanistan and Iraq. Scholarship on topics of foreign policy, international development, and military force has evolved since the 1970s and 1980s, and new studies of history and policy must take this research into account.[7] Accordingly, our aim in this book is less to criticize landmark works in the field than to revisit some of the issues they raise (as well as other questions) in a focused, rigorous, and up-to-date way.

Second, renewed exploration of the subject is necessary because historians as a whole have not done enough to cultivate sustained dialogue with the policymaking community. Scholarly books and articles that explicitly address the history-policy nexus, or attempt to engage current policy issues directly, are still the exception in a profession that generally views presentism as a sin rather than a virtue. "The American historical profession," writes Jill Lepore, "defines itself by its dedication to the proposition that looking to the past to explain the present falls outside the realm of serious historical study."[8]

Historians are often wise to be cautious about seeking to extract policy insights from a meditation on the past. The differences between two time periods are almost always more important than the similarities; lessons ripped from one context and dropped into another can easily mislead more than they can inform. Sir Michael Howard put this best when he wrote that he was "conscious above all of the unique quality of an experience that resulted from circumstances that would never, that could never, be precisely replicated."[9] Yet while the uniqueness of each historical occurrence is true enough, it is no excuse for historians to shirk engagement with contemporary policy debates and issues. As any informed observer can attest, the inescapable reality is that perceptions of history *do* influence policy—in ways both positive and negative. Whatever the limits of using history for policy, writes Jeffrey Record, "it is clear that policymakers invariably will continue to be influenced by past events and what they believe those events teach."[10] If historians as a whole seek to serve their broader society, they are therefore obligated to promote the most accurate and effective use of history in policymaking. Bringing together in this volume a group of leading scholars and practitioners to consider how this might be done, we hope to catalyze a broader and more sustained interest in these issues both within and outside the historical community.

Promoting this discussion seems all the more imperative in light of the third reason for this book: that the events of the post-9/11 era have once again demonstrated the inextricable links between history and policy, and the corresponding necessity of getting that relationship right. As one might expect, American officials have consistently sought historical reference points in their efforts to deal with the immensely challenging and often frightening problems of the present era. The administrations of both President George W. Bush and Barack Obama have regularly invoked historical analogies, narratives, and insights in choosing or justifying policies, and they have relied heavily on the presumed lessons of the past in charting routes forward. One need only look at the multitude of historical frames used by the Bush administration in devising and defending its response to 9/11: the cautionary tale of Soviet involvement in Afghanistan from 1979 to 1989, the perceived lessons of World War II and the Cold War, and the successful postwar democratizations of Japan and Germany, among many others.[11] Likewise, President Obama's administration invoked "the lessons of Iraq" in responding to uprisings in Libya and Syria, and its reading of the Vietnam War had a powerful effect on the initial "surge" and subsequent drawdown of U.S. forces in Afghanistan.[12] As the essays in this volume illustrate, there is no shortage of contemporary policy issues that demand greater historical awareness. In these circumstances, scholars have a responsibility to engage the history-policy relationship as constructively as possible.

Fourth, we believe that there is great value in exploring the history-policy nexus through a collective endeavor such as this one. The subject under consideration is broad and complex, and the multitude of cases one could study to gain a better understanding of it is virtually infinite. At best, then, any single set of studies can only be suggestive rather than exhaustive or definitive, and it is crucial to draw on a diverse set of approaches and interpretations in analyzing the questions posed above. That is what we have done in this book. The contributors have long been engaged in thinking about these issues, and here, as elsewhere, they have done so in a wide range of creative and insightful ways. Their essays cover a broad span of subjects thematically and temporally—from the use of force to anti-human trafficking efforts, from the lessons of the humanitarian interventions of the nineteenth century through the applications of history during the administrations of Bill Clinton, Bush, and Obama. To the extent that a single book draws together such diverse perspectives and insights, it casts brighter light on an often obscure and slippery subject, and demonstrates just how pervasive the history-policy dynamic truly is.[13]

Fifth, and perhaps most important, we believe that there is a need for work that treats the history-policy nexus as an authentic dialogue, not simply as an opportunity to tell policymakers what they are doing wrong and what they ought to be doing instead.[14] It should be self-evident that one cannot fully appreciate the intricacies of the history-policy relationship without fully engaging both historians and members of the policymaking community. Policymakers may understand aspects of the relationship that elude talented historians, and vice versa. And as we make clear in the forthcoming chapters, both communities have obligations to meet if this relationship is to become a healthier one. Accordingly, this book draws on contributions from both of these "tribes"—leading historians whose work represents the cutting edge of scholarship on key policy issues, and several individuals with significant, high-level experience in the shaping of American statecraft. In bringing these two groups together and putting them in dialogue with one another, the book offers positive avenues for improving the historical content of policy and the policy content of history. We see great possibility in these integrated endeavors.

Historians and Policymakers

This book is divided into three sections, each of which engages a core aspect of the history-policy relationship. In each section, a group of leading scholars and/or policymakers explores a diverse set of subjects clustered around a single overriding question or theme. This approach combines the benefits of ecumenism and of structure. It offers a sustained approach to key issues in the history-policy relationship while also leveraging the broad range of experiences and expertise that the contributors possess.

In part I, four leading diplomatic historians explore the complex and varied ways that history *does* influence U.S. foreign policy. In chapter 2, Jeremi Suri begins this section by examining how one prominent statesman—former secretary of state Henry Kissinger—has conceived of the relationship between historical knowledge and diplomatic practice. History, notes Suri, has long been essential to Kissinger's understanding of how talented practitioners can and should wield power, and Kissinger has used history to anticipate some of the deep structural forces at work in the international system. He has also made use of his historical knowledge to pursue possibilities for creative statecraft that can exploit or subtly shift broader international currents.

In chapter 3, Mark Atwood Lawrence provides a deeply textured analysis of the numerous historical "lessons" that American observers have drawn from the Vietnam War in the decades since that conflict ended. He notes that the Vietnam analogy has been interpreted in different—and often contradictory—ways by policymakers and pundits, and he evaluates the ways in which lessons drawn from that conflict have both informed and misinformed debates about post-Vietnam foreign policy. He concludes by reflecting on the utility and limits of the Vietnam analogy as a tool for informing statecraft.

In chapter 4, H. W. Brands builds on Lawrence's analysis by explicitly examining the role of analogies in U.S. policy during the Persian Gulf crisis and war of 1990–91. He reveals how two particular analogies—those of Munich and Vietnam—were pervasive in shaping the George H. W. Bush administration's confrontation with Saddam Hussein. These analogies, Brands argues, had both salutary and less salutary effects on the quality of American statecraft, demonstrating both the power of analogical reasoning and the need to treat such reasoning with great care.

Finally, in chapter 5, Jennifer Miller analyzes the interplay between historical narratives—prevailing understandings of the recent past—and U.S.-Japanese relations after World War II. Focusing on debates over Japanese rearmament, Miller shows that narratives forged from complex international interactions had a powerful role in shaping the U.S.-Japanese relationship. Shifts of policy, in turn, required efforts to revise those historical narratives. The chapters in this section thus cover a broad chronology and subject matter; together they demonstrate the rich, complex, and sometimes contradictory qualities of the relationship between history and policy.

Part II is prescriptive as well as descriptive: it engages the question of how historical knowledge *can* and *should* inform better policy. In this section four top scholars—including two with significant policymaking experience—analyze particular themes or episodes in the history of U.S. foreign policy, and they offer insights into how to make those subjects more "usable" in dealing with contemporary global challenges. Starting off the section, Thomas Mahnken and William Inboden combine the insights derived from their scholarly work with those gained during their time in government. Mahnken in chapter 6 analyzes how understandings of America's Cold War–era strategy of containment continue to inform—and mislead—discussions of contemporary problems. He suggests how policymakers and pundits might apply a firmer grasp of containment's history to clarify options, alternatives, and debates on a range of foreign policy questions today.

In chapter 7, Inboden reexamines a widely misunderstood subject—the history of the National Security Council (NSC) during the administration of President Ronald Reagan. Inboden argues that William Clark's management of the NSC in 1982–83 was actually more rational and purposeful than scholars have often assumed. He also uses this deeply researched reinterpretation of the Reagan NSC as a way of promoting creative thinking about how presidents and their national security advisers should approach the task of managing and implementing foreign policy in pivotal eras.

The final two chapters of this section deal with the history-policy relationship through the lens of humanitarian issues. In chapter 8, Michael Cotey Morgan studies the complex dilemmas that humanitarian military intervention has long posed for U.S. and British officials, and he points to several useful ways in which this history can shed light on questions about whether, when, and how to use force for humanitarian purposes today. In chapter 9, Gunther Peck examines the role of historical analogies, narratives, and symbols in current approaches to combating human trafficking. He argues that a better understanding of how these historical legacies shape current policy debates—and how they sometimes distort the nature of the challenge—can help policymakers test assumptions, identify blind spots, and elucidate opportunities for more effective action. As each of the chapters in part II underscores, history *can* play a constructive role in policy, provided that scholars and policymakers are willing to interrogate the past with self-awareness and rigor.

Part III, the final section of this book, draws out more extensively the insights that policymakers can contribute to the healthy dialogue we hope to foster. In each chapter, scholars with extensive policy backgrounds bring their experiences to bear on the central questions explored in this volume. In chapter 10, James Steinberg reflects on how various forms of history—personal history, historical analogies, and historical learning—informed U.S. responses to the wars in Yugoslavia during the 1990s. He then traces the role that the lessons drawn from those conflicts played in subsequent interventions in Afghanistan and Libya. Steinberg offers practical suggestions for how scholars and policymakers might think about the problem of incorporating historical insights into policy decisions.

Likewise, Peter Feaver and William Inboden discuss in chapter 11 the crucial role that historical knowledge, analogies, and awareness played in policy initiatives undertaken by the George W. Bush administration, particularly during the authors' time at the NSC from 2005 to 2007. They argue that "a historical sensibility pervaded the thinking of President Bush and many senior members of his administration," and that the overall quality of policy was better for this characteristic. Their analysis provides a firsthand account of how sound policy must be simultaneously prospective and retrospective, and how good historical knowledge can illuminate pathways for creative action.

Concluding this volume, Philip Zelikow describes in chapter 12 the kinds of "lessons" history actually offers. Through a sophisticated analysis that draws on his extensive experience in both the policymaking and scholarly worlds, Zelikow cautions against using history as a storehouse for facile generalizations that can be applied across time and space. Rather, he argues that the "historian's microscope" is a powerful tool for appreciating the complexity of the past, accumulating vicarious experience, and better positioning ourselves to address the possibilities, challenges, and choices of our own times. This volume illustrates how history can become a source of wisdom and perspective for policymakers. Zelikow's chapter and others provide careful analysis and concrete examples for moving a constructive history-policy dialogue forward.

Themes and Insights

As the foregoing discussion indicates, the chapters in this volume are rich and diverse. They capture a range of viewpoints on the central questions about how historical knowledge already contributes, and should contribute moving forward, to policymaking. They also come together around a number of shared themes and conclusions that anchor the book as a whole. Although the reader can trace these themes across the chapters, we have chosen to highlight several of particular importance at the outset.

The Nature of the History-Policy Relationship
The first theme is the complex, multifaceted, and often contradictory ways in which history influences policy judgments. As nearly all of the chapters in this volume demonstrate, there is no single model for how historical knowledge shapes the policymaking environment or guides particular decisions. Analogical reasoning is probably the most common way in which policymakers directly apply history to policy issues, and the chapters by H. W. Brands, Mark Atwood Lawrence, Gunther Peck, and other contributors demonstrate just how compelling—if sometimes misleading—this

type of reasoning can be. Accordingly, the potential utility of analogies, and the ways that they can be used productively, constitutes a key theme of the book. It is important to recognize, however, that analogies are but one pathway through which the past influences the present.

Personal experience—an individual's own history—is another such pathway. Past experiences provide the intellectual framing through which we interpret current events, and as James Steinberg's chapter illustrates, they powerfully shape how new challenges and opportunities are perceived. Likewise, historical narratives—the inherited accounts of what happened and why—profoundly influence the cultural milieu in which policy options are considered and decisions are made. Historical symbols and metaphors— the notion of containment, for instance—can also shape policy, by providing the reference points that pull officials toward certain solutions and away from others.[15] In some cases, policymakers even bring their own understanding of history as an intellectual endeavor to bear on their approach to contemporary problems. As Jeremi Suri notes, this was certainly true of Henry Kissinger, who relied less on simple analogies than on his studied reflections about how historical forces interacted with policy opportunities. This list of pathways for history's influence on policy could easily go on further, but the key point is that any discussion of the history-policy relationship must begin with an acknowledgment of just how many diverse forms that relationship can take.

Discussion should also begin with a recognition that the policy insights to be drawn from history are not always as objective or unarguable as we might like them to be. One of the difficulties inherent in applying historical knowledge to policy is that reasonable observers can draw entirely different—and contradictory—implications from the same historical episode. For the Clinton administration in the early 1990s, was the "correct" lesson to be drawn from 1914 that great powers should not meddle in long-standing ethnic and national conflicts in the Balkans? Or was it that decisive intervention was imperative, lest those conflicts fester, metastasize, and trigger systemic instability? Smart people could and did make both arguments based on plausible readings of the past. For decades, intelligent observers have also drawn diametrically opposed conclusions from the U.S. war in Vietnam. For some, the key lesson of that conflict is the need to respect the limits of American power; for others, the history of the war, and its aftermath, show the danger of not using American power assertively enough.[16]

We should not attribute these disagreements to bias on one side or the other, for as historians surely understand, interpretive disputes are the rule rather than the exception even when history is studied rigorously. The fact is that history does not lend itself to a single, incontestable set of policy-relevant takeaways; it lends itself—particularly with new research—to continuing contestation and debate.

These points should be a source of humility and self-awareness for historians and policymakers alike. Policymakers should realize that history shapes their actions in myriad ways, and through numerous channels, whether they perceive that to be the case or not. Policymakers and historians should also understand that history almost never produces a single correct answer to a policy problem. This need not be a cause of discouragement for those who would like to make history serve policy in concrete and useful ways, because there is still great utility in such efforts. Historical thinking about policy must, however, begin with a clear understanding of how policy and history interact, and what the limits of that relationship often are.

Historical Analogies

A second theme concerns the utility—and limits—of historical analogies. Analogies are unavoidable in policymaking, they are often misleading, but they can be immensely useful if treated with care.

As noted above, analogical reasoning is perhaps the most common way in which policymakers use history, and it is a practice that many historians view with deep suspicion. The entire endeavor seems to reek of indifference to the importance of context and complexity, to suggest that an insight—usually an oversimplified one—drawn from one distinct experience can apply accurately to another. As Jeffrey Record notes: "Reasoning by historical analogy can be dangerous, especially if such reasoning is untempered by recognition that no two historical events are identical and that the future is more than a linear extension of the past." There is much truth in this assessment. One has only to look at the influence of the Munich analogy on U.S. policy in Vietnam, or on British policy during the 1956 Suez Crisis, to understand how badly the uncritical application of historical analogies can distort policy.[17] When analogies dull policymakers' sensitivity to the particularities of their current context—to the differences between two situations separated by time and space, or to the danger of devising historical "laws" from a single episode in the past—they can have pernicious impacts indeed.

Those impacts can be especially problematic when analogies become politicized. Precisely because analogies can be so powerful and evocative, there is a temptation for policymakers to invoke them less as an opening for critical inquiry than as a blunt rhetorical object. The Munich analogy, the Vietnam analogy, and countless others have often been deployed not as a means of carefully interrogating the past for insights about the present, but as a political device to sell a particular policy or discredit an opponent's alternative.[18] This rhetorical tactic is part and parcel of democratic politics, of course, but it is an invitation to simplistic and overwrought readings of history—and a key reason why so many scholars are skeptical of whether policymakers can really use analogies with integrity.

This caution about analogies confronts both historians and policymakers with a real dilemma. Policymakers inevitably grasp for comparisons to make sense of new information and uncertainty. This is why historical analogies are so unavoidable—they help decisionmakers who are under intense pressure grapple intellectually with their challenges and opportunities. For all its drawbacks and abuses, analogical reasoning is therefore a perfectly natural way to bring the wisdom of experience to current dilemmas. As Yuen Foong Khong writes in his highly critical study of analogical reasoning during the early escalation of American intervention in the Vietnam War, "Because policymakers often encounter new foreign policy challenges and because structural uncertainty usually infuses the environment in which responses to such challenges must be forged, policymakers routinely turn to the past for guidance."[19] Other critics of analogical reasoning have reached the same conclusion.[20] Historians may deplore the way that analogies are routinely misused in policy decisions, but it is unrealistic to think that analogies will ever be purged from that process.

The good news is that this is not necessarily a bad thing. Historical analogies do not always have a negative impact on policy debates; at times, they push decisionmakers in helpful directions that open new possibilities and protect against dead ends. One can argue that the Munich analogy actually served U.S. policymakers well in the case of the Korean War, for example, by encouraging the administration of President Harry S. Truman to combat a Soviet-backed assault on South Korea that, if successful, might have seriously destabilized the postwar environment.[21] In the same vein, one interpretation of H. W. Brands's contribution to this volume is that the Munich and Vietnam analogies—both ubiquitous during the run-up to the

Persian Gulf War—had some positive effects on U.S. policy. Whatever its limitations, the Munich analogy helped inform George H. W. Bush's decision to resist Saddam Hussein's invasion of Kuwait; the Vietnam analogy motivated the president to emphasize the decisive use of military power for carefully defined and delimited objectives. Mark Lawrence, James Steinberg, Peter Feaver, and William Inboden make similar observations (with varying degrees of emphasis) in their chapters: analogies have influenced policy in beneficial as well as pernicious ways.

This point touches on a fundamental reality about historical analogies. Although the uncritical or selective deployment of analogies is obviously fraught with peril, a more discerning use can be quite illuminating. Carefully employed, analogies can help spark the intellectual curiosity that leads to sharper, textured interpretations of complex situations, integrating attention to details with insights about the relationships between different actors and events. Carl von Clausewitz famously called this the coup d'oeil (the flash of insight) that allows the skilled commander to make sense of the chaotic battlefield—understanding its development and anticipating its trajectory.[22]

The key here is to understand that analogies should serve as the beginning of an inquiry into the continuities between past and present, rather than an end to such an analysis. Observing that the present situation is "like" something that came before need not foreclose further critical examination of context and discontinuity; it can actually serve as an intellectual point of departure for interrogating how the present is both similar and different from what came before. If a leader is warned that some foreign intervention will become "another Vietnam" or "another Iraq," for instance, such admonitions can provide useful frames of reference for exploring how applicable these comparisons really are—and thus better fleshing out the true dynamics of the challenge. Likewise, the comparative use of analogies—looking at current events in light of not just one prior episode, but two, three, or four— can reveal potential continuities between past and present, while also underscoring the need to avoid becoming locked into any single analogical paradigm.

Analogies can aid decisionmaking so long as they are viewed as an invitation to scrutiny and critical assessment, rather than a means of closing off such important intellectual work. Analogies themselves are neither good nor bad, neither helpful nor harmful. It is how they are used—and how rigorously they are examined—that makes all the difference.

Historical Sensibility

The rigorous use of analogies is a starting point for understanding history as more than just a repository of facts and comparisons. May and Neustadt observed that during policy discussions President Truman frequently invoked historical details gained from his readings about other eras. He invoked these details, generally, to constrict debate and focus it on a few "necessary" options, rather than to open new questions and perspectives on pressing problems. In contrast, general (and later secretary of state) George Marshall had read little history, and he rarely based his policy arguments on facts about the past. Instead, he pushed his advisers (including Dean Acheson, George Kennan, and Charles Bohlen) to explore new opportunities and use knowledge of past efforts to inform creative adjustments in the present.[23]

The launching of the Marshall Plan stands out as an endeavor in constructive historical imagination. George Marshall's landmark speech at Harvard University in June 1947 did not include many detailed facts or any long excursions into the history of America or Europe. Rather, Marshall began with a basic proposition, drawn from an understanding of how societies had struggled to recover from war in the past. Marshall focused on what he called the "fabric of European economy":

> The feverish preparation for war and the more feverish maintenance of the war effort engulfed all aspects of national economies. Machinery has fallen into disrepair or is entirely obsolete. Under the arbitrary and destructive Nazi rule, virtually every possible enterprise was geared into the German war machine. Long-standing commercial ties, private institutions, banks, insurance companies, and shipping companies disappeared, through loss of capital, absorption through nationalization, or by simple destruction. In many countries, confidence in the local currency has been severely shaken. The breakdown of the business structure of Europe during the war was complete.

Marshall did not pretend that the events in Europe after World War II were "like" any past moment, but he drew on the historical knowledge that conditions of suffering and stagnation bred extremism and instability. He and his colleagues also drew on the historical knowledge that prolonged turmoil in Europe had negative repercussions for the United States. Despite the heavy burden of debt from World War II, and the fears of a return to the prewar conditions of economic depression, American leaders in the late 1940s used this history to justify an unprecedented commitment to European recovery. American aid was "logical" to restore "normal economic health in the world," Marshall said, "without which there can be no political stability and no assured peace."[24]

He then went one step further. Marshall had learned from his own military experiences in the Philippines and other areas that the United States could not impose solutions. Acheson, Kennan, and Bohlen learned similar lessons from their experiences in Washington and Europe during the war. The resulting emphasis on multilateralism and partnership in reconstruction was unprecedented in American history, but it was the best route forward because of the knowledge that isolationism and unilateralism had failed to produce the intended results in the past.

Many of Marshall's successors have sought to replicate the achievements of the Marshall Plan in other regions. They have been less successful, in part, because they have tried to replay past policies, rather than understand broader historical trends.[25] Marshall and his colleagues did not make that mistake in 1947. They saw strong historical reasons for why postwar turmoil in Europe was dangerous, why Washington should care, and why America should build on-the-ground partnerships with local Europeans. Their sense of historical change led them to reject the standard American separation from Europe and embrace experimentation with new and bold solutions. Historical thinking about alternatives offered an escape from the imprisonment of the past.

This is the best way to understand how a historical sensibility—rather than a mere repetition of historical facts—can help policymakers confronting enormous challenges under conditions of great uncertainty. Reading history offers an opportunity to think about the broad dynamics (economic, geopolitical, and cultural) that influence contemporary events, whether such dynamics are or are not recognized by current actors. Fernand Braudel called this perspective the *longue durée* (the long term),[26] and policymakers must indeed take the time to develop (and continually reassess) their understanding of how their immediate crises fit into the long term. Unless they do so, they will never get ahead of the daily pressures. Putting out fires is a technical skill, but anticipating where fires are most likely to occur, and how they can best be prevented, requires historical awareness.[27]

A historical sensibility is not only about broad dynamics. It focuses on contingencies and tipping points: places where a focused effort can make an enduring difference. These are the "windows of opportunity" that a policymaker can only identify correctly if he or she understands the relationships among various actors, trends, and events. In the late 1940s American policymakers perceived a window of opportunity in postwar Europe because they recognized the potential partners on the ground, the areas where their incentives would align with U.S. interests, and the extent to which the disjunctures caused by the war had created an opening for decisive action. Reading history can give policymakers the knowledge to identify similar moments and devise plans for them in the present day. A historical sensibility helps one to see the links between various crises and the potential points of leverage for pushing events toward a new result. A historical sensibility builds agency through awareness of connections, and the places where they are susceptible to influence.

This is something that the wisest analysts of statecraft have long understood. Clausewitz famously argued for a historical sensibility in generals because only that would allow them to understand the complex interplay of forces that shaped events on the battlefield, and to identify—and exploit—opportunities as they arose.[28] The same logic applies to foreign policy writ large. A sense of how the international landscape is evolving and where the spaces for productive action might exist are key issues in effective leadership. Reading history reminds us that we must lift our heads above the chaos of our in-boxes to find a broader order in events, and to exert influence at critical junctures. American policymakers did this in 1947 because they thought in historical terms about the past and future of postwar Europe. This book aims to encourage similar ways of thinking.

Responsibilities of Historians and Policymakers

Reflections on the need for a historical sensibility bring us to a final point: the reciprocal responsibilities of historians and policymakers. One often detects among historians a sense that the travails of the history-policy relationship reside primarily in the unwillingness of policymakers to engage high-quality history in a serious fashion. As the chapters in this book indicate, there is indeed some truth to this assertion, and policymakers simply must do a better job of being sensitive to the requirements of employing history effectively. They need to approach the use of history in systematic and rigorous fashion, rather than doing so selectively, carelessly, or disingenuously. As Philip Zelikow emphasizes in his chapter, policymakers cannot treat history as a grab bag of ready-made analogies or a strip mine from which universally relevant lessons can be extracted. Analogies must be carefully scrutinized and weighed against competing analogies; context must be given its due weight in determining the relevance of insights from the past; and the temptation to seek simple affirmation (or ammunition) from history's embrace must be assiduously avoided. Policymakers need to grapple meaningfully with competing interpretations of the past; they need to think seriously about the historical currents and trends that shape their world; and they must be willing to go beyond potted histories and favored writers to engage rigorous academic research on the relevant subjects. Above all, policymakers need to be explicit in recognizing that they will use history whether they acknowledge it or not. The real question is whether they will make the intellectual investment necessary to use it well.

To be clear, we are under no illusion that high-level policymakers will devote days on end to poring over back issues of academic journals; nor do we believe that any of the tasks mentioned above represent a magical formula for resolving tensions in the history-policy relationship. After all, the very nature of history is that it rarely produces a single answer to any problem, and the very nature of policy is that there remain inherent limits on how much effort policymakers can devote to the search for historical insight. To say that perfection is unattainable, however, is not to concede that progress is impossible. To the extent that policymakers can be *more* systematic, *more* rigorous, and *more* deliberate in approaching the use of history—even if only at the margins—we believe that they will be better able to profit from what the past has to offer, and more likely to avoid the common pitfalls that so often plague the history-policy relationship.

These admonitions to policymakers should not stand alone, of course, because historians have responsibilities too. They must begin by avoiding the condescension, narrowness, and insularity that frequently close off their work to policymakers eager for assistance. There are, certainly, numerous historians who avoid these characteristics and whose work combines rigorous scholarship with a policy focus. What is true of individual historians, however, is not broadly true of the discipline as a whole. It is rare indeed to find a historical journal that encourages authors to include a "policy implications" section in their articles, and the same silence can be found in most books on diplomatic history published by university presses.[29] Similarly, historians seem far less likely than their colleagues in political science or international relations to publish in influential opinion-making journals like *Foreign Affairs* or *Foreign Policy*. Nor, unfortunately, is this particularly surprising, because policy-relevant work is generally unrewarded (and sometimes penalized) within the discipline of history. Many historians, especially those who are at the early stage of their careers, are discouraged from acknowledging any policy connection in their work, for fear they might be categorized as unserious or presentist.[30]

Perhaps most problematic, the relative isolation of scholars from policymakers means that historians rarely have the opportunity to contemplate the challenges that policymakers confront: the severe time pressures and resource constraints, the competing and often irreconcilable demands, the radical uncertainty in which key decisions must be made, and the fact that the alternative to one imperfect option is often something even worse.[31] Many of these situational factors are not well represented in the extant documents, especially when they are studied as discrete topics and not integrated into a holistic understanding of what it was like for policymakers to deal with multiple issues (and crises) at the same time. From a distance, it is very hard for historians to empathize with policymakers regarding "what it was like to be there." That is, of course, why so many policymakers view academic history as unhelpful; it is simply out of touch with the realities officials face on a daily basis.

If the history-policy relationship is to work as well as it should, the historical discipline will have to meet the policy world halfway. This means cultivating a professional culture that values relevance as well as originality, and gives its members real incentives to engage directly in policy debates. It means creating attractive, prestigious outlets for such work within the discipline, while also encouraging historians—even young historians—to go beyond an audience of specialists and make their work accessible to those outside the field. Not least, it means balancing the proper and necessary desire to be critical in assessing policy, on the one hand, with empathy and a willingness to engage in constructive dialogue with policymakers, on the other.

If historians are to have real credibility in addressing policy issues, they also need to be more directly involved in the world that they describe. A profound oddity of diplomatic history is that comparatively few practicing diplomatic historians have spent time working in a policy capacity. There are exceptions, such as Melvyn Leffler, Philip Zelikow, or Richard Immerman, but these examples are notable precisely because they are exceptions. It is relatively rare to hear of young historians serving in government through a Council on Foreign Relations International Affairs Fellowship or through the Intergovernmental Personnel Act, for instance, or of historians otherwise taking a more direct role in policy issues while also maintaining good standing within academia.[32]

This state of affairs hardly disqualifies historians from producing good scholarship on policy-relevant issues, but it does have the effect of ensuring that the profession as a whole includes too few people who have firsthand knowledge of how the policy world really works on a day-to-day basis. One cannot help but think that this is not a desirable state of affairs, that it would be better for historians and policymakers alike if historians spent more time actively engaged in the sort of activities they write about.[33] More than anything else, a healthy history-policy relationship requires a sustained dialogue between these two fields. Experiences that promote such a dialogue, and make historians better able to comment intelligently on the policy world, should be cultivated by leaders in government and on college campuses.

Special meetings where historians include a token policymaker, or where policymakers call in an ad hoc group of historians, are only a start. Too often the token policymaker happens to affirm the bias of historians, just as the handpicked group of historians shares the prejudice of the policymaker. Even when there is intellectual diversity in the room, it is very difficult for a "guest" policymaker or historian to challenge the deeply held assumptions and preferences of a powerful set of hosts. We must work more diligently and systematically to overcome the entrenched professional divisions, even as we preserve intellectual integrity.

Where Do We Go from Here?

The conference that preceded this volume, and the essays that it produced, are designed to model a new approach to collaboration between historians and policymakers. Scholars and practitioners must make a concerted effort to recognize and transcend their biases by forming enduring intellectual relationships—not just one-off meetings—with major thinkers who approach the world in different ways. They must listen to each other, acknowledge differences, and make an effort to find points of agreement, as well as continued disagreement. Each chapter in this book reflects these kinds of difficult discussions.

Accuracy is the bedrock of a fruitful relationship between history and policy, and it is based on close attention to evidence. Each of the chapters in this book grapples with a big historical and policy topic by closely assessing a body of evidence. This requires a rigorous effort to understand and to explain; it also involves a serious investigation into how others, often with different views, have analyzed the same evidence. This is the only method of ensuring accuracy: close attention to evidence and broad assessment of different points of view. Accuracy does not require agreement on all things, but it does presuppose that conscientious analysis will allow agreement on many parameters.

A diverse group of practitioners and historians, like those assembled for this book, must work together to examine biases and test accuracy. This is a collaborative effort, and as such, historians should allow their community to expand beyond its disciplinary gatherings. Similarly, policymakers must make space in their offices for historians. The collaboration that we advocate is not about personality as much as it is about the structures of dialogue and the networks of association that drive professionalism. This book is a call for rigorous and intentional professional ecumenism.

Of course, the ecumenism we advocate goes beyond the communities of historians and foreign policy specialists to include other disciplines and professional endeavors. As historians and policymakers increase their level of collaboration, they must also bring in more social scientists, businesspeople, and technology experts, among many others. Our point in this volume is not to privilege historians above other disciplines, but to focus on the foundational importance of historical knowledge and dialogue in international policymaking. The chapters in this book look to open avenues for productive and rigorous cross-disciplinary and cross-cultural collaborations that build on what a more sustained dialogue between historians and practitioners can offer for each of these fields, and many others.

Wisdom comes from an ever-evolving mix of specialized research and generalized understanding. Historians and policymakers need more of both, and they can help each other in their joint pursuits. We have more confidence in a new generation of leaders who search beyond their comfort zones for wisdom, rather than familiar and predictable answers. This book is an effort in that direction.

Notes

1. George Packer, "What Obama and the Generals Are Reading," *New Yorker*, October 8, 2009 (www.newyorker.com/news/george-packer/what-obama-and-the -generals-are-reading).

2. See Peter Spiegel and Jonathan Weisman, "Behind Afghan War Debate, a Battle of Two Books Rages," *Wall Street Journal*, October 7, 2009.

3. Margaret MacMillan, *Dangerous Games: The Uses and Abuses of History* (New York: Modern Library, 2009), 8. For representative examples of history's influence on policy and policy debates, see Yuen Foong Khong, *Analogies at War: Korea, Munich, Dien Bien Phu, and the Vietnam Decisions of 1965* (Princeton University Press, 1992); Roland Paris, "Kosovo and the Metaphor War," *Political Science Quarterly* 117, no. 3 (Fall 2002), 423–50; David Hoagland Noon, "Operation Enduring Analogy: World War II, the War on Terror, and the Uses of Historical Memory," *Rhetoric and Public Affairs* 7, no. 3 (2004), 339–64; and Eliot Cohen, "The Historical Mind and Military Strategy," *Orbis* 49, no. 4 (2005), 575–88.

4. Jeffrey Record, *The Specter of Munich: Reconsidering the Lessons of Appeasing Hitler* (Washington, D.C.: Potomac Books, 2006).

5. As Scot MacDonald notes, in many cases "historical information is only retrieved because it supports current beliefs and is used solely to justify policy chosen by other means." See Scot MacDonald, *Rolling the Iron Dice: Historical Analogies and Decisions to Use Military Force in Regional Contingencies* (Westport, Conn.: Greenwood Press, 2000), 11.

6. For some of the scholarly literature, see Ernest May, *"Lessons" of the Past: The Use and Misuse of History in American Foreign Policy* (Oxford University Press, 1973); and Richard Neustadt and Ernest May, *Thinking in Time: The Uses of History for Decision Makers* (New York: Free Press, 1986). Other important contributions include Khong, *Analogies at War*; John Lewis Gaddis, *The Landscape of History: How Historians Map the Past* (Oxford University Press, 2004); MacMillan, *Dangerous Games*; Michael Howard, *The Lessons of History* (Yale University Press, 1991); Marc Trachtenberg, *History and Strategy* (Princeton University Press, 1991); Marc Trachtenberg, *The Cold War and After: History, Theory, and the Logic of International Politics* (Princeton University Press, 2012); Gordon Wood, *The Purpose of the Past: Reflections on the Uses of History* (New York: Penguin, 2008); William Bain, "Are There Any Lessons of History? The English School and the Activity of Being an Historian," *International Politics* 44 (2007), 513–30; Christopher Hemmer, *Which Lessons Matter? American Foreign Policy Decision Making in the Middle East, 1979–1987* (State University of New York Press, 2000); Jo Guldi and David Armitage, *The History Manifesto* (Cambridge University Press, 2014);

David Patrick Houghton, "The Role of Analogical Reasoning in Novel Foreign-Policy Situations," *British Journal of Political Science* 26 (1996), 523–52, and other works cited in this chapter and volume. Recent books and articles that engage the history-policy relationship head on include Francis J. Gavin, *Nuclear Statecraft: History and Strategy in America's Atomic Age* (Cornell University Press, 2012); Jeremi Suri, *Liberty's Surest Guardian: American Nation-Building from the Founders to Obama* (New York: Free Press, 2011); John David Lewis, *Nothing Less than Victory: Decisive Wars and the Lessons of History* (Princeton University Press, 2010); Hal Brands, *What Good Is Grand Strategy? Power and Purpose in American Statecraft from Harry S. Truman to George W. Bush* (Cornell University Press, 2014); Williamson Murray, James Lacey, and Richard Sinnreich, eds., *The Shaping of Grand Strategy: Policy, Diplomacy, and War* (Cambridge University Press, 2011); William Inboden, "Statecraft, Decision-Making, and the Varieties of Historical Experience: A Taxonomy," *Journal of Strategic Studies* 37, no. 2 (2014), 291–318; Jeffrey Engel, "Bush, Germany, and the Power of Time: How History Makes History," *Diplomatic History* 37, no. 4 (2013), 639–63; and Jakub Grygiel, "The Primacy of Premodern History," *Security Studies* 22, no. 1 (2013), 1–32.

7. For one recent study that does just this, see Engel, "Bush, Germany, and the Power of Time."

8. Jill Lepore, quoted in Gavin, *Nuclear Statecraft*, 2.

9. Howard, *Lessons of History*, 10.

10. Jeffrey Record, *The Perils of Reasoning by Historical Analogy: Munich, Vietnam and American Use of Force since 1945*, Occasional Paper 4 (Center for Strategy and Technology, Air War College: 1998), 23.

11. See Donald Rumsfeld, *Known and Unknown: A Memoir* (New York: Penguin, 2011), 367–68. For Bush's comments, see Michael Gordon and Eric Schmitt, "A War on a Small Scale, Possibly Long and Risky," *New York Times*, September 29, 2001; Noon, "Operation Enduring Analogy"; George W. Bush, "Address to a Joint Session of Congress," September 20, 2001, American Presidency Project, University of California–Santa Barbara; and Jacob Weisberg, *The Bush Tragedy* (New York: Random House, 2008), 235–36.

12. Michael Hirsh, "Iraq and Libya Haunt Obama's Syria Policy," *National Journal*, May 2, 2013; Dominic Tierney, "The Obama Doctrine and the Lessons of Iraq," *Foreign Policy Research Institute E-Notes*, May 2012 (www.fpri.org/enotes/05/201205.tierney.obama-doctrine-iraq.html); Spiegel and Weisman, "Behind Afghan War Debate, a Battle of Two Books Rages."

13. For a recent work that employs this approach to good effect, see Niall Ferguson, Charles Maier, Erez Manela, and Daniel Sargent, eds., *The Shock of the Global: The 1970s in Perspective* (Harvard University Press, 2010).

14. For an article that makes a closely related point, see Francis J. Gavin, "Politics, History and the Ivory Tower-Policy Gap in the Nuclear Proliferation Debate," *Journal of Strategic Studies* 35, no. 4 (2012), 573–600.

15. See Thomas Mahnken, this volume, chapter 6.

16. On these issues, see Mark Atwood Lawrence, chapter 3, and James Steinberg, chapter 10, this volume. On contrasting lessons from Vietnam, see Mark Moyar, "Grand Strategy after the Vietnam War," *Orbis* 53, no. 4 (2009), 591–610.

17. Record, *Perils of Reasoning by Historical Analogy*, 23. See also MacDonald, *Rolling the Iron Dice*, 116–17; Renee Jeffery, "Evaluating the 'China Threat': Power Transition Theory, the Successor-State Image and the Dangers of Historical Analogies," *Australian Journal of International Affairs* 63, no. 2 (2006), 310–11; and Khong, *Analogies at War*, 2–3, 12–13.

18. For a similar point, see Andrew Taylor and John Rourke, "Historical Analogies in the Congressional Foreign Policy Process," *Journal of Politics* 57 (1995), 460–68.

19. Khong, *Analogies at War*, 252.

20. Record, *Perils of Reasoning by Historical Analogy*, 23.

21. On this point, see William Stueck, *Rethinking the Korean War: A New Diplomatic and Strategic History* (Princeton University Press, 2002), 215–16; and Robert J. Donovan, *Tumultuous Years: The Presidency of Harry S. Truman, 1949–1953* (University of Missouri Press, 1996), 201.

22. Carl von Clausewitz, *On War*, edited and translated by Michael Howard and Peter Paret (Princeton University Press, 1984), 100–12.

23. See Suri, *Liberty's Surest Guardian*, 124–64; and Neustadt and May, *Thinking in Time*, 247–59.

24. "The 'Marshall Plan' speech at Harvard University, 5 June 1947" (www.oecd .org/general/themarshallplanspeechatharvarduniversity5june1947.htm).

25. On this point, see Suri, *Liberty's Surest Guardian*, esp. 165–265.

26. For a succinct statement of Braudel's historical philosophy, see Fernand Braudel, *On History*, translated by Sarah Matthews (University of Chicago Press, 1982).

27. This is a point that Gaddis makes very well in *The Landscape of History*.

28. Clausewitz, *On War*.

29. To our knowledge, there is only one historical journal—the *Journal of Policy History*—that explicitly lists informing policymakers as part of its mission. Unfortunately, this journal is generally not considered to have a great deal of prestige or influence within the historical profession, nor is it generally thought of as a forum in which leading diplomatic historians place their work.

30. In 1999, for instance, one historian attacked Melvyn Leffler and John Gaddis for having "access to the pages of the establishment's in-house organ *Foreign Affairs*." It might also be noted that this critique was made as part of the Society for Historians of American Foreign Relations' Stuart L. Bernath Memorial Lecture. See Robert Buzzanco, "What Happened to the New Left? Toward a Radical Reading of American Foreign Relations," *Diplomatic History* 23, no. 4 (1999), 597.

31. For critiques of this tendency in scholars, and arguments that academics must be more sensitive to these dynamics, see Francis Bator, "No Good Choices: LBJ and the Vietnam/Great Society Connection," *Diplomatic History* 32, no. 3 (2008), 309–40. See also Francis J. Gavin and James B. Steinberg, "Mind the Gap: Why Policymakers and Scholars Ignore Each Other, and What Should Be Done about It," *Carnegie Reporter* 6, no. 4 (2012; http://carnegie.org/publications/carnegie -reporter/single/view/article/item/308/). For a book that is emblematic of these ten-dencies, see Shane Maddock, *Nuclear Apartheid: The Quest for American Atomic Supremacy from World War II to the Present* (University of North Carolina Press, 2010). For a book that admirably mixes criticism with empathy, see Melvyn Leffler, *A Preponderance of Power: National Security, the Truman Administration, and the Cold War* (Stanford University Press, 1992).

32. During the 2012–13 and 2013–14 academic years, for instance, not a single historian served as a Council on Foreign Relations International Affairs Fellow, while numerous political science and international relations scholars took part in the program. This outcome was not particularly exceptional; similar trends have been at work for some time. In 2015, however, two historians were awarded the fellowships. See Council on Foreign Relations, "International Affairs Fellowship: The Program," www.cfr.org/thinktank/fellowships/iaf.html; and "International Affairs Fellows: 1967–2013" (http://i.cfr.org/content/thinktank/2013_IAF_Historical_List.pdf).

33. A good model in this regard is Leffler, who has written in *A Preponderance of Power*, xii, that the year he spent working in the Pentagon in 1980–81 gave him "a much better grasp of how the government functions," insights he put to good use in writing the book. Or one might look to the example of Richard Immerman, who spent two years working in high-level positions at the Office of the Director of National Intelligence from 2005 to 2007.

Part I

How History Does
Influence Policy

JEREMI SURI

2

Henry Kissinger, the Study of History, and the Modern Statesman

Businesspeople, professionals, and political observers who purchased Henry Kissinger's defense of friendly relations between Beijing and Washington, *On China*, did not get what they expected. The book contains more than 525 pages of dense prose, yet fewer than fifty of those pages touch directly on current issues. The vast majority of the book provides a thoughtful but largely traditional history of China and its relations with the outside world—particularly the United States. Kissinger's chapters hit all the common highlights: from Sun Zu and Qianlong to the Opium Wars, the Taiping Rebellion, and the collapse of the Qing dynasty before the horrors of the Japanese invasion and the Second World War.

The triumphant communist revolutionary and founder of the People's Republic of China, Mao Zedong—not Deng Xiaoping or Hu Jintao, or George W. Bush or Barack Obama—is the preponderant character in Kissinger's book. Mao gets more text and more reverence than any other figure. From the preface to the conclusion, Mao is the individual whom Kissinger believes best embodies the deeper realities of China, and its potential for both continuous domestic revolution and peaceful international relations with the United States. Kissinger explains that "no previous Chinese ruler combined traditional elements with the same mix of authority and ruthlessness and global sweep as Mao: ferocity in the face of challenge and skillful diplomacy when circumstances prevented his preference for drastic overpowering initiatives."[1]

This is a very strange way to think about contemporary international politics. As Kissinger recounts, Mao was a communist revolutionary, a dictator who unleashed the destruction of the Great Leap Forward and the Cultural Revolution, and a sworn enemy of the United States for most of his career. Mao died in 1976, with his citizens reeling from the extreme violence and dislocation of his arbitrary rule; Kissinger describes the poverty, chaos, and pessimistic prognostications about China in the 1970s. Mao's regime was a militaristic dictatorship with a failing economy; it was not a model for the current economic breadth of Chinese-American relations.

No one at the time anticipated that Mao would be remembered as the "father" of a prosperous, cosmopolitan, capitalist China. No one expected the incredibly rapid rise of Mao's starving and exhausted society from the antimodernism of the Cultural Revolution to the hypercapitalism of the early twentieth century. Kissinger admits his own astonishment:

> China's bustling cities, the construction booms, the traffic gridlocks, the un-Communist dilemma of a growth rate occasionally threatened by inflation and, at other times, looked to by Western democracies as a bulwark against global recession—all of these were inconceivable in Mao's drab China of agricultural communes, a stagnant economy, and a population wearing standard jackets while professing ideological fervor from the "Little Red Book" of Mao quotations.[2]

The United States also went through a series of major transformations from the protests, crime, and stagflation of the 1970s to the unity, innovation, and growth of the 1980s and 1990s. At the time of Mao's death and the "normalization" of relations between Beijing and Washington, the United States had just withdrawn from a long and costly war in Vietnam. The country suffered through a string of energy crises and its first prolonged economic downturn since the Great Depression. Americans were more deeply divided on major political issues, and they were profoundly uncertain about their future. As in China, the "historical trends" of 1970s America did not point with any accuracy to the triumphs and prosperity of the coming decades.[3]

The Chinese and American societies of the 1970s—when Mao and Kissinger were in power—shared little resemblance to what they would become under Deng Xiaoping and Ronald Reagan in the 1980s. The two societies did not show any obvious signs of the remarkable growth they would experience, fueled by global capital and trade, in the decades after the Cold War. Aaron Friedberg is one of many authors to describe a contemporary Chinese-American relationship that shows more overlap, interpenetration, and direct rivalry than anything even Kissinger could have expected from Chinese and American history up to the late 1970s. There is no obvious historical precedent for the current global system of trade, finance, and military force in which the United States and China are the biggest players.[4]

Why, then, does history matter so much to Henry Kissinger? Why does he believe it must matter for his readers who are trying to run successful businesses and manage international relationships? How does Kissinger conceive of historical knowledge as a foundation for effective contemporary policymaking?

No American figure in the last century has used historical analysis more explicitly to formulate policy. Nearly every one of the books and articles in Kissinger's enormous oeuvre—more than ten thousand pages of text—begins with an effort to place a foreign policy crisis or question in a deeper historical context. Nearly every one of these books and articles concludes with a set of historical lessons, translated into policy instructions for government officials. There is little theory and even less data in Kissinger's influential writing. His evidence is all historical. It is drawn from interpretations of past leaders—Klemens von Metternich, Viscount Castlereagh, Otto von Bismarck, Winston Churchill, Charles de Gaulle, Mao, and, of course Kissinger himself—and how their actions shape contemporary policymaking.

The paradox is that Kissinger is not a historian by training or inclination. His formal and informal education has been in philosophy, politics, and policymaking, not careful research about the past. Kissinger has, in fact, never examined primary documents in an archive. He has never paid close attention to historiography—the evolving debates among professional historians about sources and interpretations. Most of all, Kissinger has written in a selective way about particular events and personalities. For all the pages he has produced, he has never systematically analyzed the complex and contradictory record of a topic—the multiple perspectives and sources that define deep historical analysis. Kissinger's narratives are simple, linear, and outcome-driven. They rely on few sources, and even fewer competing interpretations.

This observation does not mean that Kissinger's long book narratives are somehow untrue. Sophisticated explanations do not have greater purchase on truth than do simpler analyses. Kissinger's narratives are, however, very different from the standard writings of historians (even "public historians"), who generally favor complexity and contingency over determinism. Kissinger's account of U.S.-China relations has few actors and even fewer surprising twists and turns. Historians generally look beyond the top leaders, and they generally emphasize events outside the control of the figures Kissinger most closely considers. Even traditional diplomatic historians cover a wider range of actors and events than those described in *On China* and other Kissinger books.[5]

Kissinger is, therefore, like the renowned healer who does not practice traditional medicine. He is the most respected public historical thinker of the late twentieth century who does not work like a historian. For this reason, above all others, Kissinger's writings are consistently criticized (and frequently disdained) by professional historians. His writings lack sufficient evidence, analysis of historiography, and attention to diverse actors. None of his books would make it through a history department dissertation defense, a rigorous historical peer review, or a university tenure committee. Kissinger's historical thinking is impressionistic and presentist, rather than systematic and academic.

The Power of Kissinger's Historical Thinking

Dismissed by most professional historians, Kissinger's historical analysis has always had its greatest influence on nonhistorians. They are the people who buy his books, invite him to speak, and appoint him to powerful positions. Although he often appears as a charlatan in the eyes of scholars who study the past, he is an oracle (now a legendary prophet) for those who want to anticipate the future. Even after turning ninety years of age, Kissinger continues to draw eager crowds of upwardly mobile professionals across the globe who believe that his words will help them advance. He is a powerful monument for awestruck audiences; to touch him is to connect with larger political forces.

This observation applies to Kissinger's public detractors as well as his defenders: both groups of policy partisans want to connect their arguments to him. For detractors and defenders, he is a key historical actor in the continuing evolution of American foreign policy. His interpretations, his actions, and his advocacy have shaped American relationships with China, the Middle East, and other regions. To understand and master those relationships today, one must grapple with Kissinger's histories. Is he correct in his definition of inherited American national interests? Have he and other powerful Americans acted effectively to pursue those interests? What are the lessons from past American actions, and what are the alternative paths forward? Although enigmatic, Kissinger's historical interpretations of foreign policy define current debates.

For those on different sides of key issues, Kissinger articulates the deeper forces—both good and bad—moving American policy. That is the power of his historical interpretations. Other writers use history to meditate on details, complexities, and dilemmas; Kissinger uses history to articulate vast, tectonic interpretations for major developments in the international system. His history integrates different issues, it offers clear coherence, and it is prescriptive; it is precisely the kind of historical knowledge that people concerned with contemporary policy need. Every president since Dwight D. Eisenhower has used Kissinger's interpretations to define, at least in part, what he is for and what he is against. Kissinger's history ignores parochial scholarly debates and instead frames policy discussions.[6]

On China is representative of his approach and its appeal. He writes, "The appropriate label for the Sino-American relationship is less partnership than 'co-evolution.' It means that both countries pursue their domestic imperatives, cooperating where possible, and adjust their relations to minimize conflict. Neither side endorses all the aims of the other or presumes a total identity of interests, but both sides seek to identify and develop complementary interests."[7]

This capsule paragraph, repeated in different forms throughout this and other long works by Kissinger, offers a clear and coherent framework for understanding the emergence of friendly relations between Washington and Beijing that began in the early 1970s; it also explains continued rivalries, tensions, and uncertainties. Instead of assessing contemporary foreign policy by focusing on sources of conflict and cooperation alone, Kissinger defines a pattern of historical "co-evolution" that rejects alliance or war, but embraces diplomacy, patience, and compromise above all. Kissinger's history of the U.S.-China relationship is an imperative for continuing what he calls "the normal interactions of major power centers" since the 1970s. This involves what he describes as the successful balancing of "long-term moral convictions [especially human rights] with case-to-case adaptations to requirements of national security."[8]

Kissinger's histories are populated by large impersonal forces—economic development, military capability, demographics, and geography—and he defines the systematic and enduring ways in which these forces work upon each other to explain openings for human agency. His histories allow readers to escape determinism by showing how leaders of insight and courage ("statesmen")—including Mao and Kissinger himself—have understood the system and exploited its dynamics for their purposes. Historical understanding and manipulation, Kissinger argues, are the sources of effective leadership; all of his great statesmen were historical thinkers. Ideological zealotry, national chauvinism, and other ahistorical motivations are, according to Kissinger, sources of international failure; all of his failed leaders (including Louis Napoleon, Woodrow Wilson, and Nikita Khrushchev) were idealistic and historically ignorant.

The almost unparalleled influence of Kissinger's historical thinking derives from his deep engagement with the past, combined with a sharp focus on present application. He does not address specific issues but instead the big questions about relations between societies and the avenues for effective leadership. He does not meditate on the contradictions and complexities of the past, but instead articulates coherent and actionable frameworks to explain the options available for policymakers today.

Kissinger's historical thinking is more art than science, more image and description than rigorous research, more impression and interpretation than careful reconstruction of the documentary record. His artistry is his attraction for readers who are struggling to escape the seeming chaos of our contemporary world. His models have always been more literary and philosophical than technical and scientific. Literary and philosophical history is, ultimately, most widely used by citizens and policymakers.[9]

Does History Repeat Itself?

On China offers a revealing window into Kissinger's artistry, his thinking about history, and his application of history to contemporary policy. It merits close attention as a culmination of his lifelong engagement with history

[margin note: How Kissinger views / approaches history]

and policy. It also deserves close scrutiny because of its influence on contemporary thinking about U.S.-China relations.

Kissinger closes his long account with an epilogue titled "Does History Repeat Itself?" This is probably the most widely read part of the book—the concluding "lessons" many readers wanted when they purchased this tome. It is Kissinger's summation statement about how to understand the future of U.S.-China relations: the dangers and the opportunities.

What is the "history" that Kissinger warns against repetition in his epilogue? It is not U.S.-China relations during the Cold War, but the origins of the First World War. Pointing to the history of the period, when a rapidly rising Germany triggered a destructive war with its neighbors, Kissinger warns against a simple application of this searing experience to the rise of China a century later. He calls this kind of analogical reasoning a "surrender to the presumed mechanism of history."[10] After five hundred pages of historical details on China and the United States, Kissinger wants to remind readers that the past is not determinative of the future; we are not locked into an inevitable pattern of Great Power conflict, as some have claimed.[11]

Kissinger abruptly shifts from his focus on U.S.-China relations to the Anglo-German rivalry before the First World War in order to explain the different possibilities for these two periods. Great Power conflict was avoidable in the early twentieth century, just as it is, according to Kissinger, a hundred years later. He wishes to show how knowledge of history can prevent its undesirable repetition. He is not alone. The unintended and enormously destructive conflict in the early twentieth century inspired an enormous quantity of scholarship, and it remains a central nightmare of those who study contemporary international relations.

For Kissinger, the events around 1914 offer an enduring warning that the world does not need a reckless leader, like Adolf Hitler or Hideki Tōjō a generation later, to descend into a nearly uncontrolled maelstrom of violence and bloodletting. Kissinger is in good scholarly company when he depicts World War I as the central historical warning about uncontrolled international competition among powerful, insecure states. The Great War cautions against a laissez-faire approach to Great Power rivalries. It also cautions against assumptions about an "organic" international system that is either peaceful or destructive, cooperative or conflict-ridden. Kissinger rejects both the liberal assumption of order and the realist assumption of anarchy.[12]

Kissinger's earlier book, *Diplomacy*, elaborated in these terms on the lessons of the early twentieth century. In it he emphasized the mismatch between intentions and capabilities among the Great Powers, and the failures of policymakers to control escalating fears, insecurities, and arms races. For Kissinger, the uncertainty of international affairs opened possibilities for peace and war, but powerful figures in multiple societies made choices, both intentional and unintentional, that contributed to conflict escalation rather than peaceful dispute resolution. The First World War erupted, according to Kissinger, from a "doomsday mechanism" of international rivalries that festered and built on themselves, where one act of aggressive defense triggered another, until a momentum toward war became very difficult for diplomats to resist. None of the most powerful monarchs and ministers had the foresight and courage to step back from this process and rethink basic assumptions.

Tit-for-tat escalation, rather than creative diplomacy, was particularly common in a period when the largest powers had relatively weak and uncertain political leaders. Europe on the eve of the First World War lacked strong strategic thinkers to restrain war pressures. The continent suffered, according to this analysis, without a Metternich, a Bismarck, or even a Kissinger:

> By 1914, the confrontation between Germany and Austria-Hungary on the one side, and the Triple Entente on the other, had turned deadly earnest. The statesmen of all the major countries had helped to construct the diplomatic doomsday mechanism that made each succeeding crisis progressively more difficult to solve. Their military chiefs had vastly compounded the peril by adding strategic plans which compressed the time available for decision-making. Since the military plans depended on speed and the diplomatic machinery was geared to its traditional leisurely pace, it became impossible to disentangle the crisis under intense time pressure.[13]

The First World War was not inevitable, but it also was not easily avoidable without strong strategic leaders. Kissinger holds politicians culpable above all. They are the historical actors who make the key choices;

they are the historical actors whom Kissinger conceives as the source of creativity in a complex international system with strong tendencies toward destruction.

Kissinger's world is filled with the stubborn inertia of cultures and civilizations, pushed and pulled at key moments by statesmen of varying power and insight. Most policymakers are failed statesmen, according to Kissinger, because they do not understand when and how to shift the dominant forces around them. The great statesmen—like Mao, Metternich, and Bismarck—are the ones who exert well-chosen leverage to nudge the "stream" of history in a new direction. They read the history around them carefully and find the pressure points where targeted stops and releases can help control the currents of geopolitics. Great statesmen, according to Kissinger, have historical wisdom, artistic creativity, and the strategic eye of a structural engineer building on unforgiving terrain. Even the most skilled statesmen cannot predict the future; they adapt, they create new options, and they reject the apparent inevitability of the world as it is. Kissinger's statesman is, by necessity, radical in his means, even if he remains conservative in his ends.

Historical Opportunism

Kissinger defines the major wars of the twentieth century as consequences of historically informed decisionmaking without historically courageous statesmen. This is one of Kissinger's key points. To study history is not enough; leaders must be prepared to identify and seize opportunities for changing the trajectory of history to their advantage. This requires analysis of the pressures for continuity and identification of the possible sources for change. Articulating this argument in his writings, and applying it in his own policymaking, Kissinger's emphasis on historical opportunities for leadership echoes Niccolò Machiavelli's famous advice to Lorenzo de Medici:

> I judge that it might be true that fortune is arbiter of half of our actions, but also that she leaves the other half, or close to it, for us to govern. And I liken her to one of these violent rivers which, when they become enraged, flood the plains, ruin the trees and the buildings, lift earth from this part, drop in another; each person flees

before them, everyone yields to their impetus without being able to hinder them in any regard. And although they are like this, it is not as if men, when times are quiet, could not provide for them with dikes and dams so that when they rise later, either they go by a canal or their impetus is neither so wanton nor so damaging. It happens similarly with fortune, which demonstrates her power where virtue has not been put in order to resist her and therefore turns her impetus where she knows that dams and dikes have not been made to contain her.[14]

Kissinger laments that the early twentieth-century leaders of Europe failed to contain and redirect the onrushing currents of war, and he warns against repeating similar passivity. The figures who made policy understood the historical forces around them, but they surrendered to the easy and disastrous paths of predictable action. They failed to find leverage for effective leadership in their historical analyses, as Kissinger recounts. The "generation of 1914" was resigned to its fate and mired in internal controversies, rather than focused on measures to extricate their societies from rising militarism.

Above all, Kissinger affirms the historical lesson that strong civilian leaders must limit the autonomy of their armies and seek vigorous diplomatic negotiations during the periods of highest tension. As a scholar and a practitioner, Kissinger consistently emphasizes the importance of seizing the initiative and defining the diplomatic discussions around difficult strategic issues. The "generation of 1914" failed to act in this way, and it brought disaster upon itself.

Kissinger recounts this history because he fears its repetition in contemporary U.S.-China relations. He sees himself as a wise man who can use his learning and experience to prevent descent into conflict. His historical analysis is directly relevant for his argument, and it is also a measure for lending credence to his advice.

Crowe and Kennan

In an effort to connect contemporary U.S.-China relations to the disturbing history of the early twentieth century, Kissinger invokes the famous 1907 "Memorandum on the Present State of British Relations with France and Germany," written by a high-ranking member of the British Crown's Foreign Office, Eyre Crowe. Crowe diagnosed a century-long pattern of "one-sided aggressiveness" by Germany and its Prussian predecessor, and he criticized British appeasement policies that allegedly displayed a "never-failing readiness to purchase the resumption of friendly relations by concession after concession" to Berlin. Crowe did not predict an inevitable war, but he saw Anglo-German conflict as unavoidable:

> It might be deduced that the antagonism is too deeply rooted in the relative position of the two countries to allow of its being bridged over by the kind of temporary expedients to which England has so long and so patiently resorted. On this view of the case it would have to be assumed that Germany is deliberately following a policy which is essentially opposed to vital British interests, and that an armed conflict cannot in the long run be averted, except by England either sacrificing those interests, with the result that she would lose her position as an independent Great Power, or making herself too strong to give Germany the chance of succeeding in a war. This is the opinion of those who see in the whole trend of Germany's policy conclusive evidence that she is consciously aiming at the establishment of a German hegemony, at first in Europe, and eventually in the world.

Crowe's final recommendation to the British prime minister, at the end of more than twenty pages of dense text, was *not* to prepare for immediate war. That was too rash, and perhaps unnecessary, according to Crowe. He believed that there was a definite historical pattern to German expansionist aims, but that they were not irreversible. German leaders were rational, he explained, and they responded to obvious and overwhelming force. Crowe renounced diplomatic concessions, counseling for strict limits on Germany, enforced by British military power, and accompanied by frank recognition of the adversarial relationship between the two nations.

Anticipating George F. Kennan's advice to American policymakers about the Soviet Union forty years later, Crowe called for firm British containment of German power as the only viable alternative to war or British decline. He predicted that Germany would be encouraged if she meets on England's part with unvarying courtesy and consideration in all matters of common concern, but also with a prompt and firm refusal to enter into any one-sided bargains or arrangements, and the most unbending determination to uphold British rights and interests in every part of the globe. There will be no surer or quicker way to win the respect of the German Government and of the German nation.[15]

Kennan offered parallel advice for Americans on the "sources of Soviet conduct" and the wisdom of firm containment policies after 1945. His words echoed Crowe's in their use of history to discern a pattern of adversarial behavior and a method for consistent resistance, short of war. Based on a close assessment of the Kremlin's action and aims, Kennan argued,

It is clear that the United States cannot expect in the foreseeable future to enjoy political intimacy with the Soviet regime. It must continue to regard the Soviet Union as a rival, not a partner, in the political arena. It must continue to expect that Soviet policies will reflect no abstract love of peace and stability, no real faith in the possibility of a permanent happy coexistence of the Socialist and capitalist worlds, but rather a cautious, persistent pressure toward the disruption and weakening of all rival influence and rival power.

Kennan counseled for a policy of "firm containment, designed to confront the Russians with unalterable counter-force at every point where they show signs of encroaching upon the interests of a peaceful and stable world."[16] He predicted that the Soviets would respect force and avoid war. Kennan, like Crowe, believed that the enemy could be managed if opportunities for expansion were closed and temptations to make trouble were deterred. His advocacy of containment echoed Crowe's rejection of one-sided bargains (that was how Kennan viewed the Yalta agreement), and it reiterated Crowe's determination to uphold rights and interests against continued efforts at enemy encroachment.

Both strategists saw strength as the source of successful diplomacy (not the reverse), and both saw strategic value in recognizing the historical trends toward conflict and working forcefully—sometimes aggressively—to restrain and manage those trends. Most of all, both strategists gave pride of place to displays of national power and resolve, not the maneuverings of diplomats or other figures. For Crowe and Kennan, the strategic alignment of incentives and penalties mattered more than the personal relationships, negotiations, and initiatives of individual actors. Diplomacy was an extension of national strategic judgments; it did not alter the fundamental aims of states in conflict.

Diplomacy and the Statesman

Kissinger praises Crowe and Kennan for their learned efforts to understand the deep sources of German and Soviet international behavior in the twentieth century. He also affirms their astute and eloquent explanations of historical trends toward Great Power conflict in their times. He warns, however, against the firmness of their judgments and the rigidity of their prescriptions. He argues that they leave too little room for maneuvering, too little opportunity for compromise, and too little margin for controlled risk-taking.

Treating diplomacy as more of an art than a science, Kissinger argues that displays of strength and postures of containment are too passive, too conservative, and too reactive; he looks for statesmen who are willing to pursue a more active agenda that includes discussions and overtures—even when dealing with dangerous adversaries—to redefine international relations. For Kissinger, strength and containment cannot encompass an effective foreign policy, especially if leaders aim to improve—not just preserve—the strategic circumstances that they have inherited.[17]

Kissinger's main point of difference is his belief that individual diplomats can exert more leverage over historical forces than Crowe and Kennan concede in their analyses of geopolitics. He places much more emphasis on personality, negotiation, and creativity than do Crowe and Kennan. In his writings, Kissinger attributes extensive power to the vision, charisma, and energy of great leaders—Metternich and Bismarck in the nineteenth century, Mao and Anwar Sadat in the twentieth century. He treats them as men who reordered the forces of history that they inherited, linking issues formerly separated, and separating possible contentions from one another. They bent history to serve their purposes, according to Kissinger, and they found the leverage to pursue limited but significant change on their own terms. That was how Metternich managed the Congress of Vienna,

Bismarck the unification of Germany, Mao the Communist Revolution in China, and Sadat the creation of a U.S.-Egyptian alliance. Kissinger has written prolifically about the need for contemporary American policymakers to do the same.

That was his aspiration when given the chance. In his work as a policymaker, Kissinger tried to act as he imagined his heroes would: traveling ceaselessly to meet with adversaries, negotiating tirelessly to forge compromises, articulating threats to cajole concessions, and dispensing aid to encourage deal making. Kissinger spent his years as national security adviser and secretary of state embroiled in complex diplomatic meetings. No modern American policymaker invested so much time and thought in mastering the negotiations and Great Power relations of his era.

In some ways, Kissinger's diplomacy crowded out space for strategy, as he flew rapidly from one negotiation to another. His energetic personal diplomacy also encouraged a tendency toward micromanagement of negotiations, a trait that was often criticized by his subordinates. Reading the record of Kissinger's years in office, it does appear that his emphasis on the historical role of the creative statesman raised inhuman demands on his time, attention, and crisis management. Even if Kissinger could embody the insights of Metternich or Bismarck, applying that wisdom to the vast array of modern policy pressures proved too difficult. The limitations of American policies in Southeast Asia, South America, and sub-Saharan Africa—three regions Kissinger understood poorly—reflect the shortcomings of applying a Eurocentric vision of the statesman to a global landscape with very diverse historical experiences.[18]

Kissinger's marathon discussions with Arab, Chinese, Israeli, North Vietnamese, and Soviet leaders framed what he perceived as the range of possible policy options in the 1970s. He brought a clear sense of the opportunities for American military and economic power to each of these negotiations, but also recognized the limits of American control over events on the ground. Like other Great Powers in the past, the United States needed to restrain its excessive commitments and build effective relationships with powerful regional actors. In this context, Kissinger's summaries of his travels for President Richard Nixon were acts of policy in themselves, defining international openings and outlining paths for American action through other states—what observers called the Nixon Doctrine.

Kissinger's diplomacy put flesh on the bones of the Nixon Doctrine. He did not accept the trends of the Cold War as they were, but looked to shift the trajectory of relations between the United States and the Arab states, Israel, North Vietnam, the Soviet Union and, of course, China. He wanted the United States to become the indispensable broker between these different regimes, and to secure its interests by convincing (and, if necessary, bribing) other states to act on its behalf. His core aim was to direct cooperative interstate efforts through discussion and, when necessary, coercion. Although Kissinger's efforts were met with very mixed results, he raised American expectations for diplomacy and defined an era—for better and for worse—by the pursuit of détente.[19]

Détente, for Kissinger, was an effort to convert the bipolar Cold War conflict into a multilateral set of Great Power negotiations. He sought to return the international system to a "normal" historical mode of politics, where the biggest states managed conflicts, traded territories, and avoided major wars. This system required historically informed statesmen, and Kissinger believed he had found them in Mao Zedong, Anwar Sadat and, of course, himself. For this reason, American foreign policy in the early 1970s was highly personalized; it focused intensively on order and stability, rather than democracy and justice. Kissinger believed that was the core wisdom of modern diplomatic history.[20]

Before and After the Cold War

Kissinger's writings reach back before his Cold War years as a policymaker, and they stretch forward into the twenty-first century. In his self-conscious references to a long and enduring history, Kissinger is a romantic thinker who rejects the "scientific" presumptions of exactness, predictability, and structural necessity. His historical philosophy is largely derived from nineteenth-century Germany, emphasizing an inner spirit, the power of genius, and the possibilities of charisma. In his writings and his self-fashioning as a strategic wise man, he searches for the "transcendent" figures in the past who can guide present leaders to a new conceptualization of their society's future, liberated from "surrender to the presumed mechanism of history."[21]

Kissinger clings to his faith in "great men"—or at least great statesmen—and their ability to shape history. For him the vectors of change and the institutions of power are more susceptible to individual shifts than Crowe and Kennan recognized. The First World War and the Cold War were, at least in part according to Kissinger, results of policies that assumed Great Power conflict was unavoidable and required forceful containment. In both historical cases, Kissinger argues, policymakers devoted insufficient attention to the opportunities for shifting the nature of international relationships and creating an alternative to contained conflict. Those correctly diagnosing historical pressures toward discord were too content to accept the status quo, rather than undertake measures to direct the vectors of historical change. The romantic in Kissinger sees power in the flow of history, and charisma in the ability of certain men to move history.

At critical moments, however, men have failed to move history. Kissinger criticizes political leaders during the years before the First World War for failing to restrain their militaries and pursue a new set of diplomatic agreements to manage conflicting interests. That is, of course, what Metternich and Bismarck had done decades earlier. Alas, there were no Metternichs or Bismarcks in the European chancelleries on the eve of August 1914.[22]

During the early years of the Cold War Kissinger criticized American leaders, including George F. Kennan and Secretary of State Dean Acheson, for emphasizing "situations of strength" rather than possible areas of agreement with Soviet leaders on the postwar division of Europe and the management of nuclear weapons. According to Kissinger, Kennan and Acheson were prudent in their defense of American interests in Europe and Asia, but they were not creative or imaginative about alternative arrangements to the conflicts they took for granted. Kissinger argues that Americans should have sought more agreement with the Soviet leaders than they did, especially in the years after 1945 and the months after Joseph Stalin's death in 1953. Working as Nixon's chief foreign policy aide, Kissinger pursued broader American agreements with the Soviet Union, as well as the Chinese Communist regime, than at any time since the Second World War.[23]

This history is useful for Kissinger in examining contemporary U.S.-China relations because it captures the default trajectory toward conflict between these two societies, and the possibilities for cooperation if leaders can break away from their resignation to the apparent inevitability of discord. Leaders in Washington and Beijing have the opportunity to build a new "Pacific Community," Kissinger argues, if they turn insecurities and threats into reasons for negotiation, agreement, and long-term relationship building. Kissinger explains that this is the appropriate historical precedent to apply from postwar Europe to contemporary East Asia:

> One of the great achievements of the generation that founded the world order at the end of the Second World War was the creation of the concept of an Atlantic Community. Could a similar concept replace or at least mitigate the potential tensions between the United States and China? It would reflect the reality that the United States is an Asian power, and that many Asian powers demand it. And it responds to China's aspiration to a global role.[24]

This is, of course, the path that the United States, Canada, and their European partners learned to follow after the Second World War, when they rejected inherited patterns of conflict in Western Europe. This is also what Kissinger proudly argues that he, Nixon, Mao, and Zhou Enlai achieved, turning away from twenty years of mutual recriminations, direct combat in Korea, and recurring crises in the Taiwan Strait to create a new "opening" between their societies. As a young Kissinger reflected in his very revealing undergraduate thesis, history is about both conflict and opportunity, decline and renewal. Leaders, he then wrote, must turn conflict and decline into opportunity and renewal.[25]

Kissinger's thinking about history and policy has always been dialectical. That is reflected in the density of his prose, his positioning between academic and policy expertise, and his fundamental romanticism about the human condition. It is evident in his intensive, elaborate, and prolific reflections on the power of historical trends, and his passionate commitment as a policymaker and a public intellectual to the uses of leadership initiatives—often in secret, out of the public eye—to shift historical trends toward new purposes. History has a definite direction for Kissinger, but well-informed, courageous leaders can shift it in important and enduring ways.

Kissinger and History

Kissinger has published a mountain of articles and books throughout his career, and he continues to add to this intimidating edifice.[26] His writings are almost all historical and self-serving. They are an accurate, although incomplete, representation of his behavior as a policymaker. Kissinger leaves a lot out, but he fairly faithfully recounts what he thought he was doing: his analysis of the international system, his understanding of American purposes, and his vision of statesmanship.

Kissinger's conceptualization of history is built around large states and the sources of military, economic, and cultural power that they possess. He sees the evolving balance of power between large states as the fuel for international relations, and he asserts that policymakers must read the evolving balance of power in an accurate and dynamic manner. They must shape their preferences to take account of the opportunities and limits created by the balance of power at a given moment.

Statesmen, according to Kissinger, read the system in this way, and they do something more: they recognize that history is not determinative, but presents a range of possibilities. The statesman pursues creative and beneficial possibilities for the national interest, using diplomacy and coercion to encourage a particular result. During the Cold War, this approach underpinned Kissinger's effort to move beyond containment and forge cooperative relations with both the Soviet Union and Communist China—what became known as détente. Kissinger's post–Cold War thinking points to focused efforts on U.S.-China partnership—a "Pacific Community" on the model of the Cold War Atlantic Community, underpinning the North Atlantic Treaty Organization, the Conference on Security and Cooperation in Europe, and the European Union. These institutions were historical achievements of multilateral diplomacy, he recounts, and they provide a precedent for what he hopes to encourage in East Asia today.

In Kissinger's conceptualization, history is an inspiration for imagining diplomatic initiatives that can nudge the balance of power in new directions. It is also a license for dynamic, creative, and even somewhat radical leaders. Kissinger's statesman is a forward-looking risk taker who is willing to act in nontraditional ways to further inherited interests. Kissinger's statesman is energetic, not cautious; he pursues positive results amid systemic imperfections.

The controversies surrounding Kissinger are a result, in part, of his historical thinking. His worldview gives little agency to democracy or human rights. His understanding of power is hierarchical, not egalitarian. Within an American society that fetishizes "eternal" political truths about constitutionalism and rights, Kissinger's approach offers an alternative keyed to the historical evolution of power and leadership. His writings fascinate readers because they are so different from standard political fare. His writings frequently fail to persuade, however, because their historicism is hard for idealistic Americans to swallow.

Kissinger remains an "outsider" to mainstream American thinking, and this is what makes him such a controversial, curious, and uncommon figure. It is also what makes his influence so overwhelming and so limited at the same time. On current U.S. policy toward China, key actors must contend with Kissinger's historical arguments, but his words will not shape the fundamental choices. His big books add to the debate; they do not change the dominant currents of national behavior.

Historical consciousness has its constraints. Kissinger would predict that himself, in a society uncomfortable with what another historical thinker, Reinhold Niebuhr, identified as the unavoidable ironies of history.[27]

Notes

1. Henry Kissinger, *On China* (New York: Penguin, 2011), 131.

2. Ibid., 368.

3. The literature on the United States at home and abroad in the 1970s is rapidly growing. See, among others, Daniel J. Sargent, *A Superpower Transformed: The Remaking of American Foreign Relations in the 1970s* (Oxford University Press, 2015); Thomas Borstelmann, *The 1970s: A New Global History from Civil Rights to Economic Inequality* (Princeton University Press, 2012); Jefferson Cowie, *Stayin' Alive: The 1970s and the Last Days of the Working Class* (New York: New Press, 2010).

4. Aaron Friedberg, *A Contest for Supremacy* (New York: Norton, 2011).

5. Some of the most widely respected diplomatic histories of U.S.-China relations are Odd Arne Westad, *Restless Empire: China and the World since 1750* (New York: Basic Books, 2012); Michael H. Hunt, *The Genesis of Chinese Communist Foreign Policy* (Columbia University Press, 1998); Warren I. Cohen, *America's Response to China: A History of Sino-American Relations*, 5th ed. (Columbia University Press, 2010); and Michael Schaller, *The United States and China: Into the Twenty-First Century*, 3d ed. (New York: Oxford University Press, 2002).

6. On this point, and Kissinger's influence on policy debates since the 1950s, see Jeremi Suri, *Henry Kissinger and the American Century* (Belknap Press of Harvard University Press, 2007).

7. Kissinger, *On China*, 526.

8. Ibid., 527, 526.

9. On this point, see Suri, *Henry Kissinger and the American Century*, chapter 1.

10. Kissinger, *On China*, 518.

11. For an influential theoretical argument about the determinative historical pressures toward Great Power conflict, see John Mearsheimer, *The Tragedy of Great Power Politics* (New York: Norton, 2001). Kissinger rejects the systemic determinism of realist theorists like Mearsheimer.

12. For an influential statement of the liberal internationalist position, see G. John Ikenberry, *Liberal Leviathan* (Princeton University Press, 2011). For an influential statement of the realist position, see Mearsheimer, *The Tragedy of Great Power Politics*.

13. Henry Kissinger, *Diplomacy* (New York: Simon and Schuster, 1994), 201.

14. Niccolò Machiavelli, *The Prince*, translated by Harvey C. Mansfield, 2d ed. (Chicago: University of Chicago Press, 1998), 98–99.

15. Eyre Crowe, "Memorandum on the Present State of British Relations with France and Germany," in *British Documents on the Origins of the War*, vol. 3, edited by G. P. Gooch and Harold Temperley (London: His Majesty's Stationary Office, 1928), 397–420 (http://tmh.floonet.net/pdf/eyre_crowe_memo.pdf).

16. X [George F. Kennan], "The Sources of Soviet Conduct," *Foreign Affairs* 25, no. 4 (1947), 566–82.

17. For more elaboration on these points and their roots in Kissinger's writings during the 1950s and 1960s, see Suri, *Henry Kissinger and the American Century*, chapter 4.

18. On this point, see Jussi Hanhimäki, *The Flawed Architect: Henry Kissinger and American Foreign Policy* (Oxford University Press, 2004); and Raymond Garthoff, *Détente and Confrontation: American-Soviet Relations from Nixon to Reagan*, rev. ed. (Brookings Institution Press, 1994).

19. See Garthoff, *Détente and Confrontation*; and Suri, *Henry Kissinger and the American Century*, chapter 5.

20. This is the historical record of détente and the foreign policies of the Great Powers, especially the United States, that is analyzed in Jeremi Suri, *Power and Protest: Global Revolution and the Rise of Détente* (Harvard University Press, 2003).

21. Henry Kissinger, *A World Restored: Metternich, Castlereagh, and the Problems of Peace, 1812–1822* (London: Phoenix Press, 2000), 329. Kissinger uses the same words in his Ph.D. dissertation, upon which *A World Restored* is based; see Henry Alfred Kissinger, "Peace, Legitimacy, and the Equilibrium (A Study of the Statesmanship of Castlereagh and Metternich)," Ph.D. dissertation, Harvard University, April 1954, 541–42.

22. Kissinger, *Diplomacy*, 201–03.

23. Suri, *Kissinger and the American Century*, chapters 4–5.

24. Kissinger, *On China*, 528.

25. Henry A. Kissinger, "The Meaning of History (Reflections on Spengler, Toynbee and Kant)," B.A. thesis, Harvard University, 1950.

26. After *On China*, Kissinger published another four-hundred-page book; see Henry Kissinger, *World Order* (New York: Penguin, 2014).

27. See Reinhold Niebuhr, *The Irony of American History* (New York: Scribner's, 1952).

3

Policymaking and the Uses of the Vietnam War

"**I**raq is George Bush's Vietnam." So declared Senator Edward M. Kennedy in a speech on January 9, 2007, one day before President George W. Bush was due to announce his plan to send twenty thousand U.S. troops to shore up the faltering American military effort in Iraq. Like many other critics of the nearly four-year-old war in Iraq, Kennedy staunchly opposed the "surge." The Bush administration's plan, insisted the critics, flew in the face of common sense as well as the desires of the American people, as had been demonstrated most recently in Democratic gains in the 2006 midterm elections. Speaking at the National Press Club in Washington, Kennedy phrased his reservations in a way bound to generate headlines. The Massachusetts Democrat insisted that, just like Lyndon Johnson forty years earlier, Bush was responding to frustration and setback by doubling down on a failed enterprise: "In Vietnam, the White House grew increasingly obsessed with victory, and increasingly divorced from the will of the people and any rational policy." In fact, he continued, in Indochina "there was no military solution" to be had. "But we kept trying to find one anyway. In the end, 58,000 Americans died in the search for it. The echoes of that disaster," Kennedy concluded, "are all around us today."[1]

Seven months later, President Bush responded in kind. Confident that the surge was bringing positive results in Iraq, Bush drew no less assertively on the history of the Vietnam War in making the case that the United States must stick with his policy. During the Vietnam War, just as at present in Iraq, "people argued that the real problem was America's presence and that if we would just withdraw, the killing would end," Bush declared in a speech on August 22, 2007, to the annual convention of the American Veterans of Foreign Wars. In fact, asserted the president, the problem in Vietnam was that U.S. forces had not fought long enough. He contended that giving up before the fight was won had damaged American credibility in the eyes of its Cold War adversaries, but the core of his argument had to do with the impact of pullout on the people of Indochina. "One unmistakable legacy of Vietnam," Bush declared, "is that the price of America's withdrawal was paid by millions of innocent citizens whose agonies would add to our vocabulary new terms like 'boat people,' 're-education camps,' and 'killing fields.'"[2]

Thus did two powerful voices in American politics invoke utterly contradictory lessons of America's lost war in Vietnam. For Kennedy the Vietnam War taught the need to understand the limits of American power; for Bush it taught the need to use that power boldly. The starkness of this debate was, of course, nothing new in the annals of American efforts to draw on the history of American involvement in Vietnam in weighing later policy dilemmas. Since even before the end of the war in 1975, Americans have been arguing about the implications for the future conduct of U.S. foreign policy. The answers range across a broad spectrum of possibilities: policymakers and politicians, journalists and scholars have invoked Vietnam to warn against action abroad and to urge bold intervention, to decry the influence of domestic politics on policymaking and to highlight the need for greater popular involvement, and to champion counterinsurgency methods and to advocate audacious conventional operations (to cite just three of the most jarring contradictions).

The remarkable malleability of the Vietnam analogy flows from at least two basic characteristics of the war and its place in American life since 1975. First, the Vietnam War was a sprawling event—or, more accurately, a long series of events—that persisted over at least two decades and subsumed an enormous variety of experiences. It is therefore hardly surprising that, in retrospect, different observers draw conflicting lessons. Much depends on which aspects of the war—and which period of time—one examines, and which reminiscences one trusts. In this regard the Vietnam analogy functions differently from the other historical point of reference cited frequently by U.S. policymakers over the last seven decades: the Munich Conference of 1938. Whereas the Munich analogy generally carries just one message—appeasement encourages aggression—the Vietnam analogy contains any number of meanings.

Second, policymakers draw different lessons from the war because conflicting points of view are sustained passionately in the larger political culture within which they operate. Although most academic writing on the war advances the view that the political failings of the South Vietnamese state made it virtually impossible for the United States to achieve its objectives, the larger body of literature—popular studies, battle accounts, and memoirs—points to a wide range of interpretive possibilities. At the same time, ordinary Americans continue to hold an array of basic attitudes about the war. Although majorities of Americans have viewed the war as a mistake ever since the fighting ended, polls show that substantial segments of the population have clung to the idea that the United States could have won if only the military had been allowed to wage the war free of constraints imposed by civilian leaders in Washington.[3] Divisions over the basic meaning of the war are tenacious in part because Vietnam remains a proxy for disputes over fundamental political and cultural values, attitudes that are rarely altered by historical scholarship.[4] Debates over the lessons of the war tap into deep cleavages about the nature of the American political system, the obligations of citizens toward their governments, and the validity of traditional patriotic values.

The enormous variation with which the Vietnam analogy is deployed invites scholars to weigh in on the question of what Americans *should* understand as the correct lessons of the war. In playing this role, historians can help inform policy debates in which policymakers and politicians often stray far beyond expert opinion.[5] This chapter, however, takes a different tack; rather than argue for the accuracy of a particular understanding of the war or criticizing policymakers for faulty analogizing, the following pages attempt to bring greater clarity and order to the debate over the lessons of the Vietnam War by systematically examining the ways in which the war has been used in policymaking deliberations—especially public discussions of major foreign policy problems that have received extensive media attention.[6] This effort may help promote greater rigor and self-awareness in a debate that is unlikely to be resolved any time soon.[7] At a minimum, this exercise demonstrates the sheer difficulty of drawing lessons from the war and therefore the need for skepticism whenever policymakers invoke the Vietnam analogy. The point of this chapter is not to provide a detailed narrative of the ways in which policymakers have drawn on the history of the Vietnam War; rather, the goal is to lay out a scheme for categorizing the diverse arguments that policymakers and politicians (and in many cases journalists and members of the larger public) make about the latter-day relevance of the Vietnam War.

Conflicting uses of the Vietnam analogy flow fundamentally from contrasting ideas about why the United States failed to achieve its objectives in Vietnam. Broadly speaking, Americans cluster around three explanations. Many Americans believe that the U.S. defeat in Vietnam resulted from a failure to understand the basic political situation in Vietnam. Many others attach central importance to a failure of decisionmaking about how to fight the war. Meanwhile, a much smaller group, with virtually no adherents in elite policy circles, contends that America's defeat stemmed from a failure among American leaders to act on the basis of honorable and appropriate motives. This chapter describes these three points of view and, more important, attempts to demonstrate via selective examples how policymakers and politicians have deployed these points of view in arguing about later foreign policy challenges.

A Failure of Understanding

Scholars, journalists, memoirists, and other commentators who see America's defeat in Vietnam as the result of a failure of understanding take an essentially tragic view of the war. This group, probably representing a slight majority among the American public, generally expresses sympathy for the containment policy and views the American intervention in Vietnam as a logical application of the broader approach to resisting communist expansion around the world. They acknowledge that, given the mind-set of the time, protecting an independent, noncommunist South Vietnamese state from communist assault seemed to make sense. Advocates of this school of thought assert, however, that American leaders erred badly in viewing containment as the appropriate American response to turmoil in Vietnam.

Acting on mistaken assumptions, the argument runs, Americans became ever more thoroughly ensnared in an unwinnable war from which they would extract themselves only after years of frustration, bloodshed, and national crisis.[8]

Scholarship and other commentary advocating this view of the war vary in the answers different authors offer to the basic question of precisely what U.S. policymakers misunderstood. One variant emphasizes that Americans failed to appreciate the peculiar history of Vietnam, whether because of a general myopia about foreign cultures or a more specific lack of expertise owing to purges of Asia experts from the State Department during the 1950s. This line of thinking emphasizes that Americans failed to appreciate Vietnam's long history of anticolonial nationalism and the intricate blending of nationalism and communism in the revolutionary movement led by Ho Chi Minh. Blind to these complexities, the argument runs, U.S. policymakers wrongly categorized the insurgency against the South Vietnamese government as a simple case of communist aggression. In fact, the insurgents enjoyed considerable legitimacy and support within South Vietnam, even if they received aid from North Vietnam and, less directly, the communist superpowers.[9]

A second, closely related point of view emphasizes that American leaders failed to understand that the principal challenge in Vietnam was political rather than military in nature. This line of reasoning suggests that U.S. officials, especially in the Johnson administration, believed that dramatic military escalation could achieve U.S. objectives in Vietnam by inflicting unsustainable losses on communist forces and intimidating the North Vietnamese government. In fact, critics have repeatedly argued, the core problem for the United States in Vietnam was always the failure of the Saigon government to win the backing of the population below the seventeenth parallel. More specifically, the persistent unwillingness of the South Vietnamese government to broaden its political base, enact democratic reforms, and address economic grievances among the rural population alienated the population from the government and ensured that the revolutionaries, rather than Saigon leaders, would win the competition for legitimacy. In this view, the war was fundamentally a contest for the "hearts and minds" of the South Vietnamese population, but the government—regardless of how much assistance the United States poured into the country—never came close to challenging the National Liberation Front in that arena.[10]

A third variant of the view that Americans failed to understand crucial aspects of the war they were fighting offers an even harsher vision of U.S. misperceptions. Proponents of this line of thinking argue that American forces fell short in Vietnam due to an inability to grasp that U.S. material prowess was inappropriate to the basic challenges that confronted them in the war. This position emphasizes that in the mid-1960s, American leaders— like the broader population—were brimming with confidence in their ability to bring progress to third world nations. They prided themselves in part on their know-how, but the sheer material abundance of the American lifestyle also convinced them that other societies—and surely an especially benighted one like Vietnam, which both Lyndon Johnson and Henry Kissinger labeled a "fourth-rate" country[11]—would bend before the spectacular power of American technology and material abundance. Yet such power, critics suggest, proved ineffective in satisfying the desires that motivated ordinary Vietnamese to take up arms against the Saigon regime, including the yearning for national unity and independence. Hubris, then, prevented Americans from seeing the limits on their own capabilities and the inappropriateness of their immense power to address grievances among a distant population.[12]

Policymakers and politicians attuned to each of these three interpretive traditions draw the same broad lesson from the Vietnam War: the United States must recognize the limits on its ability to intervene effectively overseas and undertake such endeavors only with great caution. Close inspection reveals, however, that policymakers and politicians have made the case differently at different times, invoking one (or occasionally more than one) of the three particular views described above. These three arguments are deeply interwoven in deliberation of American foreign policy since 1975, but it is revealing to disentangle them. The goal in the following paragraphs is by no means to provide a rigorous or complete overview of debates about the lessons of the Vietnam War. Rather, it is to offer striking examples of distinct interpretive strands as they have informed latter-day debates.[13]

The failure to understand the history of complex and distant societies. Wary of embroiling the United States in distant societies about which Americans know little, policymakers and politicians have often invoked the Vietnam War as a cautionary tale about the risks of inadvertently becoming bogged down in another nation's civil war. This theme was notably prominent in the spring of 1999, when Congress debated a proposal to send four thousand U.S. troops to participate in a UN peacekeeping operation in Kosovo once a U.S.-led bombing campaign had evicted Serbian forces from the territory. Critics of the administration of President Bill Clinton warned that the plan risked entangling thousands of American troops in a complex situation similar to that in Vietnam thirty-five years earlier. "How many more young men and women are going to go [to] faraway places to get in the middle of civil wars where there is a dubious reason to be there to start with and no way home?" asked Republican representative Lindsey Graham of South Carolina. The complexities of Kosovo, Graham added, were far more reminiscent of Vietnam three decades before than they were of Kuwait, where U.S. forces had achieved a resounding success in 1991.[14] Representative Stephen Horn, a Republican from California, called Kosovo "a quagmire of ethnic and religious rivalries that we cannot solve alone. Let us remember Dien Bien Phu," Horn asserted, "when many of his key advisers pressured President Eisenhower to send our armed forces to help bail out the French. He was a wise president; he turned them down."[15]

The failure to understand the essentially political nature of the problems facing the United States. Since 1975, policymakers have invoked the Vietnam analogy to suggest that Americans are too quick to resort to military solutions and must recognize that many of the problems they face abroad are fundamentally political. Senator Kennedy's 2007 speech opposing the surge in Iraq centered on this point. "Injecting more troops into a civil war is not the answer," Kennedy averred. "Our men and women in uniform cannot force the Iraqi people to reconcile their differences." In fact, argued Kennedy, sending more U.S. troops only heightened political difficulties in Iraq by encouraging Iraqi dependency on the United States and making ordinary Iraqis more resentful of the American presence.[16] Kennedy's reasoning echoed reservations about the deployment of American ground troops voiced during the aforementioned debate over Kosovo. Representative Jerry Costello, a Democrat from California, insisted that the war "has to be settled by those who are most affected—those who live there" and added that "it will be impossible for us militarily from the outside to impose a successful solution on the problems faced by the people of this area."[17]

The failure to appreciate the limits of American know-how and power. The final variant of the "failure of understanding" school of thought—that Americans simply lack the wherewithal to solve problems in distant parts of the globe—is more common outside of governmental institutions than within them. If taken to its extreme, after all, this line of argument might stymie all activity in the international arena, and that is clearly not an option for individuals who must respond in some way to challenges from abroad. Nevertheless, policymakers and politicians have occasionally argued that the United States must respect the limits on its ability to effect change in the world and see beyond the hubris that led Americans to think otherwise in Vietnam. Perhaps the most striking expressions of this opinion came in the late 1970s as the administration of President Jimmy Carter sought to inject a new spirit of humility into the conduct of U.S. foreign policy. "There can be no going back to a time when we thought there could be American solutions to every problem," Secretary of State Cyrus Vance asserted in 1979, obviously referring to the Vietnam era.[18] Similar arguments surfaced in more recent years after U.S. forces began waging a counterinsurgency war in Iraq. "Since I fought in Vietnam, I have not seen an arrogance in our foreign policy like this," Senator John Kerry, the Massachusetts Democrat and Vietnam veteran who became secretary of state in 2013, told a radio interviewer in 2004.[19] Two years later Republican senator Chuck Hagel of Nebraska—another Vietnam veteran, one who would become a cabinet member in the administration of President Barack Obama—wrote in the *Washington Post*, "We have misunderstood, misread, misplanned and mismanaged our honorable intentions in Iraq with an arrogant self-delusion reminiscent of Vietnam. Honorable intentions," Hagel added, "are not policies and plans. Iraq belongs to the 25 million Iraqis who live there. They will decide their fate and form of government."[20]

A Failure of Decisionmaking

Adherents to the second broad school of thought about the lessons of Vietnam reject the idea that the United States misunderstood the situation there and stumbled into an unwinnable war. This view, probably held by a substantial minority within the American population, maintains instead that American leaders got it exactly right: South Vietnam was a victim of communist aggression that was consistent with communist expansionism elsewhere in the world; the reason the United States failed to achieve its objectives in Vietnam was a failure to wage the war in the proper way. Indeed, according to this line of thinking, the U.S. government could have achieved its objectives if only it had made different decisions about the military and political conduct of the war. This view originated during the fighting, when hawkish critics of the Johnson administration blamed the president for failing to wage the war with adequate determination and skill.[21] Since 1975 this idea has formed the kernel of "revisionist" scholarship, which argues that the war was both necessary and winnable for the United States.[22]

Variation within this school of thought flows from divergent answers to the question of exactly who prevented the United States from seizing the opportunity for victory. By far the most common position blames weak or overly cautious civilian leaders—especially President Johnson. Critics of Johnson frequently argue that he escalated American involvement too gradually, imposed excessive restrictions on the ability of the military to wage the war as U.S. commanders wished, and did too little to mobilize the American people for what he knew would likely be a long and difficult war. Some express a degree of sympathy for Johnson's behavior, acknowledging his genuine desire to prevent the conflict in Vietnam from growing into a major war between the United States and China and his concern with keeping the war from diverting attention from his highest presidential priority, the array of domestic reform programs known as the Great Society. Others offer harsher judgments, blaming Johnson for irresolute leadership and badly exaggerated fears of China, both of which denied the military an opportunity to do what was necessary to achieve victory. In any case, flawed conduct in the war originated from excessive caution exercised by the American commander in chief.[23]

A second interpretive tradition also takes a dim view of presidential leadership but pins most of the blame for the failure in Vietnam on segments of the American public—especially the antiwar movement, whose activism is alleged to have constrained Washington's ability to wage the war more effectively. In this view, U.S. leaders made the right decision to commit combat forces in order to prevent the collapse of South Vietnam, and even came close to achieving U.S. goals in the early 1970s, only to have defeat stolen from the jaws of victory by declining popular support for the war. Besides blaming antiwar activists themselves, adherents of this view single out three institutions as especially responsible for swaying larger numbers of Americans toward the antiwar camp—universities, the media, and Congress. Commentators who focus on universities usually note that rapidly growing access to higher education in the post–World War II era created arenas in which young people had unprecedented opportunities to question established authority, while growing draft calls gave college-age men extra incentive to challenge U.S. foreign policy. Meanwhile, critics of American journalism suggest that television and print encouraged dissent by painting an excessively negative picture of the war, especially during and after the Tet Offensive. Similarly, commentary that focuses on the role of Congress argues that liberal politicians bought into an unreasonably gloomy view of the fighting and wrongly constrained the executive branch's ability to wage the war.[24]

The final two variants of the "failure of decisionmaking" school focus on military leadership. Both make the same basic point: military commanders fundamentally misjudged the nature of the Vietnam War and chose the wrong strategies. But the two variants make the case in starkly different ways. One group of commentators suggests that the U.S. military erred in viewing the war as essentially a guerrilla conflict that did not require an all-out military commitment by American forces. In fact, say military analysts such as Harry Summers, Bruce Palmer, and Philip R. Davidson, the core of the problem facing the United States in South Vietnam was an invasion by a major conventional military force, the North Vietnamese Army.[25] This view maintains that, to the extent that South Vietnamese guerrillas were major players in the war, they were sustained by support from Hanoi and lacked anything close to the strength and legitimacy that many Americans assumed they had. U.S. commanders should therefore have focused American power on North Vietnam by bombing it more intensively and using American ground forces to block the infiltration of troops and supplies into the south. Commentary of this sort often berates civilian leaders for escalating U.S. military involvement too gradually, imposing too many restrictions on the use of American firepower, and failing to mobilize the public. But much of it is at least as critical of the military for failing to provide sound or compelling advice.[26]

The other line of argument concerned with military decisions makes precisely the opposite point, contending that the United States erred by treating the war as a conventional struggle when it fact it was essentially a guerrilla war that required counterinsurgency methods. In sharp contrast to the champions of conventional warfare, proponents of counterinsurgency such as Andrew Krepinevich and Guenter Lewy contend that the most important military challenge to South Vietnam came from indigenous guerrilla forces and the communist political apparatus under the control of the

National Liberation Front. But U.S. commanders, steeped in an institutional culture that prioritized conventional warfare and inhibited creativity and innovation, downplayed pacification and nation-building activities in favor of major "search and destroy" operations in more remote areas. The key goal of U.S. forces was to kill as many enemy soldiers as possible rather than control territory and win the "hearts and minds" of the local population. This argument bears some resemblance to the view (described in the previous section) that emphasizes Americans' inability to see that the key problem in Vietnam was political rather than military. But there is an important distinction. The group analyzed above argues that the war was fundamentally unwinnable because the political problems were so severe; the group described here maintains that the war would have in fact been winnable if the military had only chosen the right methods. For evidence, adherents to the latter school often point to the relative effectiveness of the U.S. Marines, who emphasized pacification in their area of responsibility (the northernmost sector of South Vietnam), and of the U.S. Army after 1968, when new commanders accorded a higher priority to counterinsurgency methods.[27]

As with adherents to the "failure of understanding" school, those who champion various strands of the "failure of decisionmaking" interpretation have invoked the lessons of Vietnam in various ways as they have tried to influence policy choices. In many cases, proponents of the latter school have deployed more than one of the interpretive variations sketched above, but it is nevertheless possible to disentangle distinct lines of argument. It is, in fact, much easier to do so with this group than with adherents to the "failure of understanding" school. In part, this greater ease flows from the notable stridency with which commentators have often pinned blame for the American failure in Vietnam on a particular set of culprits. The "failure of understanding" school, by contrast, tends to engage in more abstract kind of reasoning since it is principally concerned with broad matters of ideology and institutional behavior. Another reason why it is easier to sort the "failure of decisionmaking" school into distinct strands is the greater quantity of such commentary in the policymaking record over the years. To be sure, "failure of understanding" arguments predominate in the academy and have found frequent expression in Congress. But "failure of decisionmaking" arguments have been more frequently and forcefully articulated within the executive branch, where policymakers facing the need to respond to crises are less likely to be drawn to arguments for caution or inaction.[28] Rather, they have generally argued in the following four ways.

A failure to commit fully to war. Since 1975, policymakers have frequently drawn on the history of the Vietnam War in advocating that the United States must act with decisiveness in international affairs, especially when deploying American forces overseas. Indeed, this idea sat at the core of the best-known articulation of the "failure of decisionmaking" outlook on the Vietnam War—Ronald Reagan's campaign speech at the annual convention of the Veterans of Foreign Wars in August 1980. After declaring that the American war in Vietnam was a "noble cause," Reagan insisted that "we will never again ask young men to fight and possibly die in a war our government is afraid to let them win."[29] This idea was also enshrined in the Weinberger Doctrine, the set of principles laid down by Defense Secretary Caspar Weinberger in 1984 specifying conditions under which the United States would commit troops abroad. Weinberger's speech has often been depicted as an attempt to constrain the use of American military force, but he aimed his declaration first and foremost at making U.S. strength more usable by spelling out preconditions that must prevail before American troops could be sent into harm's way. The doctrine sprang from the belief that the Vietnam debacle was the result of bad decisions—decisions that could be made differently in the future. "If we decide it is necessary to put combat troops into a given situation, we should do so wholeheartedly, and with the clear intention of winning," Weinberger declared. "If we are unwilling to commit the forces or resources necessary to achieve our objectives, we should not commit them at all."[30]

Reagan's and Weinberger's general prescriptions echoed in policy deliberations in the decades that followed. For example, President George H. W. Bush invoked Reagan's words one week into the 1991 Persian Gulf War. Vowing that the war would "not be another Vietnam," Bush declared in a speech: "Our troops will have the best possible support in the entire world, and they will not be asked to fight with one hand tied behind their back."[31] In public and in secret deliberations, administration officials spoke frequently of the need to strike boldly and decisively.[32] President George W. Bush's comments more than a decade later about the surge in Iraq hit the same theme, warning of the horrors that might ensue, as in Southeast Asia, if U.S. leaders grew wobbly in the face of difficulties. "We'll succeed, unless we quit," Bush said in late 2006.[33] In 2014 Senator

John McCain, Republican from Arizona, likewise demanded boldness as the Obama administration gradually increased aerial bombing of Islamic extremists in Iraq and Syria. The president's "incrementalism," said McCain, reminded him of "another war we lost . . . and that was the war in Vietnam."[34]

A failure to manage public opinion. While adherents to the "failure of decisionmaking" school have usually pointed to the need for the nation to act vigorously in order to achieve military objectives abroad, many have also urged the necessity of strong leadership in order to generate popular backing for overseas ventures. The Weinberger Doctrine suggested that political leaders should send U.S. forces abroad only if they are confident in advance of solid public and congressional support. But much commentary from U.S. policymakers and politicians since 1975 has insisted that leaders can—and must—play an active role in generating that backing. Clearly, the Pentagon has viewed the Vietnam War as an object lesson in the pitfalls of allowing journalists relatively unfettered access to all aspects of U.S. combat operations. As a consequence, the U.S. military tightly restricted the activities of journalists covering the interventions in Grenada (1983), Panama (1989), the Persian Gulf (1991), and Iraq (2003–11).[35]

A good deal of commentary has, however, emphasized the need for bold assertions of national purpose and clear articulation of exit strategies in order to keep the public firmly behind American military operations. In the run-up to the 1991 Persian Gulf War, for example, Colin Powell, the chairman of the Joint Chiefs of Staff, insisted on "a clear statement of what political objective you're trying to achieve" so that "you know when you've accomplished it."[36] Powell was, of course, pushing on an open door, and the Bush administration, fearful of becoming bogged down in a complex political entanglement, notoriously held back from overthrowing Saddam Hussein's regime once the immediate goal of liberating Kuwait had been accomplished. A few years later, critics of the Clinton administration worried that Washington was not achieving the same clarity of purpose in Kosovo and therefore risked going to war without adequate public support. "More than thirty years ago in Vietnam, we also lacked clear and specific objectives," declared Senator Max Cleland, a Democrat from Georgia, insisting that as a result "our policy was never fully understood or fully supported by the American people. . . . I cannot, in good conscience, sit here and watch it all appear to be happening again."[37]

A failure to understand the true nature of the war. Policymakers, espe-cially military officers and analysts of military affairs, have frequently invoked the Vietnam War in arguing that the United States needs to un-derstand the nature of battlefield challenges that it faces, and to fight appropriately. Such arguments have been made sometimes to urge that the nation recognize the need to eschew limited war and embrace a major conventional effort; at other times such arguments have supported the reverse—the necessity to switch from a conventional approach to a coun-terguerrilla strategy. A good example of the former arose in the run-up to the 1991 Persian Gulf War. Powell, a Vietnam veteran so vocally wedded to the Weinberger Doctrine that it later became known as the Powell Doctrine, astonished other senior Bush administration officials by recommending that the United States assemble a huge force of half a million U.S. troops and "five or six carrier task forces" in the Middle East before moving against Iraq. Bush went along with Powell's approach. "I did not want to repeat the problems of the Vietnam War," Bush later wrote, "where the political lead-ership meddled with military operations. I would avoid micromanaging the military."[38]

The reverse logic prevailed several years later during the second war with Iraq, especially after the United States, having achieved dramatic success with its initial conventional invasion of the country, became bogged down in a grueling fight with Iraqi insurgents. While some U.S. generals remained wedded to a conventional strategy emphasizing big forces and heavy firepower, others—a group of officers dubbed the "crusaders" by military analyst Andrew Bacevich—urged that the war be reconceived as a counter-insurgency.[39] This group shared the view that the United States had es-sentially won the Vietnam War after it abandoned the search-and-destroy method in favor of a counterinsurgency approach, though declining pub-lic and congressional support ultimately squandered that victory. They hoped to achieve the same sort of turnaround in Iraq by emphasizing nation building and the quest to win Iraqi "hearts and minds." In 2006 Pres-ident George W. Bush threw his support behind champions of counterin-surgency even though he worried about embracing a limited-war approach that he associated with previous defeat in Vietnam. He later explained the reason for his decision to back the change in course: "I worried we might not succeed [in Iraq]. We could be looking at a repeat of Vietnam—a humiliating loss for the country, a shattering blow to the military, and a dramatic setback for our interests."[40]

Another Possibility: A Failure of Motives

A third interpretive tradition suggests that the American failure in Vietnam stemmed from neither misunderstanding nor bad choices but from improper or ignoble motives for fighting the war. Despite all their disagreements, advocates of the "failure of understanding" and "failure of decisionmaking" schools share something crucial: they suggest that the American commitment to war in Vietnam stemmed from an understandable and reasonable desire to block communist expansion. Advocates of the third school reject this characterization of American motives as far too generous to U.S. officials and propose instead that American leaders committed the nation to war on the basis of reprehensible motives pursued by unrepresentative parts of the American population—usually business interests, politicians pursuing narrow personal or party agendas, or an out-of-control national security apparatus. The argument focused on economics suggests that U.S. leaders sought to defend South Vietnam in order to protect a global capitalist system designed to serve the interests of the United States.[41] Meanwhile, the argument focused on politics rests on the idea that the United States went to war in order to protect the electoral interests of political parties or individual politicians whose prospects might have been damaged by defeat in Vietnam. Proponents of this view often argue that U.S. leaders did not aim so much to achieve victory in Vietnam as to avoid a defeat that would have called into question their personal dedication to the anticommunist cause and handed their political opponents potent weapons to use against them.[42] The argument about the national security establishment suggests that the military, backed by industry and government, made decisions to protect and expand its prerogatives rather than on the basis of any sound understanding of actual threats to the United States.[43]

"Failure of motives" arguments are staples of academic writing about the Vietnam War, and some of the most innovative studies to be published about the war in recent years have developed the argument about personal credibility and domestic politics more fully than ever before.[44] Occasionally such views also find expression on op-ed pages.[45] They are common too among dissent movements—first during the Vietnam War itself and then among antiwar activists who have deployed the history of American intervention in Vietnam to protest U.S. activities in other places and periods.[46] In political and policy circles, however, these themes have received scant attention. Indeed, even the most progressive and iconoclastic leaders, while frequently invoking the Vietnam War in arguing against later interventions, have almost entirely avoided suggesting that electoral or economic considerations propelled U.S. commitments overseas.[47] This reasoning probably has less to do with the actual views of the most critical members of the political and policymaking communities than with their sense of what sorts of arguments stand any chance of resonating with peers or, for members of Congress, the general public. To impugn the motives of American leaders is to step outside what the communications theorist Daniel C. Hallin has dubbed the "sphere of legitimate controversy" and thereby to invite quick rejection and jeopardize one's future credibility.[48]

The difficulties of raising "failure of motives" arguments in political or policy circles is well illustrated by an episode not from the years since 1975 but from the months between autumn 1964 and summer 1965, when one high-ranking member of the U.S. policymaking establishment, Undersecretary of State George Ball, repeatedly invoked the French defeat in Vietnam as evidence that the United States should avoid escalating its military commitment to the country. In making this case, Ball—a trusted insider whose dislike of escalation flowed not from iconoclasm but from a Eurocentric disdain for distractions in Asia—insisted in a series of memoranda for President Johnson that the United States was essentially walking in the footsteps that the French had followed several years earlier and was in danger of becoming similarly bogged down in a grueling war against an implacable enemy. Sending combat forces to Vietnam would, Ball insisted in October 1964, make the U.S. position "in the world's eyes, approach that of France in the 1950s—with all the disastrous political connotations of such a posture." If Americans themselves could not see the parallels with French colonialism, he warned, "Asians would not miss the point."[49] Ball recognized in a later memo that France had fought a "colonial war" in Vietnam, whereas the United States was fighting "to stop aggression." But he hastened to add that the Americans lay open to accusations of waging a "white man's war" against Asians, just like the French before them.[50] His contention was clear: American motives in Vietnam, even if not brazenly colonial in nature, were ambiguous enough to embolden the enemy and raise questions about the entire enterprise.

Ball's assertions—in a rare instance of a senior policymaker casting even the most banal sort of doubt on U.S. motives—provoked immediate and unanimous rejection from the rest of Johnson's senior advisors.[51] "To them,"

Ball later recalled of his October 1964 memo, "my memorandum seemed merely an idiosyncratic diversion from the only relevant problem: how to win the war."[52] In June 1965, the National Security Council prepared a report for the president entitled "France in Vietnam, 1954, and the U.S. in Vietnam, 1965—A Useful Analogy?" The answer, predictably, was a definitive "no." Above all, the report insisted that American purposes bore no resemblance to those of the French. France was a "colonial power seeking to reimpose its overseas rule," it asserted, whereas the United States was "responding to the call of a people under communist assault." The report went on to reiterate criticism of the French that American officials had been insisting upon ever since the late 1940s: France had refused to concede a meaningful degree of independence to Vietnam and, as a consequence, had failed to lure Vietnamese nationalists away from the Marxist agenda pursued by the revolutionaries led by Ho Chi Minh. It was therefore little wonder that the anticolonial cause had gained strength and ultimately prevailed. By contrast, the report stated, "the United States was sincerely dedicated to Vietnamese independence and struggling to prevent a new kind of foreign domination, this time by the communist bloc."[53]

Conclusion

American policymakers are powerfully drawn to the Vietnam analogy in weighing decisions about international affairs, but the analogy can be used to support an extraordinarily wide array of policy options. Strong critics of America's participation in the Vietnam War who are drawn to "failure of motives" explanations use the war to call for a fundamental overhaul of American democracy, while strong proponents of the "failure of decision-making" school deploy the war to urge bold use of the U.S. military. Even within political and policymaking arenas, where officials draw on only part of the larger spectrum of interpretive possibilities, the Vietnam War has been used in starkly contradictory ways, and this is a pattern that is unlikely to change anytime soon. So searing was the Vietnam War to many policymakers, and so well-entrenched are opinions about the reasons for the American failure in Vietnam, that it is hard to imagine the war will not remain the go-to analogy for many years to come whenever the United States faces decisions about intervention in less-developed parts of the world. Indeed, it is conceivable that views about the war are so passionately held that not even the passing of the generations who had direct experience with it will do much to dampen the tendency to invoke it in the service of latter-day policy debates.

The ubiquity and persistence of the Vietnam analogy cut two ways. On the one hand, it gives both the public and policymakers a common language and set of reference points with which to discuss controversial matters of the moment. The benefits were arguably on display in the fall of 2009, when Obama administration officials debated the future of U.S. policy in Afghanistan partly by weighing similarities and differences between the Afghanistan effort and the Vietnam War four decades earlier—a relatively constructive and sophisticated debate that drew on scholarly studies.[54] On the other hand, there is something discouraging about the ways in which politicians and policymakers draw upon the history of the Vietnam War. Invocations of the earlier conflict often have a scripted, predictable quality to them, reflecting not so much a desire to uncover useful information as a determination to mobilize support among like-minded individuals within the bureaucracy or the public at large. Equally discouraging is the fact that the best scholarship on the war seems to have little carryover into the policymaking and political realm—the result, no doubt, of scholars' failures to make their work accessible, as well as a distinct unwillingness in the broader political culture to consider the possibility that American motives may sometimes have been at fault.

One might, of course, throw up one's hands and complain that there is little to be gained by returning again and again to the Vietnam War as a point of comparison for later policy dilemmas. It may in fact be, as former National Security Council aide James Thomson once quipped, that the key lesson of the Vietnam War is never again to "take on the job of trying to defeat a nationalist anti-colonial movement under indigenous communist control in former French Indochina."[55] Given the inevitability of Vietnam analogies, however, the better course seems to lie in doing as much as possible to make sure that history is used in as sophisticated and illuminating a manner as possible. One path toward this goal is, of course, for scholars to weigh in via op-eds and other accessible forms of writing to ensure that policymakers' analogical forays are informed by a reasonably sophisticated grasp of history, even—and perhaps especially—if good history involves confronting uncomfortable realities that lie outside the sphere of legitimate controversy. Using the same means, scholars can bring to light analogies other than the Vietnam War that may be less shrouded in controversy and therefore better able to provide insight into contemporary dilemmas. Finally, and perhaps most important of all, historians should endeavor to remind policymakers of the problems associated with analogizing of any sort and warn of the need to avoid analogical thinking becoming a substitute for deep knowledge about the historical background of present-day problems. These solutions are, of course, unlikely to have a momentous effect, but better uses of historical knowledge can hardly hurt the process—and might even promote more reasoned, careful, and effective policy choices.

Notes

1. Edward M. Kennedy, "Escalation Is Not the Answer: Time for Congress to Act to Ensure Real Change in Iraq," January 9, 2007, Archives of the National Press Club, Washington, D.C.

2. George W. Bush, "Address to the Veterans of Foreign Wars National Convention," August 22, 2007, *Public Papers of the Presidents: George W. Bush, 2007*, part 2 (Government Printing Office, 2011), 1102–04.

3. For an overview of trends in American opinion in recent decades, see Mark Atwood Lawrence, "Too Late or Too Soon? Debating the Withdrawal from Vietnam in the Age of Iraq," *Diplomatic History* 34, no. 3 (2010), 591–92.

4. This point is elegantly developed in Bernard von Bothmer, *Framing the Sixties: The Use and Abuse of a Decade from Ronald Reagan to George W. Bush* (University of Massachusetts Press, 2010).

5. Superb studies of this sort are Jeffrey Record, *Making War, Thinking History: Munich, Vietnam, and Presidential Uses of Force from Korea to Kosovo* (Annapolis, Md.: Naval Institute Press, 2002); and Lloyd C. Gardner and Marilyn B. Young, eds., *Iraq and the Lessons of Vietnam: Or, How Not to Learn from the Past* (New York: New Press, 2007).

6. It is conceivable that policymakers have used the Vietnam analogy in different ways in secret discussions inaccessible to historians because of security classification; only the release of relevant policymaking documents could settle the matter. Yet available documentation and memoirs do not suggest major differences between the public and private ways in which policymakers draw lessons from Vietnam. Neither does Neustadt and May's classic study of the uses of historical analogies by decisionmakers. See Richard E. Neustadt and Ernest May, *Thinking in Time: The Uses of History for Decision-Makers* (New York: Free Press, 1986).

7. This approach is inspired by William Inboden, "Statecraft, Decision-Making, and the Varieties of Historical Experience: A Taxonomy," *Journal of Strategic Studies* 36, no. 5 (2013), 1–28.

8. One of the classic formulations of this view is Arthur M. Schlesinger Jr., *Bitter Heritage: Vietnam and American Democracy, 1941–1966* (New York: Houghton Mifflin, 1967). For a later study emphasizing the misapplication of containment, see George C. Herring, *America's Longest War: The United States and Vietnam, 1950–1975*, 4th ed. (New York: McGraw-Hill, 2001).

9. Perhaps the most famous work to make this point is Frances FitzGerald, *Fire in the Lake: The Vietnamese and the Americans in Vietnam* (Boston: Little, Brown, 1972). From a different ideological perspective, former secretary of defense Robert S. McNamara made a similar point in his memoir *In Retrospect: The Tragedy and Lessons of Vietnam* (New York: Times Books, 1995).

10. Works emphasizing the persistent unpopularity of the South Vietnamese government during the peak years of U.S. involvement include Eric M. Bergerud, *The Dynamics of Defeat: The Vietnam War in Hua Nghia Province* (Boulder, CO: Westview, 1991); Jeffrey Race, *War Comes to Long An: Revolutionary Conflict in a Vietnamese Province* (University of California Press, 1972); and James Trullinger, *Village at War: An Account of Conflict in Vietnam* (Stanford University Press, 1993).

11. For these quotes and illuminating discussion of racial stereotyping, see Yaacov Vertzberger, *The World in their Minds: Information Processing, Cognition, and Perception in Foreign Policy Decisionmaking* (Stanford University Press, 1993), 126.

12. See, for example, Loren Baritz, *Backfire: The Myths That Made Us Fight, the Illusions That Helped Us Lose, the Legacy That Haunts Us Today* (New York: Ballantine, 1986), and James William Gibson, *The Perfect War: Technowar in Vietnam* (New York: Atlantic Monthly Press, 1986). A more recent variation on the theme is Mark Philip Bradley, *Imagining Vietnam and America: The Making of Postcolonial Vietnam, 1919–1950* (University of North Carolina Press), 2000.

13. A superb scholarly expression of these arguments is Robert K. Brigham, *Is Iraq Another Vietnam?* (New York: Public Affairs, 2006).

14. Lindsey Graham, Transcript of debate on March 11, 1999, *Congressional Record* 145, part 3, House of Representatives (Government Printing Office, 1999), 4289.

15. Stephen Horn, quoted in Roland Paris, "Kosovo and the Metaphor War," *Political Science Quarterly* 117, no. 3 (2002), 444. For a journalist's perspective, see Thomas L. Friedman, "ISIS and Vietnam," *New York Times*, October 29, 2014.

16. Kennedy, speech to the National Press Club.

17. Jerry Costello, quoted in Paris, "Kosovo and the Metaphor War," 444.

18. Cyrus Vance, quoted in Donald Wallace White, *The Rise and Decline of the United States as a World Power* (Yale University Press, 1999), 342.

19. Farah Stockman, "Democrats Draw a Vietnam Parallel in Denouncing U.S. Strategy," *Boston Globe*, April 8, 2004 (www.boston.com/news/nation/washington/articles/2004/04/08/democrats_draw_a_vietnam_parallel_in_denouncing_us_strategy/).

20. Chuck Hagel, "Leaving Iraq, Honorably," *Washington Post*, November 26, 2006 (www.washingtonpost.com/wp-dyn/content/article/2006/11/24/AR2006 112401104.html).

21. See Sandra Scanlon, *The Pro-War Movement: Domestic Support for the Vietnam War and the Making of Modern American Conservatism* (University of Massachusetts Press, 2013), especially chapters 1–2.

22. The best recent example of revisionist scholarship on the Vietnam War is Mark Moyar, *Triumph Forsaken: The Vietnam War, 1954–1965* (Cambridge University Press, 2006). For a useful critique, see Andrew Wiest and Michael Doidge, eds., *Triumph Revisited: Historians Battle for the Vietnam War* (New York: Routledge, 2010). For superb analysis of historiographical debates over Vietnam, see Gary R. Hess, *Vietnam: Explaining America's Lost War* (Malden, Mass.: Wiley-Blackwell, 2009).

23. For a relatively sympathetic view, see Michael Lind, *Vietnam: The Necessary War* (New York: Free Press, 1999), chapter 6. For a more critical perspective, see Moyar, *Triumph Forsaken*, especially chapter 14.

24. On universities and the antiwar movement see, for example, Adam Garfinkle, *Telltale Hearts: The Origins and Impact of the Vietnam Anti-War Movement* (New York: Macmillan, 1997). For a superb overview of commentary critical of the media and Congress, see Hess, *Vietnam*, chapters 6 and 8. For negative attitudes toward the American media among U.S. military officers, see Douglas Kinnard, *The War Managers: American Generals Reflect on Vietnam* (New York: Da Capo, 1991), 124–35.

25. Harry G. Summers, *On Strategy: A Critical Analysis of the Vietnam War* (Novato, Calif.: Presidio, 1982); Bruce Palmer Jr., *The 25-Year War: America's Military Role in Vietnam* (University of Kentucky Press, 1984); and Philip R. Davidson, *Vietnam at War: The History, 1946–1975* (Novato, Calif.: Presidio, 1988).

26. H. R. McMaster, *Dereliction of Duty: Johnson, McNamara, the Joint Chiefs of Staff, and the Lies That Led to Vietnam* (New York: Harper, 1998); Hess, *Vietnam*, 91–98; and George C. Herring, "American Strategy in Vietnam: The Postwar Debate," *Military Affairs* 46, no. 2 (1982), 57–63.

27. Andrew F. Krepinovich, *The Army and Vietnam* (Johns Hopkins University Press, 1988), and Guenter Lewy, *America in Vietnam* (Oxford University Press, 1978). For a general discussion of this school, see Hess, *Vietnam*, chapter 5. A more oblique contribution to this body of work is John A. Nagl, *Learning to Eat Soup with a Knife: Counterinsurgency Lessons from Malaya and Vietnam* (University of Chicago Press, 2005). For challenges to the idea that U.S. commanders waged the war in appreciably different ways after 1968, see Gregory A. Daddis, *Westmoreland's War: Reassessing American Strategy in Vietnam* (New York: Oxford University Press, 2014); and Nick Turse, *Kill Anything That Moves: The Real American War in Vietnam* (New York: Metropolitan, 2013).

28. It is hardly surprising that the first study of the lessons from Vietnam, a 1977 collection of reflections by U.S. policymakers who had presided over the war, strongly emphasized failures of decisionmaking rather than more incisive kinds of criticism. See W. Scott Thompson and Donaldson D. Frizzell, eds., *The Lessons of Vietnam* (New York: Crane, Russak, 1977).

29. Ronald Reagan, "Restoring the Margin of Safety," August 18, 1980, Ronald Reagan 1980 Presidential Campaign Papers, box 227, Ronald Reagan Presidential Library, Simi Valley, California.

30. Caspar Weinberger, "The Uses of Military Power," November 28, 1984 (www .pbs.org/wgbh/pages/frontline/shows/military/force/weinberger.html).

31. George H. W. Bush, "Remarks to the Reserve Officer Association," January 23, 1991, in *Public Papers of the Presidents: George Bush, 1991*, vol. 1 (Government Printing Office, 1991), 20.

32. For such commentary, see Marvin Kalb and Deborah Kalb, *Haunting Legacy: Vietnam and the American Presidency from Ford to Obama* (Brookings Institution Press, 2011), 127–49; and Record, *Making War, Thinking History*, chapter 7.

33. George W. Bush, quoted in Robert Scheer, "Bush's Vietnam Analogy," *The Nation*, December 4, 2006 (www.thenation.com/article/bushs-vietnam-analogy#).

34. Akbar Shadid Ahmed, "John McCain: Obama's Iraq Strategy Reminds Me of Vietnam," *Huffington Post*, November 11, 2014 (www.huffingtonpost.com/2014 /11/11/mccain-obama-vietnam_n_6141008.html).

35. For example, Philip M. Taylor, *Global Communications, International Affairs, and the Media since 1945* (London: Routledge, 1997), chapter 3.

36. Colin Powell, quoted in Kalb and Kalb, *Haunting Legacy*, 132–33.

37. Max Cleland, quoted in Paris, "Kosovo and the Metaphor War," 444.

38. George Bush and Brent Scowcroft, *A World Transformed* (New York: Knopf, 1998), 354.

39. Andrew J. Bacevich, "The Petraeus Doctrine," *Atlantic*, October 2008 (www .theatlantic.com/magazine/archive/2008/10/the-petraeus-doctrine/306964/?single _page=true). For a critical view of counterinsurgency and the ways in which its champions drew on the Vietnam War, see Douglas Porch, *Counterinsurgency: Exposing the Myths of the New Way of War* (Cambridge University Press, 2013). The other side of the argument is forcefully presented in Nagl, *Learning to Eat Soup with a Knife*.

40. George W. Bush, *Decision Points* (New York: Crown, 2010), 367.

41. See, for example, Gabriel Kolko, *Anatomy of a War: Vietnam, the United States, and the Modern Historical Experience* (New York: New Press, 1994); and Andrew J. Rotter, *The Path to Vietnam: Origins of the American Commitment to Southeast Asia* (Cornell University Press, 1989).

42. See, for example, Leslie H. Gelb and Richard K. Betts, *The Irony of Vietnam: The System Worked* (Brookings Institution Press, 1979).

43. See, for example, Gareth Porter, *The Perils of Dominance: Imbalance of Power and the Road to War in Vietnam* (University of California Press, 2005).

44. See, for example, Robert Dean, *Imperial Brotherhood: Gender and the Making of Cold War Foreign Policy* (University of Massachusetts Press, 2001); David Kaiser, *American Tragedy: Kennedy, Johnson, and the Origins of the Vietnam War* (Harvard University Press, 2000); and, especially, Fredrik Logevall, *Choosing War: The Lost Chance for Peace and the Escalation of War in Vietnam* (University of California Press, 1999).

45. See, for example, Fredrik Logevall and Gordon M. Goldstein, "Will Syria Be Obama's Vietnam?" *New York Times*, October 8, 2014.

46. Antiwar activists during the Vietnam era frequently assailed the war as the product of unrepresentative forces that were out of touch with America's real needs and best traditions. See, for instance, Martin Luther King Jr.'s famous antiwar speech, "Beyond Vietnam: A Time to Break Silence," April 4, 1967, in Clayborne Carson and Kris Shepard, eds., *A Call to Conscience: The Landmark Speeches of Dr. Martin Luther King, Jr.* (New York: Warner, 2001), 133–64. Democratic representative Dennis Kucinich of Ohio invoked King's words in a speech on January 8, 2007, the same day as Ted Kennedy's speech condemning the surge; see Kucinich, "Out of Iraq and Back to the American City" (www.democrats.com/Out-of-Iraq--and-Back-to-the-American-City).

47. A striking exception is President Jimmy Carter who, as part of his effort to cleanse American politics and call the nation back to its best traditions, obliquely questioned the motives underlying the Vietnam War. See especially Jimmy Carter, "University of Notre Dame—Address at Commencement Exercises at the University" (www.presidency.ucsb.edu/ws/?pid=7552).

48. For the "sphere of legitimate controversy" concept, see Daniel C. Hallin, *The "Uncensored War": The Media and Vietnam* (University of California Press, 1989), 114–26.

49. George Ball, "How Valid Are the Assumptions Underlying Our Vietnam Policies?" (memo), October 5, 1964, National Security File, Vietnam Country File, box 222, Lyndon Baines Johnson Library (hereafter LBJL), Austin, Texas.

50. George Ball to President Johnson, June 18, 1965, in *Foreign Relations of the United States, 1964–1968*, vol. 3 (Government Printing Office, 1995), 18.

51. Ball's memoranda and their reception by the rest of the Johnson administration are examined in Yuen Foong Khong, *Analogies at War: Korea, Munich, Dien Bien Phu, and the Vietnam Decisions of 1965* (Princeton University Press, 1992), 150–62; and Neustadt and May, *Thinking in Time*, 75–90.

52. George Ball, quoted in William C. Gibbons, *The U.S. Government and the Vietnam War: Executive and Legislative Roles and Relationships*, vol. 2 (Princeton University Press, 1986), 362.

53. National Security Council, "France in Vietnam, 1954, and the U.S. in Vietnam, 1965—A Useful Analogy?," June 30, 1965, National Security File, NSC History: Deployment of Major U.S. Forces to Vietnam, July 1965, box 43, LBJL.

54. Peter Spiegel and Jonathan Weisman, "Behind Afghan War Debate, a Battle of Two Books," *Wall Street Journal*, October 7, 2009 (http://online.wsj.com /news/articles/SB125487333320069331). The books in question were classic expressions of the "failure of understanding" and "failure of decisionmaking" schools. These were, respectively, Gordon M. Goldstein, *Lessons in Disaster: McGeorge Bundy and the Path to War in Vietnam* (New York: Times Books, 2008); and Lewis Sorley, *A Better War: The Unexamined Victories and Final Tragedy of America's Last Years in Vietnam* (New York: Harcourt, 1999). See the introduction to this volume.

55. James Thomson, quoted in Richard N. Pfeffer, ed., *No More Vietnams? The War and the Future of American Foreign Policy* (New York: Harper and Row, 1968), 258.

H. W. BRANDS

4

Neither Munich nor Vietnam
The Gulf War of 1991

Coming as it did at the apparent end of an era of modern history—namely, the Cold War—the Persian Gulf Crisis of 1990–91 struck participants and observers as redolent with historical significance. Looking forward, President George H. W. Bush described a "new world order" in which the United Nations and countries sympathetic to its goals would deter or reverse aggression by rogue states or miscreant despots, free of the paralysis that had seized the UN during the Cold War. To establish this new dispensation, however, the United States would have to avoid repeating two glaring mistakes of the past as it formulated its response to Saddam Hussein's invasion and occupation of Kuwait.

The first mistake was summarized, as it had been since the 1940s, by a single word: Munich. Much of American Cold War policy had been premised on the belief that dictators were basically all alike and that aggression had a predictable dynamic. The democracies had failed to stop Adolf Hitler from seizing the Sudetenland in 1938, and World War II had been the result. Joseph Stalin thus had to be contained, as Hitler had not been, lest World War III ensue. Saddam lacked the means of Hitler or Stalin, but his motives were presumed to be similar, and the appropriate response was the resolve that had not been applied against Hitler at the time of the Munich Conference.

The second mistake was Vietnam. To many Americans, especially the Republicans who controlled the White House during the 1980s and early 1990s, Vietnam signified a war that had been lost because it had been half-heartedly fought. Avoiding another Vietnam required choosing wars carefully but then waging them energetically.

From the outset of the Gulf Crisis, these two analogies—Munich and Vietnam—shaped American policy toward Iraq. They informed the thinking of the Bush administration and permeated its rhetoric. They shaped the larger political context as well, partly by the design of the administration but also as a result of the experience those on the outside of the administration shared—directly and vicariously—with those on the inside. Sometimes the analogies influenced decisions; at other times they chiefly provided the language in which decisions were couched and explained. At the end of the crisis, the administration judged that its interpretation and application of the lessons of Munich and especially Vietnam had served the country well.

This was debatable. Historical analogies gain their power by simplifying the present to fit templates imported from the past. But they risk *oversimplifying*, for the fit is never perfect: the present is never just like the past. Saddam was like Hitler in some ways, but he was quite unlike him in others. A war in the Persian Gulf might resemble the war in Vietnam, but Southwest Asia in the 1990s was a far cry from Southeast Asia in the 1960s. As the Bush administration discovered, analogies come with baggage that can threaten to outweigh the benefits the analogies afford.

Shades of the 1930s

George H. W. Bush and Brent Scowcroft later admitted to being caught off guard by the Iraqi invasion of Kuwait in August 1990. In their joint memoir, the former president and national security adviser explained that during their first year in office they had tried to extend President Ronald Reagan's policy of engagement with Iraq. Bush issued a directive, NSD-26, in October 1989 that declared, "Normal relations between the United States and Iraq would serve our longer-term interests and promote stability in both the Gulf and the Middle East."[1] During the next several months the administration pursued this goal by—among other measures—providing credit to Iraq for purchases of American grain. The effort elicited no reciprocal goodwill gesture on the part of Saddam Hussein. "In early 1990, it gradually became apparent to me that Saddam had made an abrupt change in his policy toward the United States," Bush wrote. "The relative moderation he had adopted earlier, perhaps mostly to curry favor with us was abandoned. His behavior became even less predictable."[2]

It was this unpredictability that caused Bush and his administration to be surprised when Saddam ordered his troops into Kuwait. Saddam had complained about Kuwait's oil policies and linked these to border disputes, yet he told U.S. ambassador April Glaspie, according to Glaspie's account of the meeting, that he would take no action against Kuwait ahead of a conference that was being organized by the government of Egypt to defuse the dispute.[3] "Diplomacy seemed to be working, if slowly," Scowcroft recalled later, and other intelligence from the region supported this view. "The Arab leaders were insisting that they had matters well in hand and that unilateral steps by the United States would only complicate matters," Scowcroft noted.[4] King Hussein of Jordan called Bush personally to counter any thoughts of American intervention. "The atmosphere is good," Hussein said of the prospects for a peaceful resolution of the Iraq-Kuwait dispute. "It looks tense but it will ease up."[5]

Yet Saddam ordered the invasion anyway. Bush got the news from Scowcroft shortly before 5:00 a.m. on August 2, 1990, and Scowcroft summoned the National Security Council (NSC) to consider the American response. Going into the meeting, Bush paused for a photo opportunity and took a few questions from reporters. Helen Thomas of United Press International asked if he was considering military intervention.

"We're not discussing intervention," Bush responded. He added that he wouldn't talk publicly about intervention even if he were considering it. "One of the things I want to do at this meeting is hear from our Secretary of Defense, our Chairman [of the Joint Chiefs of Staff], and others. But I'm not contemplating such action."

Thomas pressed the issue. "You're not contemplating any intervention or sending troops?" she demanded.

"I'm not contemplating such action, and again I would not discuss it if I were," Bush responded.[6]

Bush proceeded into the NSC meeting, where he heard reports on his diplomatic, economic, and military options. The State Department was already working at the United Nations and in friendly capitals to isolate Baghdad diplomatically. The Treasury Department was investigating the prospects for an international boycott of oil shipments from Iraq and Kuwait.

Joint Chiefs chairman Colin Powell and the head of the U.S. Central Command, Norman Schwarzkopf, laid out military responses ranging from air strikes and naval bombardment to the introduction of U.S. ground forces.

Scowcroft judged the meeting to be quite unsatisfactory. "I was frankly appalled at the undertone of the discussion, which suggested resignation to the invasion and even adaptation to a *fait accompli*," he wrote later. "There was a huge gap between those who saw it as the major crisis of our time and those who treated it as the crisis *du jour*."[7] But he apparently raised no such objections at this meeting, which ended with nothing important decided.

Bush had previously agreed to speak that afternoon at the Aspen Institute in Colorado, and he flew directly to the mountain resort (aboard a borrowed Gulfstream, as Aspen's runways couldn't accommodate *Air Force One*). Margaret Thatcher was waiting for him when he arrived; the British prime minister was scheduled to speak two days later, but she had come early to see Bush. Thatcher spent the morning reflecting on the news from the Gulf, a region the British had long considered themselves expert on. As she recalled later,

> By the time I was due to meet him at the main ranch I was quite clear what we must do.
>
> Fortunately, the President began by asking me what I thought. I told him my conclusions in the clearest and most straightforward terms. First, aggressors must never be appeased. We learned that to our cost in the 1930s. Second, if Saddam were to cross the border into Saudi Arabia he could go right down the Gulf in a matter of days. He would then control 65 per cent of the world's oil reserves and could blackmail us all. Not only did we have to move to stop the aggression, therefore, we had to stop it quickly.[8]

Thatcher's vigorous antiappeasement position reflected her reading not simply of the 1930s but also of the early 1980s, when Argentina had invaded the Falkland Islands. Thatcher had resisted calls then for a mediated settlement, even when proposed by the United States and presented by Secretary of State Alexander Haig. "In the drawing room at No. 10 Downing Street, after I had explained the American proposals to Mrs. Thatcher,"

Haig remembered, "she rapped sharply on the tabletop and recalled that this was the table at which Neville Chamberlain sat in 1938 and spoke of the Czechs as a faraway people about whom we know so little and with whom we have so little in common. A world war and the death of over 45 million people followed."[9] Thatcher's adamancy had prompted initial criticism but subsequent praise after the British force she dispatched to the South Atlantic retook the Falklands, with great positive results for her politically (and disastrous consequences for the Argentine government, which collapsed following the defeat).

Thatcher adduced the lessons of Munich and the Falklands in her meeting with Bush in Aspen. She had learned of the ambivalence he had expressed that morning, and she deemed it utterly wrongheaded, and said almost as much in the joint news conference they held after their meeting: "Iraq has violated and taken over the territory of a country which is a full member of the United Nations. That is totally unacceptable, and if it were allowed to endure, then there would be many other small countries that could never feel safe."

Bush wasn't yet willing to be so categorical, though his position appeared to have firmed up since that morning. A reporter queried, "Isn't Saddam Hussein at the root of this problem?" Before the president could answer, the reporter continued, "Would you like to see him removed? What can you do about him?"

"I would like to see him withdraw his troops, and the restoration of the legal government in Kuwait," Bush replied. "We find his behavior intolerable in this instance." He added, "The reaction from around the world is unanimous in being condemnatory. So, that speaks for itself."

"Are you still not contemplating military intervention?" another reporter asked.

"We're not ruling any options in, but we're not ruling any options out," Bush responded.[10]

The administration subsequently denied that Bush had required Thatcher's encouragement to take a hard line against Saddam. The White House contention was that the president's careful language in the immediate aftermath of the Kuwait invasion reflected not indecision but unwillingness, as Scowcroft put it, to "telegraph his thinking" to Baghdad.[11] This is plausible; Bush might well have decided on his own to make Saddam cough up Kuwait. But Thatcher's intimation that Bush would be viewed as the Neville Chamberlain of the 1990s if he appeased Saddam certainly must have enhanced his resolve.

Bush flew back to Washington, where he met again with the NSC. "It's been a remarkable twenty-four hours," the president told the group. "It's fortunate Mrs. Thatcher is at Aspen. I am glad we are seeing eye-to-eye.... She shared her views one hundred percent with me." Bush was now closer to a decision to deploy the American military in one form or another. "Diplomatic efforts are under way to get Saddam to back off. He is ruthless and powerful. Others' efforts might not succeed to get his troops out and Kuwait's ruler back in. We need to weigh the implications of taking this on directly. The status quo is intolerable."

After discussing diplomatic and economic options, the group turned to military force. Defense Secretary Dick Cheney said that the U.S.S. *Eisenhower* was headed from the Mediterranean to the northern Arabian Sea and would arrive in two days, but its planes could have no more than a modest effect: "Where they will be located, there is not a lot you can do with naval aircraft. They can reach some targets, but they won't alter the military situation."

Powell agreed, citing two distinct objectives. The first was to deter an Iraqi strike against Saudi Arabia. The surest method of achieving this objective was to place U.S. forces on the ground in that country. The troops probably would not have to fight; their presence would be a sufficient deterrent. The second objective was more ambitious and daunting: to drive the Iraqi Army out of Kuwait. "This is harder than Panama and Libya," Powell said, referring to the limited operations against those countries in the previous few years. "This would be the NFL, not a scrimmage. It would mean a major confrontation. Most U.S. forces would have to be committed to sustain, not for just one or two days." Powell added that Saddam was "professional and megalomanic" and that the Iraqi Army was battle hardened after eight years of war against Iran.

Bush was less impressed by Saddam than Powell was. "I am not certain he is invincible," Bush said. He added that Iraq had failed to defeat Iran despite years of trying.

"But Iran paid in manpower," Powell rejoined.[12]

Scowcroft was happier with this meeting than the previous one. "The tone of the NSC discussion was much better than the day before," he remarked later.[13] Though Powell was skittish, the president seemed convinced that Iraqi control of Kuwait was intolerable.

Bush flew by helicopter to Camp David for a short weekend, returning on Sunday, August 5. He hadn't planned on making a statement as he exited the aircraft, but reporters shouted questions at him and he felt obliged to respond. At that moment he appeared not to make the connection to Chamberlain's return from Munich in 1938, also by air, after which the prime minister asserted that his bargain with Hitler had achieved "peace for our time." But others saw the symbolism when Bush, fresh off the helicopter, made it clear that he was no Chamberlain. "I'm not going to discuss what we're doing in terms of moving of forces, anything of that nature," he told the reporters, adding,

> I view it very seriously, not just that but any threat to any other countries, as well as I view very seriously our determination to reverse out this aggression. And please believe me, there are an awful lot of countries that are in total accord with what I've just said, and I salute them. They are staunch friends and allies, and we will be working with them all for collective action. This will not stand. This will not stand, this aggression against Kuwait.[14]

Saddam as Hitler

Bush may or may not have required the Munich analogy to make up his mind about Saddam and Iraq. He might well have decided to rescue Kuwait without help from the memory of Hitler—although, as a veteran of World War II, he presumably felt that memory more personally than did those whose recollection of the war was simply vicarious.

Whatever the role of Munich in Bush's decisionmaking, he found the parallel between Hitler and Saddam irresistible in explaining his decision: "We all know the grave economic consequences of Iraq's occupation of Kuwait. But as serious as these consequences may be, what is ultimately at stake is far more than a matter of economics or oil. What is at stake is whether the nations of the world can take a common stand against aggression." The world had been down this path before. "Hitler revisited," Bush said in his typically telegraphic style. America had stepped up then, if too slowly: "Remember, when Hitler's war ended, there were the Nuremberg trials." And it would step up now: "America will not stand aside. The world will not allow the strong to swallow up the weak."[15]

Bush told an audience in Burlington, Vermont, that he had been studying the history of World War II, "And there's a parallel between what Hitler did to Poland and what Saddam Hussein has done to Kuwait." The Nazi SS had nothing on Saddam's thugs when it came to brutality, Bush asserted:

> Do you know what happened in Kuwait the other day? Two young kids, mid-teens, passing out leaflets—Iraqi soldiers came, got their parents out and watched as they killed them. They had people on dialysis machines, and they ripped them off of the machines and sent the dialysis machines to Baghdad. And they had kids in incubators, and they were thrown out of the incubators so that Kuwait could be systematically dismantled.

Critics of the administration's policy were saying its principal worry was oil, but Bush denied this: "It isn't oil that we're concerned about. It is aggression. And this aggression is not going to stand."[16]

After Saddam seized hundreds of Americans in Iraq and was said to have placed some of them near military installations, Bush escalated his rhetoric. "They are held in direct contravention of international law, many of them reportedly staked out as human shields near possible military targets," the president declared. "Brutality that—I don't believe Adolf Hitler ever participated in anything of that nature."[17]

Some listeners thought Bush was getting carried away. Did he really think Saddam was worse than Hitler? "Is there a chance that you might be exaggerating a bit for effect?" a reporter asked.

Bush defended his choice of words. "I don't think I'm overstating it," he replied. Tipping his hand emotionally, he added, "I know I'm not overstating the feelings I have about it."

Another reporter pressed the issue, asking, "Can you tell us what Saddam Hussein has done that can be compared to the Holocaust?"

"Well, I didn't say the Holocaust," Bush explained, but he defended his basic point: "I was told—and we've got to check this carefully—that Hitler did not stake people out against potential military targets."[18] And he stuck to his antiappeasement theme. "We're not talking about oil," he insisted. "We are talking about standing up against aggression. And if the United States can't do it and cannot lead, nobody can. We do not need another Hitler in this time of our century."[19]

Bush's statements to reporters could be expected to reveal what he wanted the public to know of his thought processes; sometimes a president's private remarks tell a different story. In this case, though, Bush's public and private statements track each other closely. On the last day of 1990 he wrote a letter to his children. The United Nations Security Council had given Saddam a deadline, January 15, 1991, to evacuate Kuwait. Sixteen days before that deadline Bush told his children that the prospect of war weighed heavily upon him. He explained why he thought war might be necessary:

> My mind goes back to history: How many lives might have been saved if appeasement had given way to force earlier on in the late '30s or earliest '40s? How many Jews might have been spared the gas chambers, or how many Polish patriots might be alive today? I look at today's crisis as "good" vs. "evil"—yes, it is that clear.[20]

Yet Bush's very attachment to the Hitler comparison made some in the administration uncomfortable. The United States had eventually waged an all-out war against Hitler that entailed the utter destruction of the German government and an extended occupation of Germany (where American troops still remained in 1990). Powell was reasonably sure the president had no similar plans for Iraq, and he feared that the harping on Hitler would raise expectations that would be difficult to meet. As Powell later recalled,

> I suggested to Cheney and Scowcroft that they might try to get the President to cool the rhetoric. Not that the charges were untrue, but the demonizing left me uneasy. I preferred to talk about the "Iraq regime" or the "Hussein regime." Our plan contemplated only ejecting Iraq from Kuwait. It did not include toppling Saddam's dictatorship. Within these limits, we could not bring George Bush Saddam Hussein's scalp. And I thought it unwise to elevate public expectations by making the man out to be the devil incarnate and then leave him in place.[21]

Dick Cheney had a different problem with the Hitler comparison. While Bush cited Hitler to generate congressional support for resistance to Saddam, potentially including war, Cheney thought the Nazi era showed the unreliability of Congress and therefore the imprudence of resting policy on the legislature. "I told Garrick Utley that I loved the Congress," Cheney recalled of a November 1990 appearance on *Meet the Press*. "I had served there for ten years. But I also had a sense of its limitations." Cheney had reminded Utley of some pertinent history:

> I take you back to September 1941, when World War II had been under way for two years; Hitler had taken Austria, Czechoslovakia, Poland, Norway, Denmark, the Netherlands, Belgium, France and was halfway to Moscow. And the Congress, in that setting, two months before Pearl Harbor, agreed to extend the selective service system, the draft for twelve more months, by just one vote.[22]

A Pivot toward Southeast Asia

Partly to meet these objections, but also to assuage another set of concerns, Bush looked to a different chapter of history to explain what a war for Kuwait would *not* become. As U.S. troops arrived in the vicinity of the Persian Gulf, critics of the administration's policy warned that the region could turn into another Vietnam. Bush asserted that it would not. "I have to tell you, I understand where these kids are coming from," he said after encountering some protesters. "We've been through a couple of agonizing periods with the Korean war and the Vietnam war. So, their view shouldn't be entirely written off." But heeding the critics would allow aggression to flourish, just as it would have at an earlier time: "They've got it wrong. They've got the facts wrong. They're looking introspectively in a bit of an isolationistic way. We can't do that. We have the responsibility to lead—the United States does." Bush rejected assertions that the United States intended a protracted occupation of the Gulf or the Middle East:

> Saddam Hussein will be held accountable. And the legitimate government of Kuwait will be restored. And America will remain in the Persian Gulf not one single day longer than necessary. I look forward to the day that every single man and woman serving there now with pride—and beautifully trained—every single one of them comes home. But we must stay for as long as it takes to complete our mission.[23]

Bush cited the spirit of the early Cold War, before Vietnam, to appeal for unity behind the effort in the Gulf. Campaigning for Pete Wilson, the Republican nominee for governor of California, the president applauded the support of the candidate and Republicans generally for the administration's Middle East policy. "Pete's been in the forefront on this one," he said, adding,

> Our party has always stood for strength at home and strength abroad. And today it's no different. But partisanship, as Senator Vandenberg said, stops at the water's edge. We got away from that a little bit in the Vietnam days.... I like that concept that when it comes to foreign affairs, the partisanship should, indeed, stop at the water's edge. And so, I think in a spirit of fair play—given what we're facing halfway around the world—I ought to say, and I say it proudly, that I am very grateful for the bipartisan support for our stand against aggression in the Persian Gulf.[24]

Bush liked the Vandenberg model of pre-Vietnam bipartisanship well enough to repeat it. "I believe, as Arthur Vandenberg did long ago—Senator Vandenberg—that politics ends at the water's edge," he told a Republican rally in Massachusetts. "That's a noble sentiment. It's strong. It makes sense today. We crept away from that because of the agony of Vietnam. Now we are united."[25]

Bush intended for America to remain united, as it had not been during the Vietnam years. In the autumn of 1990 the administration's emphasis shifted from defending Saudi Arabia to ejecting Iraqi forces from Kuwait, and as American troop numbers in the Gulf continued to grow, Bush took care to explain his thinking. "I've been asked why I ordered more troops to the Gulf," he told reporters. "I remain hopeful that we can achieve a peaceful solution to this crisis. But if force is required, we and the other twenty-six countries who have troops in the area will have enough power to get the job done." He understood that the escalation engendered worries based on American history, but felt that such worries were exaggerated: "I know that there are fears about another Vietnam. Let me assure you, should military action be required, this will not be another Vietnam. This will not be a protracted, drawn-out war." A fight against Iraq would be nothing like the conflict in Vietnam, he explained: "The forces arrayed are different. The opposition is different. The resupply of Saddam's military would be very different. The countries united against him in the United Nations are different. The topography of Kuwait is different." American strategy would, this time around, be different:

I want peace. I want peace, not war. But if there must be war, we will not permit our troops to have their hands tied behind their backs. And I pledge to you: There will not be any murky ending. If one American soldier has to go into battle, that soldier will have enough force behind him to win and then get out as soon as possible, as soon as the U.N. objectives have been achieved. I will never—ever—agree to a halfway effort.[26]

As the president prepared Congress for a vote on the use of force in the Gulf, he reiterated that a war there would not be like Vietnam. At a news conference, a reporter relayed a question from a young reader: "It's from an eighteen-year-old from Birmingham, Michigan. And his question is: If the war in the Gulf escalates, how will you get the American people to support the war?" The reporter then added, "It's a common theme of our readers' questions, and it seems to ask whether you think the American public is as willing to accept war as an option as your policies seem to be."

"I don't want war as an option; I want peace as an option," Bush responded. "I think some of those questions stem from the fact that some believe this will be another Vietnam. And the agony of Vietnam is still with us. People remember a protracted war. They remember a war where individuals were asked to fight with one hand tied behind their back, in essence. This will not be, in my view, that kind of a confrontation."[27]

The Vietnam analogy was for public consumption, but it also shaped discussions within the administration. During the Reagan years Caspar Weinberger had formulated a set of guidelines he thought should govern the use of American military power abroad. "The war in Vietnam, with our 'limited objectives' and yet our unlimited willingness to commit troops, reinforced my belief, which I expressed many times when I was Secretary of Defense, that it was a very terrible mistake for a government to commit soldiers to battle without any intention of supporting them sufficiently to enable them to win, and indeed without any intention to win," Weinberger wrote after leaving office. His guidelines, articulated in a 1984 speech, insisted that for the United States to commit combat troops to a conflict, six standards must be met: its vital interests or those of its allies must be at risk; sufficient resources must be committed to allow victory; the military and political objectives must be clear; the commitment must be flexible enough to accommodate changing circumstances; Congress and the American people must support the commitment; and force must the last resort.[28] As Powell, Weinberger's senior military adviser at the time, summarized, "Is the national interest at stake? If the answer is yes, go in, and go in to win. Otherwise, stay out."[29]

Weinberger's dicta influenced Powell and other members of the Bush administration as they weighed war plans for the Gulf. Powell and some of his uniformed colleagues worried that the Weinberger conditions hadn't been met, and their worries came to the attention of the White House. "As we moved nearer to the possibility of war, there were several incidents which could be interpreted to suggest that at least some among our military were less than enthusiastic about the prospect," Scowcroft later observed. "They occurred against the backdrop of the Vietnam conflict. There was considerable sentiment that the military had been ordered into Vietnam by the civilian leadership and then left holding the bag when the political climate shifted."[30]

Powell himself made no secret of his unwillingness to fight another war like that in Vietnam, where he had served two tours and been wounded and decorated. As soon as the administration began talking of war in the Persian Gulf, he felt obliged to test the resolve of the president. At the NSC meeting following Bush's return from Aspen, Powell listened to Cheney, Scowcroft, and others talk about forcibly evicting Saddam from Kuwait. As he later recalled,

> I then asked if it was worth going to war to liberate Kuwait. It was a Clausewitzian question which I posed so that the military would know what preparations it might have to make. I detected a chill in the room. The question was premature, and it should not have come from me. I had overstepped. I was not the National Security Advisor now; I was only supposed to give *military* advice. Nevertheless, I had wrestled with the politics and economics of crises for almost two years in the White House, in this very room. I had participated in superpower summits. More to the point, as a midlevel career officer, I had been appalled at the docility of the Joint Chiefs of Staff, fighting the war in Vietnam without ever pressing the political leaders to lay out clear objectives for them. Before we start talking about how many divisions, carriers, and fighter wings we need, I said, we have to ask, to achieve what end?

After the meeting, Cheney took Powell to task. "Colin," he said, "you're Chairman of the Joint Chiefs. You're not Secretary of State. You're not the National Security Advisor anymore. And you're not Secretary of Defense. So stick to military matters." Powell admitted that he had gone too far. "I was not sorry, however, that I had spoken out," he remembered. "What I had said about giving the military clear objectives had to be said."[31]

Powell spoke not simply for himself but for the military rank and file. As American troops arrived in Saudi Arabia, reporters and visitors asked them how they felt about the deployment. "I am proud to represent our nation by being over here, and I'd like our nation to be proud of me," a young army lieutenant told a reporter. "But I had a brother and an uncle who fought in Vietnam, and we all know what happened to the Vietnam vets. They were disrespected by the American people for being there. Well, that's a big concern to us out here, and we talk about it every night. We are ready to defend our country, but we want to be supported and respected for what we are doing." Another said, "I have a lot of friends who were Vietnam vets. Some of us are scared that once we start going home in body bags, the country will turn against this and it will become another Vietnam."[32] John Murtha, a Democratic congressman from Pennsylvania and a Marine Corps veteran of Korea and Vietnam, visited Saudi Arabia to assess the soldiers' morale. They repeatedly asked him if the people back home supported them. "The aura of Vietnam hangs over these kids," Murtha remarked. "Their parents were in it. They've seen all these movies. They wonder, they wonder."[33]

The American media wondered, too. From the start, reporters and news organizations probed American thinking on the conflict. The *New York Times* conducted a poll of attitudes toward the crisis in the Gulf, giving respondents a choice of two historical analogies. The first was, "Saddam Hussein is like Adolf Hitler of Germany in the 1930s and it is important to stop him." This statement elicited agreement from 61 percent of the respondents, while 33 percent said it was not a good comparison. The second assertion was, "The current situation in the Middle East is a lot like Vietnam in the 1960s." To this 42 percent agreed, while 52 percent disagreed.[34]

Pundits took up the historical cudgels in opinion columns. Jeane Kirkpatrick urged the Bush administration to steer between the Scylla of Munich and the Charybdis of Vietnam. "No law of war compels the president to choose between a strategy of appeasement and a Vietnam-style ground war," the neoconservative professor and Reagan-era ambassador to the United Nations declared. "Viable alternatives exist between the two extremes."[35] Alexander Haig, who had scrapped with Kirkpatrick during Reagan cabinet meetings, now agreed. "International conflicts attract historical analogies the way honey attracts bears, because the 'lessons learned' from such analogies are supposed to help us avoid past mistakes," he wrote. "The Persian Gulf crisis is no exception, and two analogies in particular—Munich and Vietnam—might have something to tell us." What these analogies said, according to Haig, was that both outcomes must be avoided: "The Munich analogy teaches us not that Saddam Hussein is already a Hitler but that we must act now to prevent him from becoming one. The Vietnam analogy instructs us not that we should refrain from using force but that if our purposes are just and clear, we should use it decisively."[36]

No More Vietnams

In Dick Cheney's mind, the most important audience for the historical analogies—the only one that really mattered—was George Bush. Journalist and author Bob Woodward often refuses to cite sources for his books on the inner workings of government, but readers have long guessed which insiders have spoken to him from the amount and favorability of the coverage he accords them. His book *The Commanders* casts Cheney as a prime mover behind the push for war, and Cheney evidently told Woodward that Bush took the Vietnam analogy quite seriously. "By now Cheney had come to realize what an impact the Vietnam War had had on Bush," Woodward writes of the shift in strategy from the defense of Saudi Arabia to the liberation of Kuwait—from Desert Shield to Desert Storm. "The President had internalized the lessons—send enough force to do the job and don't tie the hands of the commanders. In a September 12 speech in California, Cheney had said, 'The President belongs to what I call the "Don't screw around" school of military strategy.' Though this perhaps was inelegantly stated, Cheney was certain that the President didn't want to screw around. That meant a viable offensive option."[37]

Cheney and others in the administration conveyed this message to America's allies in the move against Iraq. The government that most wanted to know was that of Saudi Arabia, which risked the wrath of other Arabs and Muslims if it sided with the United States against Saddam. Saudi ambassador Prince Bandar bin Sultan visited the Pentagon to meet with Powell and measure Americans' intentions. As Woodward wrote, apparently relying on interviews with Bandar,

> It seemed to him that Powell and [Secretary of State James] Baker were the members of the Bush inner circle least inclined to go to war against Saddam. "If we don't have to fight, it will be better," Powell told the prince. "If we have to, I'll do it, but we're going to do it with everything we have." Powell said that the President had ordered that this not turn into another Vietnam. The guiding principle was going to be a maximization of firepower and troops. Later, Cheney told Bandar, "The military is finished in this society if we screw this up."[38]

Bush himself conveyed the same message to the leaders of Congress. "We don't need another Vietnam War," he said in a White House meeting in late November. "No hands are going to be tied behind backs. This is not a Vietnam. . . . I know whose backside's at stake and rightfully so. It will not be a long, drawn-out mess."[39]

Congress accepted the assurance, though not without argument. In debate in the House of Representatives over authorizing the president to use force against Iraq, Illinois Republican Robert Michel employed the Munich analogy explicitly and Vietnam implicitly:

> I speak from the prejudice of being a combat veteran of World War II. And those of our generation know from bloody experience that unchecked aggression against a small nation is a prelude to an international disaster. Saddam Hussein today has more planes and tanks and, frankly, men under arms than Hitler had at the time when Prime Minister Chamberlain came back from Munich with that miserable piece of paper—peace in our time. I'll never forget that replay of that movie in my life.

America needed to act decisively against Saddam, Michel said. "Either we stop him now, and stop him permanently, or we won't stop him at all."[40]

Democrat Paul Simon of Illinois hadn't fought in World War II, but he had been deeply involved in the political struggles surrounding the

Vietnam War. "There is a grim mood here in Congress," he told the Senate. "When you and I were elected to the House, Mr. President, in 1974, we were already involved in the Vietnam War." That had been a divisive time, but it was no more divisive than the present. "I have not experienced this kind of a mood before in Washington, D.C.," Simon said, noting that he didn't want to see things get any worse. Alongside most of the opponents of the use-of-force resolution he argued not for ignoring the Iraqi aggression but for giving the economic option—sanctions—additional time to work. "The evidence is pretty overwhelming that this has a chance to succeed if we stick with it," Simon said.[41]

Edward Kennedy employed different analogies. Speaking in the Senate against the use-of-force resolution, the Massachusetts Democrat warned that a war against Iraq would prove bloodier than the administration's supporters were predicting: "Military experts have used Israel's two recent desert wars as reliable indicators of the casualties we will suffer. In the Six Day War in 1967, Israel suffered 3,300 casualties out of a force of 300,000, including 700 dead. In the heavier fighting that lasted 20 days in the 1973 war, Israeli casualties were 11,000 out of a force of a similar size, with 2,600 dead." Kennedy thought the arithmetic translated directly. "In other words," he added, "we're talking about the likelihood of at least 3,000 American casualties a week, with 700 dead, for as long as the war goes on."[42]

Most other members of Congress didn't say which analogies they were voting for or against, but the president eventually won his resolution. The vote in the Senate was close: 52 in favor and 47 against. In the House the administration's margin was more comfortable: 250 to 183.

Saddam Hussein ignored the American resolution, as well as the operative NSC resolutions, and his troops remained in Kuwait after the deadline of January 15, 1991. On January 16 Bush ordered American air forces to commence the assault on Iraqi forces and positions. As he announced his decision, he stressed again what he had learned from history:

> Prior to ordering our forces into battle, I instructed our military commanders to take every necessary step to prevail as quickly as possible, and with the greatest degree of protection possible for American and allied service men and women. I've told the American people before that this will not be another Vietnam, and I repeat this here tonight. Our troops will have the best possible support in the entire

world, and they will not be asked to fight with one hand tied behind their back. I'm hopeful that this fighting will not go on for long and that casualties will be held to an absolute minimum.[43]

The lessons of Vietnam stuck with Bush throughout the air war. Three weeks in, he met with his national security team to consider if and when a ground offensive should begin. "The President was torn," Scowcroft later remembered. "He did not want to appear to be second-guessing the military experts. Still vivid in his mind was the image of Lyndon Johnson during Vietnam, hunched over aerial charts selecting individual targets for air strikes." But Bush was the president, and he knew he couldn't abdicate a decision as fundamental as when and whether to launch a ground war.[44]

The decision was complicated by signals from Saddam that he might finally heed the UN eviction demand. Had Saddam sent the signals before the war started, Bush might have followed up on them and claimed a diplomatic victory, but the onset of fighting changed his calculus; mission creep set in, as it often does. "The question is, what comes next?" he wrote in his diary. "We've got some unfinished business. How do we solve it? How do we now guarantee the future peace? I don't see how it will work with Saddam in power, and I am very, very worried."[45]

Scowcroft and Cheney didn't want to let Saddam off the hook with a mere evacuation of Kuwait. "It was essential that we destroy Iraq's offensive capability," Scowcroft recounted. "This was also a major objective, though it had not been feasible to list it openly as such while a peaceful solution to the crisis was possible." Scowcroft persuaded the president, who didn't require much nudging; American intelligence made plain that the air war was going very well. As he later recalled,

Estimates indicated that Iraq's military capability had been reduced by at least 40 percent. If Saddam would evacuate Kuwait, our objectives would be largely achieved and without the need for land combat. The President, however, saw the dangers of an Iraqi withdrawal before its army had been destroyed. It would then remain a menace on the Kuwaiti border and in the region. Our forces were too large to rotate, and the Saudis would never tolerate a huge alien presence on their soil indefinitely to contain Saddam. We had to act now while we were mobilized and in place.[46]

Bush brushed off Saddam's overtures and unleashed the ground offensive. As he did so he conceived the issue in the context of history. "We don't want to have another draw, another Vietnam, a sloppy ending," he wrote in his diary. "Our credibility is at stake." U.S. and coalition forces scored dramatic victories, prompting the president to reflect on the meaning of it all. "I'm thinking, good God, isn't it exciting?" he wrote. "Isn't it marvelous that this little country will be liberated?" Much of Bush's thrill reflected his belief that America was turning a historic corner. "We're doing something decent, and we're doing something good," he later wrote, "and Vietnam will soon be behind us. . . . It's surprising how much I dwell on the end of the Vietnam syndrome. I felt the division of the country in the 60s and 70s. . . . I remember the agony and the ugliness; and now it's together."[47]

The desire for a definitive ending tempted the president toward further mission creep: a march to Baghdad and the destruction of Saddam Hussein's regime. "I worried he would emerge from the war weakened but as a 'hero' still in charge," Bush wrote later. But taking Baghdad might be costly—certainly in comparison with the war thus far—and there was no guarantee of easy success, as a comparable experience had demonstrated. "We had had problems locating [Dictator Manuel] Noriega in Panama, a place we knew well," Bush wrote. "Saddam was far more elusive and better protected."[48] The United States would outrun its UN mandate and likely would fracture the anti-Saddam coalition; and it would probably have to occupy Iraq for some time.

So Bush, after allowing the American military some last licks against the Iraqis, called the war off. "Kuwait is liberated," the president told the country. "Iraq's army is defeated. Our military objectives are met. Kuwait is once more in the hands of the Kuwaitis, in control of their own destiny. We share in their joy, a joy tempered only by our compassion for their ordeal."[49]

In fact, the administration's joy was tempered by something else as well. "Still no feeling of euphoria," Bush wrote in his diary the next day. "It hasn't been a clean end—there is no battleship *Missouri* surrender. This is what's missing to make this akin to WWII, to separate Kuwait from Korea and Vietnam."[50] Saddam remained in power in Baghdad; his army was battered but intact. Bush hadn't wavered from his belief that Saddam must not be appeased, but he belatedly appreciated Powell's concern about portraying Saddam as the modern Hitler, since this Hitler had survived his war. Bush hoped the Iraqis would overthrow him, yet he couldn't count on it.

The Iraqis did not topple Saddam, eventually prompting Bush's son, President George W. Bush, to finish the job. By then his father's failure to take Baghdad seemed to many in America more significant than the liberation of Kuwait. But the elder Bush and Scowcroft still defended what they had done on behalf of America and the world. "The United States had recognized and shouldered its peculiar responsibility for leadership in tackling international challenges, and won wide acceptance for this role around the globe," they wrote. "American political credibility and influence had skyrocketed."[51]

Much of that influence resulted from the removal of a historical monkey from America's back. Ironically it was this part of Bush's accomplishment that, for better or worse, made his son's later accomplishment possible. "It's a proud day for America," Bush had declared as the fighting ended; the country had stood up for what was right and had prevailed. "And, by God, we've kicked the Vietnam syndrome once and for all."[52] In a radio address to America's armed forces in the Persian Gulf, the president repeated this theme. "Americans today are confident of our country, confident of our future, and most of all, confident about you," he said. "We promised you'd be given the means to fight. We promised not to look over your shoulder. We promised this would not be another Vietnam. And we kept that promise. The specter of Vietnam has been buried forever in the desert sands of the Arabian Peninsula."[53]

History's Lessons

Bush claimed too much. He had not quite laid to rest the ghost of Vietnam; it would shadow the next president, Bill Clinton, as his administration responded to war in the Balkans. It would haunt the administrations of George W. Bush and Barack Obama when wars in Afghanistan and Iraq dragged on much longer than expected. Yet the Gulf War of 1991 created its own lessons, foremost of which, as interpreted by Bush's son and Dick Cheney, by then vice president, was that it was a mistake to leave a dictator in power in the Gulf.

The larger lesson was that historical analogies have to be handled with care. Analogies are powerful tools: they distill experience into a few words that typically convey emotion as well as intellectual argument. Appeals to Munich summoned not simply the misguided reasoning of appeasement but the horrors of the war that followed. Vietnam conjured more than the failure of policy on the ground in Southeast Asia; it also revived the wrenching American politics of the 1960s and 1970s. It was doubtless significant that each of these analogies could be summarized in a single word, giving them greater impact in the Gulf Crisis than analogies of, for instance, the early Cold War or the Arab-Israeli wars, which required lengthier explanations.

Linguists and psychologists have long debated the role of words in shaping thought. Which comes first, the thought or the words? A similar uncertainty surrounds the use of historical analogy in policymaking. Did Bush go to war against Saddam because he recalled the consequences of Munich, or did he use the language of Munich to justify a decision he would have made anyway? It is impossible to say, for the words and the thoughts were inextricably entangled, as words and thoughts always are.

This entangling has particular consequences for the use of historical analogy. Bush discovered that he couldn't call Saddam another Hitler without raising the expectation that the United States should do to Saddam what it had done to Hitler. The power of such an analogy is its ability to compress experience and emotion, but that is also its weakness, for extraneous elements get dragged along with the pertinent.

The problem is knowing which parts of the analogies are pertinent. The Munich analogy was always suspect, for it extrapolated from one person, Hitler—arguably (and thankfully) one of the least representative people in the history of the twentieth century—to other persons. America's Cold War policies were founded on the belief that Stalin was essentially Hitler in red. There was little reason to believe that this was true, and much that could cause one to believe it was false. Hitler's policy was consistently aggressive, and Stalin's almost as consistently defensive. But the assertion couldn't easily be disproved, and its lack of disproof was thus taken as proof. Was Saddam another Hitler? This was far easier to assert than to disprove, and in American policy since Pearl Harbor, the burden has always been on the skeptics of intervention. In the case of the Gulf War, they lost, albeit not by much in the Senate.

The Vietnam analogy was more solidly grounded, for it dealt not with the character of individual foreign rulers but with the American body politic. The lesson of Vietnam, as taken by those who cited it during the Gulf Crisis, was that the United States should not initiate wars it was not willing to fight to the finish. The basis for this conclusion was that the American people wouldn't tolerate long, indecisive conflicts, and given that the American people had not collectively changed very much between the early 1970s and the early 1990s, this was a reasonable inference.

Yet it still left something to be desired, as would become clear after the United States invaded Afghanistan in 2001. If the Vietnam analogy held, the American people should have rejected the war in Afghanistan long before 2014, when the U.S. combat role in that country officially ended. In fact, they did reject it: during the second half of the conflict, opinion polls consistently showed that Americans wanted to be done with Afghanistan. But they didn't do so effectively. Something crucial had changed since Vietnam, and that thing was probably the termination of the draft. Because the Afghanistan war was fought with volunteers, it provoked far less opposition than the Vietnam War had. This suggests that even the Vietnam analogy wasn't what it was cracked up to be.

The upshot of all this for policymakers is that historical analogies are tools that can be useful if employed with discretion. The discretion is critical, for the analogies can mislead as easily as lead. They are no substitute for close analysis of the situation at hand. Better one expert on Arab politics, in a crisis among Gulf Arabs, than a dozen students of Nazi Germany.

Notes

1. National Security Directive 26, "U.S. Policy Toward the Persian Gulf," October 2, 1989, George Bush Presidential Library, College Station, Texas.

2. George Bush and Brent Scowcroft, *A World Transformed* (New York: Vintage, 1998), 307.

3. Baghdad to State Department, July 25, 1990, George Bush Presidential Library, College Station, Texas.

4. Bush and Scowcroft, *A World Transformed*, 312.

5. Memorandum of telephone conversation with King Hussein of Jordan, July 31, 1990, George Bush Presidential Library, College Station, Texas.

6. George H. W. Bush remarks and exchange with reporters August 2, 1990, Public Papers of the Presidents, American Presidency Project (http://www.presidency.ucsb.edu/ws/index.php?pid=18726&st=&st1=).

7. Bush and Scowcroft, *A World Transformed*, 317, emphasis in the original.

8. Margaret Thatcher, *The Downing Street Years* (New York: HarperCollins, 1993), 817.

9. Alexander M. Haig Jr., *Caveat: Realism, Reagan, and Foreign Policy* (New York: Macmillan, 1984), 272.

10. George H. W. Bush and Margaret Thatcher remarks and question-and-answer with reporters in Aspen, Colorado, August 2, 1990, Public Papers of the Presidents, American Presidency Project (http://www.presidency.ucsb.edu/ws/index.php?pid=18727&st=&st1=).

11. Bush and Scowcroft, *A World Transformed*, 315.

12. Minutes of NSC meeting, August 3, 1990, George Bush Presidential Library, College Station, Texas.

13. Bush and Scowcroft, *A World Transformed*, 324.

14. George H. W. Bush remarks and exchange with reporters in Washington, August 5, 1990, Public Papers of the Presidents, American Presidency Project (http://www.presidency.ucsb.edu/ws/index.php?pid=18741&st=&st1=).

15. George H. W. Bush remarks in Dallas, October 15, 1990, Public Papers of the Presidents, American Presidency Project (http://www.presidency.ucsb.edu/ws/index.php?pid=18931&st=&st1=).

16. George H. W. Bush remarks in Burlington, Vermont, October 23, 1990, Public Papers of the Presidents, American Presidency Project (http://www.presidency.ucsb.edu/ws/index.php?pid=18954&st=&st1=).

17. George H. W. Bush remarks in Mashpee, Massachusetts, November 1, 1990, Public Papers of the Presidents, American Presidency Project (http://www.presidency.ucsb.edu/ws/index.php?pid=18983&st=&st1=).

18. George H. W. Bush remarks in Orlando, Florida, November 1, 1990, Public Papers of the Presidents, American Presidency Project (http://www.presidency.ucsb.edu/ws/index.php?pid=18985&st=&st1=).

19. George H. W. Bush remarks in Albuquerque, New Mexico, November 3, 1990, Public Papers of the Presidents, American Presidency Project (http://www.presidency.ucsb.edu/ws/index.php?pid=18992&st=&st1=).

20. George H. W. Bush to George W. Bush, Jeb Bush, Neil Bush, Marvin Bush, and Doro Bush Koch, December 31, 1990, George Bush Presidential Library, College Station, Texas.

21. Colin Powell, *My American Journey* (New York: Ballantine, 1996), 478.

22. Dick Cheney, *In My Time: A Personal and Political Memoir* (New York: Threshold, 2011), 204–05; Eleanor Randolph, "Cheney Cautions Congress on Debate of Gulf Policy," *Washington Post*, November 19, 1990.

23. George H. W. Bush remarks in Des Moines, Iowa, October 16, 1990, Public Papers of the Presidents, American Presidency Project (http://www.presidency.ucsb.edu/ws/index.php?pid=18934&st=&st1=).

24. George H. W. Bush remarks in Irvine, California, October 26, 1990, Public Papers of the Presidents, American Presidency Project (http://www.presidency.ucsb.edu/ws/index.php?pid=18963&st=&st1=). Senator Arthur Vandenberg of Michigan was a Republican apostle of bipartisanship in the early Cold War.

25. Bush remarks in Mashpee, Massachusetts, November 1, 1990.

26. George H. W. Bush news conference, November 30, 1990, Public Papers of the Presidents, American Presidency Project (http://www.presidency.ucsb.edu/ws /index.php?pid=19119&st=&st1=).

27. George H. W. Bush news conference, December 18, 1990, Public Papers of the Presidents, American Presidency Project (http://www.presidency.ucsb.edu/ws /index.php?pid=19166&st=&st1=).

28. Caspar W. Weinberger, *Fighting for Peace: Seven Critical Years in the Pentagon* (New York: Warner Books, 1990), 8–9, 441–42.

29. Powell, *American Journey*, 292.

30. Bush and Scowcroft, *A World Transformed*, 431.

31. Powell, *American Journey*, 451–52, emphasis in the original.

32. James LeMoyne, "Troops in Gulf Talk of War, and of Vietnam and Respect," *New York Times*, September 30, 1990.

33. R. W. Apple Jr., "Views on the Gulf: Lawmakers Versed in Vietnam," *New York Times*, September 16, 1990.

34. Michael Oreskes, "Poll on Troop Move Shows Support, and Anxiety," *New York Times*, August 12, 1990.

35. Jeane Kirkpatrick, "Will We Liberate Kuwait . . ." *Washington Post*, November 12, 1990.

36. Alexander M. Haig Jr., "Gulf Analogy: Munich or Vietnam?" *New York Times*, December 10, 1990.

37. Bob Woodward, *The Commanders* (New York: Simon and Schuster, 1991), 306–07.

38. Ibid., 324.

39. Ibid., 339.

40. "War and Peace: A Sampling from the Debate on Capitol Hill," *New York Times*, January 11, 1991.

41. Ibid.

42. Ibid.

43. George H. W. Bush address, January 16, 1991, Public Papers of the Presidents, American Presidency Project (http://www.presidency.ucsb.edu/ws/index .php?pid=19222&st=&st1=).

44. Bush and Scowcroft, *A World Transformed*, 466.

45. Ibid., 471.

46. Ibid., 463, 477–78.

47. Ibid., 483–84.

48. Ibid., *A World Transformed*, 463.

49. George H. W. Bush address, February 27, 1991, Public Papers of the Presidents, American Presidency Project (http://www.presidency.ucsb.edu/ws/index .php?pid=19343&st=&st1=).

50. Bush and Scowcroft, *A World Transformed*, 486–87.

51. Ibid., 491–92.

52. George H. W. Bush remarks in Washington, March 1, 1991, Public Papers of the Presidents, American Presidency Project (http://www.presidency.ucsb.edu /ws/index.php?pid=19351&st=&st1=).

53. George H. W. Bush radio address, March 2, 1991, Public Papers of the Presidents, American Presidency Project (http://www.presidency.ucsb.edu/ws /index.php?pid=19355&st=&st1=).

JENNIFER M. MILLER

5

Narrating Democracy

Historical Narratives, the Potsdam Declaration, and Japanese Rearmament, 1945–50

When the U.S. military began its occupation of Japan in the fall of 1945, the occupation authorities prioritized demilitarizing Japan both institutionally and culturally. With firm determination, U.S. officials disbanded the military, destroyed weaponry, purged and tried military leaders, and sought to eradicate the military's social, political, and cultural prestige. This process culminated with the writing of a new constitution drafted by the occupation authorities. As the centerpiece of this new constitution, article 9 explicitly renounced war and prohibited the "belligerency of the state," including the creation of military forces.[1] In pursuing these ambitious goals the occupation authorities drew from a clear historical narrative about the causes and consequences of World War II in the Pacific. Specifically, the July 1945 Potsdam Declaration, signed by China, Great Britain, and the United States, enumerated surrender terms for Japan and put forth a particular version of the nation's wartime history. The declaration blamed Japan's military leaders for waging an irresponsible and aggressive war—not only against countries and peoples throughout the Pacific but also against the Japanese people themselves. It called on the occupation authorities to restore and revitalize the "democratic tendencies" of the Japanese people by purging Japan of its misguided,

99

militarist leadership, thus assuring that Japan would not again wage an aggressive war.[2]

Within five years, however, occupation policy had changed dramatically. As the certitude of postwar victory gave way to the tensions, divisions, and violence of the Cold War, especially in Northeast Asia, U.S. policymakers decided that demilitarization was no longer in the interests of the United States or Japan. After the shocking outbreak of war in Korea in June 1950, General Douglas MacArthur, head of the U.S. occupation authorities, ordered the Japanese government to create the National Police Reserve (NPR), a new defensive force that would ultimately develop into Japan's contemporary Self-Defense Forces (SDF). In light of the Potsdam Declaration's argument that Japan's militarist wartime leadership was solely responsible for a horrific war, the creation of the NPR required a dramatic ideological refashioning of the military's role in the postwar Japanese state. Working together to repurpose the Potsdam narrative, U.S. and Japanese officials performed a volte-face and argued that this new military was not the primary danger to Japanese democracy but instead the primary protector of a democratic Japanese people. The NPR, these officials claimed, was possible because of Japan's successful postwar democratization. Moreover, only the presence of military power could secure this peaceful and democratic order against the domestic and foreign threat of international communism.

Historians have framed the creation of the NPR as the culmination of a larger shift in U.S. policy toward Japan, commonly called the *reverse course.* In using this critical term they claim that the occupation shifted away from the original Potsdam Declaration goals of democratization and demilitarization to focus on fighting communism, economic growth, and rearmament in order to stabilize Japan as an important Cold War ally. According to this narrative, American policymakers, fueled by a growing Cold War panic, were willing to sacrifice democracy to secure military cooperation in Asia, and thus shifted their focus away from instilling democratic norms and rights in Japan.[3] This chapter argues, however, that the shift in occupation policy did not mean that Japanese democracy ceased to matter in the minds of U.S. policymakers. As evidenced by the debates surrounding rearmament and the NPR, many Americans remained convinced that only a democratic Japan could secure American geostrategic goals and resist the allure of communism or a return to militarism. To be sure, this does not mean that U.S. policymakers cared about democracy as the Japanese themselves sought to engage and develop it. Moreover, American views of Japan's domestic politics were always tied to U.S. security calculations. In the early years of the occupation, democratization was the key to securing U.S. power in the Pacific and preventing a revival of Japanese militarism. With the rise of the Cold War, U.S. policymakers hoped that by publicly valuing a Japanese democracy premised on popular support and representation, they could shore up the Japanese fight against communism and secure Japanese support for U.S. Cold War policy and a U.S.-Japanese security alliance premised on Japanese rearmament. American visions of Japanese democracy—and the Potsdam narrative they drew from—did not evaporate in the late 1940s; rather, they remained a fundamental cornerstone of U.S. thinking about Japan.

U.S. officials were not alone in rethinking the relationships among history, democracy, and military power. In the aftermath of a devastating defeat, Japanese of all political camps engaged in a process of writing and rewriting Japan's wartime past. Echoing the language of the Potsdam Declaration, many Japanese argued that postwar democratization was explicitly antimilitarist. A true democratic regime, they argued, was premised on peace, an active and critical public, and the "authentic" will of the people, all of which would be undermined by the return of military aggression, violence, and hierarchies. Despite a shared terrain of popular democracy, this historical narrative soon clashed with the growing U.S. focus on rearmament and U.S. attempts to repurpose remilitarization as a constituent element of democratization. This usage of recent history, especially its call for a demilitarized and pacifist future, deeply shaped the U.S. approach to rearming Japan. Indeed, the fact that Japan was now a democracy, and one that the United States had helped create, meant that U.S. policymakers felt that they could not simply ignore Japanese opinion if they wanted to maintain legitimacy, especially as they sought to encourage active Japanese participation in the Cold War as a firm U.S. ally. Unintentionally, then, the historical narrative developed at Potsdam and instilled during the early years of the occupation emerged as the key tool in Japanese challenges to the United States' own political, ideological, and diplomatic goals. International interactions therefore shaped the development of historical narratives on all sides of this relationship: within the United States and Japan, and within both government policy and popular understanding. In creating their understandings of recent history, Americans and Japanese constantly borrowed from, influenced, and contested each other.

To uncover the mutual constitution of American and Japanese understandings of their intertwined histories of empire, war, and occupation, this article will examine early discussions over Japanese rearmament, culminating in the creation of the National Police Reserve in 1950. In particular, it will examine how historical narratives both drove and justified security policy by analyzing the seemingly contradictory relationship between the antimilitarist narrative that emerged from the war and the decision to begin rearming Japan in 1950. In both historical and popular discussions, World War II is often treated as an event of such momentous proportions that the historical lessons for policymakers were—and still are—obvious and clear. For example, the most famous lesson of the war, the 1938 Munich Agreement, has long been taken as a rallying cry for preemptive intervention against authoritarian regimes. Yet the case of the NPR emphasizes that the lessons of World War II were, in reality, flexible and contested. Historical events did not lead to one obvious or specific policy outcome; indeed, the events of the war in the Pacific seemed to directly caution against rearmament. Rather, it is the historical narratives that diverse actors develop to explain, understand, and justify these events; the way these narratives condition understandings of the past and its relationship to future policy possibilities; and—most crucially—the fact that narratives are always subject to revision, change, and repurposing that is key to understanding how the "lessons" of World War II could ultimately facilitate calls for Japan's remilitarization.

Narrating War and Defeat

The process of writing the official history of Japan's war and defeat began with the Potsdam Declaration, signed by U.S. president Harry Truman, British prime minister Winston Churchill, and Chinese chairman Chiang Kai-shek on July 26, 1945. Written as U.S. planes continued to bomb Japanese cities into ash, this document laid out the guiding principles for the surrender of Japan and forecast key occupation reforms. The Potsdam Declaration was not simply a dry list of military plans or political conditions; rather, it articulated a specific historical narrative of Japan's actions before and during the war, arguing that sole responsibility lay with Japan's "self-willed militaristic advisers." As the declaration stated, the "irresponsible militarism" of these leaders had "deceived and misled the people of Japan into embarking on world conquest." In this narrative, war and atrocities stemmed directly from the military's dominant position in the fabric of the Japanese state. While Japan had democratic institutions like a parliament, the military was not accountable to them (it reported directly to the emperor), and this allowed military leaders to ignore and subvert the wishes of the people. In contrast to the military leadership, however, the people of Japan were not responsible for the war. In fact, they were inherently democratic and, in the minds of the declaration's authors, inherently peaceful. The Potsdam Declaration stated that, after the war, "The Japanese Government shall remove all obstacles to the revival and strengthening of democratic tendencies among the Japanese people."[4] In arguing that an irresponsible, irrational, and militarist leadership had deceived the Japanese people to lead them into war, the declaration sought to create a usable past of democratic possibility.[5]

While this historical narrative was far from accurate—the military adventurism that caused empire and war drew from popular support and voluntary mobilization—the Potsdam Declaration served as the foundation for the central goals of the occupation—democratization and demilitarization—and these two goals were deeply intertwined.[6] U.S. policymakers believed that only "true" democratization—which included not merely the creation of democratic laws and institutions but the embrace of "democratic" norms such as individualism, local and popular autonomy, and broad public engagement in political affairs—could prevent the Japanese people from again being seduced by the allure of war and empire; only by removing the cancer of militarism could democracy truly take root. The occupation authorities therefore pursued both goals simultaneously. To eradicate the military from its central role in Japan's government and civil society, they immediately dismantled the imperial army and navy, ended military conscription, and purged military, economic, industrial, and political leaders deemed responsible for war and militarism from both public and private institutions. This process reached its symbolic highpoint in the Tokyo War Crimes Tribunal, which lasted from 1946 to 1948 and convicted key figures of Japan's wartime military and civilian leadership of waging aggressive war.[7]

Instigating what scholars have called a "revolution from above," occupation authorities also sought to instill democratic practices and institutions by allowing women to vote, breaking up industrial monopolies and cartels, legalizing the Communist Party, encouraging labor unionization, revising education curriculum, and encouraging local autonomy, especially in policing.[8] They negated the 1925 Peace Preservation Law, which had allowed the arrest of government critics, lifted restrictions on speech and assembly, released political prisoners, and abolished the imperial political police (known colloquially as the thought police).[9] As the culmination of these reforms, the occupation authorities legally codified Japan's new status as a "democratized and demilitarized" state by writing a new constitution; article 9 stated that "the Japanese people," the new sovereign of the democratic state, "forever renounce war as a sovereign right of the nation," and declared that "land, sea, and air force, as well as other war potential, will never be maintained."[10] This radical pacification reflected how deeply U.S. officials drew from the antimilitary narrative of the Potsdam Declaration. While in the United States it remained widely accepted that military capabilities were necessary to defend and protect democracy, U.S. occupation authorities remained convinced that Japanese democratic politics depended on the eradication of military power. Historical narratives, then, did not simply provide rhetorical justification for policy choices; they deeply informed U.S. officials' conceptualization of the necessary conditions to sustain democracy in Japan.

In order to transform postwar Japan, U.S. officials believed that it was equally important to change Japanese patterns of thought and memory; just as vital as political and institutional measures was the demilitarization of Japan's cultural sphere. U.S. authorities sought to strip the Japanese population of military memories, experiences, and cultural norms; given the mass conscription of the war, this was a task of herculean proportions. The occupation's censorship bureau laid down strict rules for all public discussions and depictions of the military and its wartime behavior. In contrast to policies in Germany, those in Japan did not encourage discussion of Japan's wartime atrocities;[11] instead, all mentions of the military had to reinforce the Potsdam narrative. The censorship bureau instructed filmmakers who dealt with the war to "emphasize 'how the Japanese people were blindly led into a war of aggression' and that 'the guilt of war rests with the past military leaders of Japan.'"[12] After the conclusion of the Tokyo Trials, the occupation's Civil Information and Education Section planned and edited a newsreel to emphasize this narrative; as a draft script asserted, "there is also no room to doubt the deceptive attack on Pearl Harbor. With this attack as a fuse, the ambitions of the Japanese militarists for domination of the whole of Asia were bloodily begun. In order to carry out this war of aggression, [wartime prime minister] Hideki Tōjō and the other accused first carried out a deceptive attack on even we Japanese."[13] In elevating the Pearl Harbor attack—rather than Japan's 1931 invasion of Manchuria—as the beginning of the country's quest for regional dominance, the occupation authorities also rewrote the larger Asian war as a U.S.-Japanese conflict.[14] In this telling, the United States and the Japanese people were natural allies; both suffered equally, and thus had the mutual goal of eradicating Japanese militarism.

Throughout the occupation this historical narrative accrued immense power and meaning as the Japanese themselves enthusiastically adopted it. In seeking to process the experience of war and defeat, many Japanese politicians, intellectuals, and activists came to argue that Japan's military leaders had victimized the Japanese people; the only way to achieve honor and meaning in the total devastation of defeat was to create a new order in Japan, one devoted to peace, democracy, and demilitarization.[15] This argument echoed the Potsdam Declaration's separation of the military leadership from the Japanese people. Speaking at a 1946 memorial service for students killed in the war, for example, Nanbara Shigeru, head of the prestigious Tokyo Imperial University, stated bluntly that "Japan had been led into war by ignorant, reckless militarists, and ultranationalists; that people, including those from the university had followed along believing that they were fighting for truth and justice; that, unfortunately, truth and justice had been on the side of the United States and Britain."[16] This assertion of wartime Japan's "collective irrationality," a belief that simultaneously posited a shared experience yet placed responsibility with the wartime government, became a widespread way to grasp the devastation of Japan's defeat while blaming now-purged military and wartime leaders.[17] As John Dower asserts, the Potsdam narrative, occupation reforms, and the new constitution "possessed a compelling psychological attraction to a shattered people sick of war."[18]

Throughout the occupation, the removal of the military from Japan's history, memory, and everyday experience—and, seemingly, its future—was an enterprise shared by both occupier and occupied. This did not mean that Americans and Japanese adopted this narrative for the same reasons; nor would they extract the same lessons. The U.S. occupation authorities used the Potsdam narrative not only to evoke democratic possibility but also to argue that such a future necessitated American guidance. Indeed, this historical narrative undergirded occupation policy to such extent that it was written into Japan's new constitution. A different telling of the war—for example, one that placed responsibility on the people themselves—might well have led to different policies that emphasized educating the public about their wartime "sins" or the reform, rather than the destruction, of the military.[19] For many Japanese, however, the Potsdam narrative not only blamed the military but would also become the foundation of calls for the public to actively protect a pacifist democracy. In this telling, democracy and military power were contradictory. Still, the Potsdam Declaration's elevation of the democratic Japanese "people" laid out key foundations of Japan's postwar sociopolitical order and served as a site of cooperation between the occupation authorities and many Japanese. Yet as Cold War tensions changed American attitudes toward Japanese militarization, the pervasiveness of the Potsdam narrative would raise difficult questions about the relationship between Japanese democracy and Cold War security.

Rearmament, Democracy, and Cold War Security

Japan's new constitution came into effect on May 3, 1947, but a rapidly changing world would soon make its emphasis on demilitarization a relic of the past. With international tensions growing—Soviet pressure on Berlin, a series of communist takeovers in Eastern Europe, the resumption of civil war in China, and collapsing European empires throughout Asia—U.S. policymakers foresaw a different future for the United States and Japan, one in which Japan would play a central role in U.S. security. In particular, U.S. policymakers began to discuss the possibility of rearming Japan as the central U.S. ally in East Asia. This new policy direction, however, contradicted the intertwined narratives of democratization and demilitarization that undergirded the occupation. Seeking to reconcile recent Japanese history with their desire for an armed ally, U.S. policymakers therefore embarked on a series of discussions about the virtues and dangers of Japanese rearmament. These discussions illuminate how historical narratives continued to influence U.S. decisionmaking; even as they faced new global conditions and unfamiliar dilemmas, U.S. officials pondered what the events of recent history meant for shifting policy goals—both their possibilities and their limits. Policymakers thought seriously about the relationships among Japan's wartime history, its postwar democracy, and U.S. Cold War security. Their discussions—held behind closed doors, and thus removed from the need to mobilize Japanese public support—reveal that these policymakers did not abandon democracy, or the lessons of Potsdam, in thinking about the future of the U.S.-Japanese relationship. Rather, they debated how best to channel Japanese democracy toward U.S. Cold War security—essentially, how to transform Japan into a militarized democracy.

In 1947–48, MacArthur began to argue that the goals laid out in the Potsdam Declaration had been secured. It was therefore time to end the occupation by signing a peace treaty; Japan should be a neutral and demilitarized state.[20] Other U.S. officials, however, disagreed that the time had come to grant Japan independence. As a U.S. Army study asserted in 1948, "Today, Japan is a bastion of pro-American sympathy in the Far East. Were Japan to succumb to Soviet domination, our only effective 'foot in the door' in the Far East would be lost and the remainder of the Far East would have little hope of resisting eventual Soviet domination."[21] With this anxiety in mind, and at the urging of policymakers like George Kennan, head of the State Department's policy planning staff, U.S. policymakers began to think about Japan as an important future ally.[22] Kennan argued that Japan's unique position as an industrial power and regional stronghold made any talk of Japanese independence pure madness. In keeping with his belief of inherent Soviet aggression and expansion, an independent and weak Japan was deeply vulnerable to communism. Instead, the United States had to rethink how to make Japan into a strong ally; this included not only an emphasis on economic growth and stability but also the possibility of new defensive capabilities, a potentially drastic break with popular ethos of demilitarization.[23]

Growing Cold War tensions therefore radically changed U.S. policymakers' understanding of the main threat posed to and by Japan. While MacArthur's early attempts to displace militarism included legalizing the Communist Party and fostering labor organization, U.S. officials now asserted that external and especially internal communism, not militarism, was the biggest threat to Japan. As the State Department commented in 1949, in case of war, "The threat to Japan . . . comes from agitation, subversion, and coup d'etat. The threat is that of a conspiracy inspired by the Kremlin, but conducted by Japanese. It is essentially a conspiracy from within—and whether it succeeds depends primarily on the political, economic and social health of Japan itself."[24] In the efforts to confront this threat, purges that the U.S. authorities had once directed at militarists shifted to focus on leftists and alleged communists. It was this shift that led Japanese observers to coin the term *reverse course*.[25] Stabilizing Japan as an ally against communist expansion and internal subversion became the primary goal in U.S. policy.

This new conviction that Japan's main threat was no longer militarism, combined with a growing desire for Cold War allies in Asia, redirected American attention to the question of Japanese rearmament. Over the next several years, U.S. policymakers debated this question, clashing over the relationships among military power, democratic politics, and the need to mobilize the Japanese government and public in support of U.S. Cold War policy. Those who spoke in favor of rearmament—especially military planners—often cited military necessity as the key rationale. A U.S. Army study in spring 1948 claimed that "solely from a military perspective," rearmament would not only act as a deterrent to communist incursion but would also create a Japanese armed forces that would "share the burden" of defending Japan from potential Soviet aggression.[26] The army also asserted that rearmament could contribute to the "revival of national prestige" within Japan, which would then strengthen U.S. leadership in Asia. Despite concerns that such national sentiments would again fuel aggressive expansionism, the Army study claimed that Japanese armed forces could be at the core of a postwar, postimperial, independent Japan that nevertheless actively supported U.S. Cold War policy.[27] Indeed, U.S.-led rearmament, the authors argued, could *dilute* the power of wartime militarism by assuring that remilitarization would be channeled in support of U.S. hegemony and international stability. "Rearming Japan by the creation of small Japanese military units," the army claimed, "equipped with light weapons and organized, initially trained, and strictly supervised with the U.S. Army would safeguard against the reemergence of the Japanese military clique and tend to alleviate the fears of other western Pacific nations of a resurgence of Japanese aggression."[28] In this telling, Japan's recent history was not a reason to avoid rearmament; American supervision would assure that these military forces would support, rather than challenge, Japanese democracy. According to this logic it was preferable to begin rearmament while Japan was still occupied to ensure that the United States could control the outcome by assuring that a "properly" trained, structured, and indoctrinated military acted as a bulwark against not only communism but the return of militarism.

At the same time, other U.S. officials, both military and civilian, continued to argue that Japan's actions during World War II had demonstrated the deep risks of rearming Japan. As a report on early rearmament for the Joint Chiefs of Staff asserted, "a Japan with a right to rearm and intent on rebuilding her munitions factories would, in the absence of a guarantee of sound friendship with the United States, again constitute an extreme military hazard to this nation and to other non-Communist Pacific nations."[29] In part this assessment drew from racialized assumptions about Japanese "character," specifically "the inbred Japanese habit of submission to autocratic authority" that rendered Japan equally susceptible to communist or militarist takeover.[30] In thinking about a future U.S.-Japanese relationship, U.S. policymakers further worried that rearmament would undermine the legitimacy of U.S. democratization efforts—and by extension, U.S. power—in Japan. Rearmament required Japanese participation, yet by so glaringly contradicting the early occupation narrative of democratization and demilitarization it could also undermine the legitimacy of U.S. leadership and thus Japanese willingness to actively support U.S. security planning. The rise of Cold War tensions only made these questions more acute; democratic Japanese participation was imperative not only to U.S. security goals but also to assuring that Japan itself remained strong against communist incursion and subversion without returning to wartime militarism. As the Joint Chiefs of Staff asserted, "the continuing Soviet policy of aggressive communist expansion makes it essential that Japan's democracy and western orientation first be established beyond all question."[31] In this telling, Japanese democracy and close U.S.-Japanese security cooperation were natural partners.

MacArthur, who strongly opposed rearmament, further warned against "untimely" militarization. The danger of rearmament, he claimed, was not the revival of Japanese militarism, which under his guidance had been "eliminated and . . . destroyed."[32] Rather, by abandoning the demilitarization principles of the early occupation, rearmament would undermine the U.S. position in Japan. As he asserted, "Abandonment of these [occupation] principles now would dangerously weaken our prestige in Japan and would place us in a ridiculous light before the Japanese people."[33] Ironically, the primary rationale against rearmament was that it would endanger U.S. security by undermining Japan's willingness to support U.S. Cold War policies. Notably, in MacArthur's telling, U.S. power in Japan was both absolute—it had completely "eliminated" militarism—and utterly dependent on Japanese support and consent. This contradictory conceptualization of American power reflected the ambiguous relationship between the Potsdam narrative and the future of U.S.-Japan policy.

Regardless of the lessons learned from the experience of war and occupation, the point remained that U.S. officials did not see rearmament as a dichotomy of emphasizing democracy or eschewing democratization by focusing on remilitarization and security. Indeed—unlike in Latin America, for example—policy for Japan never discussed restoring the nation's militarist and authoritarian wartime regime in order to secure communist repression and regional stability.[34] Rather, the debates of U.S. policymakers and military leaders centered on the position of the military in securing or threatening this larger relationship between democracy and security. Policymakers from the Joint Chiefs to the State Department to MacArthur continued to genuinely believe that Japanese democracy was the key to preventing both communist subversion and the return of aggressive militarism. Only three years after World War II, the fresh memories of the conflict cautioned against a headlong rush to remilitarization in Japan. These officials also framed democracy as a useful political tool to secure Japanese consent and support of American policies and to demonstrate the "benevolence" of American leadership on the Japanese—and even a global—stage.[35] They assumed that a democratic Japan would not only be inherently peaceful but that it would see the United States as a natural ally. In debating rearmament, then, U.S. policymakers constantly confronted the thorny relationships among U.S. leadership, security, and Japanese democracy: even military leaders asserted that Japanese democracy was vital to U.S. security.

More broadly, this debate over Japanese rearmament focused on the question of how best to understand Japan's recent history of militarism, war, and occupation, especially in light of shifting Cold War policy. U.S. policymakers could not come to a consensus about the value of rearmament in the late 1940s in part because the historical narrative did not seem to firmly counsel in favor of or against it. Perhaps only one thing was clear: Japan needed continued American guidance. Indeed, policymakers arguing both in favor of and against rearmament paternalistically agreed that Japan needed to remain under U.S. supervision to ensure that it would not again fall prey to militarism and threaten American security.[36] By reinforcing this belief in the necessity of American tutelage rather than facilitating Japanese independence, these discussions—and the historical narratives they drew upon—assured that the United States would continue to play a central role in the rebuilding of Japan's military and, more broadly, Japanese security throughout the occupation and beyond.

[margin note: Impact of hist. narrative]

The Korean War and Japanese Debates about Rearmament

History—both narrative and experience—deeply informed how the Japanese government and public thought about rearmament. As U.S. policymakers debated the future of the Japanese military, rearmament was also becoming a growing point of Japanese public attention, especially after the start of the Korean War in June 1950. Similar to U.S. policymakers' opinions about rearmament, those of the Japanese diverged, dependent in part on differing interpretations of Japan's wartime past. Some Japanese, especially conservative politicians, elevated rearmament as necessary to Japanese security and as the key to regaining Japan's purpose and prestige. Others, especially intellectuals and activists on the left, highlighted the lessons of the war and the Potsdam narrative, especially the need for a critical and democratic public that would hold the government accountable to the Japanese people. In this telling, rearmament—like the war itself—was against the peaceful wishes of the people and was thus a prime test of the power of postwar democracy and popular representation. This vision of Japan's postwar sociopolitical order soon became a prominent critique of U.S. security planning, as many Japanese clamored for their country to oppose its growing Cold War bond with the United States. In an unexpected turn, the Potsdam narrative turned from a source of consensus to the core of urgent conflict.

The start of the war on June 25, 1950, with North Korea's invasion of South Korea, resolved U.S. policymakers' debate in favor of rearmament. Fearing that communism was aggressively seeking to dominate Asia, the United States immediately sent troops to defend South Korea. The continued occupation of Japan was vital to this quick response; the first U.S. troops departed directly from occupation duty. These troop movements drastically reduced the number of soldiers guarding Japan, heightening U.S. fears of a security vacuum primed for communist subversion. In light of this new security situation MacArthur reversed his earlier hesitations about rearmament; on July 8, 1950, he instructed Japanese prime minister Yoshida Shigeru (who governed Japan under MacArthur's supervision) to create a new policing force of 75,000 men—the National Police Reserve (NPR)—to help ensure domestic security.[37] Within a few years, this police force would evolve into Japan's Self-Defense Forces, which remain Japan's military today. According to MacArthur's letter to Yoshida, the United States had succeeded in building a stable democratic order in Japan; Japan was therefore ready for the defensive forces necessary to "safeguard the public welfare in a democratic society."[38]

Yet the NPR also reflected the belief that Japanese remilitarization had to be closely supervised by the United States. This was not only due to the dangers of remilitarization but also the latent vulnerabilities of a democratic system. Despite MacArthur's claim that the NPR was evidence of Japan's democratic progress, it was not the product of democratic choice. To create the NPR, the occupation authorities chose not to introduce parliamentary legislation in Japan's Diet, and the Japanese cabinet instead issued an order on August 10, 1950. As U.S. military officials asserted, issuing a cabinet order "was necessary and desirable" because "the freedom of discussion and debate enjoyed by [the Diet] would undoubtedly have been seized by the Communists and other leftist members to criticize not only the Government's proposal but actually to attack by inference or by thinly veiled reference the motives of the Supreme Commander and of the United States for propaganda purposes both in Japan and abroad."[39] Democracy may have been a necessary precondition to the creation of the NPR, which would in turn ensure the survival of this political system in Japan. At the same time, democracy was dangerous; the NPR—and Cold War security more broadly—was far too delicate and important to subject to the democratic process. These hesitations highlight the fundamental limits of Americans' belief in Japan's democratization; their visions of a democratic Japan did not extend to a wholesale embrace of open debate or respect for democratic choice but instead sought to utilize popular legitimacy for strengthening and expanding state power. This tension between a deep belief in the superiority of democracy and an equally deep fear of democratic subversion fundamentally shaped U.S. Cold War policy—not only in Japan but also in the United States and across the globe.

U.S. resistance to opening rearmament to Japanese parliamentary and public debate was not merely a manifestation of paternalism; it also stemmed from the intense and heated discussions that surrounded rearmament among the Japanese people. For some Japanese—especially conservatives who never fully embraced the Potsdam Declaration's condemnation of the wartime regime and had long believed that Japan lay under the shadow of communist threat—rearmament was a way to regain national honor and purpose. Ashida Hitoshi, who briefly served as prime minister during the occupation, argued that the Korean War had forced Japan to reassert itself as a powerful nation on the global stage. He asserted that "the war in Korea is not just the battle for the Korean peninsula but also the prelude to the coming struggle for Japan. Standing at the middle of a fierce confrontation between two worlds, the people who do not defend themselves will ruin the nation."[40] Rearmament, Ashida argued, would be the key to rebuilding the sense of national purpose necessary to survival in the world, especially under the looming threat of the Cold War. As he wrote in a 1950 opinion paper requested by the occupation authorities, "Present-day Japan is in urgent need of unifying its national will, without which we cannot ride out the crisis . . . the task of the government is to take the initiative to tell the people that Japan is on the brink of danger, to remind them that we must defend the country by our own efforts."[41] By identifying defense, and by extension military capabilities, as the key to "unifying the national will," Ashida harked back to a different version of Japan's prewar history, one in which militarized empire, expansion, and war paved Japan's path to international prominence and fostered national unification.[42] Ashida's language, especially the term "national will," sought to reclaim the unity and purpose of the war to stabilize and restore Japan as a major international power.

Ashida was not alone in this advocacy for national defense and a renewed popular "will." As historian Masuda Hajimu asserts, the Korean War coincided with—and furthered—resurging conservative sentiments, which many Japanese expressed by openly longing for their country's recent military past. Indeed, many now advocated for public support of war widows and veterans, for the enshrinement of those killed in the war, and for the release of war criminals.[43] The war also bolstered public sentiment for rearmament, with newspaper surveys reporting at some points that 53.8 percent of the people agreed that Japan should establish defensive forces.[44] Moreover, with the start of the Korean War, the occupation authorities "depurged" thousands of prewar and wartime conservative political leaders and military figures. Many of these "depurgees" advocated for rearmament as a way to reenter the public sphere by developing a new political conversation.[45] To do so they sought to heighten public fears of communist subversion, especially after the successful Chinese Communist Revolution in 1949 and the Japanese Communist Party's adoption of a policy of armed revolution following a blistering critique from the Cominform (a Soviet-dominated organ for the international communist movement) in January 1950.[46] As one ex-general claimed, "if war happened [in Japan] it would be guerilla warfare at home rather than conventional military battles, and . . . riots led by 'Red-Japanese' would occur everywhere in the country."[47] Rearmament, these conservative politicians and former military leaders argued, was the solution to these fears by assuring that Japan had not only the national will but also the capabilities to resist and suppress these threats.[48]

The impact of the Korean War, however, was equally strong in fostering anti-rearmament and antiwar sentiment among many Japanese, further solidifying the prominence of the Potsdam narrative. Though Japan's peace movement—which called not only for pacifism but also international neutrality—had started in the late 1940s, the Korean War elevated and expanded its impact. To many, the start of war so close to Japan only further proved that Japan had to pursue a future of neutrality and peace or again be engulfed in conflict. The leaders of this movement, particularly the intellectual group Heiwa Mondai Danwakai (Peace Problems Study Group), drew directly from the experience of World War II and especially the idea that the war—and the Japanese government—had victimized the Japanese people. In their first statement, issued in March 1949, the group committed itself to "plac[ing] our trust in the people and walk[ing] in step with them." Like the writers of the Potsdam Declaration, the members of Heiwa Mondai Danwakai conceived of the "people" as inherently democratic and peace-seeking. This commitment to the people was the foundation of their expression of collective guilt as intellectuals and national leaders: "we as a whole succeeded little in serving as a brake upon the country's march into the war of aggression and certainly showed ourselves lacking in both courage and effort in actively attempting to prevent such a war."[49] Their belief that the Japanese people had to be an active and critical public in order to prevent war, assure Japanese neutrality, and protect postwar democracy stood at the foundation of Japan's peace movement.

In the minds of many peace activists, leftist politicians, and intellectuals, this emphasis on a critical public was inherently connected to the need to prevent the Japanese state from regaining war-making capabilities. As the prominent political scientist Maruyama Masao asserted, "the people's power of control over the government in order to prevent war" was the key to building a democratic political order.[50] Peace movement leaders argued that the Japanese state had to represent the wishes of the people; the development of military force was therefore no longer a legitimate use of state power, not only due to the imperial military's overseas aggression, violence, and emphasis on total obedience to leadership but also its historical position outside the boundaries of democratic and parliamentary oversight.[51] Essentially, they sought to turn the Potsdam narrative against the U.S. goal of rearmament, asserting that democratization was not simply an end to be achieved but instead a process that necessitated constant public engagement to protect democracy and peace.[52] Though U.S. policymakers would come to see the Japanese peace movement, and especially its emphasis on Japanese neutrality, as a major obstacle in the U.S.-Japanese relationship, this movement's foundational premise—that the true roots of Japanese democracy lay in the active engagement of the Japanese people—was not far removed from the narratives that undergirded the occupation.

Intellectual leaders were not alone in using the experience of World War II to frame the threat of war in Korea and the dangers of rearmament. Politicians, especially in the Socialist Party, also drew from war memories—specifically the harm that had come to the Japanese people—to articulate their vision of a neutral, demilitarized Japan. In the early 1950s, the left wing of the Socialist Party routinely deployed such slogans as "We are opposed to rearmament—youth! Don't take up arms."[53] In emphasizing the war's impact on Japan's youth, the Socialists complemented the increasingly visible antiwar activism of groups such as Wadatsumikai (Japan Memorial Society for Students Killed in the War), which bemoaned how students' "priceless youth and lives were wasted and buried by war."[54] The Socialist Party also issued a 1951 statement directly criticizing conservative advocacy of rearmament as reminiscent of the path to war and as an inaccurate repetition of the true feelings of the Japanese people. "How can we ask the people of our country to take up guns and swords?" it decried. The government demanded mobilization from "people whose homes burned, whose property was lost, whose fathers, husbands, and brothers' lives were taken in war. . . . The calls for rearmament and patriotism are degeneracy [that] bring us back to . . . the defeat of the war."[55] In arguing against rearmament and, more broadly, Japanese support for the United States in the Cold War, the Socialists thus drew from the Japanese people's experiences of living through the death and destruction of World War II.

This melding of historical narrative, popular experience, and democratic advocacy set important parameters around public debate in Japan, especially as the postwar expansion of voting rights left the parliamentary government even more dependent on public support. Japanese prime minister Yoshida Shigeru epitomized these conflicting pressures as he sought to balance diverse Japanese opinions about rearmament while trying to sustain his own political legitimacy. Publicly, Yoshida rarely spoke in favor of rearmament. From the creation of the NPR in 1950 until he left office in 1954, he repeatedly clashed with U.S. policymakers over the size of Japan's military forces, countering U.S. demands for swifter military growth by arguing that rearmament would undermine Japanese stability because of its economic cost, its unpopularity, and its sociopolitical disruption.[56] At the same time, Yoshida privately stated that Japan would eventually need to rearm and was deeply involved in certain components of the NPR. In particular, he wanted to assure that rearmament would not lead to the rise of neomilitarist sentiments that would challenge the postwar state and by extension, his own leadership. In a desire to curb neomilitarism, Yoshida became personally involved with the creation of Japan's new military academy, arguing that the prewar education of officers had failed by inculcating a commitment to the military rather than a commitment to the Japanese nation.[57] In a meeting with General Matthew Ridgway, head of the occupation forces (having replaced MacArthur in April 1951) and of the United Nations command in Korea, Yoshida argued that "it was very important that Japan carefully select its future officers and insure their proper education in the democratic spirit."[58] Yoshida's divided position on rearmament—and the diverse social, cultural, and political consequences that he highlighted—were a testament to broader divisions running through Japanese politics and society.

The intense Japanese debates regarding rearmament simultaneously demonstrate the depth and limits of U.S. influence over Japan's use of historical narratives and their political consequences. The related shocks of the Korean War and the creation of the NPR exacerbated ongoing debates about peace, democracy, and Japan's future—debates channeled through diverse interpretations of Japan's wartime past. Some Japanese hoped that rearmament could restore the sense of national unity and purpose destroyed by Japan's defeat. For others, the narratives that U.S. authorities developed in the early occupation years became a political tool and public rallying point to criticize both Japanese politicians and U.S. policymakers. This did not mean, however, that U.S. policymakers abandoned their emphasis on rearmament or, more broadly, Japanese public engagement in the Cold War. Rather, Japanese discussions over rearmament played a constitutive role in the development of U.S. policy. They complicated the question of using democracy as a tool to legitimate and strengthen the U.S.-Japanese alliance, deeply shaped the United States' approach to the NPR and, ultimately, would prevent Japan from rearming to the extent desired by U.S. policymakers.

A Military for Peace and Democracy

With both Americans and Japanese engaged in complex debates about democracy, history, and military power, the NPR became a key site for U.S. policymakers' attempts to reconcile Japanese democracy with Cold War security. Japan's new constitution, combined with vibrant Japanese discussions over rearmament, meant that U.S. policymakers believed they could not build the NPR without reference to postwar democracy and the Potsdam narrative.[59] In publicly presenting the NPR, U.S. and Japanese authorities therefore sought to appropriate the concept of the democratic Japanese people, an idea that had not only been developed through the Potsdam Declaration and the occupation but also stood at the foundation of the postwar antimilitary movement. This approach demonstrates the deep influence of the Potsdam narrative in defining the contours of political and democratic legitimacy and thus the continued influence of democracy on U.S. policy. Indeed, even as democratic concepts and symbols became political tools used to foster public consent, they continued to drive key elements of NPR policy—including advertising, language, dress and, most important, the fact that this force could not be deployed overseas. Having originally separated the military from state legitimacy, U.S. and Japanese policymakers set about trying to reinstate the military as a central element of the postwar order by framing the NPR as a product and protector of peace and popular democracy.

From the beginning, U.S. occupation authorities were deeply involved in the creation, training, and publicizing of the NPR, to the extent that U.S.

military adviser Frank Kowalski dubbed the force a "little American Army."[60] The deep reach of earlier U.S. demilitarization policies meant that the Japanese government was not logistically or politically able to recruit, fund, arm, or train a new military. Instead, the occupation's Civil Affairs Division supervised the creation and training of the new force, which was headquartered in offices adjacent to the division's and trained by U.S. soldiers.[61] Working closely together, the civilian Japanese director general of the NPR and U.S. military representatives from the Civil Affairs Division planned the NPR from the ground up, debating issues such as uniforms, cars, and command structures.[62] While the Japanese government provided pay, allowances, lodging, and transportation, the Civil Affairs Division provided U.S. officers as instructors, along with ordnance, ammunition, and communications technology.[63]

Reflecting earlier hopes that the NPR could neutralize militarism, and seeking to disarm popular and political criticism of the NPR, both U.S. and Japanese authorities dedicated extensive energy to subsuming this new force into broader narratives of peace and democratic possibility. NPR recruitment posters and advertisements linked Japanese democracy, peace, and NPR service by using such slogans as "Peace-loving Japan wants you!"[64] Posters showed NPR members with images that reflected peace and representative democracy, including the NPR symbol of a dove (which also decorated uniform caps) and the Japanese Diet building, and were emblazoned with the slogans "Protect the public order in a democratic Japan" and "Peace and law and order is by our hand!!"[65] These slogans not only sought to co-opt the theme of popular democratic responsibility but also played on a growing Japanese desire for the end of the U.S. occupation by emphasizing Japan's independent obligation to protect itself. To be sure, it is not clear whether the ideas expressed in these slogans actually drew people to join the NPR. In a country still reeling from war and destruction, the majority of recruits cited economic rationales, not ideological commitment, as their rationale for joining this new force. Regardless of members' motivation, however, the occupation authorities and the Japanese government did not struggle to find recruits for the NPR. MacArthur's letter had set the initial quota at 75,000. When recruitment opened, half of this quota was met the first day; within a month, 380,000 people had applied to join the NPR.[66]

These efforts to separate the NPR from Japan's wartime past by intimately connecting it to postwar democracy not only shaped its public presentation but also permeated its language and dress, its everyday management and self-conceptualization. As was shown by using *Police* in the name National Police Force, another way the NPR sought to hide its ultimately military nature was through the use of neologisms, a process that has continued into today's SDF. Though it was organized like a military force (with battalions, regiments, and divisions), the NPR did not use military titles, instead relying on police ranks, such as inspector second class (for second lieutenant) or superintendent (for colonel).[67] Foreign soldiers, such as the U.S. occupation forces, were "soldiers," but members of the Japanese force were—and still are—referred to as "group members."[68] A desire to demonstrate that the NPR was not a creation of the imperial Japanese military permeated even the everyday language of this new force. Moreover, to contrast the NPR with the imperial military, and with U.S. occupation forces, whose uniforms the NPR emulated closely, an officer's rank was indicated not with stars but with cherry blossoms.

While military leaders intended these choices to symbolize the NPR's difference from a conventional military force, they unintentionally maintained a connection to Japan's wartime past. During the years of war and imperialism, for example, the cherry blossom was a widespread symbol in the Imperial Japanese Navy. Cherry blossoms decorated the sides of kamikaze planes, and Japanese soldiers were extorted to "fall like cherry blossoms for the emperor"; successive governments used cherry blossoms as "the master trope to encourage soldiers to fight to the death."[69] Similarly, the images on recruiting posters—the Diet building, a dove—had a longer history that U.S. officials likely did not recognize. During the 1930s, as Japan aggressively pursued empire and war in mainland China, "the government seized on the [new Diet building] as a banner for national unity and promoted images of it abroad as proof of the nation's democratic government. . . . The Diet building emerged from the war as an unhappy reminder of failed military adventurism."[70] Doves (or pigeons, which are the same word in Japanese) and war also were deeply connected in prewar and wartime Japan; the Imperial Japanese Army used them widely in the Russo-Japanese War and the Second Sino-Japanese War. The military even introduced awards for pigeons that performed well during Japan's aggressive expansion into China in the 1930s.[71]

The history surrounding these symbols therefore complicated efforts to repurpose them as emblematic of the NPR's democratic character. The military had been so central to the political, social, and cultural order in prewar Japan that it was difficult to find symbols that connected democracy and the military without replicating prewar images and cultural trappings; these difficulties reflected the larger contradiction of rearming Japan with an ostensibly *nonmilitary* military. It is no wonder that an April 1952 poll conducted by the newspaper *Mainichi* reflected ongoing confusion about the character and the role of the NPR: 59.6 percent of men and 41.5 percent of women called the NPR an army, while 24.5 percent of men and 17.5 percent of women said it was not an army and 11 percent of men and 36.3 percent of women were unsure.

Ultimately, the NPR's confused position in Japan's postwar political and cultural order reflected the tensions innate to U.S. and Japanese efforts to repurpose Japan's wartime history. The Potsdam narrative of a democratic Japanese people continued to shape U.S. policy, even as U.S. policymakers subverted this narrative by unilaterally restoring defensive and military capabilities in Japan. Indeed, U.S. and Japanese officials did not simply use the concept of postwar democracy as a rhetorical tool to justify the creation of the NPR, though this was a key component of their approach. They also sought to weave the concept of a democratic military into the language and trappings of this new force. Only democracy, they believed, would give this force the popular legitimacy necessary to become an active component of U.S.-Japan security policy while also assuring that it would not resurrect militarism and Japanese aggression.

Yet these efforts to present the NPR force as the protector of peace and democracy clashed not only with the occupation's earlier emphasis on popular democracy and demilitarization but also memories and experiences of World War II. Using the language and ideas laid out in the Potsdam Declaration, many Japanese would continue to foreground the concept of popular democracy to criticize the NPR as an attack on Japan's postwar values and order. Indeed, throughout the 1950s, U.S. attempts to use postwar democracy to legitimate the NPR were fundamentally limited by these Japanese debates and criticisms, by Japanese assertions that postwar democracy eschewed military force. The NPR, and later the SDF, therefore continues to be a central point of controversy in the U.S.-Japan alliance well into the twenty-first century. Even today, the SDF remains largely a defensive force, and its actions overseas are constitutionally constrained by article 9 of the Japanese constitution. This continued insistence on equating Japanese democracy with limits on military power demonstrates the long legacies and deep impact of the Potsdam narrative.

Conclusion

Even today, seventy years after World War II and the dawn of the U.S. occupation of Japan, historical narratives about Japanese military power continue to play a central role in the contemporary U.S.-Japanese relationship, U.S.-East Asia security discourses, and international politics across Asia. Ironically, after censoring and suppressing discussions of the military during the occupation, U.S. political leaders now censure Japan for failing to acknowledge its wartime behavior; in June 2007, for example, the House of Representatives passed a "comfort women" resolution calling on the Japanese government to "formally acknowledge, apologize, and accept historical responsibility . . . for its Imperial Armed Forces' coercion of young women into sexual slavery" during the war in the Pacific.[72] Americans and Asians alike also express deep discomfort at some contemporary Japanese historical interpretations of the war; they routinely lament the habit of Japanese leaders to visit the World War II museum at Yasukuni Shrine, which notoriously celebrates war criminals and presents Japan as the liberator of Asia against foreign aggression. Across the Asia-Pacific region, these actions have raised questions about the nature of Japan's democracy and whether contemporary Japan truly differs from the regime that waged an aggressive and horrific war. As historian Alexis Dudden notes, "Critics wonder how supposedly free, open, and democratic Japan can reconcile state-sponsored worship of men who perpetuated the decimation of tens of millions of lives and entire regions."[73]

The history of the Potsdam narrative—its genesis, transformation, and misappropriation—offers useful insights into the lasting presence of Japan's past in shaping the continued tensions and controversies of Pacific politics. Potsdam's definition of democracy rested on a firm delineation between the Japanese people and the Japanese military. The U.S. occupation, and the historical narrative that justified it, elevated U.S.-Japanese democratic reconciliation and sought to obscure the centrality of the military—and Japan's imperial war—from prewar Japanese history, a narrative deepened by active Japanese participation. The gap between this narrative and historical reality, however, has limited and perverted the public discussion about Japan's path to war; military actions during the war, including wartime atrocities; and the war's meaning and consequences. On the one hand, it sparked an active peace movement in Japan, which has elevated pacifism as the only logical response to the violence of World War II. On the other hand, in displacing the military so fully, it has obscured critical reflections on the role of military power or popular engagement with the military state while sparking a desire to glorify wartime morale and commitment, to nostalgically recall imperial Japan's position as a regional and global leader, and to restore the military as a constitutive element of Japanese history and the Japanese state. While it would be far too simple to draw a direct line from the Potsdam Declaration to contemporary discussions of World War II, examining the development, usage, and consequences of the Potsdam narrative reflects the strange careers and unintended consequences of historical narratives.

Examining the intersections between history and policymaking during the U.S. occupation of Japan also provides a new and necessary perspective on the relationship between democracy and security, two concepts that are often treated as opposed to one another. Despite the prominence of the "reverse course" narrative, in which U.S. policymakers ceased to care about Japanese democracy with the rise of the Cold War, U.S. debates over rearmament and history tell a different story. This was in part because of recent wartime experiences; it had taken four bloody years to dislodge Japan from its Pacific empire, and Americans therefore had a vested interest in assuring that militarist forces did not rise again in Japan. U.S. policymakers also hoped that Japanese democracy would insure a malleable yet strong political and social system, one that stood firm against the return of authoritarian militarism, resisted the threat of communist incursion, and remained open to U.S. Cold War power. Finally, the power of the Potsdam narrative offered a framework through which U.S. officials sought to foster Japanese support and consent even as they advocated policies far removed from the Potsdam Declaration's original demilitarized intentions. Ultimately, for these U.S. policymakers, Japanese democracy was not the opposite of U.S. security; instead, it was a crucial tool to achieve it. This does not mean that U.S. policymakers understood or even respected democracy as Japanese people themselves embraced it, or that they treated all countries in the same way they did Japan. The narrative of Japan's path to war was simultaneously a lens through which policymakers understood policy choices; a call to take certain actions, like democratization and demilitarization; and a tool to foster public support. As a case study of the intersections among history, democracy, and security in the aftermath of World War II, the U.S.-Japanese relationship highlights the diverse ways that democratic narratives and security goals became deeply interdependent.

More broadly, the evolution of the Potsdam Declaration and the historical lessons that emerged from it highlight the international dynamics that simultaneously shape both historical narratives and global politics. The narratives that sought to explain Japan's past—and the policies that stemmed from these narratives—were not merely the product of domestic or national debates. This is not simply a story of the projection of American power and ideas, nor of Japanese resistance to American hegemony; rather, in the aftermath of a devastating war and an unprecedented occupation, American and Japanese of all political convictions continuously borrowed from each other, appropriated each other's language, and challenged each other's stories. Even when they fiercely disagreed with each other's vision of military power and democratic politics, they routinely utilized the same terminology, symbols, and historical references. The "lessons" of war and occupation were therefore forged through interactions that crossed political and national boundaries. It is these broad similarities that gave—and continues to give—the Potsdam narrative such power in historical and contemporary understandings of World War II in both Japan and the United States.

Notes

1. The Constitution of Japan, November 3, 1946 (www.kantei.go.jp/foreign /constitution_and_government_of_japan/constitution_e.html).

2. The Potsdam Declaration, July 26, 1945 (www.ndl.go.jp/constitution/e/etc /c06.html).

3. See for example, J. Victor Koschmann, *Revolution and Subjectivity in Postwar Japan* (University of Chicago Press, 1996), 21–22, 205–08. Even in discussing the early years of the occupation of Japan within a democratization framework, historians have highlighted that these early policies were themselves riddled with contradictions—especially the decision to preserve the imperial system and the broader irony of imposing democracy under military fiat. See, for example, John Dower, *Embracing Defeat: Japan in the Wake of World War II* (New York: Norton, 1999), 65–68, 277–373.

4. The Potsdam Declaration, July 26, 1945 (www.ndl.go.jp/constitution/e/etc /c06.html).

5. The Potsdam Declaration represented the thinking of the United States' leading Japan specialists, such as former Japan ambassador and under secretary of state Joseph Grew and Japan historian and State Department planner Hugh Borton. They believed that a fanatic "militarist oligarchy" had risen to the fore,

perverted Japan's political system, and forced the Japanese people into aggressive imperialism and war, a historical construct reflected in the declaration itself. See Hugh Borton, *Spanning Japan's Modern Century: The Memoirs of Hugh Borton* (Lanham, Md.: Lexington, 2002), 95–96; and Takamae Eiji, *Inside GHQ: The Allied Occupation of Japan and Its Legacy* (London: Continuum, 2002), 203, 214–15.

6. See, for example, John Dower, *War without Mercy: Race and Power in the Pacific War* (New York: Pantheon, 1987); Sheldon Garon, *Molding Japanese Minds: The State in Everyday Life* (Princeton University Press, 1997); Barak Kushner, *The Thought War: Japanese Imperial Propaganda* (University of Hawai'i Press, 2006); Alan Tansman, ed., *The Culture of Japanese Fascism* (Duke University Press, 2009); and Louise Young, *Japan's Total Empire: Manchuria and the Culture of Wartime Imperialism* (University of California Press, 1999).

7. For more on Hirohito's wartime actions, including the debates over Japan's surrender, see Herbert Bix, *Hirohito and the Making of Modern Japan* (New York: Harper Perennial, 2001), 235–532.

8. Dower, *Embracing Defeat*, 80–82.

9. Ibid., 81.

10. The Constitution of Japan, November 3, 1946 (www.kantei.go.jp/foreign/constitution_and_government_of_japan/constitution_e.html).

11. Dower, *Embracing Defeat*, 428–29; Kyoko Hirano, *Mr. Smith Goes to Tokyo: Japanese Cinema under the American Occupation, 1945–1952* (Washington, D.C.: Smithsonian Institution Press, 1992), 51.

12. Hirano, *Mr. Smith Goes to Tokyo*, 51.

13. Draft film script of International Military Tribunal in the Far East Newsreel, quoted in Hirano, *Mr. Smith Goes to Tokyo*, 51.

14. As part of this larger agenda the occupation authorities forbade the use of the Japanese designation "Great East Asia War," substituting "Pacific War," which further elevated the U.S.-Japanese conflict over Japan's expansion into China, Korea, and Southeast Asia. Dower, *Embracing Defeat*, 419.

15. Dower, *Embracing Defeat*, 487–90. This narrative of Japanese victimization also became key to the peace movement in the late 1940s and the antinuclear movement in the 1950s, the latter of which drew from Japan's position as the sole country to experience the ravages of a nuclear bomb. See James J. Orr, *The Victim as Hero: Ideologies of Peace and National Identity in Postwar Japan* (University of Hawai'i Press, 2001).

16. Dower, *Embracing Defeat*, 489.

17. Ibid., 492, 495.

18. Ibid., 398.

19. "Popular responsibility" was a key component of the early months of the U.S. occupation of Germany. The occupation authorities forced German citizens to view images and films from concentration camps and to evacuate and

rebury bodies from the camps, and it forced entire towns to tour the camps to witness the death and destruction firsthand. While these policies focused on popular responsibility for mass atrocities rather than the war itself, they differed considerably from the approach in Japan. See Giles MacDonough, *After the Reich: The Brutal History of the Allied Occupation* (New York: Basic Books, 2007).

20. Some members of the State Department began to advocate for a peace treaty in 1948–49, arguing that ending the occupation by signing an "early" treaty would be the key to securing Japan's "western orientation." "Department of State Comments on Current Strategic Evaluation of U.S. Security Needs in Japan (NSC 49)," September 30, 1949, in *Rearmament of Japan, Part One, 1947–1952*, edited by Hiroshi Masuda (Congressional Information Service, 1998), document no. 1-A-119, Microfiche Collection, Congressional Information Service.

21. Department of the Army, Plans and Operations Division, "Limited Military Armament for Japan," 1948, in Masuda, ed., *Rearmament of Japan, Part One*, document no. 1-A-46, Microfiche Collection, Congressional Information Service.

22. Michael Schaller, *Altered States: The United States and Japan since the Occupation* (Oxford University Press, 1997), 15–16.

23. Peter Mauch, *Sailor Diplomat: Nomura Kichisaburō and the Japanese-American War* (Harvard University Press, 2011), 231. Kennan further asserted that MacArthur's reforms had only destabilized Japan and did little for Japan's war-torn economy, leading policymakers to elevate economic recovery as the key to Japan's future stability. The National Security Council made this shift clear in its new guidelines for Japan, NSC 13/2. Schaller, *Altered States*, 17.

24. "Department of State Comments on Current Strategic Evaluation of U.S. Security Needs in Japan (NSC 49)," September 30, 1949, in Masuda, ed., *Rearmament of Japan, Part One*, document no. 1-A-119, Microfiche Collection, Congressional Information Service.

25. Masuda Hajimu, "Fear of World War III: Social Politics of Japan's Rearmament and Peace Movements, 1950–3," *Journal of Contemporary History* 47 (2012), 558.

26. Department of the Army, "Limited Military Armament for Japan." This rhetoric of burden sharing remains a common refrain in contemporary U.S.-Japan security discussions.

27. Department of the Army, "Limited Military Armament for Japan."

28. Ibid.

29. "The Impact of an Early Peace Treaty with Japan on United States Strategic Requirements: A Report by the Joint Strategic Survey Committee to the Joint Chiefs of Staff," November 30, 1949, in Masuda, ed., *Rearmament of Japan, Part One*, document 1-A-114, Microfiche Collection, Congressional Information Service.

30. Ibid.

31. Ibid.

32. "Views of General of the Army Douglas MacArthur on Rearmament of Japan," April 16, 1948, in Masuda, ed., *Rearmament of Japan, Part One*, document no. 1-A-46, Microfiche Collection, Congressional Information Service.

33. Ibid. MacArthur would assert this point again two years later, arguing, "Among the Jap people themselves [rearmament] would be accompanied by the most violent reaction as the average Jap citizen still holds the mil responsible for Japan's destruction and would not willingly see Japan remilitarized. Indeed nothing could more quickly and completely alienate the Jap people from American leadership than such a proposal." Notably, this comment came *after* he had ordered the creation of the National Police Reserve. Telegram from MacArthur, August 2, 1950, in Masuda, ed., *Rearmament of Japan, Part One*, document no. 1-C-21, Microfiche Collection, Congressional Information Service.

34. For a history of the United States' relationship with and support of authoritarian regimes overseas, see David Schmitz, *Thank God They're on Our Side: The United States and Right Wing Dictators 1921–1965* (University of North Carolina Press, 1999).

35. For a discussion of the concept of "benevolent" U.S. leadership in the Cold War, see Melani McAlister, *Epic Encounters: Culture, Media, and U.S. Interests in the Middle East Since 1945* (University of California Press, 2001), 43–83.

36. For a detailed discussion of narratives of maturity and guidance in the postwar U.S.-Japanese relationship, see Naoko Shibusawa, *America's Geisha Ally: Reimagining the Japanese Enemy* (Harvard University Press, 2006).

37. Thomas French asserts that by labeling the NPR as an army, historians have misunderstood its character; he argues that due to its connection with Japan's civil police, especially through its disciplinary system, its civilian leadership and bureaucracy, its procurement policies, and some elements of its training, the NPR is best understood as a constabulary force. It is true that both U.S. and Japanese policymakers initially conceived of the NPR as a domestic, defensive force, not only due to the security vacuum of the Korean War but also the Japanese Communist Party's recent turn toward a policy of armed resistance and violent revolution. But U.S. policymakers (along with some Japanese conservatives) saw the NPR as the core of a new Japanese army, drawing parallels, for example, between the NPR and the South Korean military during the Korean War, utilizing U.S. military training materials, and regularly discussing the future of the NPR with former members of the Japanese wartime military. See Thomas French, "Contested 'Rearmament': The National Police Reserve and Japan's Cold War(s)," *Japanese Studies* 34, no. 1 (2014), 25–36.

38. General Douglas MacArthur to Yoshida Shigeru, July 8, 1950, in Masuda, ed., *Rearmament of Japan, Part One*, document no. 1-B-126, Microfiche Collection, Congressional Information Service.

39. Courtney Whitney, "Memorandum Concerning Legal Aspects of the Implementation of the Supreme Commander's Letter of 8 July 1950," July 14, 1950, in Masuda, ed., *Rearmament of Japan, Part One*, document no. 1-B-126, Microfiche Collection, Congressional Information Service.

40. Ashida Hitoshi, quoted in Masuda, "Fear of World War III," 558.

41. Ashida Hitoshi, quoted in Ōtake Hideo, "Rearmament Controversies and Cultural Conflicts in Japan: The Case of the Conservatives and the Socialists," in *Creating Single Party Democracy: Japan's Postwar Political System*, edited by Tetsuya Kataoka (Stanford, Calif.: Hoover Institution Press, 1992), 60–61.

42. Here I am not arguing that Japan was a uniquely militarized or aggressive state, but simply that a wide variety of people and groups in Japan engaged in and supported empire and war. See Young, *Japan's Total Empire*.

43. Masuda, "Fear of World War III," 557.

44. Ibid., 559.

45. See Jennifer M. Miller, "The Struggle to Rearm Japan: Negotiating the Cold War State in U.S.-Japanese Relations," *Journal of Contemporary History* 46, no. 1 (2011), 82–108. Several of these "depurgees" became prime minister after the end of the occupation, including Hatoyama Ichirō (1954–56), Ishibashi Tanzan (1956–57), and Kishi Nobusuke (1957–60). Moreover, some noncareer military officers (U.S. policymakers determined their noncareer status based on when these men had joined the military) joined the NPR. In the last two years of the occupation, the United States would continue to "depurge" wartime military officers in order to build an experienced officer cadre in the NPR.

46. See Koschmann, *Revolution and Subjectivity in Postwar Japan*, 220–29.

47. Masuda, "Fear of World War III," 556.

48. In raising the specter of communism, conservatives harked back to another vital thread of prewar Japanese history—namely, prewar crackdowns on communism due to concerns about its impact on Japan's political, economic, and social order, and the broader belief that Japan needed to eliminate communism in East Asia.

49. Heiwa Mondai Danwakai, quoted in Glenn D. Hook, *Militarization and Demilitarization in Contemporary Japan* (New York: Routledge, 1996), 30.

50. Maruyama Masao, quoted in Hook, *Militarization and Demilitarization in Contemporary Japan*, 40.

51. Hook, *Militarization and Demilitarization in Contemporary Japan*, 41.

52. For a detailed discussion of the concept of "democratic revolution" in postwar Japan, see Koschmann, *Revolution and Subjectivity*, especially 11–41.

53. Dai kyū kai zenkoku tōtaikai, "Dai kyū kai tōtaikai sengen: surogan" [Ninth Party Congress declaration: Slogans], January 30, 1952, in *Shiryō nihon shakaitō shinjyū nenshi* [Documents—A forty-year history of the Japan Socialist Party] (Tokyo: Nihon shakaitō chūū honbu, 1986), 244.

54. Franziska Seraphim, *War Memory and Social Politics in Postwar Japan* (Harvard University Asia Center, 2006), 135–36.

55. Masuda, "Fear of World War III," 566.

56. For a detailed exploration of these negotiations after the end of the occupation, see Miller, "The Struggle to Rearm Japan," 82–108.

57. Tomoyuki Sasaki, "An Army for the People: The Self-Defense Forces and Society in Postwar Japan," Ph.D. dissertation, University of California–San Diego, 2009, 48.

58. CINCFE General Matthew Ridgway to Joint Chiefs of Staff, August 25, 1951, RG 218 Records of the U.S. Joint Chiefs of Staff, Geographic File 1951–1953, 092 Japan Sec. 2–7, Box 23, Folder: CCS 092 Japan (12-12-50) Sec. 6, National Archives and Records Administration, College Park, Maryland (hereafter NARA).

59. Unlike the occupation of Germany, the United States carried out the occupation of Japan with only minimal on-the-ground participation of other allied countries. However, the thirteen-nation Far Eastern Commission technically oversaw the development and implementation of occupation policy as laid out by the Potsdam Declaration. The FEC included the Soviet Union, which remained deeply opposed to Japanese rearmament, and this was another factor in the NPR's defensive character.

60. Dower, *Embracing Defeat*, 547.

61. Memorandum by Douglas W. Overton of the Office of Northeast Asian Affairs to the Acting Director of that Office (Johnson), "National Police Reserve," January 19, 1951, in *Foreign Relations of the United States 1951* (Government Printing Office, 1977), 6:808. See also "Organization of the National Police Reserve," Frank Kowalski Papers, Military Files: Subject Files, Folder: Japan: Reports, Misc. Reports N.D., National Police Reserve N.D., Box 9, Library of Congress, Washington D.C. (hereafter LOC).

62. For detailed notes of these discussions, see the Frank Kowalski Papers, Military Files: Subject Files, Japan, Reports, Folders: Daily, 1950–1952, and Kitamura, Morimitsu, 1951–1954, undated, Box 8, LOC.

63. Overton memorandum.

64. "Public Safety Highlights, PSD-11." Frank Kowalski Papers, Military Files: Subject Files, Japan: Reports, Folder: Misc. Reports, N.D., National Police Reserve, N.D., Box 9, LOC.

65. Posters, Frank Kowalski Papers, Speeches and Writings, Folder: Speeches, undated, Japan: National Police Reserve, Box 19, LOC.

66. Sasaki, "An Army for the People," 66. Five years after World War II, economic prospects in Japan remained grim. The NPR, however, offered a monthly salary of 5,000 yen—1,000 yen higher than the average starting salary of a college graduate—along with a 60,000 yen retirement benefit; Sasaki, "An Army for the People," 67.

67. "Japan Drills an 'Army of Sergeants,'" *Life*, February 5, 1951, 30.

68. Sabine Frühstück, *Uneasy Warrior: Gender, Memory, and Popular Culture in the Japanese Army* (University of California Press, 2007), 66.

69. Emiko Ohnuki-Tierney, *Kamikaze, Cherry Blossoms, and Nationalisms: The Militarization of Aesthetics in Japanese History* (University of Chicago Press, 2002), 13.

70. Jonathan M. Reynolds, "Japan's Imperial Diet Building in the Debate over Construction of a National Identity," in Tansman, ed., *The Culture of Japanese Fascism*, 254–55.

71. Frühstück, *Uneasy Warriors*, 172–73.

72. House Resolution 121, quoted in Kinue Tokodome, "Passage of H.Res. 121 on 'Comfort Women,' the U.S. Congress and Historical Memory in Japan," *Japan Focus*, August 30, 2007 (http://japanfocus.org/-Kinue-TOKUDOME/2510#sthash .OGBjhNyP.dpuf). For a broader discussion of the role and consequences of apologies in international relations, see Jennifer Lind, *Sorry States: Apologies in International Politics* (Cornell University Press, 2008).

73. Alexis Dudden, *Troubled Apologies among Japan, Korea and the United States* (Columbia University Press, 2008), 5.

Part II

How History Can *and* Should *Influence Policy*

THOMAS G. MAHNKEN

6

Containment

Myth and Metaphor

Containment was arguably the most influential national security concept of the twentieth century; for roughly four decades, it guided U.S. strategy toward the Soviet Union. Although the U.S.-Soviet competition has passed into history, the concept of containment remains very much alive. Policymakers and scholars continue to prescribe a strategy of containment in a variety of circumstances, including many very different from those that gave birth to the idea during the Cold War. In doing so, they often invoke the *myth* of containment, a simplified and idealized representation of the strategy as it was practiced during the Cold War, as well as the *metaphor* of containment, a rough policy and strategy analogy for dealing with current national security challenges. Although containment can be a useful strategy under some circumstances, formulating and implementing such an approach requires more than a resort to myth or metaphor. Rather, it requires that policymakers understand the nature of a particular competitor, including its objectives, and conduct a thorough assessment of its strengths and weaknesses relative to the United States.

Scholars frequently use the word *containment* as shorthand to describe a family of strategies that successive American administrations pursued over decades during the Cold War. It is beyond the scope of this chapter to recount in detail the formulation and implementation of U.S. Cold War strategy; others have extensively chronicled containment's history from the 1940s through the 1980s.[1] However, several aspects of the Cold War approach to containment are pertinent to the discussion of how foreign policymakers today invoke the concept.

First, containment was a strategy. That is, containment was formulated as a way for the United States to achieve its political aims in competition with the Soviet Union, a way for the U.S. government to pit American strategic advantages against the propensities of the Soviet political system. As originally articulated by George Kennan, containment was to be "a political war, a war of attrition for limited objectives."[2] It was a strategy that could yield either the limited aim of changing Soviet behavior or the unlimited aim of changing the Soviet system.[3] Kennan wrote that "the United States has it in its power to increase enormously the strains under which Soviet policy must operate, to force upon the Kremlin a far greater degree of moderation and circumspection than it has had to observe in recent years, and in this way to promote tendencies which must eventually find their outlet in either the breakup or the gradual mellowing of Soviet power."[4] The original formulation of containment thus contains a bifurcated theory of victory: if the United States were to oppose the further expansion of Soviet power through collective, flexible, and adaptable efforts, then over time either Soviet behavior would moderate or the Soviet system would collapse.

Second, the strategy of containment was based on an understanding of the Soviet political system and the result of a net assessment of American and Soviet strengths and weaknesses. Indeed, much of Kennan's so-called Long Telegram and subsequent article written under the pseudonym X is devoted to an assessment of the nature of the Soviet political system and its implications for U.S. strategy. In Kennan's view, Soviet behavior derived from a mix of Russian history and Marxist ideology, and he viewed the Soviet leadership as exhibiting strategic patience because they believed that time (indeed history) was on their side. Similarly, National Security Council Report 68, drafted by Paul Nitze in 1950, devotes considerable attention to assessing the international environment, the nature of the U.S.-Soviet competition, the aims of the United States and the Soviet Union, and the means available to both before exploring alternative courses of action.[5]

Third, it is worth remembering that containment is but one of a family of alternatives available to strategists—a family that includes appeasement, engagement, containment, rollback, and nonentanglement.[6] Similarly, containment was one of a set of alternatives that American policymakers explored at various times during the Cold War. These ranged from withdrawing (militarily, if not politically) from key regions to the muscular exercise of American power to roll back communism. Although American leaders repeatedly elected to pursue a strategy of containment, it is worth remembering that containment was never the only option available to the United States.

Perhaps the best-known effort to examine varieties of containment and alternatives to it was the Solarium project of the administration of President Dwight D. Eisenhower. Over the course of two and a half months, teams examined three candidate national security strategies: the existing strategy of containment, which sought to prevent Soviet expansion in Europe while minimizing the risk of general war; a more robust version of containment that nonetheless abstained from direct military action within the Soviet sphere of influence; and a strategy to diminish Soviet power and roll back Soviet control of territory, including through military means. In the end the study largely confirmed the existing strategy of containment.[7]

Fourth, the U.S. government pursued different varieties of a containment strategy during much of the Cold War. Indeed, as John Lewis Gaddis reminds us, the United States pursued not a single strategy, but strategies, of containment. That is, containment proved to be a flexible approach, one that could accommodate both more forward-leaning and more circumspect approaches. During certain periods the United States emphasized the military instrument of national strategy, while in others it emphasized diplomacy. Similarly, during some periods the nation was more active in containing the Soviet Union than at other times. In Kennan's original formulation, it would have led to a contraction rather than an expansion of U.S. interests and a focus on Western Europe and Japan. In his view, the goal was for the United States to remain active in "enough places, and in sufficiently strategic places, to accomplish our general purpose."[8]

The development of nuclear weapons greatly facilitated containment. Indeed, nuclear deterrence was a vital element of the overall strategy. In particular, the extension of U.S. nuclear deterrence guarantees to America's allies bolstered their ability to resist coercion.

Fifth, although the United States implemented a strategy of containment for much of the Cold War, it was not the only strategy that was pursued against the Soviet Union. One such alternative was détente. The strategy of détente practiced by the administration of President Richard Nixon was clearly an attempt to cope with the nation's weakness in the U.S.-Soviet competition in the wake of the Vietnam War. Moreover, Nixon and his advisers saw the strategy as a break from traditional American diplomacy, one they hoped would yield a broader modus vivendi with the Soviet government.[9]

More consequentially, the strategy toward the Soviet Union during the administration of President Ronald Reagan represented a repudiation of many of the key assumptions of both détente and containment.[10] Whereas Cold War orthodoxy held that the Soviet Union was a permanent feature of the international system, Reagan and some of his close advisers emphasized the transitory character of the Soviet regime. Whereas most believed that there was little that the United States and its allies could do to change the nature of the Soviet political system, Reagan believed that the nation had much greater leverage over the Soviet Union than many others credited it with. Indeed, he grasped that the Soviet Union was in the throes of a terminal illness.[11] Whereas many believed that efforts to confront the Soviet regime would lead to crisis and potentially conflict, Reagan was willing to accept considerable risk in standing up to it. Finally, whereas many counseled that the wisest strategy was to accommodate the Soviet Union within the international order, Reagan sought to create a fundamental change in its character by pushing the communist regime to confront its weaknesses.[12]

Reagan's personal experiences and view of history informed his willingness to break with the practice of containment. His views of the Soviet Union in particular and communism in general were shaped by his experience in Hollywood during the early Cold War. In Reagan's view, American strength had been central to countering communism and protecting the United States and its allies. American strategic superiority had bolstered peace, and the waning and loss of that superiority in the face of the Soviet Union's growing nuclear and conventional capabilities threatened that peace. As he saw it, détente was a one-way street of repeated and unreciprocated Western attempts to reduce tensions with the Soviet bloc.[13]

Reagan saw containment as something to be transcended rather than embraced; by the mid-1970s he was committed to defeating the Soviet Union. As he told Richard V. Allen, who would later serve as his national security adviser, in 1977, "My idea of American policy toward the Soviet Union is simple, and some would say simplistic. It is this: We win and they lose."[14]

Sixth, containment was highly successful as a bureaucratic strategy. That is, it was amenable to implementation by a large organization. As a buzzword, *containment* served as an easily understandable encapsulation of American strategy that applied throughout the U.S. national security bureaucracy. Moreover, the strategy of containment applied across the various instruments of national power. The U.S. armed forces were clearly in the business of containment, but so too were diplomats in the State Department, the members of the Central Intelligence Agency's clandestine service, and the members of the U.S. Information Agency. Indeed, containment's simplicity as a bureaucratic strategy was a considerable ingredient of its long-term success.

Simplicity could, of course, lead to distortion. Viewing the world through the lens of containment could lead American decisionmakers to perceive guerrillas to be communists and all communist regimes to be, a priori, hostile to the United States. It also promoted zero-sum thinking, where a gain for the Soviet Union was automatically viewed as a loss for the United States.

Finally, although containment was formulated and initially implemented as a strategy, at times American decisionmakers began to view it as a policy. In other words, containment became an end in itself rather than a means to an end. For much of the 1960s and 1970s, policymakers sought to check the spread of Soviet influence without dealing with the domestic political system and ideology that motivated it. In part this was the result of the bureaucratization of containment, but it also reflected the belief that the Soviet Union had become a permanent feature of the international environment and that threats to the Soviet system would be at best fruitless and at worst destabilizing and dangerous.

On the whole, containment proved to be a successful strategy for the United States during its long-term competition with the Soviet Union. Its success can be attributed to a good understanding of the nature of the competitor, an assessment of Soviet strengths and weaknesses, and nuclear deterrence. It is also worth noting, however, that U.S. victory ultimately came only after a break with containment during the Reagan administration.

The Myth and Metaphor of Containment

The concept of containment has endured far beyond the end of the Cold War and the demise of the Soviet Union. A quarter century later, policymakers continue to invoke containment as a foreign policy option, although in very different contexts than the Cold War and against very different competitors than the Soviet Union. Whereas Neville Chamberlain proved the folly of appeasement (a once respectable strategy), the favorable outcome of the Cold War for the United States has seemingly privileged the concept of containment. In part, this can be seen as nostalgia for a golden age when one elegant concept encapsulated the core of American foreign policy and strategy. Periodically since the end of the Cold War, foreign policy commentators have bemoaned the absence of a master concept to govern U.S. national security policy and a new Mr. X to provide a coherent lens through which to view the current international system.[15] And there have been periodic attempts to provide just such a vision.[16] The continued use of containment also signifies a desire to impose order on a disorderly international environment.

In invoking the concept of containment, today's policymakers and scholars tend to misread and simplify the historical record in a number of ways. First, they tend to perceive continuity to a greater extent than is warranted. They thus tend to imply that there was a single strategy of containment that the United States pursued consistently throughout the Cold War, rather than the varieties of containment strategy that the government pursued at various times during the Cold War.

Second, in retrospect, scholars and policymakers tend to view containment as easier and less controversial, both domestically and internationally, than it in fact was. Lost is any memory of the domestic debates over defense spending and recriminations over intervening (in Korea and Vietnam, for example) or failing to intervene (in China), as well as tension with allies over the presence of U.S. troops or the credibility of the extended nuclear deterrent. Gone is an awareness of the policy debates about determining the target of containment, whether communist ideology or Soviet power. Absent is the sense of contingency: the awareness that different policy choices could have yielded very different outcomes.

Containment has become an empty vessel, to be filled with whatever scholars and policymakers desire or fear. Since the end of the Cold War, containment has been applied to virtually every contemporary challenge. In the case of Iran it has been promoted as a reasonable option to rolling back the nation's power and interdicting its nuclear energy program. In the case of China it has been invoked as an example of a strategy the United States is not pursuing and as a way of contrasting Sino-American competition with the Cold War. Some scholars and legislators have even sought to apply the concept to the war with al Qaeda and its affiliates. For policy-makers, containment is often used as a straw man for what not to do. Scholars, by contrast, tend to view containment in a more favorable light.

Iran

Iran provides both the first and the most explicit case of the post–Cold War application of a strategy of containment. Similar to the Soviet Union in its embrace of an expansionist ideology, Iran nonetheless represents a much different competitor from the Soviet Union in terms of its weakness relative to the United States, including its lack of nuclear weapons. Moreover, the geopolitical setting of the Middle East, including the lack of alliances, differs considerably from that of postwar Europe.

Despite these differences, only a few years after the collapse of the Soviet Union the administration of President Bill Clinton undertook a policy of "dual containment," one that sought simultaneously to prevent Iran and Iraq from destabilizing the Persian Gulf region.[17] In the words of the Clinton administration's 1996 *National Security Strategy*:

> In Southwest Asia, the United States remains focused on deterring threats to regional stability, particularly from Iraq and Iran as long as those states pose a threat to U.S. interests, to other states in the region and to their own citizens. We have in place a dual containment strategy aimed at these two states and will maintain our long-standing presence, which has been centered on naval vessels in and near the Persian Gulf and prepositioned combat equipment.[18]

The primary goal of Clinton's dual containment was to isolate and delegitimize both Iran and Iraq. The hoped-for result was some time and space to bolster the U.S.-constructed regional order. The administration also hoped that Tehran's revolutionary fervor would mellow over time. The United States sought to keep the two countries out of regional politics, protecting Saudi Arabia and the smaller Persian Gulf states from the designs and ambitions of Saddam Hussein and the Iranian clerics. Making Iraq and Iran irrelevant would also allow Israel and the more moderate Arab countries to make progress on peace accords.[19]

The U.S. government attempted to isolate Iraq through the no-fly zones the United States and its allies established over the nation in the wake of the 1991 Gulf War, and also through international economic sanctions.[20] The

United States sought Iraqi compliance with UN Security Council Resolutions that ordered Iraq to eliminate its nuclear, chemical, biological, and missile programs. Content with containing Iraqi ambitions and provocations, Clinton saw little incentive in ousting Saddam.

Clinton's containment policy regarding Iran centered on generating international political opposition against Iran and unilateral economic sanctions. The administration cast its containment policy as an attempt to check Iran's nuclear ambitions, its financial support for terrorism, and its opposition to the Arab-Israeli peace process.[21]

Criticism

Dual containment was criticized on several grounds. First, observers argued that it lacked substance. Former national security advisers Zbigniew Brzezinski and Brent Scowcroft characterized it as "more a slogan than a strategy,"[22] and argued that the approach did not represent a long-term strategy but instead an expedient effort to isolate the two major opponents of an active American role in the Gulf region. They further argued that the elements of dual containment were poorly conceived. Others argued that the very notion of dual containment was nonsensical in that it took countries with radically different goals and regional interests and treated them similarly. Indeed, dual containment lumped together two countries that had recently fought against each other in the longest and bloodiest conventional war since World War II. Hisham Melhem has characterized it as "reactive, punitive, and tactical."[23]

Indeed, it was unclear whether dual containment represented a strategy (a means to an end) or a policy (an end in itself). Despite assertions from the Clinton administration that its goals were limited, it was unclear whether the United States sought to merely change Saddam Hussein's behavior or replace his regime. Indeed, the administration undertook actions supporting both aims during its time in office. Moreover, in 1998, bipartisan majorities in both houses of Congress passed the Iraq Liberation Act, declaring that the goal of U.S. policy should be "to remove the regime headed by Saddam Hussein from power."

Regarding Iran, the Clinton administration sought the limited aim of changing the behavior of that nation's government—specifically, trying to convince Iran to renounce its quest for nuclear weapons and end its support for terrorism and subversion. Here the question was whether Washington could assemble and hold together a coalition.

The Iraqi pillar of dual containment eroded under the Clinton administration. Over time, fewer and fewer of America's allies were willing to support the military enforcement of containment. By the time President Clinton launched Operation Desert Fox against suspected Iraqi nuclear, chemical, and biological weapon sites in December 1998, only Great Britain was willing to participate. Similarly, sentiment among many of America's allies increasingly turned away from the strict application of economic sanctions against Baghdad and increasingly toward weakening or removing them. Corruption within the United Nations "oil-for-food" program and allegations that sanctions had led to the deaths of thousands of Iraqi civilians only accelerated this process.

If the containment of Iraq eroded under Clinton, it collapsed under George W. Bush. The September 11, 2001, terrorist attacks on the United States changed the risk calculus of Bush and many of his advisers. As a result, containment, particularly with the political will to enforce it weakening, appeared to be an increasingly risky strategy. As Bush later wrote, "Before 9/11, Saddam was a problem America might have been able to manage. Through the lens of the post 9/11 world, my view changed.... The stakes were too high to trust the dictator's word against the weight of evidence and the consensus of the world. The lesson of 9/11 was that if we waited for a danger to fully materialize, we would have waited too long."[24] As a result, the Bush administration moved from containing to overthrowing Saddam's regime.

The overthrow of Saddam Hussein gave new voice to calls to contain Tehran's influence. On the one hand, some policymakers and scholars saw in containment a concept that could be applied to Iran. Karim Sadjadpour and Diane De Gramont, for example, have argued that the United States should use diplomacy and philanthropy to counter Iranian influence in the Gulf region,[25] while Isaiah Wilson argues that the United States should rediscover containment in its dealings with Iran.[26]

Some who advocated containment of Iran framed it as a more reasonable alternative than the kind of regime change practiced in Iraq. As then senator Chuck Hagel remarked in 2007,

Our strategy must be one focused on direct engagement and diplomacy ... backed by the leverage of international pressure, military options, isolation and containment ... not unlike the strategies that the United States pursued during the Cold War against the Soviet Union ... with Libya that has led to Libya's reintegration into the global community ... and as we are doing today through the "Six-Party" process to address the North Korea nuclear issue. The core tenets of George Kennan's "The Long Telegram" and the strategy of containment remain relevant today. This is how we should have handled Saddam Hussein.[27]

In Hagel's view, containment was a valuable strategy despite the marked differences in circumstances.

For others, differences in circumstances argued against the application of containment to Iran. Nothing resembling the U.S. Cold War alliances exists in the Gulf region. Moreover, America's allies and regional states are divided over the relative merits of containing or engaging Iran. Dalia Dassa Kaye and Frederic Wehrey, for example, have argued that states in the Persian Gulf region, although concerned about Iranian subversion and coercion, are unlikely to stand up to Tehran as a unified bloc.[28] Vali Nasr and Ray Takeyh assert that containment of Iran is both unsound and impractical; moreover, they argue that such a strategy is likely to further destabilize an already volatile region.[29]

Despite the marked differences between the Soviet Union and Iran and postwar Europe and contemporary Southwest Asia, some policymakers and scholars have promoted containment as an acceptable, if not desirable, strategy in the event that Tehran acquires nuclear weapons.[30] As James Lindsay and Ray Takeyh note, "Even if Washington fails to prevent Iran from going nuclear, it can contain and mitigate the consequences of Iran's nuclear defiance. It should make clear to Tehran that acquiring the bomb will not produce the benefits it anticipates but isolate and weaken the regime."[31] And Robert Reardon wrote optimistically in 2012,

The most appropriate frame in which to consider the United States' Iran policy is one of *containment*. Importantly, this does not refer exclusively, or even mostly, to a military strategy, but an overarching policy framework that incorporates the broad spectrum of U.S. statecraft, including military, economic, and diplomatic instruments. All of these tools can be used effectively to craft a multilateral strategy that successfully denies Iran any political or military gain from its nuclear program, maintains regional stability and upholds the international nonproliferation regime, and applies pressure on Iran that encourages positive domestic political change over the long term.[32]

Containing a nuclear Iran would, however, be a major challenge. It would likely require the United States to threaten nuclear retaliation in response to Iranian nuclear use, to extend a nuclear deterrence guarantee to regional states in exchange for a promise not to develop nuclear weapons of their own, and potentially to deploy U.S. nuclear weapons closer to the region. It would also likely entail bolstering U.S. ballistic missile defenses, maintaining a robust conventional presence in the region, and increasing security cooperation with regional states.[33] As the authors of one study of the requirements of a strategy to contain a nuclear Iran put it, "If these steps are carried out, effective containment is possible. But it would be highly complex and far from foolproof."[34]

Policymakers have been more circumspect. Indeed, both President Barack Obama and former secretary of state Hillary Clinton have explicitly ruled out containment as an option should Tehran develop nuclear weapons.[35] As Clinton put it in March 2012, "Our policy is one of prevention, not containment. We are determined to prevent Iran from obtaining a nuclear weapon."[36]

In the case of Iran, then, a resort to containment would represent an implicit concession of defeat and a failure to prevent Tehran's acquisition of nuclear weapons.

China

If containment has been seen as an acceptable, though undesirable, strategy for dealing with Iran, in the context of Sino-American relations containment is seen as the unwise alternative to engagement.

George H. W. Bush's final national security strategy explicitly discussed the prospect of containing China, arguing that the United States "must carefully watch the emergence of China onto the world stage and support, contain, or balance this emergence as necessary to protect U.S. interests."[37] Since then, however, many policymakers have emphasized that U.S. strategy is not aimed at containing China. As noted above, the loaded legacy of Cold War–era containment connotes conflict, or at least the specter of potential conflict, with an antagonistic state. As former secretary of state Clinton put it,

> There are some in both countries who believe that China's interests and ours are fundamentally at odds. They apply a zero-sum calculation . . .

so whenever one of us succeeds, the other must fail. But that is not our view. There are also many in China who still believe that the U.S. is bent on containing China and I would simply point out that since the beginning of our diplomatic relations, China has experienced breathtaking growth and development.[38]

Scholars have tended to posit strategy options for the United States in dealing with China as either containment or engagement,[39] and scholars of China have echoed this dichotomy.[40] In practice, though, the United States both contains and engages—that is, Washington has undertaken a strategy of "congagement" with China.[41] The United States tends to engage with China on trade and economic issues, while favoring containment and confrontation regarding the issues of Taiwan, Tibet, and human rights.[42]

Scholars tend to use the term *containment* to disparage features of U.S. strategy that they dislike, or as a straw man to be argued against in order to promote features of U.S. strategy that they favor. Along the former lines, Ted Galen Carpenter argues that U.S. efforts to strengthen cooperation with Australia and the Philippines,

> along with previous efforts to strengthen cooperative military ties with other traditional allies such as South Korea and Japan and one-time U.S. adversaries such as Vietnam, have all the earmarks of a rather unsubtle containment policy directed against China. It is a foolish strategy that will complicate and perhaps permanently damage the crucial U.S.-China relationship.[43]

Hugh White, while noting the differences in U.S.-Soviet relations during the Cold War and Sino-American relations today, argues that "nonetheless, at a deeper level the parallels are clear and becoming clearer."[44] Thomas Friedman was being somewhat more diagnostic when he characterized U.S. policy toward China as "pre-containment" or "containment-lite," triggered by a sudden upsurge in China's assertion of claims to the South China Sea.[45]

Along the latter lines, scholars argue that instead of containing China, the United States should be engaging Beijing. As Joseph Nye has written, "Containment was designed for a different era, and it is not what the United States is, or should be, attempting now. Containment is simply not a relevant policy tool for dealing with a rising China. Power is the ability to obtain the outcomes one wants, and sometimes America's power is greater when we act with others rather than merely over others."[46] As Nye points out, Cold War containment took place in a situation in which there was little economic interchange or social interaction between the United States and the Soviet Union. By contrast, today the United States has immense trade with China as well as huge exchanges of students and tourists. He notes, "When I worked on the Pentagon's East Asia strategy in 1994, during the Clinton administration, we rejected the idea of containment for two reasons. If we treated China as an enemy, we were guaranteeing a future enemy. If we treated China as a friend, we kept open the possibility of a more peaceful future."

Nye argues that a strategy of containment would have three fatal flaws. First, it exaggerates Chinese strength. Whereas the Soviet Union possessed an expansionist ideology and conventional military superiority in Europe, China lacks both. Second, the United States could not assemble a coalition to contain China even if it wanted to. Only if China's behavior becomes more aggressive could such a coalition be formed—that is, China would have to contain itself. Third, containment in Nye's view discounts the possibility that China can evolve into a responsible power. As he puts it, "If we treat China as an enemy now, we are guaranteeing ourselves an enemy."[47]

David Shambaugh writes that engagement is the best process to achieve the ultimate goal of "integrating China into the existing rule-based, institutionalized, and normative international system."[48] It will be difficult, he posits, but the United States must try.

Whereas American policymakers deny that the United States is interested in—let alone engaged in—containing China, Chinese commentators have regularly, since the Tiananmen Square protests of 1989, accused the United States of developing and implementing a coherent strategy of containing China.[49] They believe that such a strategy undergirds America's alliances in the Asia-Pacific region and that it animates the increasing emphasis that successive American administrations have placed on the region.

In practice, U.S. strategy has been a mixture of containment and engagement, and a combination of competition and cooperation is likely to govern Sino-American relations for the foreseeable future. Barring a major Chinese misstep, containment without engagement is difficult to imagine; there are substantial domestic and international political barriers to adopting a strategy of pure containment. Indeed, such a move could force

America's allies to distance themselves from the United States and lead to escalating competition. Conversely, a strategy of pure engagement would be tantamount to appeasement.[50]

The application of containment to China thus has few advocates. However, as Beijing's increasing assertiveness engenders responses from its neighbors, a sort of de facto containment appears to be emerging.

Al Qaeda

Finally, containment has been applied both as a straw-man approach and a prescription for dealing with al Qaeda. In a 2004 speech at the University of Virginia, Robert Hutchings, then chairman of the National Intelligence Council, used Kennan's prescriptions as a framework for examining the parallels between the threat posed by Soviet communism and that of al Qaeda's brand of virulent Islamism. Contrasting the traditional state-based threat posed by the Soviet Union with the asymmetric threat of terrorism, Hutchings concluded that Kennan's model of containment was inadequate.[51] To Hutchings, containment served as a way to highlight the differences between the past and the present.

Others, however, have framed containment as a reasonable strategy for dealing with radical Islam. Stephen D. Biddle, for example, has posited containment as an alternative to the current strategy for fighting al Qaeda, one that would settle for more modest goals in exchange for lower costs and lower short-term risks.[52]

Among politicians, Rand Paul has advocated a new strategy of containment aimed at "radical Islam." Paul's adoption of containment is ironic, however: whereas containment was originally seen as a means of keeping the United States engaged, in Paul's formulation it represents a call to disengage.

Conclusion

Containment lives on. To the extent that scholars and policymakers endorse the practice, however, it tends to be as a policy rather than a strategy—as an end in itself rather than as a means to an end. Only rarely does it emerge from a careful net assessment of the competitors. Rarer still are efforts to link a strategy of containment to a theory of victory. How, for example, would a strategy of containment lead to a mellowing of the clerical regime in Tehran or ensure its downfall? How, conversely, would a strategy of engagement produce a political effect in Beijing?

In fact, containment is all too often used as a surrogate for policy and strategy. It is used as a substitute for thinking through U.S. aims, performing a careful net assessment, and developing a strategy. The remedy is not to jettison the concept of containment but instead to be more thoughtful in its application.

Containment can be a successful strategy, but its success is hardly guaranteed. As implemented against the Soviet Union, it required persistent hard work over the course of decades. It was an active process that relied crucially on allies who shared both interests and values with the United States. Moreover, it rested on a foundation of nuclear deterrence and extended nuclear guarantees to America's allies.

These elements are likely to be no less important in the future. Whether applied to Iran or China, successful containment would require active efforts to gain and maintain domestic and international support for U.S. efforts over the course of years, if not decades; it would require persistent efforts to develop and implement a coalition strategy; and it would require a heavy reliance on deterrence and extended deterrence. It would, in other words, require U.S. leaders to recover habits of thought and action that have largely fallen into disuse.

Notes

1. See, for example, John Lewis Gaddis, *The Cold War: A New History* (New York: Penguin, 2005); and Melvin P. Leffler and Odd Arne Westad, eds., *The Cambridge History of the Cold War*, 3 vols. (Cambridge University Press, 2010).

2. George Kennan, quoted in John Lewis Gaddis, *George F. Kennan: An American Life* (New York: Penguin, 2011), 235.

3. Carl von Clausewitz differentiated between unlimited and limited aims when he wrote, "War can be of two kinds, in the sense that either the objective is to *overthrow the enemy*—to render him politically helpless or militarily impotent, thus forcing him to sign whatever peace we please; or *merely to occupy some of his frontier districts* so that we can annex them or use them for bargaining at the peace negotiations. Transitions from one type to the other will of course recur in my treatment; but the fact that the aims of the two types are quite different must be clear at all times, and their points of irreconcilability brought out." Carl von Clausewitz, *On War*, edited and translated by Michael Howard and Peter Paret (Princeton University Press, 1989), 69, emphasis in the original.

4. X [George F. Kennan], "The Sources of Soviet Conduct," *Foreign Affairs* 25, no. 3 (1947), 566–82.

5. Paul Nitze, *NSC-68: United States Objectives and Programs for National Security*, report to the president through the National Security Council, April 14, 1950.

6. See Colin Dueck, "Strategies for Managing Rogue States," *Orbis* 50, no. 2 (2006), 223–41.

7. Robert R. Bowie and Richard H. Immerman, *Waging Peace: How Eisenhower Shaped an Enduring Cold War Strategy* (Oxford University Press, 1998), 123–43.

8. George Kennan, quoted in Gaddis, *George F. Kennan*, 310.

9. See, for example, Henry Kissinger, *Diplomacy* (New York: Touchstone, 1994), 755.

10. Thomas G. Mahnken, "The Reagan Administration's Strategy toward the Soviet Union," in *Successful Strategies*, edited by Williamson Murray (Cambridge University Press, 2014).

11. Richard Pipes, *Vixi: Memoirs of a Non-Belonger* (Yale University Press, 2003), 162.

12. John Lewis Gaddis, *Strategies of Containment: A Critical Appraisal of American National Security Policy during the Cold War* (Oxford University Press, 2005), 354.

13. Ronald Reagan, "The President's News Conference," January 29, 1981 (www.presidency.ucsb.edu/ws/print.php?pid=44101).

14. Richard V. Allen, "The Man Who Won the Cold War," *Hoover Digest*, January 2000 (www.hoover.org/research/man-who-won-cold-war).

15. Eliot A. Cohen, "Calling Mr. X," *New Republic* 218, no. 3 (January 19, 1998), 17; Richard N. Haass, "Is There a Doctrine in the House?" *New York Times*, November 8, 2005; Fareed Zakaria, "Wanted: A New Grand Strategy," *Newsweek* (December 8, 2008), 40.

16. See, for example, Mr. Y, *A National Strategic Narrative* (Washington, D.C.: Woodrow Wilson Center, 2011).

17. Patrick Clawson, "The Continuing Logic of Dual Containment," *Survival* 40, no. 1 (1998), 33–47; Gary Sick, "Rethinking Dual Containment," *Survival* 40, no. 1 (1998), 5–32.

18. *National Security Strategy of the United States* (The White House, 1996), 30.

19. Zbigniew Brzezinski, "Differentiated Containment," *Foreign Affairs* 76, no. 3 (1997), 22.

20. Ibid.

21. Ibid., 23.

22. Brzezinski, "Differentiated Containment," 20–30.

23. Hisham Melhem, *Dual Containment: The Demise of a Fallacy* (Georgetown University Center for Contemporary Arab Studies, 1998), 5–6.

24. George W. Bush, *Decision Points* (New York: Crown, 2010), 229.

25. Karim Sadjadpour and Diane De Gramont, "Reading Kennan in Tehran," *Foreign Affairs* 90, no. 2 (2011), 160–63.

26. Isaiah Wilson, "Rediscovering Containment: The Sources of American-Iranian Conduct," *Journal of International Affairs* 60, no. 2 (2007), 95–112.

27. Chuck Hagel, "The United States and Iran: At a Dangerous Crossroads," speech by Senator Chuck Hagel at the Center for Strategic and International Studies, November 8, 2007 (http://csis.org/files/media/csis/events/071108_hagel.pdf).

28. Dalia Dassa Kaye and Frederic Wehrey, "Containing Iran? Avoiding a Two-Dimensional Strategy in a Four-Dimensional Region," *Washington Quarterly* 32, no. 3 (2009), 37–53.

29. Vali Nasr and Ray Takeyh, "The Costs of Containing Iran: Washington's Misguided New Middle East Policy," *Foreign Affairs* 87, no. 1 (2008), 85–94.

30. David Sanger, "Debate Grows on Nuclear Containment of Iran," *New York Times*, March 13, 2010.

31. James M. Lindsay and Ray Takeyh, "After Iran Gets the Bomb," *Foreign Affairs* 89, no. 2 (2010), 33–49; Robert S. Litwak, "Living with Ambiguity: Nuclear Deals with Iran and North Korea," *Survival* 50, no. 1 (2008), 91–118; Robert Litwak, *Outlier States: American Strategies to Change, Contain, or Engage Regimes* (Washington, D.C.: Woodrow Wilson Center Press, 2012); Robert Litwak, *Rogue States and U.S. Foreign Policy: Containment after the Cold War* (Washington, D.C.: Woodrow Wilson Center Press, 2000).

32. Robert J. Reardon, *Containing Iran: Strategies for Addressing the Iranian Nuclear Challenge* (Santa Monica, CA: RAND, 2012), xvi.

33. Colin H. Kahl, Raj Pattani, and Jacob Stokes, *If All Else Fails: The Challenges of Containing a Nuclear-Armed Iran* (Washington, D.C.: Center for a New American Security, 2013); Eric S. Edelman, Andrew F. Krepinevich, and Evan Braden Montgomery, "The Dangers of a Nuclear Iran: The Limits of Containment," *Foreign Affairs* 90, no. 1 (2011), 66–81.

34. Kahl, Pattani, and Stokes, *If All Else Fails*, 7.

35. Christi Parsons and Paul Richter, "Obama Rules Out Containment Strategy for Iran," Tribune Newspapers, March 3, 2012 (http://m.spokesman.com/stories/2012/mar/03/us-force-is-option-in-iran/).

36. "Hillary Clinton: Time Running Out for Diplomacy with Iran," *USA Today*, March 31, 2012.

37. *National Security Strategy of the United States* (The White House, 1993), 8.

38. "U.S. Not Seeking to Contain China: Clinton," Reuters, October 29, 2010.

39. See, for example, David Shambaugh, "Containment or Engagement of China?" *International Security* 21, no. 2 (1996), 180.

40. Wang Enbao, "Engagement or Containment? Americans' Views on China and Sino-U.S. Relations," *Journal of Contemporary China* 11, no. 31 (2002), 381–92.

41. Aaron L. Friedberg, *A Contest for Supremacy: China, America, and the Struggle for Mastery in Asia* (New York: Norton, 2011), chapter 4.

42. Wang, "Engagement or Containment?" 392.

43. Ted Galen Carpenter, "Washington's Clumsy China Containment Policy," *National Interest* (November 30, 2011).

44. Hugh White, *The China Choice: Why America Should Share Power* (Collingwood, Victoria, Australia: Black Inc., 2012), 115.

45. Thomas Friedman, "Containment-Lite," *New York Times*, November 9, 2010.

46. Joseph Nye, "Work with China, Don't Contain It," *New York Times*, January 26, 2013.

47. Joseph Nye Jr., "The Case against Containment: Treat China Like an Enemy and That's What It Will Be," *Global Beat* (June 22, 1998).

48. David Shambaugh, "Containment or Engagement of China?" *International Security* 21, no. 2 (1996), 180.

49. Friedberg, *A Contest for Supremacy*, 135–36.

50. Ibid., 252–53.

51. Robert L. Hutchings, "The Sources of Terrorist Conduct," speech to the Jefferson Literary and Debating Society, University of Virginia, March 19, 2004 (http://www.au.af.mil/au/awc/awcgate/nic/speeches_terrorist_conduct.htm).

52. Stephen D. Biddle, *American Grand Strategy after 9/11: An Assessment* (Carlisle, Penn.: U.S. Army War College, 2005).

WILLIAM INBODEN

7

Grand Strategy and Petty Squabbles

The Paradox and Lessons of the Reagan NSC

Early in his presidency Ronald Reagan famously joked of his administration that "sometimes our right hand doesn't know what our far-right hand is doing."[1] As with much of President Reagan's humor, this quip had a ring of truth. Especially in the realm of national security policy, in organizational terms the Reagan administration was consumed by division, acrimony, confusion, and even occasional outbreaks of criminal malfeasance, as exemplified by the Iran-Contra affair.

Even setting aside felonious misconduct by renegade staff, a cursory overview of the Reagan administration's national security system reveals pervasive dysfunction. The National Security Council (NSC) suffered a revolving door of national security advisers, totaling six different advisers in eight years, and the NSC structure itself underwent multiple reorganizations.[2] Secretary of State George Shultz and Secretary of Defense Caspar Weinberger detested each other and feuded throughout their tenures. Shultz was not the only leader at Foggy Bottom to be alienated from the rest of the administration; during his brief sojourn as secretary of state in the first eighteen months of the Reagan presidency, Alexander Haig expressed open contempt for everyone else in the administration, including the president himself. The feeling was largely reciprocated, and led directly to Haig's premature departure.

151

When considering what insights the history of the Reagan NSC might offer for statecraft today, an obvious conclusion might be that it provides a cautionary tale in what *not* to do. After all, good management practice—and plain common sense—would seem to say that leaders of large organizations (such as the U.S. government) should instill clear lines of authority, develop and maintain a stable division of responsibility, cultivate open communication and information sharing, and promote staff unity and collegiality while minimizing division and acrimony. In failing to follow these standards, the Reagan NSC could appear at first glance as a historical case study in what to avoid rather than what to emulate. Drawing this lesson would be the use of history for "error avoidance," as I have described in a previous study.[3]

But history rarely fails to surprise, and the surprise that seems to emerge amid these organizational failures is the overall success of the Reagan administration's foreign policy. John Lewis Gaddis has been at the vanguard of these reassessments; in his words,

> What one can say now is that Reagan saw Soviet weaknesses sooner than most of his contemporaries did; that he understood the extent to which détente was perpetuating the Cold War rather than hastening its end; that his hard line strained the Soviet system at the moment of its maximum weakness; that his shift toward conciliation preceded Gorbachev; that he combined reassurance, persuasion, and pressure in dealing with the new Soviet leader; and that he maintained the support of the American people and of American allies.[4]

This tension between the organizational pathologies of the Reagan NSC and the strategic accomplishments of Reagan's national security policy raises a difficult question: Could such a dysfunctional government really have produced such a successful foreign policy? Peter Rodman puts it thus: "The paradox of Ronald Reagan is that he was one of the most important presidents of the modern era, who left his bold imprint on his administration and on history, yet on issues on which he was less engaged, his management of his government has to be rated among the weakest."[5] How can this paradox of a dysfunctional NSC and a successful grand strategy be reconciled?

In terms of organizational clarity and interagency coordination, in the aggregate the Reagan NSC *was* a dysfunctional mess. But part of the reason for the ostensible paradox lies in the expectation of many scholars that the NSC serve its traditional purpose of "honest broker" in coordinating the interagency process among the Departments of State, Defense, and Treasury, the Joint Chiefs of Staff, the CIA, and other important national security actors. By this standard, the Reagan NSC did largely fail. But what has been much less appreciated is that at crucial times the Reagan NSC served the purpose that Reagan himself seems to have intended for it: helping him develop the main ideas and strategic pillars of his national security policy and posture. This raises an important question for scholars: Should the Reagan NSC be evaluated by our preferred standards, by the standards of the president who oversaw it, or by the foreign policy results it achieved?

Scholars of security studies devote abundant attention and intellectual energy to the development and content of strategy. This is appropriate, but incomplete. Arguably as important is the implementation of strategy. Incandescent strategic insights and innovations by themselves make for good reading, but unless married to effective implementation are of little use in the realm of statecraft. Alongside the development of strategic ideas, a primary concern of policymakers is how to turn those principles into meaningful policy action.

Thus, another question this chapter seeks to address is, how does a president get his government to implement a strategy? This intersection of strategic ideas and implementation also helps address the aforementioned question of the paradox of the Reagan NSC, for upon taking the oath of office in 1981, President Reagan faced the same conundrum that has bedeviled American presidents before and since: How does the chief executive impose his will on his own government? The U.S. presidency occupies its own organizational paradox in that the "most powerful man in the world" often feels powerless to control his own government.

This is partly due to the constitutional design of the American founding, with the checks and balances of Congress and the judiciary constraining executive power. In the modern postwar era the permanent bureaucracy has emerged as a second impediment to presidential authority. The rise of the United States to global superpower status brought with it the creation of the national security state, comprising the various bureaus and agencies of the defense, diplomacy, and intelligence communities all responsible for wielding national power on the international stage. The "administrative state," as some critics describe it, has a set of its own interests, as career employees such as civil servants, foreign service officers, and the uniformed military each possess their own bureaucratic and policy preferences. Mindful that they will outlast the four or eight years of any particular presidency, these bureaucratic actors often resist White House initiatives that conflict with their own policy priorities, and they can vex even the most determined of presidents.

As president, Ronald Reagan knew what he wanted. He did not value smooth organization, interagency coordination, and attention to detail as much as he valued a few big ideas and a means to develop and implement those ideas. While Reagan had been developing those ideas for much of his adult life, it was only upon assuming the presidency that he had the opportunity to refine and implement them.[6] These Reaganesque principles may appear simple—such as the moral bankruptcy of communism, the fragility of the Soviet economy, and the need for the United States to recover its strength—but they were fraught with apparent internal contradictions and severe challenges in implementation. Helping reconcile these contradictions and devise effective implementation became a primary task of Reagan's NSC.

Efforts to understand the Reagan NSC soon bump up against the even more vexing challenge of understanding Reagan himself. Elusive, distant, and enigmatic, Reagan perpetually confounded even those who knew him and worked with him for decades, just as he has confounded many biographers since.[7] His sometimes conflicted policy preferences have also contributed to these challenges of understanding the fortieth president. Many of the persistent staff and cabinet feuds in the Reagan administration boiled down to frustrated officials on opposing sides each claiming to represent the "real Reagan"—and, of course, the purported position of the "real Reagan" always happened to align with each official's own preferences. Unraveling the Reagan riddle in its infinite permutations is well beyond the scope of this chapter. Rather, the more modest hope here is to help illuminate the relationships among Reagan's foreign policy vision, its implementation, and the results it engendered.

The first step is to confront the question of just what Reagan's policy was toward the Soviet Union. The ironies and internal contradictions in

Reagan's Cold War posture are well known: the nuclear abolitionist who increased the American nuclear arsenal and practiced nuclear brinksmanship; the small government conservative who presided over a massive increase in defense spending and overall deficits; the proponent of human rights and liberty who supported many repressive anticommunist dictators; and the archrival of the Soviet Union who made continual efforts to reach out to Soviet leaders.

Reagan himself acknowledged those contradictions, and self-consciously sought to develop and implement each prong simultaneously as part of his grand strategy to defeat the Soviet Union. He articulated these tensions frequently after taking office. For example, in the first year of his presidency, Reagan met with the Vatican secretary of state, Agostino Cardinal Casaroli. Over the course of the meeting Reagan described several principles of his Cold War strategy. On nuclear arms, he told Casaroli that "the only way to deter nuclear war was to arm as strongly as the opponent. However, this was not good enough. There could be miscalculations and accidents. It was necessary to reduce the number of forces on both sides." Moreover, "we could threaten the Soviets with our ability to outbuild them, which the Soviets knew we could do if we chose. Once we had established this, we could invite the Soviets to join us in lowering the level of weapons on both sides." Reagan also revealed his strategic assumptions about Soviet vulnerability and his intention to use asymmetric tools such as human rights to undermine Soviet rule. In the words of the meeting transcript, Reagan "wondered if in our emphasis on the impressive buildup of Soviet military power whether we had failed to appreciate how tenuous was the Soviet hold on the people in its empire." Specifically, Reagan told Casaroli that he "had heard reports of the fervor of the underground Church in the Soviet Union itself. He had heard stories of Bibles being distributed page by page among the believers." On another occasion, his May 1981 meeting with West German chancellor Helmut Schmidt, Reagan observed that "for us to be successful in arms control the Russians have to see that the alternative is a buildup to match theirs." He spoke of a similar dilemma concerning his economic priorities. During a March 1981 NSC meeting, he confessed that he was "afflicted with two allergies: the allergy of wanting to control government spending and the allergy of wanting to increase our national security posture."[8]

What is one to make of such statements? In positive terms, they revealed Reagan's clear sense of the strategic principles that would guide his policies toward the Soviet Union; they also demonstrated his self-awareness of the need to balance and even reconcile the tensions among his different principles. In negative terms, internal tensions can easily become incoherent contradictions that produce policy confusion. And the statements hinted at some of the truculent feuds that would beset the Reagan administration and at times paralyze policymaking as different senior officials would seize on their favored principles from Reagan while disregarding the president's contrary principles.

In short, faced with these competing principles (and competing principals), the Reagan administration could have fallen to the same fate as its despised predecessors in the administration of President Jimmy Carter. Evaluating the challenges that both administrations faced in reconciling different models of the containment doctrine, Gaddis notes that "the obvious solution would have been to devise some new strategy of containment, neither symmetrical nor asymmetrical in character, drawing upon the strengths of each approach while rejecting their weaknesses. Jimmy Carter . . . sought to do just this and failed. Ronald Reagan, Carter's successor, attempted the same feat, and succeeded beyond all expectations."[9]

Reagan did this in part by using his NSC in his own preferred way. For several reasons—likely including Reagan's aversion to personal conflict and confrontation, his limited interest in the processes of governance, and the internal tensions within his strategic priorities—his NSC functioned poorly as an honest broker and coordinator for the first six years. But for a time, especially during the very dynamic and crucial two years under William Clark, Reagan's NSC served well in developing the president's strategic doctrines and then ensuring their implementation.

The primary strategic assumption undergirding the entire Reagan Cold War policy architecture was that the United States should try to defeat the Soviet Union rather than coexist with it. This may appear mundane in the smooth hindsight of history, but at the time it was seen as intellectually radical and operationally reckless—even dangerous. In previous decades American policy had been predicated on coexisting with the Soviet Union as a permanent fixture on the geopolitical landscape; it focused on a defensive posture to contain any further Soviet expansion while maintaining global stability. President Richard Nixon and Secretary of State Henry Kissinger's détente framework, which governed American policy throughout the 1970s even as Reagan persistently criticized it, was predicated on this assumption of the Soviet Union's durability. Thus came the need to live with the Soviet Union rather than entertain reckless fantasies of defeating it. Yet in Robert Kaplan's memorable observation, "In perceiving the Soviet Union as permanent, orderly, and legitimate, Kissinger shared a failure of analysis with the rest of the foreign-policy elite—notably excepting the scholar and former head of the State Department's policy planning staff George Kennan, the Harvard historian Richard Pipes, the British scholar and journalist Bernard Levin, and the Eureka College graduate Ronald Reagan."[10] Not coincidentally, two of these four, Reagan and Pipes, would later join together at the White House in an effort to test and implement their shared proposition.

The NSC under Reagan made two distinctive contributions to the president's overall Cold War strategy. First, it deepened and expanded the principles and ideas that constituted his strategy, embodied in a series of national security directives. Second, it oversaw the development and implementation of several specific initiatives to put his strategy into practice—in human rights and democracy, economic pressure, and strategic defense. While these strategic directives and accompanying initiatives all came to fruition in the years 1982–83 under the leadership of National Security Adviser William Clark, they set the agenda for Cold War policy during the duration of Reagan's presidency. Understanding the history of this process, in turn, can illuminate several broader insights about the management and implementation of foreign policy.

Organizing the Reagan NSC

The Reagan NSC initially got off to an inauspicious start. A few weeks before the 1980 election, campaign foreign policy staff member Richard Allen had persuaded then candidate Reagan to downgrade the position of national security adviser to staff member rather than being coequal with other cabinet principals such as the Secretaries of State and Defense. Reagan agreed to this in an effort to eliminate the notorious disputes that had bedeviled previous administrations, such as those between Henry Kissinger and William P. Rogers or Zbigniew Brzezinski and Cyrus Vance. Allen claims, plausibly, that at the time he did not have designs on the national security adviser position, or else he would not have suggested that its authority be diminished. After the election, and at Reagan's request,

Allen agreed to take the job. Further organizational confusion arose when secretary of state designate Alexander Haig made an audacious power grab (the first of many) and drafted a memo for the president assigning himself all authority over foreign policy in the administration. In Allen's recounting, the "troika" of James Baker, Michael Deaver, and Edwin Meese all summarily rejected Haig's memo. They failed, however, to establish a clear alternative decisionmaking structure for the National Security Council. Instead, in Allen's words, "the formal structure of the NSC remained unsettled for an entire year, but it didn't really matter, you just worked around it."[11]

Notwithstanding Allen's retrospective assessment of it, his short sojourn as national security adviser was marked by disorganization and ineffectiveness. Allen enjoyed neither a close relationship with nor regular access to the president, and Allen's foreign policy acumen was not accompanied by the requisite management skills. Even further handicapping the NSC under Allen was the fact that the president himself regarded foreign policy as a secondary concern during his first year. Rather, in 1981 the Reagan White House wanted to prioritize its economic agenda in an effort to revive the moribund economy. Allen recalls that "no foreign policy initiative was to be undertaken until the domestic economic reform was passed," which further stalled any foreign policy initiatives.[12]

Almost as soon as Reagan took the oath of office, tensions began to percolate between the NSC and the State Department. These partly reflected the persistent institutional rivalries that are the bread and butter of bureaucratic disputes, but they also anticipated the persistent feuding that would afflict the Reagan national security team throughout the eight years of his presidency. For example, less than three weeks after Reagan's inauguration, Allen sent him a memo warning that "a word with the Secretary of State may be in order, so that he understands clearly your wishes, and so that precise guidelines are given to the Department's bureaucracy. One does not expect the bureaucracy to carry out your policy if it is not stated in precise terms." Similarly, a week later, Deputy National Security Adviser James "Bud" Nance wrote to Allen that "the President must keep his hand on the tiller in the White House. You simply will not have the capability to beat the bureaucracy and let Mr. Reagan be president unless you do."[13]

Exacerbating this institutional distrust was Secretary of State Haig himself. The archival records virtually seethe with examples of his bureaucratic feuds with the NSC and the Defense Department; almost as soon as he took office, Haig succeeded in antagonizing virtually every other senior official in the Reagan administration. Ironically, Reagan himself had taken office hoping to employ a "cabinet government" model that empowered his cabinet secretaries, including Haig. So despite being dealt a winning bureaucratic hand at the outset, Haig's rapid alienation from the rest of the administration and from the president himself was tragic and self-defeating.

Haig's marginalization and Reagan's attention shift to foreign policy in 1982 made the NSC all the more important and useful to the president. The NSC shifted into the driver's seat in Reagan's second year primarily because the president shifted his attention to national security policy. Very few of Reagan's NSC meetings during the first year focused on strategic issues such as U.S. policy toward the Soviet Union, but a large number focused on reacting to specific issues emanating from Central America and the Middle East. Indeed, it would be but a slight exaggeration to say that the Reagan administration only began to fight the Cold War in 1982.

While this shift came about partly through strategic design as the Reagan White House had deliberately focused its first year on reviving the American economy, it also came as a product of necessity. Not only was the NSC itself ineffective in the first year, but President Reagan himself did not seem engaged on foreign policy or well served by his team. For example, Reagan and Weinberger held a press conference on October 2, 1981, to announce the strategic forces modernization program. In the assessment of longtime Reagan confidant and former NSC official Thomas Reed, "the presentation was a fiasco . . . neither man seemed to know what he was talking about," while Lou Cannon criticized it as "a sorry performance."[14] Disappointments like this converged with Reagan's interest in turning his attention to foreign policy, and he decided to make some substantial changes. Allen was dismissed, and Reagan prevailed upon Clark to take the helm of the NSC. Reagan also agreed to upgrade the national security adviser role to its historic position of reporting directly to him. In Clark's words, "I was to have direct access at any time I felt it necessary . . . [Reagan] felt that things were falling behind in foreign policy, foreign affairs, defense, intelligence, and wanted me to restructure the National Security Council."[15]

Clark assumed the position on January 4, 1982, and his tenure at the NSC played an essential role in designing and implementing the president's policies toward the Soviet Union, signifying the high-water mark in the council's policy effectiveness during the Reagan administration. Clark's tenure has received mixed treatment at the hands of scholars and in the memoirs of his Reagan administration colleagues, however. For example, George Shultz repeatedly disparages Clark as "in over his head," "invariably frustrating," and continually pushing "ill formed or unwise" ideas. Robert Gates mentions some of Clark's virtues, but then concludes that he "clearly was out of his element and did not serve the President well." But not all Reagan administration memoirs are critical; Caspar Weinberger, for example, praises Clark effusively as "ideal for the role" of national security adviser and describes in particular Clark's close relationship with Reagan.[16] Among scholars, Ivo Daalder and I. M. Destler dismiss Clark as "someone with little knowledge of or appreciation for the complexities of foreign policy," whereas David Rothkopf, otherwise disparaging of the Reagan NSC, rates Clark well for restoring discipline and authority to the organization and maintaining a very close relationship with Reagan. Paul Lettow likewise highlights Clark's strong personal ties to Reagan and observes that Clark "wielded considerable influence and authority within the government."[17]

Clark's detractors usually highlighted his lack of foreign policy experience (only one year as deputy secretary of state before taking the national security adviser position) and his conservative views, which often put him at odds with more moderate cabinet members like Deaver, Baker, and Shultz. Those same views, not surprisingly, endeared Clark to other hardliners such as Weinberger, UN ambassador Jeane Kirkpatrick, and the director of central intelligence, William Casey. The other criticism sometimes voiced of Clark related to the occasional policy confusion and the continual interagency feuding that plagued the administration. Taking stock of all of this, former Reagan NSC official and ambassador to the Soviet Union Jack Matlock offers the assessment that "the problem was not [Clark] . . . as Shultz suspected (and alleges in his memoirs), but rather the system of interagency consultation and the president's own ambiguity about many of the issues."[18]

Clark's most enduring impact came through an ambitious series of national security study directives (NSSDs) and national security decision directives (NSDDs); these represented efforts to develop what Clark knew of Reagan's own views into more robust strategies and to implement those strategies through specific policies. Just in numbers of directives alone, the

Clark NSC displayed remarkable productivity. For example, in 1981 the Reagan NSC under Allen issued only fourteen NSDDs and not a single NSSD; moreover, the NSDDs issued in 1981 addressed marginal or idiosyncratic topics such as "The Future Political Status of Micronesia" and the "Space Transportation System"; few dealt with major strategic issues. This contrasts dramatically with the 104 NSDDs and 20 NSSDs issued in the years 1982–83 alone under Clark's leadership. Moreover, these directives established the entire strategic framework of the Reagan administration's Cold War policy.[19] As Admiral John Poindexter (an NSC military aide under Clark who later served as national security adviser himself) recalled, "During the first year of the administration, we never got anywhere on NSDD issues, because there was so much disagreement. . . . But as soon as Bill [Clark] came over, the NSDD system started to operate because Bill would take items to the president and he essentially drove the process."[20]

The directive process that the NSC oversaw occurred in two stages: study and action. First, based on the president's declared interests, the NSC staff would prepare and the president would sign an NSSD ordering a comprehensive analysis of the issue at hand. The NSC would then oversee the drafting of the study, with input from relevant interagency representatives. Once agreed to by the NSC principals and signed by the president, the study paper would then be translated into an NSDD laying out the specific policies that the U.S. government would implement. At its worst it could be a simultaneously acrimonious and irrelevant exercise if the participants failed to agree on the big issues or the study never produced action. But at its best it could be an exercise of profound consequence in shaping the strategy and directing the power of the United States.

Several of these directives were especially foundational for the Reagan administration's Cold War strategy. The first pair were NSSD 1-82 and NSDD-32, developing a national security strategy for the United States. Overseen by Clark and largely drafted by senior NSC staff member Tom Reed, the study produced by NSSD 1-82 attempted to apply Reagan's principles to an analysis of the global strategic environment and its implications for U.S. policy. As Clark noted at the outset of an NSC meeting chaired by Reagan on NSSD 1-82, "[this study] will guide not only budget decisions but also national security for the balance of the century." In the same meeting Reed then outlined the main features and innovations of the strategy, which he described as "more assertive and less passive than the approach of our predecessors. For example, we call for active measures to counter Soviet expansionism, to encourage the liberalizing tendencies in the Soviet bloc, and to force the Soviet Union to bear the brunt of its economic mismanagement. The bottom line is we are helping encourage the dissolution of the Soviet Empire." The final text of NSDD-32 codified these ideas and declared a strategic goal "to contain and reverse the expansion of Soviet control and military presence throughout the world." The directive candidly acknowledged the administration's belief that Soviet military advances over the previous decade had led to "the loss of U.S. strategic superiority" and gave its imprimatur to the nascent Reagan defense buildup. In the report's words, "the modernization of our strategic nuclear forces and the achievement of parity with the Soviet Union shall receive first priority in our efforts to rebuild the military capabilities of the United States."[21]

Thirty years earlier, the presidential campaign of Dwight D. Eisenhower had criticized containment and called for a rollback of the Soviet Union, only to abandon rollback and instead fall back on containment during Eisenhower's first year in office. Now the Reagan administration made rolling back Soviet expansion and "the dissolution of the Soviet Empire" official policy. This was not mere campaign bluster, but highly classified official doctrine. It reflected the conviction of Reagan himself that the Soviet Union was dangerously aggressive, yet internally fragile, and vulnerable to concerted pressure.

Clark's tenure at the NSC did not generate immediate or unanimous accolades. Almost a year after Clark's appointment, William Safire penned a widely read *New York Times* column lamenting that "a strategy vacuum exists within the divided Reagan White House" and attacked Clark as a "crony of the President" who offered "living proof that still waters can run shallow." Titling his column "The N.S.C. after Clark," Safire predicted that Clark would soon depart and "the N.S.C. will get a new head as soon as Ronald Reagan stares down into the chasm that divides his White House staff." Safire then reviewed a lengthy list of names of possible candidates to replace Clark before declaring that "the man with the inside track to head a rejuvenated N.S.C. is Tom Reed."[22] Safire's column, which appears to have been sourced to some of Clark's bureaucratic adversaries in the administration, was accurate in its depiction of a fractious White House— something that was almost a constant throughout Reagan's presidency—but missed entirely the trust that Reagan placed in Clark, as well as the effectiveness Clark was already showing in developing the administration's strategic plans.

A very different picture of Clark emerged the next year in the *New York Times Magazine*. An August 14, 1983, cover story by Steven R. Weisman titled "The Influence of William Clark" described him as "the most influential foreign-policy figure in the Reagan Administration" and "the President's chief instrument for guaranteeing that his Administration takes a hardline approach to Communism and Soviet influence in the world." Relating how Clark's close relationship to Reagan and policy sway had inspired resentments across the administration, and especially at the State Department, the article observed that Reagan and Clark "share a basic conviction that foreign-policy breakthroughs are preceded by firmness and military resolve." Perhaps harking back to the Safire column the previous year, the article revealed that Clark had grown so frustrated by incessant disputes with Chief of Staff Baker and Deputy Chief of Staff Deaver that he had offered his resignation to Reagan. The president turned it down, reaffirming his confidence in Clark, after which Clark became "increasingly willing to assert himself."

Clark's view of the national security adviser's role had also evolved in light of his experience. In the words of the article, on first taking the job "he felt he could simply serve as an honest, anonymous broker" across the interagency. But he "took nearly a year to conclude this was impractical, a friend says, and that 'Cabinet secretaries are all parochial, so you've got to decide yourself what to do.'" To those who still caviled at Clark's operating style, he cited the issuance of more than ninety NSDDs during his tenure as a demonstration of the NSC staff's effectiveness under his leadership. Weisman's article also observed that "Clark commands enormous loyalty from his [NSC] staff," especially because of his efforts to involve them in the development of policy and provide them with access to the president.[23] Many years after Reagan had left office, Clark reflected further on the tension between the roles of honest broker and policy advocate: "So you come as National Security Advisor to a policy role once you realize what the President has decided, and then you've got to try to enforce it downward" through developing the policies and directing their implementation by the relevant departments and agencies.[24]

In this respect, having determined its overall security strategy with NSDD-32, the Reagan NSC under Clark then turned to more specific strategic assessments. The president and national security adviser both believed in the need to translate the principles and ideas in NSDD-32 into a tangible plan to take on the Soviet Union. For this, the Harvard University historian-turned-NSC staff member Richard Pipes took the lead. Pipes embodied the possibility of the "policy entrepreneur" afforded by the NSC's small size, flat structure, and proximity to the power of the presidency. Pipes was a lifelong academic specializing in Russian history whose only prior government experience before joining the NSC had been as a consultant to the CIA, including serving as one of the leaders of the "Team B" exercise of 1976 wherein outsiders had examined and provided alternatives to CIA analyses on Soviet capabilities and intentions. Having supported the Reagan campaign and then been invited by Allen to join the Reagan NSC in 1981, Pipes now had an opportunity to apply his hawkish academic theories to American statecraft as regarded the Soviet Union.

Pipes had written a substantial paper for Reagan outlining the theoretical basis for the administration's anti-Soviet policies; Reagan read the paper around the time of Allen's departure in November 1981 and told Pipes it was "very sound." Pipes summarized the four main points of the paper thus:

- Communism is inherently expansionist; its expansionism will subside only when the system either collapses or, at the very least, is thoroughly reformed.

- The Stalinist model . . . confronts at present a profound crisis caused by persistent economic failures and difficulties brought about by overexpansion.

- The successors of [Leonid] Brezhnev and his Stalinist associates are likely in time to split into "conservative" and "reformist" factions, the latter of which will press for modest economic and political democratization.

- It is in the interest of the United States to promote the reformist tendencies in the USSR by a *double-pronged* strategy: *encouraging proreform forces inside the USSR* and *raising for the Soviet Union the costs of its imperialism.*

This analysis reinforced and expanded upon many of Reagan's preexisting convictions, and illustrates how the NSC staff could serve the president's foreign policy priorities even if other NSC functions like interagency coordination did not work. These ideas also laid the groundwork for NSDD-32, and for a subsequent directive crafted by Pipes, NSDD-75, on the administration's strategy to confront the Soviet Union. Pipes also helped shape Reagan's major foreign policy speeches the next year, particularly the famous Westminster address in London on June 8, 1982, where Reagan employed this diagnosis of the Soviet Union to proleptically conclude that Marxism and Leninism would be left "on the ash-heap of history."[25]

Pipes observed that upon taking over as national security adviser, "Clark was determined to assert the authority of the NSC in the making of foreign policy" and thus responded enthusiastically to Pipes's suggestion of drafting a decision directive on Soviet policy.[26] Pipes regarded the production of NSDD-75 as his "main contribution to the Reagan administration's foreign policy." The directive was only approved after a lengthy and contentious interagency review process, which further demonstrated the need for an NSC to police and promote presidential priorities among the bureaucracy. For example, according to Pipes, most Soviet policy staff at the State Department "disliked the idea of such a paper for it smacked of 'ideology,' its bugaboo. It feared the policy paper would serve to institutionalize Reagan's belligerent anticommunism, so far confined to rhetoric, and cause no end of trouble with our allies."[27] The Pentagon also had objections. An internal State Department memo reported that both civilian policy staff and uniformed military staff officers expressed concerns "about the 'offensive' rhetoric in the paper and about the promotion of internal change in the USSR as an objective of U.S. policy."[28]

This promotion of "internal change" that caused such heartburn was also NSDD-75's main strategic innovation. Clark and Pipes overcame the bureaucratic objections to the document, and Reagan presided over an NSC meeting that led to final approval and signing the directive into effect on January 17, 1983. NSDD-75 stated that "U.S. policy toward the Soviet Union will consist of three elements: external resistance to Soviet imperialism; internal pressure on the USSR to weaken the sources of Soviet imperialism; and negotiations to eliminate, on the basis of strict reciprocity, outstanding disagreements." A memo to Reagan from Clark and Pipes described the significance of the directive:

> It has always been the objective of U.S. policy toward the Soviet Union to combine containment with negotiations, but [NSDD-75] is the first in which the United States Government adds a third objective

to its relations with the Soviet Union, namely encouraging antitotalitarian changes within the USSR and refraining from assisting the Soviet regime to consolidate further its hold on the country. The basic premise behind this new approach is that it makes little sense to seek to stop Soviet imperialism externally while helping to strengthen the regime internally.[29]

NSDD-75 also codified some emerging policies already being put into place, especially regarding support for dissidents within the Soviet Union and a global effort to promote human rights and democracy.

From Strategy to Policy

The NSC under Clark also played an essential but largely unappreciated role in turning Reagan's strategy into specific policy initiatives. Three particular areas stand out: support for human rights and democracy, ballistic missile defense, and economic warfare. Each of these may have been discrete categories that seemingly had little to do with each other—for example, the Strategic Defense Initiative appears quite dissimilar to advocacy for imprisoned Siberian Pentecostals—but each was part of a comprehensive effort to bring pressure to bear on the Soviet Union at every conceivable point, including its military, its economy, its ideology, and its internal and external legitimacy.[30] It bears emphasizing that each of these areas was presidentially driven and reflected long-standing convictions held by Reagan that predated his presidency. In each case Reagan himself provided the idea and the impetus for the policy, which was then developed into particular initiatives by Clark and the NSC staff.

Reagan had long taken an interest in political and religious dissidents within the Soviet bloc. Their individual traits of courage and idealism appealed to his sentimental side and served in his mind to personalize the brutalities of communism and the stakes of the Cold War. In political and strategic terms, he also believed that the very existence of the dissidents demonstrated the fragility of the Soviet system. Only an insecure and illegitimate government, he thought, would be so oppressive to and so fearful of its own citizens merely for seeking to exercise basic rights such as freedom to emigrate, to worship, to assemble, and to speak.

Reagan also found that his diplomatic initiatives on behalf of high-profile dissidents could serve as tests of Soviet sincerity and goodwill on other issues such as arms control negotiations. Thus the president and his senior advisers devoted countless hours to advocacy both quietly and publicly on behalf of the imprisoned Jewish dissident Natan Sharanksy, or the "Siberian Seven" Pentecostals who lived in diplomatic limbo in the basement of the U.S. embassy in Moscow for several years to avoid imprisonment. As Max Kampelman—who served as a senior emissary for the Reagan administration on both human rights and nuclear arms negotiations—recalls, Reagan "informed me that he had told Soviet ambassador Anatoly Dobrynin that the release of the Pentecostals was essential if the Soviet government wanted to have better relations with the United States." Shultz's memoirs also describe the Soviet Union's decision to allow the Siberian Pentecostals to emigrate, in exchange for Reagan's agreement to keep the deal quiet, as "the first successful negotiation with the Soviets in the Reagan administration" that laid the foundation for negotiations on a much broader set of issues.[31]

Individual human rights cases were one thing, but a global effort to promote freedom and democracy was altogether another. Yet that is what Reagan had called for in his Westminster speech in June 1982 when he proclaimed,

> We must be staunch in our conviction that freedom is not the sole prerogative of a lucky few, but the inalienable and universal right of all human beings. . . . The objective I propose is quite simple to state: to foster the infrastructure of democracy, the system of a free press, unions, political parties, universities, which allows a people to choose their own way to develop their own culture, to reconcile their own differences through peaceful means.[32]

In the context of the Soviet bloc, this represented the president's effort to develop the ideas in NSDD-32 and NSDD-75 of increasing the internal pressure on the Kremlin. But Reagan's ambitions were not confined to the communist sphere; they extended also to the American sphere of influence. Specifically, authoritarian nations that were anticommunist partners of the United States would now be encouraged to respect human rights and transition to democracy as well. In Reagan's mind this was partly born of idealism, but it also stemmed from a desire for more moral legitimacy among American partner nations and a belief that, over time, democracies would be more durable and credible allies in the conflict with Soviet communism.

The question was how to turn this lofty line of speech into a meaningful policy program, and here the NSC played an indispensable role. In the ensuing months, staff member Walter Raymond, a career CIA official detailed to the NSC, oversaw Project Democracy for the White House, out of which was born the National Endowment for Democracy and several other democracy-promoting organizations. Clark and Raymond engaged in a comprehensive campaign over the next eighteen months to "carry forward with the President's challenge as stated in his Westminster speech." This effort included corralling cantankerous nongovernmental organizations, arbitrating among feuding democracy advocates, cajoling senior members of the Senate and the House of Representatives for support, and securing authorization and appropriation of funding for the new organization. At one point Clark had to press the State Department, Defense Department, USAID, and USIA to each reprogram funds from their existing budgets to seed the new democracy organization. A few months later, in March 1983, Clark wrote individual letters to Senate majority leader Howard Baker, Foreign Relations Committee chairman Charles Percy, and other leading senators and representatives, stating that "Project Democracy is of particular interest to this President. He has asked me to convey personally to you his request for your leadership in securing Congressional approval of this bipartisan, long-range initiative." The letters concluded that "the President has also discussed this proposal with several other heads of democratic governments and has received favorable responses from them."[33]

The NSC staff's persistence on Project Democracy eventually succeeded when Congress formally chartered and funded the National Endowment for Democracy in December 1983 as a bipartisan organization committed to Reagan's Westminster call for supporting democracy globally. The NSC had not played an "honest broker" role in the process, nor had Reagan or Clark wanted it to do so. Had the NSC functioned as a coordinator or neutral arbiter, the National Endowment for Democracy would have remained nothing but a forgotten passing phrase in a presidential speech. But in this case the NSC had served the president as a zealous advocate, pushing a presidential initiative to fruition against considerable resistance from both within and without government.

Just as Project Democracy represented Reagan's challenge to the political and moral legitimacy of the Soviet Union's government, his campaign of economic warfare challenged the legitimacy and the durability of the

Soviet economy. Senior NSC staff member Tom Reed described a March 1982 NSC meeting that Reagan chaired to discuss the administration's strategy toward the Soviet Union:

> The president began to ruminate about new approaches to the Soviet problem. "Why can't we just lean on the Soviets until they go broke?" The cabinet-level elders around the table discouraged such thinking. It would not work. The Soviet Union was a stable mono-lith, etc. [National Intelligence Council chairman] Henry Rowen spoke up from a back seat, along the wall, to disagree. Rowen and his outsider colleagues felt the Soviet economic system was on the verge of collapse. Reagan thanked Rowen for his support and then, with a mere nod of his head, said to me, "That's the direction we're going to go."[34]

The Reagan administration's efforts to increase economic pressure on the Soviet Union had started three months earlier when Reagan imposed strong sanctions in the wake of the Soviet-supported imposition of martial law in Poland. Most controversial among these were the American sanc-tions imposed on NATO allies working with the Soviet Union on the mas-sive Urengoi 6 pipeline project to ship Siberian natural gas to Western Europe. The pipeline sanctions caused tremendous friction with European allies, leading even steadfast American partners like British prime minister Margaret Thatcher to vehemently protest to Reagan regarding their poten-tial harm to the British economy.[35] It marked one of the most acrimonious disputes in transatlantic relations of the entire Reagan administration. Reagan's willingness to incur the wrath of his European allies—especially France, Great Britain, Italy, and West Germany—over the pipeline sanc-tions demonstrated the fervor of his commitment to economic warfare against the Soviet Union.

On the heels of the pipeline sanctions, the White House also sought to strengthen the Coordinating Committee on East-West Trade (COCOM), a consortium of Western industrial democracies formed in the early Cold War years to coordinate technology exports with the Soviet Union. By the fall of 1982, however, it appeared that the administration's economic campaign against the Soviet bloc may have been failing. European outrage remained unabated, COCOM appeared ineffective, and Reagan's own government faced serious internal division as the State Department and many senior analysts at the CIA voiced vocal dissent against the pipeline sanctions. Yet a new combination of steps in which the NSC played a key role produced a revised and adapted set of economic warfare policies. As one of his first policy initiatives, new secretary of state George Shultz helped broker an agreement with several European allies to support other economic measures against the Soviets in exchange for the administration dropping the most onerous of the pipeline sanctions. At Reagan's direction, Clark and the NSC staff produced NSDD-66, which increased economic pressure on the Soviet Union through circumscribed gas imports, restrictions on technology sales, and increased interest rates on external loans and codified the agreements of Western European nations to do the same. Mindful of what Clark regarded as State Department intransigence in applying more economic pressure on the Soviets, NSDD-66 also bolstered the NSC's role in overseeing future implementation. Alluding to such resistance from Foggy Bottom, the NSC economic policy staff wrote that "we feel this strong NSC staff role is fully justified by our experience in the 'consultations'" with the State Department on earlier drafts.[36] Separately, NSC staff member Gus Weiss worked with CIA director Casey to develop an innovative—and at the time, highly classified—countermeasures campaign. French President François Mitterrand had told Reagan that a French intelligence source inside the Soviet Union had revealed KGB efforts to steal Western industrial technology. Based on this information, Weiss led the development of a "Trojan horse" that the CIA then deliberately embedded in some Canadian pipeline software that the Soviets were pilfering. As Reed would note later, "in order to disrupt the Soviet gas supply, its hard currency earnings from the West, and the internal Russian economy, the pipeline software . . . was programmed to go haywire, after a decent interval." Sometime after the oblivious Soviets had installed the manipulated software, "the result was the most monumental non-nuclear explosion and fire ever seen from space" as Weiss's devious countermeasure achieved its purpose in destroying a major component of the Soviet energy infrastructure.[37]

Even though the administration's initial effort to make a tactical shift from a posture of voluntary compliance to coercion of allies through the draconian pipeline sanctions had failed, Reagan still largely succeeded in making economic warfare a pillar of his Cold War strategy. As Clark later reflected, "in hindsight it had a tremendous effect in slowing down the Soviet economy and bringing them ultimately to a real cash crunch."[38]

The NSC played a similar role in these same months on a very different issue: the Strategic Defense Initiative (SDI). While part of Reagan's national security strategy involved a symmetrical buildup of nuclear and conventional arms in an effort to match Soviet capabilities, the president had also long envisioned the possibility of breaking out of the mutual assured destruction (MAD) paradigm entirely by developing asymmetric capabilities to defend against nuclear ballistic missiles. In his most audacious moments he hoped that developing such a technology might render the entire arms race—and even nuclear weapons themselves—obsolete. As he wrote to one supporter of the initiative, "with regard to the idea of defense against nuclear missiles I share your view of the mutual assured destruction policy, it makes no sense whatsoever. Hopefully a defense could result in real negotiations leading to the total elimination of nuclear weapons."[39]

Such notions—of missile defense, let alone nuclear abolition—were heretical to the arms control orthodoxies that reigned at the time, and the widely held faith that MAD ensured strategic stability and preserved the peace. Reagan realized that his dream would face massive resistance on many fronts, including much of his own government. Instead Reagan developed his ideas with a small, secretive, and informal coterie of maverick scientists, conservative businessmen, and eventually a few military officers in a highly secretive process overseen by Clark and deputy national security advisers Robert "Bud" McFarlane and John Poindexter. In Lettow's summary, "Reagan prepared and announced SDI through extraordinary use of presidential power." He instructed Clark and McFarlane to work only with a very small group of NSC staff and prepare for the SDI to be announced in a March 23, 1983, Oval Office address. Shultz and Weinberger were kept in the dark until just days before Reagan's speech. When even McFarlane urged sharing advance news with others, such as congressional and allied leaders, an "adamant" Reagan overruled him and insisted on secrecy. "This was relatively uncharacteristic of Reagan and a mark of the extreme—perhaps supreme—importance he attached to his vision of missile defense," Lettow later wrote.[40] Two days after Reagan's landmark address, he signed NSDD-85, "Eliminating the Threat From Ballistic Missiles," which ordered the "development of an intensive effort to define a long term research and development program aimed at an ultimate goal of eliminating the threat posed by nuclear ballistic missiles."[41]

Just as the concept of SDI was highly unorthodox, so was the process that conceived it. As with other presidential initiatives, such as Project

Democracy, here again Reagan used his NSC staff to incubate his ideas and then to develop them into a strategic platform to be presented to the rest of the national security system for implementation. It is another example of how the president used the NSC in the way he wanted to use it—in this case, to help protect and shepherd a key initiative rather than to vet it through a traditional interagency process. This approach was not without cost, in two ways in particular. First, it exacerbated the suspicion, division, and confusion among Reagan's own national security team, as Shultz, Weinberger, lead arms control negotiator Paul Nitze, and other important actors were all reminded yet again that they were not fully trusted nor fully in step with their president. Second, it deprived the SDI concept and program itself of the rigorous vetting, quality control, and broader base of support that a more inclusive interagency process could have produced.

In this case, however, Reagan's approach worked. Using his NSC to protect and promote SDI, he achieved the outcome he desired of a strategic surprise that led directly to the end of the Cold War even as it caught almost everyone off guard, including the Soviet leadership, American allies, the strategic studies community, and even his own government. In retrospect, the consequences were profound. As John Gaddis notes,

> As grand strategy . . . SDI was a striking demonstration of killing multiple birds with a single stone: in one speech Reagan managed simultaneously to pre-empt the nuclear freeze movement, to raise the prospect of not just reducing but eliminating the need for nuclear weapons, to reassert American technological preeminence, and, by challenging the Soviet Union in an arena in which it had no hope of being able to compete, to create the strongest possible incentive for Soviet leaders to reconsider the reasons for competition in the first place.[42]

Concluding Reflections: History and Its Elusive Lessons

The conventional wisdom about the Reagan NSC as a dysfunctional mess is not so much wrong as it is woefully incomplete. The years 1982–83 marked the zenith of the Reagan NSC's policy influence and effectiveness. During this two-year window the major pillars of Reagan's first phase of his Cold War strategy were developed, unveiled, and implemented. After these years, the locus of policy influence would shift over to the State Department under Shultz, albeit with perpetual resistance from Weinberger at the Defense Department, and with a continued strong presence from Reagan himself at key junctures and on issues of priority to him. The NSC staff, meanwhile, descended into its nadir under McFarlane, Poindexter, and the catastrophes of the Iran-Contra Affair. Some of the same strengths that the NSC displayed under Clark, such as an entrepreneurial audacity in developing policy initiatives and circumventing interagency paralysis, turned into besetting liabilities under his successors and helped contribute to an environment in which rogue staff behavior ensued. It was only after the Tower Commission report and the subsequent hiring of Frank Carlucci and then Colin Powell as national security advisers that normal functionality returned to the NSC in its more traditional coordination role in the final two years of the Reagan administration. By this point the main strategic principles for the administration had long been set, and few new policy initiatives emerged. The administration's main dynamism in these final years was instead in the realm of diplomacy, as Reagan and Shultz presided over a series of historic summits with Soviet president Mikhail Gorbachev—the reformer that Pipes and Reagan had years earlier hoped would emerge from the Kremlin— and the Cold War's peaceful denouement approached.

What might all of this mean for policymakers and scholars with an interest in learning from history? Taken in the aggregate, the insights might appear elusive at first glance. Several years of perpetual cabinet secretary feuding, poor interagency coordination, and staff engaged in felonious behavior should not inspire emulation. In that sense the lessons offered by the Reagan NSC are a cautionary tale of what not to do.

Yet that is by no means the entire story. Particularly in the 1982–83 window under Clark, the Reagan NSC offers at least one model of how a determined president with a clear set of strategic principles can impose his will on his own mechanisms of government and use his NSC staff as a vehicle to develop his ideas and ensure their implementation. The possibility of drawing usable insights from the Reagan NSC should begin with the principle that a chief executive will, by design or by default, get the organizational features that he or she values and wants.

Several specific insights for a president, or for other cabinet or executive leaders, can then emerge. For one, an effective leader should develop a clear set of strategic principles and be willing to impose them on a recalcitrant bureaucracy. The first part of that insight may seem a truism (few would argue against the value of clear strategic principles), but it is often honored in the breach by leaders unsure of what they want to accomplish. It is when married with the willingness to impose these principles on an otherwise apathetic or resistant organization that enduring effectiveness emerges. The process of imposing the executive's will on a recalcitrant implementing entity may sound appealing in the abstract, but in practice it can create demoralization, distraction, dissension, and all other manner of fractious disunity. A chief executive or other principal needs to be willing to bear these costs and make the judicious calculation of whether the strategic goals are worth the cost of implementation. The second insight follows closely from the first: a president needs to find a national security adviser committed to those principles and willing to advocate for them across the national security interagency system, just as other executives and principals need to prioritize having a deputy committed to implementing the executive's priorities. Whatever his other deficiencies, Clark fulfilled this role well for Reagan.

The third insight from the Reagan NSC may stand in some tension with the first two. This is the importance for a president of populating his or her NSC staff with "policy entrepreneurs" who share the president's strategic vision and will work to develop it into specific policy initiatives (but who remain committed to obeying the law!). The same holds for other executives in choosing their midlevel officials—finding a balance of loyalty to the principal with creativity and individual initiative is elusive, yet essential. Here Reagan and Clark were well served by entrepreneurial NSC staff such as Pipes, Reed, and Raymond, who shared the president's values and vision while being sufficiently creative to develop new initiatives in the service of that vision. This leads to the fourth insight, which draws on the damage that the feuding between Haig, Weinberger, Shultz, and Clark did to Reagan's presidency: be wary of the "team of rivals" approach in assembling a cabinet team. Admittedly, sometimes with deft management and a continually engaged president the rivals model can be constructive, but just as often it can produce profound discord and dysfunction. Such was the case with the Reagan NSC.

Finally, a president should be willing to shift the emphasis of the NSC's role at different phases of a presidential administration, just as a chief executive or principal in another realm should adapt to the different phases in an organization's growth. Sometimes what is most needed is policy development and innovation (especially early in an administration or during times of crisis or geopolitical flux), and sometimes presidential priorities need to be vigorously advanced, whereas other times honest brokerage and interagency coordination should be the priority. Put another way, Clark may not have been as effective had he served as national security adviser in the 1986–88 window, when the NSC instead needed clear organization and a focus on coordination while the State Department took the lead on diplomacy. If the historical argument of this chapter is correct, Clark's effectiveness rested not just on his closeness to Reagan and his willingness to advance Reagan's strategic priorities; it was also due to when Clark served—at a time early in Reagan's presidency, when Clark's attributes were most useful. Ultimately it is the president who needs to decide not only *what* to prioritize but *when* to prioritize it.

This case study of the Reagan NSC under Clark should at the least call into question much of the prevailing conventional wisdom that the primary or even only function of the NSC should be honest brokerage and interagency coordination. At times, especially during moments of strategic opportunity, an NSC might better serve a president as an instrument of executive will, as a laboratory to experiment with creative ideas, and as a means to implement policy innovations across the departments and agencies of the national security system. This was at least the record of the Reagan NSC under William Clark, without which Reagan's Cold War strategy and policies cannot be understood.

Notes

1. Ronald Reagan, quoted in Lou Cannon, *President Reagan: The Role of a Lifetime* (New York: Simon and Schuster 1991), 160.

2. "National Security Council" can refer to either of two distinct yet overlapping entities. In one use it describes the president chairing a meeting of cabinet principals who are statutory members of the NSC, such as the secretary of state and secretary of defense. In another use it refers to the permanent White House staff under the national security adviser who serve the president on national security issues. Both meanings will be operative in this chapter.

3. William Inboden, "Statecraft, Decision Making, and the Varieties of Historical Experience: A Taxonomy," *Journal of Strategic Studies* 37, no. 2 (2014), 291–318.

4. John Lewis Gaddis, *Strategies of Containment: A Critical Appraisal of Post-War National Security Policy* (Oxford University Press, 2005), 375.

5. Peter Rodman, *Presidential Command: Power, Leadership, and the Making of Foreign Policy from Richard Nixon to George W. Bush* (New York: Knopf, 2009), 140.

6. For background on the development of Reagan's pre-presidential anti-communism, see Peter Schweizer, *Reagan's War: The Epic Story of His Forty-Year Struggle and Final Triumph over Communism* (New York: Anchor, 2002); and Kiron Skinner, Annelise Anderson, and Martin Anderson, eds., *Reagan, In His Own Hand: The Writings of Ronald Reagan That Reveal His Revolutionary Vision for America* (New York: Free Press, 2001).

7. Paramount among these confounded biographers is Edmund Morris, who despite singular access to Reagan during the presidency produced the occasionally insightful yet overall disappointing authorized biography *Dutch: A Memoir of Ronald Reagan* (London: HarperCollins, 1999).

8. Memorandum of Conversation of December 15, 1981, meeting with Cardinal Casaroli, folder MemCons—President Reagan, 12-15-81, Box 49, Executive Secretariat, NSC: Subject File; Memorandum of conversation with Helmut Schmidt, May 21, 1981, folder MemCons—President Reagan, 5-21-81, Box 48, Executive Secretariat, NSC: Subject File; Minutes of March 19, 1981, NSC meeting, folder NSC 00005 (Sinai Peacekeeping and Pakistan), Executive Secretariat, NSC: NSC Meeting File; all in Ronald Reagan Presidential Library, Simi Valley, California (hereafter, RRPL).

9. Gaddis, *Strategies of Containment*, 343.

10. Robert Kaplan, "Kissinger, Metternich, and Realism," *Atlantic Monthly* (June 1999), 73–82.

11. Richard Allen, interview, May 28, 2002, Ronald Reagan Oral History Project, Miller Center of Public Affairs Presidential Oral History Program, Charlottesville, Virginia.

12. Richard Allen, in "The Role of the National Security Advisor," Oral History Roundtable, National Security Council Project, Center for International and Security Studies at Maryland and the Brookings Institution, December 8, 1998 (www.brookings.edu/~/media/Projects/nsc/19991025.PDF), 7. The presidential travel schedule also revealed these priorities, as Reagan's only international travel in his first year was continentally confined to Canada and Mexico. In contrast, during his second year in office Reagan traveled to a total of ten countries, including global capitals London and West Berlin.

13. February 8, 1981, memorandum from Richard Allen to Ronald Reagan, China-General 02/08/1981—05/26/1981 CF 0160, folder Meese, Edwin: Files, box 2; February 9, 1981, memorandum from Carole Farrar to Richard Allen, folder Memorandums of Conversation, President Reagan (2) [January 28, 1981], Executive Secretariat, NSC: Subject File, box 13; February 17, 1981, letter from Nance to Allen, folder 8100491-8100499, box 4, in Assistant to the President for National Security Affairs, Chronological File, box 1; all in RRPL.

14. Thomas C. Reed, *At the Abyss: An Insider's History of the Cold War* (New York: Presidio, 2005), 231.

15. William P. Clark, interview, August 17, 2003, Ronald Reagan Oral History Project, Miller Center of Public Affairs Presidential Oral History Program, Charlottesville, Virginia.

16. George Shultz, *Turmoil and Triumph: My Years as Secretary of State* (New York: Scribner's, 1993), 274, 309, 317; Robert M. Gates, *From the Shadows: The Ultimate Insider's Story of Five Presidents and How They Won the Cold War* (New York: Simon and Schuster, 2006), 285; Caspar Weinberger, *Fighting for Peace: Seven Critical Years in the Pentagon* (New York: Warner Books, 1991), 359.

17. Ivo H. Daalder and I. M. Destler, *In the Shadow of the Oval Office: Profiles of the National Security Advisers and the Presidents They Served—From JFK to George W. Bush* (New York: Simon and Schuster, 2011), 146. Revealingly, Daalder and Destler's treatment of Clark ignores almost entirely his role in crafting Reagan administration policy toward the Soviet Union while focusing on policy issues such as Latin America and the Middle East that, while noteworthy, pale considerably in importance to the U.S.-Soviet relationship. David Rothkopf, *Running the World: The Inside Story of the National Security Council and the Architects of American Power* (New York: Public Affairs, 2006), 225–27. Paul Lettow, *Ronald Reagan and His Quest to Abolish Nuclear Weapons* (New York: Random House, 2005), 62–63. For a very favorable treatment of Clark that verges on hagiography, see Paul Kengor and Patricia Clark Doerner, *The Judge: William P. Clark, Ronald Reagan's Top Hand* (San Francisco: Ignatius Press, 2007).

18. Jack F. Matlock Jr., *Reagan and Gorbachev: How the Cold War Ended* (New York: Random House 2004), 62.

19. A full list and copies of presidential directives can be found at the Federation of American Scientists' Intelligence Resource Program website (www.fas.org/irp/offdocs/direct.htm).

20. John Poindexter, quoted in Rothkopf, *Running the World*, 225–26.

21. April 16, 1982, participant list and minutes of NSC meeting on NSSD 1-82, folder NSC 00045 16 Apr 1982 (31/), box 91284, Executive Secretariat, NSC: NSC Meeting Files, RRPL. The text of NSDD-32 can be found at the Federation of American Scientists' Intelligence Resource Program website (www.fas.org/irp/offdocs/nsdd/nsdd-32.pdf). For more on NSSD 1-82 and NSDD-32, see Lettow, *Ronald Reagan and His Quest to Abolish Nuclear Weapons*, 61–70. For how these ideas shaped the overall Reagan strategy, see Francis H. Marlo, *Planning Reagan's War: Conservative Strategists and America's Cold War Victory* (Washington, D.C.: Potomac Books, 2012).

22. William Safire, "The N.S.C. after Clark," *New York Times*, November 29, 1982. I am indebted to Tom Reed for bringing this article to my attention.

23. Steven R. Weisman, "The Influence of William Clark," *New York Times Magazine*, August 14, 1983. The staff's affection and loyalty has also been confirmed

to me in several conversations with former NSC staff members who worked under Clark.

24. Clark interview, August 17, 2003.

25. Richard Pipes, *Vixi: Memoirs of a Non-Belonger* (Yale University Press, 2003), 195–200, emphasis in the original; Pipes also notes that White House speechwriter Tony Dolan used the memorandum in drafting Reagan's Westminster speech. Ronald W. Reagan, Address to Members of the British Parliament, June 8, 1982 (www.heritage.org/research/reports/2002/06/reagans-westminster-speech).

26. Pipes, *Vixi*, 200.

27. Ibid., 194, 200.

28. Memorandum from Thomas Simons to Richard Burt re: participation in IG on NSSD 11-82, folder Soviet NSSD 11-82 (1 of 3), box 5, in Pipes, Richard: Files, box 5, RRPL.

29. December 16, 1982, memorandum from William Clark to Ronald Reagan, folder NSDD 75 [2 of 4] (U.S. Relations with the USSR), box 91287, Executive Secretariat, NSC: National Security Decision Directives, RRPL. See also December 16, 1982, minutes of NSC meeting on "U.S. Relations with the USSR," folder NSC 00070, 16 Dec 1982, (2/2), box 91285, Executive Secretariat, NSC: NSC Meeting Files, RRPL. The text of NSDD-75 can be found at the Federation of American Scientists' Intelligence Resource Program website (www.fas.org/irp/offdocs/nsdd/nsdd-75.pdf).

30. These four areas were not the only ones that the Reagan strategy focused on. For example, another key part of the strategy was the various anticommunist insurgent movements that the Reagan administration supported throughout the developing world at the Cold War periphery.

31. Max Kampelman, "The Ronald Reagan I Knew," *Weekly Standard*, November 24, 2003 (www.weeklystandard.com/Content/Public/Articles/000/000/003/379ldavi.asp?nopager=1); Shultz, *Turmoil and Triumph*, 171. Ample material in the Reagan Presidential Library archives also testifies to Reagan's interest in the Siberian Pentecostals and Sharansky. On the former see, for example, "Message to Brezhnev in support of Pentecostalists" (one contains Reagan message, one contains State Department report on delivery); January 14, 1982, memorandum from William Clark to Ronald Reagan; January 14, 1982, note from Richard Darman to Ronald Reagan; and January 14, 1982, memorandum from Paul Bremer to William Clark, draft text of message; all in folder USSR: General Secretary Brezhnev (8190211, 8290012), Box 38, Executive Secretariat, NSC: Head of State File: Records, 1981–1989, box 38, RRPL. On Sharansky, see October 20, 1982, letter from Ronald Reagan to Leonid Brezhnev re: Sharansky; November 1, 1982, note from Anatoly Dobrynin to George Shultz, with attached October 30, 1982, translated response from Leonid Brezhnev; and November 2, 1982, memorandum from Bremer to Clark; all in folder USSR: General Secretary Brezhnev (8290742, 8290870), box 38,

Executive Secretariat, NSC: Head of State File: Records, 1981–1989, box 38, RRPL.

32. Reagan, Address to Members of the British Parliament.

33. September 29, 1982, memorandum from Walter Raymond to William Clark, folder Project Democracy [1] OA 85, Executive Secretariat, NSC: Subject File, box 23; October 27, 1982, memorandum to Robert McFarlane from Walter Raymond and Peter Sommer re: funding for Project Democracy, folder Project Democracy [1] OA 85, Executive Secretariat, NSC: Subject File, box 23; March 25, 1983, memorandum from Walter Raymond to William Clark on Congressional support for Project Democracy, and three attached letters from William Clark to Dante Fascell, Howard Baker, and Charles Percy, folder Project Democracy [2] OA 85, Executive Secretariat, NSC: Subject File, box 24, RRPL.

34. Reed, *At the Abyss*, 227. For more of Reed's unique perspective on Reagan, see Thomas C. Reed, *The Reagan Enigma, 1964–1980* (Los Angeles: Figueroa Press, 2014).

35. For more background on the pipeline sanctions, with a focus on the CIA's perspective, see David Kennedy and Greg Treverton, *The Reagan Administration and the Soviet Pipeline Embargo*, Harvard Kennedy School of Government case study 1016.0, January 1, 1991 (www.case.hks.harvard.edu/casetitle.asp?caseNo =1016.0).

36. November 15, 1982, action memorandum to William Clark from Roger Robinson/Dennis Blair/William Martin, folder NSDD 66 [1 of 5] (East-West Economic Relations and Poland-Related Sanctions), box 91286, Executive Secretariat, NSC: National Security Decision Directives, RRPL. NSDD-66, "East-West Economic Relations and Poland-Related Sanctions" (www.reagan.utexas.edu/archives /reference/Scanned%20NSDDS/NSDD66.pdf).

37. Reed, *At the Abyss*, 267–69. Reed also notes that he and his fellow NSC staff received reports of the explosion in the USSR and worried it may have indicated a missile launch or nuclear test, until being assured by Weiss "not to worry. It took him another twenty years to tell me why." Clark presumably alluded to this clandestine program in his oral history when he described a plan to "bring that line to a halt rather surreptitiously. I'll say no more on that subject by reason of its sensitive classification." Clark interview, August 17, 2003.

38. Clark interview, August 17, 2003.

39. Ronald Reagan to Roy Innis, June 20, 1983, in Kiron Skinner, Annelise Anderson, and Martin Anderson, eds., *Reagan: A Life in Letters* (New York: Free Press, 2003), 424–25.

40. Lettow, *Ronald Reagan and His Quest to Abolish Nuclear Weapons*, 83–110; quotations are from 83, 102. There are some indications that Weinberger had earlier been unofficially apprised by Clark of the plans for SDI; if so, Weinberger kept the secret and was not involved in the process itself. For more on the background

of the SDI announcement and the NSC's central role, see Donald R. Baucom, *The Origins of SDI, 1944–1983* (University Press of Kansas, 1992), 172–96.

41. The text of NSDD-85 can be found at the Federation of American Scientists' website (www.fas.org/spp/starwars/offdocs/nsdd085.htm).

42. Gaddis, *Strategies of Containment*, 358–59.

MICHAEL COTEY MORGAN

8

The Ambiguities of Humanitarian Intervention

In the early years of the twenty-first century, newspapers around the world published thousands of stories about genocide, torture, and cruelty in nearly every corner of the globe. During some of these incidents Western governments remained on the sidelines, avoiding intervention. In other cases they responded, sometimes militarily and sometimes diplomatically. In every instance, however, policymakers and commentators debated the morality and expediency of using force to stop brutality or to free civilians from tyranny. These arguments often coalesced around the concept of humanitarian intervention, hinging on the question of whether it makes sense to take the lives of some in order to save the lives of others.[1] Intervention's staunchest critics often question whether the use of force can ever serve humanitarian purposes, and they typically see darker motives—for example, imperial expansion or the pursuit of national interests—lurking behind the cloak of self-righteousness. They assume that humanitarian intervention requires purely altruistic goals.[2] Meanwhile, advocates for intervention usually have difficulty thinking beyond the immediate emergency toward how to rebuild broken societies and political systems once military action has stopped the immediate crisis.

Looking at humanitarian intervention's deeper history can shed some light on these problems. The record of the nineteenth century demonstrates that many contemporary dilemmas have deep roots. Two cases from this period are particularly salient. Between 1807 and 1869, Britain worked doggedly to stop the Atlantic slave trade. Successive governments used the wide range of tools at their disposal—especially the Royal Navy—to achieve a goal that most Britons regarded as self-evidently just. Fueled by popular sentiment, they sustained this effort at enormous cost over many decades. In 1898, responding to blood-curdling reports of violence in Cuba, the United States launched a brief campaign to oust Spanish forces from the island. The U.S. government went to war reluctantly, but in the firm conviction that the dictates of humanity demanded action. These cases underscore the complexities and perils of humanitarian action and offer useful insights for dealing with twenty-first-century crises.

Four lessons stand out. First, diplomacy can only do so much. British and American officials tried to negotiate solutions to the humanitarian disasters they faced. They discovered, however, that asking slave traders and Spanish counterinsurgents to change their ways made little difference, even when backed by threats of force. Without decisive military action, the crises would have continued to fester. Second, successful intervention requires public support. Because British and American citizens largely backed the military efforts, they empowered their governments to make the sacrifices necessary to achieve their humanitarian goals. Had leaders in London and Washington tried to rally uninterested voters to a cause that lacked popular appeal, their efforts would sooner or later have sputtered out. Third, the line between using force for humanitarian ends and using it for other purposes is inherently blurry. Trying to draw a sharp distinction between altruism and self-interest only distorts the complexities of international politics. In addition, pursuing a national interest within the context of a broader humanitarian effort does not invalidate that effort's claims to justice. Finally, statesmen cannot escape the constraints of power politics. Nineteenth-century leaders were never offered a neat choice between capitulating to the amoral demands of the balance of power or embarking on a moral crusade. They had to treat the maintenance of international peace as a moral good that was at least on par with humanitarian principles. They had to make compromises. They did not, however, shy away from bringing national power to bear on weaker states to uphold those principles. In spite of the political, economic, and technological differences that separate the nineteenth and twenty-first centuries, these fundamental guidelines still apply.

British Power and British Honor

In 1807, Britain outlawed the slave trade. The bill that Parliament voted into law that year represented the culmination of two decades of struggle. In 1789 William Wilberforce told his fellow members of Parliament that the injustices of the slave trade were "so enormous, so dreadful, so irremediable" that the practice had to stop, no matter the consequences.[3] Many of his colleagues acknowledged the strength of his arguments and admired the force of his oratory, but he could not overcome the entrenched interests that supported slavery on economic grounds.[4] By the end of the eighteenth century, British merchants had amassed huge fortunes by transporting millions of Africans across the Atlantic Ocean into New World slavery. Slave labor fueled the economies of Britain's Caribbean colonies, whose sugar production accounted for 4 percent of British national income. The huge costs of the war against France, which erupted in 1793, made it all the more difficult to overcome the formidable economic arguments for preserving the trade.[5]

Over time, however, Wilberforce and his supporters wore down their opponents. Acting on deep moral and religious convictions, they built a broad-based campaign for abolition by educating the British public about the slave trade's graphic realities. By the first decade of the nineteenth century, popular opinion stood solidly behind them.[6] When they finally won over Parliament, observers praised the politicians in Westminster for honoring the moral convictions of the many over the financial interests of the few. "The sense of the nation has pressed abolition upon our rulers," the *Edinburgh Review* noted. "Parliament has complied with the general feeling, after the eyes of all men were opened, and their voices lifted up against the combined impolicy and injustice of the slave trade."[7] Zealous and well-organized activists had overturned the status quo.

The abolitionists scored a major victory in 1807, but they regarded it as only a first step. Their ambitions stretched beyond the frontiers of the British Empire to the ultimate goal of liberating all slaves worldwide. From this point forward abolition became a problem for foreign policy. The campaign's ultimate success required Britain to cajole or coerce the other major slave powers, especially France, Spain, Portugal, and the United States, into following its lead. Given the depth of proslavery opinion in these countries, this was no small task. The British government could have dismissed the abolitionists' program on the grounds that it would threaten national interests or national stability, but instead it launched a military campaign to suppress the transatlantic slave trade. "With surprising swiftness Britain had gone from chief poacher to chief gamekeeper," writes Adam Hochschild.[8] Even more remarkably, it kept up the fight for six decades, relenting only when its final target, Cuba, abandoned the slave trade in 1867.[9]

Over this long period the campaign enjoyed strong public support that was nurtured by the abolitionists' ongoing efforts. In 1814 alone they presented almost fourteen hundred petitions bearing 1.375 million signatures to Parliament. In a period when Britain's population numbered 13 million and Parliament usually received about nine hundred petitions annually on all subjects, politicians found it difficult to ignore the force of the antislavery movement.[10] Translating public support into political influence, the abolitionists reached another milestone in 1833 when Britain ended slavery throughout the empire. Tactical disagreements fractured the antislavery movement thereafter, but public sympathy for slavery's victims remained widespread. Through the 1830s and 1840s, as antislavery meetings in London continued to attract crowds in the thousands, successive ministries burnished their abolitionist credentials for the sake of political survival.[11]

British leaders struggled to reconcile this pressure for action with the constraints of Great Power politics. In 1814–15 the negotiations to end the Napoleonic Wars seemed to offer a prime opportunity to stamp out the slave trade as part of the overall peace settlement. Sensitive to the abolitionists' influence in Parliament, British foreign secretary Lord Castlereagh felt compelled to put forward a multilateral antislavery pact in order to insulate himself from domestic criticism.[12] Yet he also had to distinguish between Britain's immediate objectives for the postwar order and less pressing goals that could be deferred. Forging a durable peace settlement, he concluded, had to take precedence over action to stop the slave trade.[13]

The Treaty of Paris, which restored peace between France and the victorious coalition, and the Congress of Vienna, which laid the foundations for a new international system, reflected these calculations. In Paris, Castlereagh proposed that the Great Powers agree to end the slave trade. Prince Talleyrand, representing France's newly restored monarchy, refused, as did the Spanish and Portuguese ambassadors; public opinion would not tolerate abolition. Besides, they argued, Castlereagh's plan masked strategic and commercial motives.[14] Because Britain had sent more slaves to its colonies than the other powers combined, stopping the trade now would only entrench its advantage and ruin its rivals' colonial economies. "The English have always been good at making business march alongside honor," the Spanish ambassador said.[15] The vehemence of this opposition persuaded Castlereagh that pressing his case might endanger the whole peace conference. He returned to London with little more than a French promise to halt the trade in five years' time.[16]

In Vienna the other powers' commercial interests and their resentment of British naval supremacy kept a comprehensive antislavery regime out of Castlereagh's reach. He even hesitated to propose more modest measures to extend the belligerent right of maritime search—which had allowed Royal Navy crews to board foreign ships during the war and search them for contraband—into peacetime. The very suggestion could whip up anti-British sentiment and jeopardize London's more pressing postwar goals. Castlereagh could only persuade the other powers to convene a special committee to reexamine the problem of slavery. In the meantime, the Congress of Vienna issued a vague declaration condemning the trade as "repugnant to the principles of humanity and of universal morality."[17] The fine rhetoric made little difference in practice, however. When the ad hoc committee met in 1817, it reaffirmed the principles of the Vienna declaration and adjourned. The Congresses of Aix-la-Chapelle and Verona in 1818 and 1822 declined to take any further action.[18]

Britain's early military efforts to suppress the slave trade yielded similarly meager results. Even though Parliament's 1807 law applied neither to foreign powers nor foreign-flagged ships, abolitionists expected the government to use the war against Napoleon Bonaparte to advance their cause. By invoking the belligerent right of search, they argued, the Royal Navy could liberate the captives it found aboard slave ships and prosecute the crews.[19] Besides, the slave traders plied well-known routes and the Royal Navy had ample experience in intercepting maritime traffic. But the Royal Navy strained to meet the demands of fighting both France and, after 1812, the United States. It could spare only a handful of ships to patrol the West African coast.[20] Even after the war, the navy was stretched too thin to mount a major campaign, but it established a permanent squadron with a mandate to interdict slave ships—for instance, ordering H.M.S. *Inconstant* to sail for Sierra Leone and seize "such ships or vessels as may be liable thereto, under the authority of the several Acts of Parliament prohibiting the slave trade."[21]

But in its first decade of service, the squadron numbered no more than six vessels, hardly enough to patrol hundreds of miles of African coastline.[22] Although it liberated nearly 2,000 slaves a year, it could not stop the trans-Atlantic trade, which delivered 60,000 Africans into North and South American bondage annually.[23]

Even when the Royal Navy captured a slave ship, British courts could turn victory into defeat. Judges questioned the legality of searching and seizing foreign ships in international waters in peacetime. True, British law forbade the slave trade, but the naval campaign violated the sovereignty of the countries whose ships it targeted. In 1817, the High Court of Admiralty concluded that "to force the way to the liberation of Africa by trampling on the independence of other states in Europe . . . to produce an eminent good by means that are unlawful is as little consonant to private morality as to public justice."[24] The court ordered the release of the French slave ship *Le Louis*, which the *Queen Charlotte* had seized at the cost of eight British lives.[25]

Domestic courts and Great Power congresses alike had stymied the British government's plans. For those who still dreamed of stamping out the slave trade, few options remained. An indirect diplomatic strategy held out the most hope. In the absence of a comprehensive multilateral antislavery agreement, which the Great Powers had already ruled out, the British government could seek bilateral treaties granting reciprocal rights to search vessels at sea. If every slave-trading state consented to such an arrangement, the Royal Navy would gain legal authority for its interdiction efforts. One treaty at a time, Britain could build what amounted to a comprehensive international regime and, by oblique means, put teeth in the Great Powers' vague promises to outlaw the trade.[26]

The campaign's compromises and inconsistencies underscored the mercurial relationships among diplomacy, power politics, and international law. Abstract reasoning might have suggested that the slave traders' countries of origin did not affect their moral culpability and that Britain should therefore pursue all perpetrators with equal vigor, but the logic of international affairs complicated the simplest ethical calculations. Britain could not treat all slave-trading powers equally because they were not equal in power. The cases of Portugal and France illustrated the difficulty of applying the same moral principle to different states.

In 1810, as the Peninsular War left Portugal dependent on British protection, Lisbon signed a treaty with London to ban Portuguese ships from taking on slaves anywhere other than Portuguese ports. Five years later it agreed to ban the slave trade north of the equator and, in 1817, signed a reciprocal right of search treaty. An 1823 follow-on agreement authorized the seizure not just of ships that still had slaves aboard but also of those merely carrying the equipment of the trade—for instance, iron shackles and excess supplies of food and water. (In the absence of a so-called equipment clause, slave traders might try to avoid prosecution by throwing their human cargo overboard at the sight of a vessel flying the navy's Red Ensign.) Joint Anglo-Portuguese courts sat in Sierra Leone to punish the sailors aboard captured slave ships.[27] Separate Anglo-Spanish and Anglo-Dutch treaties established similar courts in Cuba and Suriname.[28]

These agreements did not mean that Portuguese officials had suddenly become abolitionists. Rather, they surrendered to London's pressure for fear of incurring its wrath. They cooperated, but only halfheartedly, and refused to ban the slave trade in the Southern Hemisphere, which included the lucrative routes to Brazil. To make matters worse, ships from countries that had already banned the trade outright flew the Portuguese colors in the hope of dodging Royal Navy inspection. Consequently, the numbers of slaves transported under Portuguese cover rose dramatically. Lisbon's stubborn defense of the trade south of the equator threatened to hollow out the diplomatic system that Britain was working painstakingly to build.[29]

By the late 1830s, after years of Portuguese foot-dragging, the British government's patience ran out. Further progress demanded firmer action, and in 1838 British foreign secretary Lord Palmerston warned the Portuguese that unless they agreed to comprehensive measures to stop the slave trade everywhere, the British would do everything necessary to stop it themselves, including seizing Portuguese ships and trying their crews for piracy. "The Portugueze [sic] would not find such a course of proceeding redound much to their honor and dignity as a nation," Palmerston noted.[30] If the British government followed through, it would commit an act of war against Portugal and invite Lisbon to retaliate in kind. Nevertheless, because Anglo-Portuguese negotiations remained at an impasse, and because the threat of military action had not induced a change of heart in Lisbon, in 1839 Palmerston introduced a bill empowering the Royal Navy to confiscate Portuguese slave ships on the high seas. Despite some qualms in the House of Lords about violating international law, Parliament approved the bill.[31] In the following year the British captured more than sixty slave ships flying Portuguese colors. "Within a short time the flag of Portugal was swept from the seas," writes Christopher Lloyd.[32]

The episode spoke volumes about Palmerston's character, but it said more about the gulf between Portuguese power and British power. The Royal Navy could easily have handled an armed conflict between the two countries. Palmerston even welcomed the possibility. "There are several of her colonies which would suit us remarkably well," he noted.[33] No matter how violent, Portugal's fury could not upset the European order. Because the country lacked the strength either to challenge London or to destabilize the international system, neither its sovereignty nor its attitude to the slave trade could impede British policy.

The French nut proved harder to crack. In the three decades after Napoleon's ouster, the French government plunged repeatedly into turmoil. The perennial threat of revolution compelled officials in Paris to calibrate their foreign policy to satisfy the demands of domestic stability. Volatile public opinion meant volatile diplomacy. The mixture of official anxiety and popular Anglophobia ensured that Paris greeted London's overtures on slavery with acute suspicion. These obstacles, combined with the well-worn economic case for the slave trade, routinely trumped arguments based on moral principles or human rights. The trade's French defenders insisted that perfidious Albion never acted altruistically. Whatever London's motives, they were sinister by definition. In the best-case scenario, the French argued, abolition would cripple France's colonial economies and erode its power. France could not afford to cede one jot of its sovereignty by bowing to British demands.[34]

These trends played out during the Bourbon Restoration and July Monarchy alike. In 1827, Charles X banned the slave trade and ordered the *Marine* to enforce the measure, cutting the volume of traffic from seventy-two French slave ships in 1825 to twenty-three in 1828. Nevertheless, official corruption and the difficulty of taking ships at sea allowed the trade to persist. Much to London's irritation, the French government refused to take stronger action or to cooperate with the Royal Navy for fear of inciting a domestic backlash.[35] The 1830 revolution, which brought Louis-Philippe to the throne, revived British hopes. Perhaps the new regime would agree to sign a reciprocal search treaty, which many in Britain concluded was the only way to stamp out French involvement in the trade for good. Now serving as ambassador in London, Talleyrand advised Louis-Philippe to declare that his government would "redouble its efforts to prevent the trade" for the sake of preserving Anglo-French relations.[36] Louis-Philippe was caught in a dilemma: turning a blind eye to the trade would antagonize London, but giving in to the British could alienate French public opinion. He concluded that he could not afford to anger the British. With a view to bolstering his regime's international legitimacy, he signed a treaty with Britain granting the reciprocal right of search in 1831. Two years later, he agreed to add an equipment clause.[37]

It was one thing to sign a treaty, but another to act, and the new measures were only as good as the overall health of Anglo-French relations. In the early years of his reign, Louis-Philippe played along with Britain. In 1840, however, the two countries nearly came to blows over the fate of the Ottoman Empire, and French Anglophobia returned to the fore. Parisian newspapers denounced the Royal Navy's alleged mistreatment of French crews, and French officers described their "profound repulsion" at allowing a foreign navy to search French ships. Foreign minister François Guizot decided, despite his abolitionist sympathies, that French interests superseded humanitarian concerns. He resolved to punish his counterpart in London, Lord Palmerston. By 1845 France had abrogated its earlier undertakings with Britain, halted all cooperation at sea, and repudiated a new Great Power convention on the right of search that Palmerston had drafted.[38]

These circumstances limited Britain's options. Palmerston resolutely opposed slavery and, as foreign secretary, worked to bring the trade to a definitive end. "As long as England remains pre-eminent on the ocean of international affairs, there are none, be they ever so unfortunate, none, be their condition ever so desperate or forlorn, who do not turn with a look of hope to the light that beams from here," he told the House of Commons in 1841. Among the Great Powers, only the British were prepared to do what was necessary to suppress the slave trade, so they had to act.[39] At the same time, however, they could not dictate to the other Great Powers, nor could they run roughshod over their desires. The greater a country's power, the more Britain had to heed its policies. So long as the French were willing to cooperate, as was the case throughout the 1830s, realpolitik and humanitarianism coincided. But in the teeth of French intransigence, diplomacy could only do so much and Britain could only push so hard without risking a war. Palmerston could threaten Lisbon with impunity, but he, like Castlereagh before him, had to handle Paris delicately. He refused to use force against France in the way he had used it against Portugal. Incurring a Great Power's wrath, even in a just cause, could have pulled the whole continent into a major conflict, and so soon after defeating Napoleon, no British government could incur that risk lightly. When the tenor of Anglo-French relations enabled cooperation to suppress the slave trade, the British took advantage of the opportunity. When relations soured, however, British activism bowed to the exigencies of power politics. International stability was more important than abolition.

Despite this setback, the fight to stop the slave trade progressed throughout the 1840s and 1850s. France refused to let Britain search its vessels, but it nevertheless sent a naval squadron to the West African coast with a mandate to seize slave ships flying the tricolor. In the late 1840s Palmerston dealt with Brazil, one of the last remaining slave-trading states, much as he had earlier dealt with Portugal. By 1850, the Royal Navy had reduced the flow of slaves into Brazil by nearly 80 percent. Due to a combination of British pressure and a rise in domestic abolitionist sentiment, Brazil stopped its slave trade entirely within a few years.[40] In the Western Hemisphere only Cuba continued to import slaves. The numbers fluctuated with the attitudes of its Spanish governors, some of whom tolerated the practice, while others worked to stamp it out. The Crimean War drew the Royal Navy's attention away from Africa, but Britain kept urging Madrid to act decisively against the Cuban trade, which depended heavily on American smugglers. After the U.S. Civil War, Cuban opinion turned heavily against slavery. By the end of the 1860s, the Spanish government had halted the import of slaves to the island. The transatlantic trade had finally come to an end.[41]

The campaign to stop the slave trade took far longer and proved far more difficult than anyone in Britain had anticipated when it began. Its financial and human costs were steep. By one estimate Britain sacrificed 2 percent of its annual income every year for more than sixty years and lost five thousand soldiers, sailors, and officials in pursuit of its goal.[42] The trade posed no threat to British security, and the ships and men deployed to interdict it might well have been better used elsewhere. Suppressing the trade did nothing to preserve international stability or advance Britain's economic interests—quite the opposite. As Benjamin Disraeli later put it, the campaign for abolition "was virtuous, but it was not wise."[43] How, then, did the country sustain the effort for so long, and why did it pay a heavy price so willingly? Part of the explanation undoubtedly lies in British domestic politics. Wilberforce and his acolytes accrued considerable influence in Westminster and enjoyed widespread public backing. No British government could easily ignore them if it wanted to maintain parliamentary support.

Public opinion ebbs and flows, however, as did the fervor of British abolitionism in the first half of the nineteenth century. If the antislavery campaign had relied solely on public opinion, it might have foundered long before the 1860s. The source of its tenacity, therefore, ran deeper than public opinion. It depended on the intertwining of abolitionism with British identity and the power of British honor. In *The Slave*, a popular musical that brought throngs to Covent Garden in 1818 and 1826, a character sings,

> *Sons of Freedom!*
> *Hear my story,*
> *Mercy well becomes the brave:*
> *Humanity is Britain's glory*
> *Pity, and protect the slave!*

The fight against slavery vindicated British power and flattered Britons by giving them reason to think that their empire served not just the country's interests but those of humanity too.[44] In making the case against slavery, Wilberforce appealed not just to Britons' senses of justice, humanity, and Christian duty but also to their sense of honor. He and his fellow campaigners created what Kwame Anthony Appiah calls an "honor world" of their own. By taking a public stand against slavery, rich industrialists could "express pride in their freshly acquired civic standing." Middle-class men and women could show themselves to be people of feeling and "paragon[s] of virtue." Members of the burgeoning working class could advance their own demands for respect and "claim their share of the nation's honor" by fighting for the rights of all working people, slave and free alike.[45] Conversely, abandoning the fight for abolition would have meant betraying an essential component of Britishness and British honor. The ultimate success of Britain's sixty-year campaign owed much to the tight connection that developed between its citizens' identity and the righteousness of the abolitionist cause.

If British honor and identity sustained the campaign over so many years, the exigencies of power politics prevented Britain from stamping out the slave trade more quickly. The country's leading statesmen felt compelled to weigh the demands of Wilberforce and his successors as they crafted policy on some of the most important questions of the age. But moral clarity had its limits. Castlereagh, Palmerston, and other British decisionmakers went to great lengths to make the abolitionist dream a reality, but they carefully calibrated the risks that Britain incurred in the process. They refused to steer the country into a Great Power war or undermine the international system, even if keeping the peace entailed tolerating the sale of hundreds of thousands of Africans into bondage. The British effort to stop the trade was therefore not a matter of putting an absolute moral good ahead of the amoral concerns of Great Power diplomacy, but of weighing the moral good of abolition against another moral good—international peace—with which it could not always be reconciled. It demonstrated that humanitarian commitments can shape international politics and that international politics, especially the desire to maintain peace among the Great Powers, can limit those commitments in turn.

American Interests and American Altruism

In February 1895, Cuban revolutionaries launched an insurrection against the Spanish government, which had ruled the island since the sixteenth century. They demanded complete independence. Although they appealed to their compatriots for support, their call to arms failed to trigger a general uprising, initially confining the insurrection to one corner of the island.[46] The government in Madrid swiftly dispatched thousands of soldiers to the island to crush the rebels. Prime Minister Antonio Cánovas declared that Spain would "sacrifice to the last *peseta* of its treasure and to the last drop of blood of the last Spaniard" to preserve "its sacred territory."[47] Nonetheless, the insurrection continued to smolder. In response, Spanish commanders resorted to increasingly draconian measures that targeted insurgents and civilians alike. These, too, failed to pacify the island.

As the war dragged on and the death toll rose, the conflict drew the attention of politicians and journalists in the United States. By early 1898, American newspapers were calling for military action to stop what they regarded as unjustified Spanish violence against ordinary Cubans. President William McKinley tried to find a diplomatic solution to the crisis. He failed. In April, after the publication of an intercepted Spanish letter that mocked McKinley, and following the sinking of the battleship U.S.S. *Maine* in

Havana harbor, the president bowed to congressional calls for action. He sent an expeditionary force to Cuba with orders to evict the Spanish, but the campaign against Spain stretched far beyond the island's shores. American forces soon routed Madrid's forces not just on the island but also in Puerto Rico and the Philippines. Washington's victory marked its arrival as a major international player. The humanitarian and hardheaded motives that led it into the conflict reinforced each other and cannot be disentangled.

The brutality of Spain's campaign against the rebels reflected its determination to stop the uprising and its desperate search for a military solution to the crisis. Its counterinsurgency strategy was developed by General Valeriano Weyler y Nicolau, who arrived in Cuba in 1896 after a year of inconclusive and largely defensive efforts under his predecessor. With a mandate to restore order, Weyler worked ruthlessly to cut off the rebels' civilian support and strangle their supplies of food and ammunition. He built a network of trenches and watchtowers in order to block the movement of insurgent reinforcements.[48] In the countryside he forcibly relocated civilians from their farms to fortified towns, where the authorities could monitor them and prevent them from aiding the rebels. In a matter of months the reconcentration program destroyed the rural economy and displaced hundreds of thousands of Cubans. They had lost the means to feed themselves and now lacked access to adequate sanitation and shelter. They quickly began to starve and succumb to disease, dying by the thousands. Within a year, as John Offner puts it, "the concentration centers had become death camps." Weyler had earned his nickname: "the Butcher."[49]

In waging this counterinsurgency campaign the Spanish government hoped to repeat the success it had enjoyed against an earlier Cuban uprising. During the Ten Years' War, which broke out in 1868, Cubans similarly demanded independence, but the rebel leaders failed to attract substantial international support or coordinate the efforts of their sympathizers abroad with those of the forces fighting the Spanish on the island.[50] Slowly but inexorably the Spanish prevailed. When the hostilities finally ended, they tried to purchase Cuban loyalty with a promise to grant the island autonomy at some future date. Despite a series of postwar reforms, that future date never came, provoking a series of smaller-scale rebellions through the 1880s and early 1890s that quickly fizzled out. When fighting began afresh in 1895, many Cubans regarded it as a renewal of hostilities after an extended truce rather than an entirely new conflict. In Madrid the authorities assumed that they would eventually stamp out this latest eruption of violence too.[51]

The rebels' goals had not changed since the Ten Years' War, but Cuba's place in the world had. During the 1880s and 1890s the flow of American capital into Cuba rose dramatically. By the midpoint of the latter decade, American investments in cattle ranching, mining, tobacco and, above all, sugar operations on the island reached $50 million. Bilateral trade amounted to $100 million annually.[52] Cuba's reliance on the United States rose alongside America's economic stake. The abolition of slavery had raised the cost of sugar cane cultivation in Cuba at the same time as sugar beet production in Europe was expanding. The combination of these changes left Cuba's sugar industry particularly dependent on American capital and export markets. When Washington tightened its tariffs in 1895, therefore, Cuba's sugar exports to the United States fell by more than 70 percent. The downturn exacerbated the already poor economic situation on the island and revived popular calls for independence. In the 1870s Americans had paid little attention to the uprising against Spain, but twenty years later their substantial economic interests meant they could not ignore the events across the Straits of Florida.[53]

Reports of extraordinary violence in Cuba also attracted American journalists. Front-page coverage of the reconcentration camps in mass-circulation newspapers outraged government officials and private citizens alike. Some of these stories turned out to be false or exaggerated, especially in the tabloid press, but most of the information that the American public received about the conflict accurately captured the gravity of the situation in Cuba. The *New York Journal* published reports with such headlines as "Spaniards' Inhuman Cruelty," "Heartrending Narrative of a Butchery by Brutish Troops," and "Fiendish Cruelty in Cuba."[54] "Even if the American public had received nothing but dry, unemotional, and unembellished accounts, had they only seen the images of women lying dead in the streets and of children with distended abdomens and emaciated limbs," Robert Kagan writes, "it is unlikely they would have been less outraged than they were by the stories in the yellow press." Individual Americans traveling on the island corroborated the newspapers' reports that, by early 1898, hundreds of thousands of civilians had already perished.[55]

Compared to their comrades from the 1870s, the Cuban fighters of the 1890s benefited from broad popular support in the United States. Many

American citizens sympathized with their cause because of its rough parallels with the thirteen colonies' struggle against Britain a century earlier. Like the Americans of the 1770s and 1780s, the underdog Cubans were trying to free themselves from imperial tyranny.[56] Because the United States owed its very existence to "the right of insurrection," the rebels deserved Washington's support, argued Daniel E. Sickles, the former American representative in Madrid.[57] Alternatively, some pro-Cuban politicians from the American South likened Spain's despotic treatment of the island to the Union's policy for Reconstruction after 1865.[58]

In many ways this popular sympathy was the fruit of a carefully crafted strategy. The most important figures in the Cuban independence movement lived in New York City, where they worked to rally the support of the thousands of Cuban émigrés in the United States and beyond. These activists raised money for the rebels, published pamphlets, gave speeches, and lobbied members of Congress.[59] The American public responded enthusiastically. Echoing events in Britain a hundred years earlier, petitions from every corner of the United States poured into Washington, urging the federal government to endorse Cuban independence. Members of Congress responded with bipartisan resolutions demanding that the executive branch press Spain to grant the Cubans their freedom.[60] As the war dragged on, however, calls for diplomatic support turned into demands for military action. In early 1898, *Harper's Weekly* reported that "the awful deeds of Spanish soldiers and officers; the horrible tales of cruelty that have been told and verified; the miseries that resulted from Weyler's order of concentration; [and] the starvation and the resulting deaths to which trusted Americans have borne testimony" had produced a "wild frenzy of desire" in the United States to evict Spain from the island by force.[61]

Neither President Grover Cleveland, who occupied the White House when the insurrection began, nor William McKinley, who succeeded him in 1897, shared their compatriots' zeal for Cuban independence. During his two presidential terms, Cleveland regarded the prospect of American intervention abroad—whether in Hawaii or Venezuela—with skepticism. In line with the Democrats' general commitment to minimizing the power of the federal government, he strove to keep the United States from embroiling itself in foreign crises. In 1895, when Cleveland received word of the rebellion in Cuba, he refused to look into the matter lest anyone conclude that he cared about the outcome. Besides, he reasoned, the ragtag Cuban rebels were incapable of governing the island, and supporting their hopeless cause against Spain might damage the American economy, which was still recovering from an economic slump. Many businessmen, including some with investments in Cuba, feared a conflict with Spain for similar reasons.[62] When William McKinley took office he shared Cleveland's assessment. McKinley, whose main interests lay in domestic policy, regarded jingoes and imperialists as fools. He appointed moderates like John Sherman, the new secretary of state, to oversee foreign affairs.[63] "It has been the policy of the United States since the foundation of the Government to cultivate relations of peace and amity with all the nations of the world, and this accords with my conception of our duty now," McKinley said in his inaugural address. "Wars should never be entered upon until every agency of peace has failed; peace is preferable to war in almost every contingency."[64] He felt genuine concern for the island's suffering civilians but saw no reason to rush to their aid. The leading Republicans in Congress agreed.[65]

As the fighting continued, however, and as American sympathies for the rebels grew and the evidence of Spain's horrific conduct mounted, McKinley's views shifted. Sensitive as ever to the currents of domestic opinion, he concluded that the United States had to try—by diplomatic means, at least—to restore peace. At his direction, Sherman drafted a diplomatic note accusing Madrid of violating the most fundamental humanitarian principles.[66] Weyler's conduct of the war amounted to "a policy of devastation and interference with the most elementary rights of human existence," it said. Through the "deliberate infliction of suffering on innocent noncombatants" and the "resort to instrumentalities condemned by the voice of humane civilization," Spain was consigning Cuban civilians to the "doom of privation and distress."[67] Later, as the violence in Cuba continued unabated, Sherman insisted that, for the sake of "humanity and justice," the United States could not ignore the counterinsurgency campaign's human cost: "It is no merely sentimental or interested consideration which moves this Government to raise its voice in earnest remonstrance against so harsh and so futile a policy as this, which, to the inevitable hardships and woes of war, superadds extermination by starvation."[68] These efforts yielded some results. Toward the end of 1897, the Spanish government allowed the American National Red Cross onto the island to distribute relief supplies.[69] More significantly, it also ordered an end to the policy of reconcentration and offered to grant Cuba autonomy. Perhaps officials in Madrid wagered that these concessions might reduce the pressure from Washington or sap the rebels' popular support.[70]

None of these changes brought a negotiated peace any closer. Sentiment on both sides of the conflict had hardened to the point that the prospect of autonomy satisfied neither the Cuban rebels nor the Spanish officer corps.[71] As hopes for a diplomatic solution faded, calls for intervention rose in the United States. Some businessmen worried that the longer the war dragged on, the more it would damage their assets. Besides, if the revolution actually succeeded, who could predict whether an independent Cuban government would respect American businesses or property on the island?[72] Washington's representative in Madrid, General Stewart L. Woodford, told his British counterpart that American assets in Cuba "were being destroyed alike by Spanish authorities and by the insurgents . . . and that all investments and loans of American capital are thus practically unproductive and in great danger of being finally and completely lost," to say nothing of the "irreparable injury inflicted upon our commercial interests."[73] By the end of 1897 McKinley began to doubt whether he could keep the United States out of the war, though he did not relish the prospect of intervention.[74]

The events of early 1898 brought matters to a head. In February, the *New York Journal* published an intercepted letter from Madrid's ambassador in Washington that insulted McKinley's conduct of diplomacy. If that were not bad enough, it also suggested that Spain's promises of reform in Cuba were insincere. A week later, the *Maine* went to the bottom of Havana harbor. Although McKinley suspected the explosion that sank the ship had been an accident, he ordered the government to prepare for war, a move that Congress enthusiastically endorsed.[75] He considered a few last-minute ploys to avoid a conflict, including an offer to purchase Cuba from Spain, but exasperated members of Congress convinced him that he had to act decisively in order to avoid embarrassing his party and undermining his own authority. At his request, Congress declared war on Spain in April 1898, and the first American soldiers landed in Cuba two months later.[76] In August, after a string of decisive American victories on land and at sea, the two countries signed an armistice.[77]

Historians have found it easier to explain why the Spanish lost the war than why the United States intervened in the first place. Over the last century, some have argued that Washington acted for cynical reasons, including strategic advantage and economic gain.[78] It is true that, in making the case for war, McKinley insisted that the United States had a duty to protect American citizens, property, and commercial interests in Cuba. It also had to stabilize the island in order to eliminate the "constant menace" that the insurgency posed to regional stability.[79] Yet the war's contemporary advocates insisted that the United States took up arms for the sake of lofty principles. "We intervene . . . not for conquest, not for aggrandizement, not because of the Monroe doctrine; we intervene for humanity's sake," said Senator John Spooner.[80] William James wrote that the motive for the war was "perfectly honest humanitarianism, and an absolutely disinterested desire on the part of our people to set the Cubans free."[81] In his April 1898 request for a declaration of war, McKinley argued that the United States had to act "in the cause of humanity, and to put an end to the barbarities, bloodshed, starvation, and horrible miseries now existing there."[82] He presented himself as a Christian warrior, urging Americans to do their God-given duty.[83]

One-sided explanations of American motives—idealistic or otherwise—ignore the possibility that the United States acted out of both self-interest and humanitarian concern. Though it is difficult to establish precisely which factor weighed most heavily in McKinley's calculations, his various motives reinforced each other to the point that drawing sharp distinctions between them obscures more than it illuminates. It is fair to say, however, that had Spain not adopted such cruel tactics in fighting the insurgency, and had it not subjected Cuban civilians to such violence, the war would not have attracted nearly the same attention in the United States. The rebels would have found it harder to win Americans' sympathy. Members of Congress would not have lobbied the president so strenuously to intervene. McKinley himself might have found it easier to follow his initial instincts and remain above the fray. The crimes that the Spanish perpetrated in Cuba made it impossible for Americans to look away, even if it cannot on its own entirely explain American intervention. In every conflict, including the Spanish-American War, belligerents' motives are always complicated. But the complexity of the United States' reasons for going to war cannot call into question the genuinely humanitarian impulses that shaped how American politicians and average citizens alike thought about events in Cuba.

The public outcry over Spanish brutality forced officials to weigh the humanitarian costs of inaction. The rebels' supporters in the United States did everything possible to sway citizens' views, but even without their efforts Americans could have reached their own conclusions about what basic ethical considerations, informed by religious faith, required.[84] As in the case of Britain's effort to suppress the slave trade, popular support for military action went deeper than the passing currents of public opinion. As one newspaper put it, the war against Spain was based on "the preservation of honor."[85] Reflecting on a speech that vividly detailed the suffering of Cuban civilians, Senator Francis Warren felt "a raising of the blood and temper as well as of shame that we, a civilized people, an enlightened nation, born in a revolt against tyranny" could stand idly by and refuse to take action.[86] By this logic, staying out of the conflict would both dishonor the country and contradict the core principles of its national identity. The force of these sentiments meant that, once the war began, American decisionmakers could count on strong domestic support for the cause, which in turn made it possible to bring the necessary force to bear against the country's newfound enemy and force the Spanish to concede defeat.

Pragmatism and Humanitarianism

Many features of nineteenth-century diplomacy—the British Empire, the steamship, and the telegraph, to name a few—have passed into oblivion. Old assumptions about the proper role of the state and the hallmarks of advanced society became outmoded decades ago. The pace of communications, travel, and commerce today would be unimaginable to Castlereagh, Palmerston, and McKinley, and international organizations such as the United Nations have transformed the conduct of diplomacy and the regulation of global affairs since their day. Nonetheless, it is dangerous to assume that these nineteenth-century leaders have nothing to teach us, or that the problems of their era have lost their relevance. Even if our understanding of ethical conduct in international affairs and the requirements of civilization have evolved, the dilemmas that the British faced in dealing with the slave trade and the considerations that Americans weighed in responding to the war in Cuba persist.

In both cases, British and American leaders tried diplomacy first. But perfect diplomatic solutions to the most serious international challenges—including humanitarian crises—are elusive. Castlereagh's bid for a multilateral antislavery convention failed, as did McKinley's overtures to Madrid.

The politicians in London and Washington recognized that diplomacy could not solve every problem. They did not rush into using force against their adversaries, but neither did they shy away from it once it became clear that no other options were available.

When the leaders did give the orders for military action, they enjoyed strong public support. Indeed, in both cases they felt that the ardor of popular opinion compelled them to act. If they ignored those who were suffering overseas, they ran the risk of damaging their own political standing. These examples suggest that, in dealing with humanitarian crises, democratic politicians should contemplate using force only if a majority of their fellow citizens would endorse it. One cannot easily imagine that the British would have spent sixty years pursuing slave traders—at considerable cost in lives and money—had the British public not regarded the effort as a fundamental matter of national honor and identity. The same can be said for McKinley and the war against Spain. Similarly, if voters oppose sending troops to a distant country for the sake of human rights, politicians cannot easily conjure the public enthusiasm necessary for such a mission. In humanitarian crises, public opinion can cajole otherwise reluctant politicians to act, and it can sustain such action over long periods of time, especially when honor and identity are at stake. These are great virtues. But voters' commitment to a cause can evaporate even more quickly than it appeared, especially once the immediate emergency has passed. Once the transatlantic slave trade ended, the British electorate took little interest in the fates of those whom they had freed from bondage. Once the Spanish had been pushed out of Cuba, Americans showed little concern for the living standards of the island's citizens or, as the Platt Amendment suggested, their claims to self-determination. Because democratic public opinion is so powerful, politicians must heed it. But because it is so fickle, they must not rely on it.

They must also resist the temptation to draw sharp distinctions between altruistic and pragmatic arguments for intervention, because the two often reinforce each other. In an era when American influence spans the globe, it is difficult to imagine a case in which going to war against a sovereign state to protect human rights could not be construed as advancing Washington's interests or expanding its power. Gary Bass asserts that humanitarianism "is not the same thing as imperialism, even when it uses military force," but in practice the difference between the two is not always clear-cut.[87] In

Cuba in 1898, Washington's motives were simultaneously altruistic and pragmatic. The U.S. government used the tools of imperialism out of genuine humanitarian concern, but its conduct was also opportunistic and served American purposes. By extension, policymakers should not confuse complexity with amorality. "Humanitarian action is not unmasked if it is shown to be the instrument of imperial power," writes Michael Ignatieff. "Motives are not discredited just because they are shown to be mixed."[88] In making a public case for action to stop a genocide or to help an insurgency, leaders are hard-pressed to explain the many reasons—humanitarian and otherwise—for intervening. Rhetorical simplicity is usually a virtue in democratic politics, but the seduction of simple explanations should not prevent leaders from acknowledging the complexity of foreign policymaking. Because cynics criticize the United States for cloaking discreditable objectives in the rhetoric of liberty, it is dangerous for a president to pretend that any decision to use force is easy or an unambiguous matter of right against wrong. Reductionist explanations risk discrediting the genuine humanitarian impulses that inform such a decision.

These nineteenth-century cases also attest that no statesman is immune to the pressures—or should ignore the advantages—of power politics. In 1898, growing U.S. economic and military might gave the government every reason to believe that it could easily defeat Spain, then in its imperial twilight. Washington did not have to worry about the reactions of the other Great Powers in the region, and fighting the Spanish was unlikely to provoke a major conflict. But the benefits of preponderant power engendered countervailing dangers. For one thing, simply having the means to act can spawn demands for action. Some American advocates for war insisted that because the United States had the wherewithal to stop the suffering of Cuban civilians it necessarily had a duty to do so. The country's justified self-confidence made McKinley's calculations about intervention much simpler than they would have been had American and Spanish power been more evenly matched or had the international system been less stable. But statesmen must not confuse the ability to intervene with a reason to intervene. Since the end of the Cold War, the huge gulf between the military power of the United States and that of its nearest competitors has underscored this point. When humanitarian crises break out, the spotlight naturally falls on Washington because, in most cases, only the United States has the capacity to act. In many of these cases the arguments for intervention prove hard to ignore. But as Disraeli observed, wisdom and virtue are not the same thing.

The British campaign against the slave trade illustrated the compromises that power politics can impose. Competing interests pulled the country's leaders in opposite directions. On the one hand, the imperative of rebuilding the international system in the wake of the Napoleonic Wars required Britain to collaborate with the other Great Powers and respect their interests. Castlereagh deemed it more important to persuade the French to accept the postwar settlement than to push abolition forward at any cost. Palmerston feared the consequences of alienating a volatile French government against the backdrop of international instability, even if placating Paris meant delaying universal abolition. On the other hand, no one in the British government disputed the moral case against slavery or doubted that Britain would have to use force to enforce the ban on the trade, nor could any official in London ignore the power of the abolitionist lobby. But neither Castlereagh nor Palmerston regarded British policy as a matter of choosing the moral good of abolition or bowing to the amoral logic of the state system. Preserving that system and abolishing slavery were both moral goods.

The most pressing question, then, is how to decide which of these competing goods to pursue. The norm of the Responsibility to Protect, which diplomats and scholars began to elaborate in the first decade of the twenty-first century, starts from the premise that, in certain situations, the international community has a duty to defend those who cannot defend themselves, and sets out a series of prerequisites that must be satisfied before an intervention can be considered legitimate. At best this doctrine offers an ethical, but not a practical, guide for statecraft. The most significant constraints on humanitarian intervention usually spring from the limits of power politics rather than the parameters of the Responsibility to Protect. In Rwanda, Yugoslavia, and Syria building a moral case for action proved far easier than negotiating the diplomatic pitfalls that stood in the way of intervention. Only a fool would rush in to help the suffering at the cost of setting off a Great Power war, especially in the nuclear age. In light of the devastation that the Napoleonic Wars inflicted on Europe, one can easily understand why the British valued international stability ahead of the ethical imperative of suppressing the slave trade. They deserve particular credit for finding a way, albeit over a period of decades, to achieve both goals. As was the case in the nineteenth century, the core challenge of humanitarian intervention today is to juggle sometimes irreconcilable moral goods. The best way to live with this tension is to acknowledge that messy solutions are sometimes the only ones possible, that the practice of statecraft can never be perfect, and that the task of defending the rights of others will never be complete.

Notes

1. In one representative definition, humanitarian intervention encompasses "the threat or use of force across state borders by a state (or group of states) aimed at preventing or ending widespread and grave violations of the fundamental human rights of individuals other than its own citizens, without the permission of the state within whose territory force is applied." J. L. Holzgrefe, "The Humanitarian Intervention Debate," in *Humanitarian Intervention: Ethical, Legal, and Political Dilemmas*, edited by J. L. Holzgrefe and Robert O. Keohane (Cambridge University Press, 2003), 18.

2. See, for example, Noam Chomsky, "Drain the Swamp and There Will Be No More Mosquitoes," and Arundhati Roy, "Wars Are Never Fought for Altruistic Reasons," in *The Iraq War Reader: History, Documents, Opinions*, edited by Micah L. Sifry and Christopher Cerf (New York: Touchstone, 2003), 301–04 and 339–44, respectively.

3. William Wilberforce, *The speech of William Wilberforce, Esq., representative for the county of York, on Wednesday the 13th of May, 1789, on the question of the abolition of the slave trade* (London: Logographic Press, 1789), 18.

4. Adam Hochschild, *Bury the Chains: Prophets and Rebels in the Fight to Free an Empire's Slaves* (New York: Houghton Mifflin, 2005), 160–62.

5. Chaim D. Kaufmann and Robert A. Pape, "Explaining Costly International Moral Action: Britain's Sixty-Year Campaign against the Atlantic Slave Trade," *International Organization* 53, no. 4 (1999), 631.

6. Paul Michael Kielstra, *The Politics of Slave Trade Suppression in Britain and France, 1814–48* (New York: St. Martin's, 2000), 7–9.

7. "A Letter on the Abolition of the Slave Trade, addressed to the Freeholders and other Inhabitants of Yorkshire. By W. Wilberforce, Esq." *Edinburgh Review* 10 (1807), 206.

8. Hochschild, *Bury the Chains*, 310.

9. David Murray, *Odious Commerce: Britain, Spain and the Abolition of the Cuban Slave Trade* (Cambridge University Press, 1980), 324–26; W. E. F. Ward, *The Royal Navy and the Slavers: The Suppression of the Atlantic Slave Trade* (New York: Schocken, 1970), 224–27.

10. Kielstra, *The Politics of Slave Trade Suppression*, 30.

11. Ibid., 185–86, 196–97, 209–10.

12. C. K. Webster, *The Foreign Policy of Castlereagh 1815–1822: Britain and the European Alliance* (London: Bell, 1925), 21–22; Adam Zamoyski, *Rites of Peace: The Fall of Napoleon and the Congress of Vienna* (London: HarperCollins, 2007), 411.

13. Maeve Ryan, "The Price of Legitimacy in Humanitarian Intervention: Britain, the Right of Search, and the Abolition of the West African Slave Trade, 1807–1867," in *Humanitarian Intervention: A History,* edited by Brendan Simms and D. J. B. Trim (Cambridge University Press, 2011), 235–36.

14. Brian E. Vick, *The Congress of Vienna: Power and Politics after Napoleon* (Harvard University Press, 2014), 196–98.

15. Zamoyski, *Rites of Peace,* 200.

16. Ibid.; Jenny S. Martinez, *The Slave Trade and the Origins of International Human Rights Law* (Oxford University Press, 2012), 28–30.

17. "Déclaration des 8 Cours, relative à l'Abolition Universelle de la Traite des Nègres," February 8, 1815, in *British Foreign and State Papers, 1815–1816* (London: Ridgway, 1838), 971.

18. Ryan, "The Price of Legitimacy," 236–37; John Bew, *Castlereagh: Enlightenment, War, and Tyranny* (London: Quercus, 2011), 388–89, 393–94, 451–52; and Vick, *The Congress of Vienna,* 201–12.

19. Ward, *The Royal Navy and the Slavers,* 38–39; and Ryan, "The Price of Legitimacy," 232–35.

20. Ward, *The Royal Navy and the Slavers,* 43.

21. Ibid., 43–44.

22. Christopher Lloyd, *The Navy and the Slave Trade: The Suppression of the African Slave Trade in the Nineteenth Century* (London: Cass, 1968), 280–81; and Ward, *The Royal Navy and the Slavers,* 45.

23. Lloyd, *The Navy and the Slave Trade,* 275; Ward, *The Royal Navy and the Slavers,* 59.

24. High Court of Admiralty, quoted in Leslie Bethell, *The Abolition of the Brazilian Slave Trade: Britain, Brazil and the Slave Trade Question 1807–1869* (Cambridge University Press, 1970), 16.

25. Kielstra, *The Politics of Slave Trade Suppression,* 70–71; Martinez, *The Slave Trade,* 27–28.

26. Bethell, *The Abolition of the Brazilian Slave Trade,* 16–19.

27. Ward, *The Royal Navy and the Slavers,* 77–79; and Ryan, "The Price of Legitimacy," 242.

28. Martinez, *The Slave Trade,* 67–98.

29. Bethell, *The Abolition of the Brazilian Slave Trade,* 96–97.

30. Lord Palmerston, quoted in David Brown, *Palmerston: A Biography* (Yale University Press, 2010), 239.

31. Kielstra, *The Politics of Slave Trade Suppression*, 191–92.

32. Lloyd, *The Navy and the Slave Trade*, 47–48.

33. Bethell, *The Abolition of the Brazilian Slave Trade*, 155.

34. Kielstra, *The Politics of Slave Trade Suppression*, 37–38.

35. Ibid., 138–48.

36. Prince Talleyrand, quoted in Kielstra, *The Politics of Slave Trade Suppression*, 150.

37. Kielstra, *The Politics of Slave Trade Suppression*, 149–58; Lloyd, *The Navy and the Slave Trade*, 48–49.

38. Kielstra, *The Politics of Slave Trade Suppression*, 207–60.

39. Lord Palmerston, quoted in Brown, *Palmerston*, 237–38.

40. Bethell, *The Abolition of the Brazilian Slave Trade*, 327–63; and Ward, *The Royal Navy and the Slavers*, 164–66.

41. Murray, *Odious Commerce*, 323–24; Lloyd, *The Navy and the Slave Trade*, 163–76; Ward, *The Royal Navy and the Slavers*, 224–27.

42. Kaufmann and Pape, "Explaining Costly International Moral Action," 631.

43. Benjamin Disraeli, quoted in Kwame Anthony Appiah, *The Honor Code: How Moral Revolutions Happen* (New York: Norton, 2010), 107.

44. Kielstra, *The Politics of Slave Trade Suppression*, 2.

45. Appiah, *The Honor Code*, 111–13, 126–33.

46. David F. Trask, *The War with Spain in 1898* (New York: Macmillan, 1981), 1–3.

47. Antonio Cánovas, quoted in Trask, *The War with Spain*, 6–7, emphasis in the original.

48. John L. Offner, *An Unwanted War: The Diplomacy of the United States and Spain over Cuba, 1895–1898* (University of North Carolina Press, 1992), 12.

49. Offner, *An Unwanted War*, 13.

50. Trask, *The War with Spain*, 2.

51. Robert Kagan, *Dangerous Nation: America's Place in the World from Its Earliest Days to the Dawn of the Twentieth Century* (New York: Knopf, 2006), 375.

52. Offner, *An Unwanted War*, 15.

53. Ibid., 1–3.

54. Evan Thomas, *The War Lovers: Roosevelt, Lodge, Hearst, and the Rush to Empire, 1898* (New York: Little, Brown, 2010), 105.

55. Kagan, *Dangerous Nation*, 390–91.

56. Louis A. Pérez Jr., *The War of 1898: The United States and Cuba in History and Historiography* (University of North Carolina Press, 1998), 73–74.

57. Daniel E. Sickles, quoted in Kagan, *Dangerous Nation*, 379.

58. Offner, *An Unwanted War*, 43.

59. George W. Auxier, "The Propaganda Activities of the Cuban Junta in Precipitating the Spanish-American War, 1895–1898," *Hispanic American Historical Review* 19, no. 3 (1939), 286–305; Offner, *An Unwanted War*, 5–6, 62–63, 73–74, 83.

60. Kagan, *Dangerous Nation*, 379–80.

61. "The War Spirit of the People," *Harper's Weekly*, April 16, 1898, 362–63.

62. Kagan, *Dangerous Nation*, 357–74, 377–78, 380.

63. Ibid., 386–87.

64. William McKinley, First Inaugural Address, March 4, 1897 (http://avalon .law.yale.edu/19th_century/mckin1.asp).

65. Kagan, *Dangerous Nation*, 389.

66. Offner, *An Unwanted War*, 47–48.

67. John Sherman to Enrique Dupuy de Lôme, June 26, 1897, in *Foreign Relations of the United States* [hereafter *FRUS*] *1897* (Government Printing Office, 1898), 507–08.

68. John Sherman to Enrique Dupuy de Lôme, November 6, 1897, in *FRUS 1897*, 509–10.

69. Keith Pomakoy, *Helping Humanity: American Policy and Genocide Rescue* (Lanham, Md.: Lexington, 2011), 44–48.

70. Offner, *An Unwanted War*, 68–71.

71. Kagan, *Dangerous Nation*, 396–97.

72. George C. Herring, *From Colony to Superpower: U.S. Foreign Relations since 1776* (Oxford University Press, 2008), 311.

73. Stewart L. Woodford to John Sherman, September 13, 1897, in *FRUS 1897*, 564.

74. Kagan, *Dangerous Nation*, 396–97.

75. Offner, *An Unwanted War*, 111–31.

76. H. Wayne Morgan, *America's Road to Empire: The War with Spain and Overseas Expansion* (New York: John Wiley and Sons, 1965), 37–63; Kagan, *Dangerous Nation*, 401–04.

77. Pérez, *The War of 1898*, 21–22.

78. See, for example, Pérez, *The War of 1898*, 34–44.

79. William McKinley, Message to Congress, April 11, 1898, in *FRUS 1898* (Government Printing Office, 1899), 750–60.

80. John Spooner, April 15, 1898, *Appendix to the Congressional Record*, vol. 31, part 4, 301.

81. Letter from William James to Theodore Flournoy, June 17, 1898, in Ralph Barton Perry, *The Thought and Character of William James*, vol. 2 (Boston: Little, Brown, 1935), 307.

82. McKinley, Message to Congress, 757.

83. Andrew Preston, *Sword of the Spirit, Shield of Faith: Religion in American War and Diplomacy* (New York: Knopf, 2012), 214–16.

84. Ibid., 211–14.

85. Kagan, *Dangerous Nation*, 411.

86. Francis Warren, quoted in Lewis L. Gould, *The Spanish-American War and President McKinley* (University Press of Kansas, 1982), 40.

87. Gary Bass, *Freedom's Battle: The Origins of Humanitarian Intervention* (New York: Knopf, 2008), 344.

88. Michael Ignatieff, *Empire Lite: Nation-Building in Bosnia, Kosovo, and Afghanistan* (London: Vintage, 2003), 23.

GUNTHER PECK

9

The Shadow of White Slavery

Race, Innocence, and History in Contemporary Anti–Human Trafficking Campaigns

History forms a vital part of contemporary efforts to stop human trafficking. Activist journalist David Batstone, whose book *Not for Sale: The Return of the Global Slave Trade—And How We Can Fight It* helped galvanize the public's attention to millions of coerced, trafficked workers across the globe in 2000, directly compares their plight to enslaved Africans transported across the Atlantic Ocean centuries earlier. Not only are today's trafficked migrants—those moved across international borders "by force, fraud, and coercion"—indeed slaves, according to Batstone, but their numbers, some 30 million by his reckoning, dwarf the size of the better-known African slave trade, which transported some 9 million Africans to the Americas. If today's trafficked workers are slaves, those seeking to help them are a new generation of abolitionists, directly aiming to duplicate the historical success of the original abolitionists. Indeed, the Trafficking Violence Protection Act (TVPA), originally passed in 2000 at the end of Bill Clinton's presidency, was recently reauthorized and renamed in 2009 as the William Wilberforce Act. It seems that progressive history can repeat itself.[1]

And yet there are important and profound differences between African slaves of the eighteenth century and today's trafficked migrants, differences that are obscured by contemporary abolitionist language. First, the coercion that today's trafficked migrants endure is not, for the most part, legal, unlike the African slave trade. Consequently, the "slavery" experienced by contemporary migrants cannot be eliminated with the passage of a single emancipatory law, however well intended, especially when state actors are frequently the villains in contemporary trafficking stories. Second, the insistence by activists and policy officials that today's trafficked subjects are slaves has generated the moral and historical challenge of seeing enslavement in the present, of making slavery visible and real to an alternately indifferent and aroused public. Abolitionists in the eighteenth century had to persuade a doubting British public that African bodies jammed into the holds of slave ships were indeed souls, subjects worthy of moral rescue. Today's abolitionists similarly seek to awaken society's desire for moral rescue, but they first have to make slaves visible, lacking clear legal markers that define contemporary enslavement or racial criteria that make slave status allegedly recognizable. What exactly is the difference between a trafficked migrant, defined as a slave according to the TVPA, and the undocumented migrant who works for subpar wages throughout the North American economy? Which migrants are worthy of rescue, and which are unworthy (and therefore deportable)?[2]

The historical antislavery campaign that best illuminates contemporary dilemmas among human trafficking activists is not abolitionism, I will argue, but the campaign to end "white slavery" in the nineteenth and early twentieth centuries. This reform movement comprised two campaigns: the first was an effort to ameliorate work conditions for child and transient factory workers during the Industrial Revolution in Great Britain and the United States in the 1820s and 1830s, and the second was an effort to outlaw the importation and trafficking of immigrant prostitutes in both British and North American cities during the Progressive Era. In both campaigns, the language of white slavery helped define the terrain of reformers' moral rescue work, even as white slavery abolitionists struggled to articulate the precise differences among factory workers, prostitutes, and so-called white slaves. Like contemporary abolitionists, these white slavery reformers struggled with forms of unfree labor that could not be abolished through law, but which required new ways of seeing and interpreting the boundary between free and unfree workers.[3]

This chapter examines the cultural representations of human trafficking produced since 2000, focusing on the U.S. State Department's efforts to abolish human trafficking as authorized by the Trafficking Violence Protection Act (TVPA) of that year. In particular, I examine the way the State Department has represented the problem of human trafficking in its annual Trafficking in Persons (TIP) Reports. Although the term "white slavery" has largely disappeared from contemporary legislative efforts to control human trafficking in the United States, notions and images of white female victimhood—the historical heart of white slavery discourse—continue to infuse efforts to curtail human trafficking. The persistence of white slavery tropes—sexual innocence, imperial rescue, and anxieties about racial purity—reflect not so much self-conscious racism as an effort to solve enduring problems of visibility within human trafficking campaigns. How can we "see" modern slavery—and know that it is slavery—without the obvious legal markers or racial criteria of the past? By focusing on the travails of helpless female victims, contemporary actors seek to secure the moral purpose that contemporary abolitionist language invokes but rarely clarifies.[4]

The article proceeds in three sections. First, I examine the enduring power of Progressive Era discourse about white slavery and human trafficking since 2000. Using texts and images produced by far right nationalists and white supremacists, I consider how contemporary discourse on human trafficking has proven fertile ground for replotting Progressive Era white slavery mythologies for a variety of political purposes in post-9/11 America. In the second section, I examine the complex ways that government authorities have sought to represent the problem of human trafficking in annual TIP Reports and United Nations public safety announcements, locating both continuities and differences between white slavery abolitionists and contemporary policymakers. In a brief final section, I analyze the significance of white slavery abolitionism for the broad array of activists and government officials fighting the contemporary "war" against human trafficking today. Rather than claim that the history of white slavery abolitionism contains transparent lessons for the present, I instead argue that this history suggests ways of rethinking how we evaluate and see the agency of trafficking victims, as well as the efficacy of humanitarian interventions more broadly. What would a bottom-up antitrafficking policy that truly supported the agency of victims, rather than the aspirations of rescuers, look like? Given the multiple authors and stakeholders of the State Department's current humanitarian war on human trafficking, how might policymakers and activists alike learn from the ironies and unintended

consequences that have long pervaded the history of white slavery abolitionism? If history can provide guideposts for the present, I conclude, it
is by stimulating questions for scholars, teachers, practitioners, reformers,
and activists alike that can help us rethink the complex contours of
victim agency and its troubled relationship to the diverse community of
reformers and humanitarians, both in and outside formal channels of state
power.

White Slavery in Contemporary Political Discourse

Contemporary white slavery discourse is alive and well in journalism and
print media, and on the Internet, serving as a powerful tool for a diverse
cohort of conservative activists in both the United States and United King-
dom to articulate frustrations with what they see as a politically correct approach to history that minimizes the reality of white suffering and maxi-
mizes white guilt in the history of slavery. According to former Ku Klux
Klan grand wizard David Duke, white slavery—which he defines as the
deliberate trafficking and enslavement of millions of white Europeans to
North America in the colonial era under the misnomer of indentured
servitude—has not only been deliberately concealed from most white and
black Americans but also silences any claims blacks have to reparations for
chattel slavery. This so-called white slavery was not only injurious to millions of white migrants but also far worse than black slavery, according to
Duke, precisely because it was unacknowledged and hidden in the past and
the present. White slavery serves as a kind of mythology of white victimhood, a potent scar capable of marshaling a virtually bottomless font of
righteous anger in which white suffering trumps and silences any guilt over
historical injustices crafted in the past by white people toward people of
color. According to this mythology, Klansmen, like all whites, have been
history's greatest victims, and unlike politically correct white liberals, they
are the ones who have the guts to unmask the conspiracy of silence that surrounds white slavery. One of the architects of this potent mythology is
Michael Hoffman, whose book *They Were White, and They Were Slaves* ostensibly "proves" the existence of white slavery by citing cases of cruelty to
indentured servants and quoting the occasional British servant who claimed
to have been enslaved when transported to America. Far more influential
and widely read has been the work of two British journalists, Don Jordan

and Michael Walsh, whose *White Cargo: The Forgotten History of Britain's White Slaves in America* avoided explicitly embracing Duke's or Hoffman's hostility to black history but affirmed their hierarchy of white victimhood and a notion of white innocence.[5] In all of these retellings of the history of indentured servitude, cruelty to individual white bodies is equated with the experience of chattel slavery, despite the obvious fact that not a single indentured servant ever passed his or her status on to offspring, as was the case for all African slaves in the Americas by 1680.

Stories of working-class white slavery comprise just one portion of a larger contemporary discourse about white slaves that locates white innocence in terms of sexuality and virginity. These tales owe their origins to the Progressive Era white slavery crusades in which a diverse alliance of feminists and social purity advocates sought to protect women from the snares of immigrant pimps who allegedly seduced and enslaved young women. This international campaign to combat a "traffic in women" began with internationalist ideals on behalf of women in the 1890s, but it quickly fueled nationalist and racist anxieties as white victimhood was deemed infinitely worse than that endured by blacks or, as one reformer put it, "a slavery blacker than the African slave trade." Several scholars have illuminated the racist and imperial dimensions of the global white slavery panic, as well as the ways that emerging notions of women's consent were refashioned by the concerns of social purity advocates. Less explored has been the reemergence of white slavery discourse to frame the contemporary crusade against human trafficking.[6] This was especially apparent after the events of September 11, 2001, when white slavery discourse expanded dramatically on the Internet, especially among far right political groups. Two weeks after the 9/11 attacks, for example, the Omdurman, a group formally dedicated to the total victory of Christian civilization over Islamic culture, recast white slavery as a story of human trafficking involving the sexual predations of Middle Eastern Muslim men. The threat generated by sex trafficking was countered not only by the white girls' American parents, who protect the girls' virginity by pulling their guns on male Saudi attackers, but ultimately by an American invasion of Saudi Arabia and the larger Middle East. Defending white American virgins served to justify a call for preemptive war in the Middle East, more than a year before the United States invaded Iraq and scholars began debating whether the so-called Bush Doctrine was consistent with just-war theory.[7]

The Omdurman's demonization of Saudi men closely reworked older forms of antisemitism featuring Jewish men as white slavers preying on the sexual innocence of white Christian girls, a trope exploited by American progressives as well as Adolf Hitler in *Mein Kampf.* Such associations were not new in the weeks following the 9/11 attacks, but they became far more powerful and ubiquitous. The Omdurman did not have to look back to Hitler or the Progressive Era, but simply to the writings of David Duke, who just three years earlier had focused on the miseries of "a beautiful blonde Ukrainian girl" in his 1998 autobiography *My Awakening: A Path to Racial Understanding.* Emigrating to Israel with a promise of work, the unnamed girl was soon thrown into a brothel and her papers burned, Duke tells us, while her new Israeli master stated "I own you. . . . You are my property. . . . Don't try to leave. You have no papers and you don't speak Hebrew. You will be arrested and deported. Then we will get you and bring you back." This story of false enticements, passport shredding, and compulsory sex work is a familiar part of contemporary antislavery campaigns, as is the moral that Duke generated: "The White slaver is thus protected by the . . . system, while the victims are punished." Although liberal Senator Paul Wellstone eschewed Duke's racism, he nonetheless reiterated Duke's framing of human trafficking as a form of contemporary slavery in the Senate bill that would become the TVPA in 2000.[8]

The potency of these images of Middle Eastern men trafficking in white women perhaps explains why State Department photographers have largely avoided the region in representing the problem of human trafficking in the annual TIP Reports since 2001. Both Saudi Arabia and Israel remain central allies for the United States in the region, and sex trafficking imagery that demonizes either Israeli or Saudi men not only fuels antagonisms between the two countries but makes the hard work of American diplomacy in the region even harder. Hostility toward Middle Eastern traffickers presents the State Department with a particular challenge that cuts to the heart of the TVPA's national dimensions and purposes. Since 2002, State Department officials have graded all nations' antitrafficking efforts and placed them into three tiers of compliance with the U.S. law—with the important exception of the United States, which remained ungraded until 2010. Under President George W. Bush's leadership, the TVPA was used to make the United States into a kind of international vice cop, forging global alliances against legalizing prostitution and for keeping it criminalized.

Since 2001, both Israel and Saudi Arabia have consistently been located in the lowest tier. But the State Department has been reluctant to sanction either of its two chief allies in the Middle East, despite a protocol that clearly indicates they warrant sanctions. As Anthony DeStefano has noted, the enforcement of the TVPA's sanctioning power has been highly selective, with only traditional American enemies—Cuba, Iran, and North Korea—actually receiving penalties from failures to curb human trafficking.[9]

State Department efforts to publicize the spread of human trafficking, and especially sex trafficking, in its annual TIP Reports have nonetheless provoked a proliferation of cultural narratives about the contemporary dangers of sex trafficking, many of them cinematic blockbusters. Perhaps the most conspicuous narrative involving white virgins and men from the Middle East and the Balkans is the movie *Taken*, starring Liam Neeson as Bryan Mills, a man whose teenage daughter is captured by an Albanian gang while on vacation with a blond friend in Paris. In the forty-eight hours after she is taken, the consummately skilled Mills, a former CIA officer who had put country ahead of family during his career, enacts a kind of fantasy of imperial and paternal redemption and rescue. In his desperate quest to liberate his captive daughter, the determined father single-handedly kills twenty-seven sex traffickers, virtually all of them Albanians, along with a few complicit French authorities. He finally succeeds in rescuing his daughter from the arms of a decrepit oil-rich sultan who had purchased his daughter when she was sold at auction, where her virginity and whiteness had brought top dollar for the evening. While the term "white slavery" is not used in *Taken*, it is only because script writers did not need to mention it. The girl's whiteness, virginity, and innocence are the conspicuous commodities that organize not only the final auction but Neeson's character's righteous bloodletting throughout the movie. Mills's successful rescue of his daughter redeems not only her virginity and his own paternal fantasies but the righteous purpose of U.S. antitrafficking policy and its support for "raid and rescue" interventions around the globe. In effect, all trafficked women are slaves, the movie suggests, and if it takes selling a white virgin to arouse a public to action, then so be it.[10]

The trouble with virginity narratives is not simply that they can be explicitly racist in the hands of a David Duke or the Omdurman but that they mislead viewers about the complex terrain from which human and sex trafficking emerge. First and foremost, images of sexual innocence valorize one method of intervention—raid and rescue—while confining the roles that trafficked women and men are allowed to inhabit. If commodifying virgins helps make slavery visible, what of the trafficked who are not white or not virgins, or who claim to choose sex work willingly? Are they in fact less coerced while working in a brothel or less worthy of help if they reject rescue? And what of the millions of migrants who are trafficked for non-sexual labor, for laying bricks or building sewers?[11] State Department officials have been quite mindful of such complexities and the trade-offs that emerge from valorizing only white, female victims, as the next section will examine.

Representing Antislavery: Government Narratives

Analyzing the roles that images of sexual innocence and race may be playing in U.S. antitrafficking policy is hard to do. At first blush, State Department officials working to enforce the TVPA seem to have put some distance between their current efforts and older campaigns to stop the trafficking of white slaves. Not only is there not a single mention of "white slavery" in any of the annual State Department TIP Reports between 2001 and the present, but the vast majority of people featured as victims in the TIP Reports are from third world countries. If the face of the white slavery crisis in 1910 was a trapped white virgin on the cover of Ernest Bell's best seller *Fighting the Traffic in Young Girls; or, the War on the White Slave Trade,*[12] the faces of contemporary antitrafficking efforts are most often women, boys, and girls from India and Southeast Asia. Indeed, just 10 percent of the images of trafficking victims within the TIP Reports are white, while over half are Asian and nearly a quarter are black. If one compares the race and region from which trafficking victims in the TIP Reports come from during the presidencies of George W. Bush and Barack Obama, one also discovers remarkable continuities across regions and races (see figure 9-1). The only exception involves a slight increase in the number of victims hailing from the United States during Obama's presidency, a reflection of the policy shift in 2010 to stop exempting the United States from its tiered country evaluations.[13]

Yet, before imagining that contemporary policymakers have transcended the racist pitfalls of older white slavery abolitionists, we need to pay careful attention to the particular ways that trafficking has been represented in the annual TIP Reports. If one combines analysis of the reports'

Figure 9-1. Photographs in TIP Reports: Origins of Trafficked Persons by Continent, 2004–14

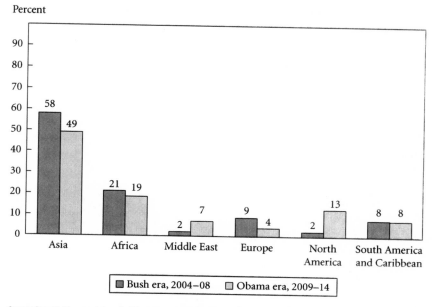

Percent

Bush era, 2004–08 □ Obama era, 2009–14

Source: Compiled by examining all of the TIP photographs published in the TIP Reports for the following years: 2004, 2006, 2008, 2010, 2012, and 2014. The total number of photographs during the Bush era was 150, and there were 139 during the Obama years. The increase in the number of North American victims was visible primarily in the 2014 TIP Report, which contained 8 photographs from North America out of a total of 55. Not all of the 289 photographs examined indicate where the victim hailed from or was trafficked. The percentages were based on the photographs of known origin, 91 from the Bush years and 91 from the Obama years.

photographs with the captions that accompany them, striking differences emerge along racial and regional lines. Three terms emerge to describe or modify the kind of trafficking that the photographs represent: sex trafficking, labor trafficking, and child trafficking. The profile of the reports' white victims is strikingly different from that of their black and Asian victims. Three-fourths of the white victims represented in the TIP Reports were trafficked for sex, in comparison to less than one-fourth of black victims and just over one-third of Asian victims. By contrast, just one-eighth of white victims were trafficked for labor, while almost three-fourths of black victims and two-thirds of Asian victims were trafficked for labor. One might conclude that these racial disparities among the reports' images reflect distinct regional patterns of human trafficking. White women, one could argue, are more likely to be trafficked for sex than for labor, while black bodies are trafficked for labor more than sex. But such conclusions would be

Figure 9-2. Photographs in TIP Reports: Type of Trafficking among Victims by Race, 2004–14

Percent

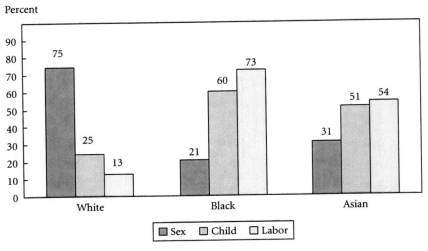

Source: Compiled by examining all of the TIP Report photographs for selected years. Rather than assigning race or location to photographs on the basis of how they appeared in the TIP Reports, especially ones where the origin of the victim was not specified, I relied on the racial and geographic designations that were indicated by textual references in the reports. Percentages were based on the photographs of known race and geographic identity. The categories of trafficking—sex, child, and labor—were also determined by textual descriptions in the TIP Reports. These categories were not mutually exclusive, and some photographs were coded for two categories, such as "sex" and "child" for underage sex workers.

erroneous and at the very least unsupported by any evidence presented within the TIP Reports. Although far fewer white victims appear in the reports than in public campaigns against white slavery during the Progressive Era, the shadow of older white slavery representations is alive and well in the images that the State Department does publish: white female bodies are trafficked for sex, while black bodies are trafficked for labor (see figure 9-2).

The continuity of such images in the TIP Reports under both the Bush and Obama presidencies complicates the critiques that scholars have made of the antitrafficking work of the State Department. While a great deal of scholarship on contemporary antitrafficking work is just emerging, much of the first wave of scholarly attention examined President Bush's conservative and evangelical supporters, who used the TVPA to criminalize prostitution globally and to silence those who would advocate for sex workers' rights.[14] Analyzing the images and captions of trafficked victims in the reports, however, complicates that picture substantially. First, in only one

TIP Report (for the year 2006) have images of sex trafficking been more numerous than those of labor trafficking.[15] Second, clear trend lines emerge in the type of trafficking portrayed in the TIP Reports, but they do not conform to presidential administrations. There is a broader shift from sex to labor in the photographs of trafficking victims, but that trend was clearly under way by 2008, the last year of Bush's presidency. Conversely, a new trend began to emerge in the reports' images after 2008, a slow but steady increase in images of sex trafficking, further complicating those who have critiqued President Bush's allegedly single-minded focus on sex trafficking. Perhaps the most important change in how trafficking has been represented is not so much in the kind of trafficking portrayed but in the gender of the victims. Most TIP images of trafficking victims were female between 2004 and 2008, but between 2010 and 2014 a small majority were male, suggesting the greater focus on labor trafficking during President Obama's presidency.[16]

Pervading both the Bush-era and Obama-era TIP Reports are challenges associated with making the slavery of human trafficking visible in pictures and in the testimonies of victims. One of the most striking trends over the years is the growing importance of slavery language to descriptions of all human trafficking, whether for sex or labor. In 2001, "slavery" and "modern-day slavery" were mentioned just seven times in the TIP Report; this increased to fifty times in 2004, and ninety-five times in 2010—a fourteenfold increase in nine years.[17] Across the same period of time there was no corresponding upsurge in the level of violence or severity of trafficking, however. Perhaps more revealing is that while descriptions of slavery proliferated in the reports, the number of actual victims describing themselves as slaves has remained fixed. Although victim testimonies featured in the reports were certainly harrowing and filled with violence and coercion, not a single trafficked subject referred to him- or herself as a slave between 2002 and 2010. The constructed nature of slavery as the discursive frame for trafficked subjects' suffering is perhaps most apparent in the captions that accompany many of the photographs that appear within the reports. A disclaimer in the 2004 TIP Report, tucked away as a footnote, described that framing in remarkably candid terms: "The photographs of this Report's cover and most uncaptioned photographs in the Report are not images of confirmed trafficking victims, but are provided to show the myriad forms of exploitation that help define trafficking and the variety of cultures in which trafficking victims can be found." Images of third world poverty emerge as signs of trafficked "slaves," even though most of these same subjects do not apparently identify themselves as slaves or even as trafficked subjects.[18]

One reason the photographs have been left uncaptioned is to protect the identity of actual trafficking victims; insisting on publishing only verified trafficking victims and their testimonies would potentially endanger these victims and certainly not help emancipate anyone. Efforts to represent the experience and agency of trafficking victims within the TIP Reports have thus consistently walked a tightrope, with some victims' advocates insisting on anonymity and others urging victims to come out into the open and to attack the public stigma that has kept many trafficked subjects in the shadows. How advocates should represent the agency or testimonies of victims of sex trafficking remains an especially vexing challenge. Whereas abolitionists tend to define all migrant sex workers as victims without consent or voice until rescued, advocates for sex workers tend to inscribe agency into virtually all testimonies that women in the global sex trade provide, ignoring the pervasive existence of coercion within the trade that relies extensively on the work of underage girls. The challenge of deciding what constitutes agency in the testimony of trafficking victims, then, has not only reflected a broader problem of making both slavery and consent visible in stories about human trafficking but also political battles among feminists to clarify what the agency of sex workers looks like—with consequences apparent on a world stage.[19]

We can see those challenges manifest in government efforts to craft public service announcements (PSAs) that educate viewers about how to see and avoid sex trafficking. The first such PSA, produced by the United Nations in 2006, featured what appeared to be firsthand images of sex trafficking. No voices or testimonies emerge in the PSA; we see only the faces of silent and motionless women whose exploitation we largely imagine. Underneath each woman's emotion-drained face appear captions illustrating the false promises made to them as migrants, such as "nice co-workers," while cutting away to hardened brothel workers looking drugged and demoralized. Accompanying the text "excellent salary" are images of used syringes and a pimp taking money from a once-again silent, immobile woman. Throughout the minute-long PSA, a continuous musical loop of descending minor-key chords evokes a world of decadent dangers and, unintentionally perhaps, pleasures that onlookers see as they tour the brothel. As a single tear emerges in the eye of a still motionless victim, a sentence flashes across the screen indicating that "more than 700,000 women are trafficked every year for the purposes of sexual exploitation and forced labour." The numbers are staggering, but the individual tear holds our focus, like the tear that flowed out of the eye of Iron Eyes Cody, the Native American whose silent witness to pollution initiated the Keep America Beautiful campaign in 1968.[20]

Despite its high-end Hollywood production values, this PSA closely resembles older Progressive Era moralistic admonitions about the traffic in women. Like Ernest Bell's 1910 classic *Fighting the Traffic in Women*, which featured a beautiful white girl on the cover clasping her hands together as a lustful man looks on, the effort to represent sex trafficking has also ironically fueled a traffic in images of seduction. While the UN's captions attempt to spell out a clear moral message about human trafficking, the glossy images also create a pornographic underworld of subdued lighting, forbidden pleasures, and erotic dancing that ironically glamorizes the very traffic it seeks to police. Determining exactly who has watched these PSAs is a challenging endeavor, but the male gaze it employs suggests that it may not have reached its intended audience of young female migrants. Like older Progressive Era admonitions, the PSA is also misleading. Not only is the figure of 700,000 women not attributed to any source, but the images of women in a brothel stand in as the representative for a much larger and more diverse whole of trafficked women—most of whom, according to the UN's own estimates, have been trafficked for forced labor rather than sexual exploitation. These inaccuracies, no greater nor less than the distortions in the movie *Taken*, have historically spurred ironic results in which the boundary between moral admonition and pornography, white slavery investigators and white slavers, has sometimes been difficult to determine. One of the most ironic applications of the 1910 White Slave Law, or Mann Act, was to censor moralistic publications ostensibly aimed at stamping out white slavery. The most celebrated target of that censorship campaign was the early blockbuster *The Traffic in Souls*, which featured a white woman being trafficked by a sinister immigrant from Eastern Europe who drugged her after buying her an ice cream in his candy shop.[21]

Perhaps aware of the striking parallels between contemporary PSAs and Progressive Era exposés of white slavery, subsequent UN PSAs have deliberately sought to de-eroticize their portraits of sexual traffic and slavery. Rather than relying on the insights or testimonies of sex workers or sex "slaves" to do so, however, the UN has turned to well-known celebrities to make their case. One of the most interesting efforts has been spearheaded by actress Emma Thompson, who grapples with two of the thorniest debates among contemporary feminists: how to de-eroticize portrayals of sex trafficking, and how to make testimonies of trafficked victims more prominent while respecting victims' privacy. Thompson's first PSA begins with a warning to viewers about the graphic nature of its contents, and features the face of Thompson, prone, expressing the chilling and poignant words of two different women: Elena, a young woman who is seeking a better life, and Maria, an abused and trafficked prostitute. We soon realize they are the same person, as Thompson's performance suggests that trafficked women "lose more than their names." The PSA is resolutely anti-erotic; Thompson's words are continuously broken and interrupted by what seem violent and convulsive blows to her body and the unmistakable rhythm of a male patron having sex as Thompson, in the guise of Maria, winces in pain. The violence is powerful and graphic, but since we only see Thompson's face, and some blood on a sheet, there is little to distract the viewer from the trauma and pain associated with Maria's sexual slavery. The PSA's abolitionist perspective is highlighted by Maria's spare words and her desire for rescue as she mouths "help me" during a particularly wrenching sequence. Thompson tackles the problem of finding voices for trafficking victims in another UN PSA, once again appearing with only her face in the frame. This time Thompson lip-synchs to the recorded words of five different victims of trafficking—some of them for sex, but others for labor and child soldiering. The constantly morphing voice of trafficked men and women, combined with the earnest and sad face of Thompson's lip-synching, create a powerful portrait of human trafficking, one that attempts to capture the varieties of labor that victims perform.[22]

Thompson's PSAs suggest the power of certain feminist complaints about the global antitrafficking movement, that antitrafficking work has ignored or silenced the testimonies of the very victims they seek to help. The text that emerges at the end of the PSA sums up its moralistic intention: "Giving a voice to the victims of human trafficking." Yet certain ironies persist in Thompson's earnest efforts to empower victims and to make the true horrors of sex slavery visible to an alternately aroused or indifferent public. Thompson may provide a voice to five trafficked subjects, but they remain faceless and anonymous in her representation, unable or unwilling to speak on their own behalf, with a script that might complicate the ostensibly clear and bright moral boundaries that undergird Thompson's intervention. Likewise, the familiarity of Thompson's face makes it virtually impossible to see her powerful portrayal as anything but a fiction. Her portrayal of Maria and Elena may redress the eroticism of previous PSAs, but we are constantly aware that Thompson is acting, whether ventriloquized by Elena, Maria, or an unnamed boy soldier in Africa. In all of her PSAs, the sympathetic face of the trafficked victim remains Thompson's, a famous white woman who in a long and distinguished line of female victims displays her pain, suffering, and innocence while exhorting us to rescue her.

The potential mischief that celebrity activism generates for trafficking victims, governmental agencies, and even the celebrities themselves comes into sharper focus when examining the State Department's use of celebrities Demi Moore and Ashton Kutcher to spearhead its antitrafficking campaign in 2010–11. Seeking to generate a viral response to their PSAs, Moore and Kutcher recruited a star-studded lineup of male actors to produce the controversial Real Men Don't Buy Girls campaign. If the number of downloads on YouTube is one measure of success, these "real men" PSAs have been quite successful, with twenty times as many views online as the UN PSAs and regular promotion by CNN's Freedom Project, which is devoted entirely to antitrafficking activism and journalism. But any coherent message about childhood sexual slavery—how to see, know, and prevent it— has been obscured by celebrity activists using humor and caricature to make the heavy-handed point that "real" men do not have sex with children. In Kutcher's PSA, we see him in a motel room opening a package of new socks after taking off his old ones and throwing them in the trash. The voiceover declares humorously, "Real men do their own laundry," and then a few seconds later, with bold text blotting out Kutcher's face, we see and hear, "Real men don't buy girls." An equally ironic PSA features Justin Timberlake applying shaving cream, then starting a chainsaw and holding it next to his face while a voice intones "Real men prefer a close shave . . . real men don't buy girls." At the end of each PSA, a glamorously dressed Eva Longoria states that "Justin Timberlake . . ." or "Ashton Kutcher is a real man," then asks, "Are you?" By attacking the masculinity of the pedophiles who create a demand for child sex slavery, these PSAs seek to stigmatize the men who fuel such traffic. They use irony deliberately in so doing, suggesting that hipster men like Ashton Kutcher are the "real men" who would never buy girls. But the PSAs seem oblivious to the larger irony of their function—namely, that they succeed by intensifying the very masculine insecurities that fuel such traffic in the first place. Gone from the Moore and Kutcher PSAs, moreover, are any representations of victims or their testimonies. Indeed, apart from the brief mention of "buying children," it is virtually impossible to tell what the PSAs are really about beyond the beauty of the celebrities who pose for the camera. The chatter they have inspired on YouTube illustrates this point: most posts do not even mention childhood sex trafficking, but simply comment on each celebrity's attributes. Typical were these responses to Bradley Cooper's spot: "My future husband here" and "OMG Bradley Cooper is so hot!"[23]

The remarkable instability of sexuality as a representational field is hardly new to crusaders against human trafficking. Many of the best-intentioned reformers of the Progressive Era expressed exasperation when carefully constructed efforts to help impoverished women became tools for policing their choices and behavior. Feminist Emma Goldman expressed the frustration of many activists in 1910 when she described the commotion surrounding the white slavery scare as a kind of distraction from harder and more pressing political questions, a politics, as she put it, for "baby people." But if contemporary efforts to change public awareness of human trafficking with public safety announcements seem self-defeating, we would do well to recall the enduring consequences of white slavery abolitionism, which included not only the passage of the Mann Act but also the dramatic expansion of the nascent Federal Bureau of Investigation, which used the white slavery problem to hone its capacity to investigate and police people's private lives. Indeed, the young J. Edgar Hoover used the FBI's open-ended white slavery mandate to advance his ambitions within the bureau by federalizing antimiscegenation laws and prosecuting interracial couples in as many states as he could on the grounds that black men were necessarily trafficking their white partners. As a result, state-based antimiscegenation laws became federalized. Such outcomes were not anticipated by Emma Goldman and belied her sense of the relatively innocuous nature of white slavery abolitionism. Indeed, Goldman would come to lament the growing power of the FBI, which would deport her and other labor radicals in the midst of a moral panic of even greater intensity, the First Red Scare, in 1920.[24]

Learning from Shadows: Rethinking Victim Agency

Recognizing the historical mischief done in the name of fighting slavery does not mean that every governmental effort to police sex trafficking as slavery has necessarily produced an ironic or nefarious result. One might argue, moreover, that antislavery framing is a tool that the State Department has no choice but to use given its cultural ubiquity in public discussions of trafficking and the power of such narratives to generate public action. Deploying antislavery tropes is an adroit use of history that builds public support for a complex and challenging global policy initiative. There are at least two problems with this practice, however. First, there is no single lesson from the history of antitrafficking policy, nor one morally correct version waiting to be plucked from the archive. To search for a single lesson suggests that the past is itself a stable and fully transparent terrain, a formation that white slavery abolitionists themselves frequently used in galvanizing support for their policy objectives, only to find themselves unprepared for the ironic consequences of their policy "successes." Feminists who hailed the passage of the Mann Act as a historic victory for women, for example, were perplexed by one of the first applications of the law, the jailing of black boxing champion Jack Johnson and the silencing of his white mistress, Lucille Cameron. Rather than emancipating a "white slave," the Mann Act effectively imposed racist notions of moral rescue upon the bodies of a prominent interracial couple. Recognizing the plasticity and elasticity of white slavery abolitionism helps historians make better sense of such ironies in hindsight, but activists at the time were unprepared to contest such outcomes precisely because they assumed their historically minded policy work had achieved its stated purpose.

Rather than proclaiming one transparent lesson from the history of white slavery, then, the shadow of white slavery suggests that contemporary activists, scholars, and government actors might use the past to inform a set of questions about the work of antislavery framing and the contours of victim agency that it structures. What, for example, would a bottom-up antitrafficking policy look like, one that enabled victims to articulate their ideas of coercion, opportunity, and rescue in terms they could recognize and embrace? Answering that question would not only necessitate rethinking the history of white slavery abolitionism but also turn a spotlight on the ironic consequences of antislavery framing past and present. The shadow of white slavery extends over contemporary antitrafficking efforts not because those of us committed to stopping human trafficking are secretly right-wing vigilantes, racists, or avowed imperialists (though those groups do play into the issue), but because the history of white slavery abolitionism exemplifies the political mischief that occurs when attempting to make "modern" slavery visible. Too often, antislavery discourse valorizes the heroism of the rescuers while ignoring or even silencing the voices of the trafficked. Defenders of abolitionist framing have deployed powerful arguments to explain how and why "rescued" women frequently resist their rescue and return to brothels, citing such psychological theories as the Stockholm Syndrome or, like Nicholas Kristof, the lack of viable economic alternatives for trafficked women in their home villages. But rarely have advocates cited testimonies of the trafficked or considered their agency and voices ascriptively, without the moralistic premises that have long defined humanitarian rescue and emancipatory intervention.

Imagining a bottom-up trafficking policy necessitates carefully considering the political and legal constraints that shape trafficked subjects' voices and testimonies as well as cultural and economic factors shaping their actions. Those constraints are not hard to find. For State Department officials trying to enforce the Trafficking Violence Protection Act, testimonies of trafficked workers, when they do emerge, comprise vexing kinds of evidence. The trafficking visa, or T visa, remains a tool through which trafficking victims' testimony is welcomed and might indeed help liberate them from their oppressors. But as the only visa in the entire panoply of immigration visas that is underutilized, it is worth asking why so few migrants take advantage of the opportunity to speak. Here the framing of each victim's testimony remains hugely important: T visa applicants must not only prove via testimony that they have been trafficked but also must agree to prosecute their traffickers, a tall order for many migrants with family connections to their oppressors. If T visa applicants are unpersuasive, moreover, they are deported or held in U.S. detention centers, where some have undergone horrible mistreatment. There is little wonder, then, that so few trafficked migrants avail themselves of the T visa or present their testimony to U.S. authorities.

To imagine a truly emancipatory and fully subscribed T visa, one needs to imagine testimonies by trafficked migrants that could not be used against them—that would, if only for a moment, stand outside the power of border bureaucracies to police and regulate migrants' movements across borders. That may indeed seem a tall order, a utopian fantasy that very few political leaders or border authorities could or would support. Conservative critics of the T visa have, after all, called its limited avenues for redress a form of amnesty, a back door to immigration reform. Perhaps the T visa survives precisely because it remains underutilized or because of its power as a symbol of humanitarian values. But if the T visa is to begin realizing its humanitarian purpose, border bureaucrats need to rethink how they use applicants' testimonies and how they see the agency of trafficking victims in the first place. Here two dimensions of trafficked migrants' agency are significant. Despite the moral rescue imbedded in most popular narratives of trafficking as slavery, a large number of victims do not call themselves slaves and resist the rescue provided by well-meaning authorities and advocates. Sometimes the reason for that resistance is obvious: providing testimony that could prosecute traffickers would endanger family relations in home villages where trafficking networks often begin. But more often, immigration authorities and many advocates are simply in the dark about why migrants resist rescue. Purely from a diagnostic perspective, it would be enormously beneficial for border bureaucrats and advocates to seek out candid testimonies from trafficking victims that could empower migrants and advocates alike to diagnose the complex reasons people become trafficked in the first place.

The second reason authorities and advocates need more candid and unscripted testimonies from trafficked migrants is that the "agency" of migrants and the "agency" of both advocates and authorities have historically conditioned each other. To ignore the ways that trafficking victims understand their own agency, and refuse even to apply for a T visa, limits the success of immigration agents and nongovernmental advocates alike. To imagine humanitarian interventions purely in terms that celebrate the heroism or the goodness of rescuers, as most PSAs and popular portrayals of trafficking do, does little to empower victims to offer their testimonies to advocates. As even a cursory history of the global effort to combat human trafficking suggests, there are a great number of actors who possess agency in shaping the formation and implantation of antitrafficking law and foreign policy. This cohort includes more- and less-well-known actors, from State Department officials to interns with various faith-based organizations and nongovernmental organizations trying to stop human trafficking. The campaign against human trafficking is simultaneously a social movement and a set of bureaucratic interests actively collaborating and sometimes fighting with one another. But arguably the most important actors in that campaign, the victims of human trafficking, remain largely absent or silent in that collaboration, making the story about human trafficking more about the rescuers than the rescued. Hearing such testimonies is crucial for crafting better antitrafficking policies. While the lessons learned from the history of antislavery activism may seem less heroic, the results are likely to be more effective and recognizable for the subjects who struggle daily with bad bargains and the predicaments generated by selling oneself for a pittance.

What, finally, does the history of antitrafficking work suggest for foreign policymakers more generally? If the misreading of history by contemporary abolitionists serves as a kind of cautionary tale, how might policy professionals more productively engage the past in waging humanitarian campaigns? Rather than striving to find the best historical analogy, policymakers would do better to use the past to test out assumptions about the present, to inform a series of empirically verifiable inquiries about *how* our current "humanitarian" policies do in fact work. Here recent and older histories of antitrafficking intervention suggest several productive starting points for foreign policy analysts and practitioners. First, we need to understand better the historical origins and consequences of framing in foreign policy formation. Indeed, humanitarian frames that frequently justify foreign policy interventions can also constrain the process of thinking through alternatives that might achieve better short- and long-term results. Rarely have such frames been put to the test by examining empirically what difference they make in assessing the outcomes of policy intervention. Contemporary activists and State Department actors alike would benefit from an explicit comparison of how UN efforts against the international trafficking in women and children worked between 1947 and 1999, for example—a half century of global activism when slavery was not the primary moral frame. That comparison would almost certainly illustrate the success of antislavery framing in generating action and awareness after 1999. But it would also shift the focus away from raid and rescue and the prosecution of traffickers to the root causes of human trafficking: poverty, insufficient educational opportunities for children and women, and global immigration policies.

Better attention to the history of humanitarian and foreign policy interventions would also improve how and when policy professionals diagnose *why* unintended consequences occur. Claims about slavery and antislavery are themselves historical analogies with ostensibly transparent moral value. But they have frequently obscured harder policy choices. Most trafficked subjects have eschewed the label of "slave," for example. If one purpose of antitrafficking intervention is to mobilize a social movement against trafficking, policy professionals might ask questions about the effects of antislavery framing on social behavior. Researchers might discover that in today's globalized and segmented labor markets, antislavery framing is a truly miserable organizing tool among the world's most exploited groups. Indeed, a great many victims resist that label—even those who desire some kind of intervention. When girls working in newly built textile factories in Lowell, Massachusetts, went on strike in 1836, their organizing motto was "We are not slaves!" If the U.S. State Department and a much larger community of antitrafficking nations are to win the "war" on human trafficking, they must first use the past to ask tough questions about the present, about the efficacy of framing all victims as slaves and about the roles of state policies in fostering traffic in the first place. Foreign policy professionals should likewise use the past to question assumptions about current foreign policies and to examine how they have been implemented. Historically minded policy questions will not generate one-dimensional historical analogies as answers, but will better prepare policymakers to understand the roles of audience, agency, and contingency in defining the outcome of nearly all foreign policy interventions.

Notes

1. David Batstone, *Not for Sale: The Return of the Global Slave Trade—And How We Can Fight It* (New York: Harper Collins, 1999). On the passage of the TVPA, see Anthony DeStefano, *The War on Human Trafficking: U.S. Policy Assessed* (Rutgers University Press, 2007).

2. On the history of abolitionism and the challenge of making the horrors of transatlantic slavery visible to an indifferent British public, see Christopher Brown, *Moral Capital: Foundations of British Abolition* (University of North Carolina Press, 2006). On the discursive and unstable visibility of slavery in the current movement, see Jo Doezema, *Sex Slaves and Discourse Masters: The Construction of Trafficking* (London: Zed Books, 2010).

3. On the history of working-class iterations of white slavery in the 1820s and 1830s that focused on labor trafficking, see David Roediger, *The Wages of Whiteness* (London: Verso, 1994); and Gunther Peck, "White Slavery and Whiteness: A Transnational View of the Sources of Working-Class Radicalism and Racism," *Labor: Studies in Working-Class History of the Americas* 1, no. 2 (2004), 41–63. On the history of white slavery as a crusade against sex trafficking, see Brian Donovan, *White Slave Crusades: Race, Gender, and Anti-Vice Activism, 1887–1917* (University of Illinois Press, 2006); Pamela Haag, *Consent: Sexual Rights and the Transformation of American Liberalism* (Cornell University Press, 1999); and Gunther Peck, "Feminizing White Slavery in the United States: Marcus Braun and the Transnational Traffic in White Bodies, 1890–1910," in *Workers Across the Americas: The Transnational Turn in Labor History*, ed. Leon Fink and Julie Greene (Oxford University Press, 2011).

4. My argument builds on the work of Jo Doezema, who has long critiqued U.S. trafficking policy as a reprise of white slavery discourse and mythology. See Doezema, *Sex Slaves and Discourse Masters*; and Jo Doezema, "Loose Women or Lost Women? The Re-emergence of the Myth of White Slavery in Contemporary Discourses of Trafficking in Women," *Gender Issues* 18, no. 1 (2000), 23–50. My work differs from Doezema's, however, in focusing on the importance of historical contingency and unintended consequences that accompanied the expansion of bureaucratic capacities for investigating "slavery" and trafficking. Doing so helps me better understand how reformist impulses evolve over time and end up harnessed to reactionary agendas. On critiques of U.S. trafficking policy that, like Doezema, focus primarily on trafficking discourse, see Gretchen Soderlund, "Running from the Rescuers: New U.S. Crusades against Sex Trafficking and the Rhetoric of Abolition," *National Women's Studies Association Journal* 17, no. 3 (2005), 64–87.

5. David Duke, *My Awakening: A Path to Racial Understanding* (Baton Rouge, La.: Free Speech Press, 1998); Michael Hoffman, *They Were Slaves and They Were White* (Covington, La.: Independent Publishing, 2000); Don Jordan and Michael Walsh, *White Cargo: The Forgotten History of Britain's White Slaves in America* (London: Mainstream Publishing, 2010). White supremacist writers not only use the trafficking issue to inflate and exaggerate the historical suffering of white people but also approach the topic of race ahistorically, presuming that all people with phenotypically light skin have been known and seen as whites. On the anachronism of much whiteness discourse, see Nell Painter, *The History of White People* (New York: Norton, 2010). Painter, 40–42, notes that Hoffman's work is racist, but nonetheless relies on his findings to suggest that "white slavery" was in fact pervasive among some servants, a lapse in her otherwise useful history of white racial ideology.

6. On the history of international feminist efforts to make trafficking in women a subject of both national and international concern and action, see

Stephanie Limoncelli, *The Politics of Trafficking: The First International Movement to Combat the Sexual Exploitation of Women* (Stanford University Press, 2010). For a critique of the ways national leaders appropriated social purity concerns in the United States, see Haag, *Consent*. On the "blackest war," see Ernest Bell, *Fighting the Traffic in Young Girls; or, the War on the White Slave Trade* (Chicago: G. S. Ball, 1910), cover insert.

7. The images produced by the Omdurman, a sequence of six, are titled "White Slavery in Saudi Arabia," and are available online (www.omdurman.org /leaflets/whiteslv.html).

8. Adolf Hitler, *Mein Kampf* (New York: Reynall and Hitchcock, 1939); Duke, *My Awakening*, 17, 20.

9. U.S. Department of State, *Trafficking in Persons Report* (2002, 2003, 2004, 2005; www.state.gov/j/tip/rls/tiprpt/); DeStefano, *The War on Human Trafficking*, 120–21; see also the appendix on the three-tiered ranking system, 147–49.

10. Pierre Morel, dir., *Taken* (Los Angeles: 20th Century Fox, 2008). There is little academic commentary on the film, but see Robert Uy, "Blinded by Red Lights: Why Trafficking Discourse Should Shift away from Sex and the 'Perfect Victim' Paradigm," *Berkeley Journal of Gender, Law, and Justice* 26 (2011), 204–19.

11. On the political work of sexual innocence in white slavery discourse, see Haag, *Consent*; Doezema, *Sex Slaves*, 77–98; and Frederick Grittner, *Myth, Ideology, and American Law* (New York: Taylor and Francis, 1990). On the power of discourse about sex to displace concerns about labor and class within antitrafficking campaigns past and present, see Peck, "Feminizing White Slavery." Perhaps the best history of trafficking that links the power of cultural discourse about trafficking with women's agency and the struggle to find agency in structures they do not author is Judith Walkowitz, *City of Dreadful Delight: Narratives of Sexual Danger in Late-Victorian London* (University of Chicago Press, 1992).

12. Bell, *Fighting the Traffic in Young Girls*.

13. U.S. Department of State, *Trafficking in Persons Report* (2002–10; www .state.gov/j/tip/rls/tiprpt/); Bell, *Fighting the Traffic in Young Girls*, cover, with image of young white girl clasping hands in prayer behind bars above the following caption, "My God, if only I could get out of here."

14. See Doezema, *Sex Slaves*; Soderlund, "Running from the Rescuers"; and Elizabeth Bernstein, "The Sexual Politics of the 'New Abolitionism,'" *Differences* 18, no. 5 (2007), 128–51. For a foundational text that equates prostitution with sex slavery, see Kathleen Barry, *Female Sexual Slavery* (New York University Press, 1979).

15. In 2006, twenty-six of fifty-one photographs where the type of trafficking was specified involved sex work, a slim majority of 51 percent. By 2008, the last year of Bush's presidency, that number had slipped to 42 percent. The Obama years witnessed initially a sharp decrease in the number of photographs of sex

trafficking and an increase in those devoted to labor trafficking. In 2010, for example, just 19 percent of TIP photographs were for sex and 75 percent were for labor. The number of photographs where the type of trafficking was specified was greater than the 182 where the race and geographic origin of the victim was also specified. Out of 252 total photographs, 243 specified the type of trafficking. U.S. Department of State, *Trafficking in Persons Report* (2004, 2006, 2008, 2010, 2012, 2014; www.state.gov/j/tip/rls/tiprpt/).

16. Designation of the gender of the victim in TIP photographs was easier than determining the race, geographic origin, or type of trafficking for each victim in large measure because pronouns identified the victim's gender. Photographs were put into one of three categories: "female victim," "male victim," and "male and female victims." During the Bush years, victims in TIP Reports were more likely to be female, with 90 out of 150 photographs (60 percent) portraying girls and women, while 66 (44 percent) of the photographs portrayed male victims. During the Obama years, male victims slightly outnumbered female victims in TIP Reports, with 55 percent of 135 photographs featuring male victims and 49 percent featuring female victims. U.S. Department of State, *Trafficking in Persons Report* (2004, 2006, 2008, 2010, 2012, 2014; www.state.gov/j/tip/rls/tiprpt/).

17. U.S. Department of State, *Trafficking in Persons Report* (2001, 2004, 2008, 2010; www.state.gov/j/tip/rls/tiprpt/). Other terms indicating unfree labor also increased over the same period. "Coercion" increased from three references in 2001 to thirteen in 2004 and eighteen in 2010, while "involuntary" also increased from one reference in 2001 to twelve in 2010.

18. U.S. Department of State, *Traffic in Persons* (2004; http://www.state.gov/j/tip/rls/tiprpt/2004/index.htm).

19. On the origins of that conflict among feminists and its impact on international visions of justice, see Limoncelli, *The Politics of Trafficking*.

20. The UN's first sex trafficking PSA can be seen on YouTube (www.youtube.com/watch?v=mqo7OlzVsAk).

21. On Jack Johnson's prosecution under the Mann Act, see David J. Langum, *Crossing Over the Line: Legislating Morality and the Mann Act* (University of Chicago Press, 1994); and Doezema, *Sex Slaves*, 88–89. George Tucker, dir., *The Traffic in Souls* (1913; West Conshohocken, Penn.: Alpha Video DVD, 2014). On censorship of white slave films in Hollywood, see Lee Grieveson, *Policing Cinema: Movies and Censorship in Early Twentieth-Century America* (University of California Press, 2004). On the controversies surrounding the representation of sex trafficking in movies, see Eric Olund, "Traffic in Souls: The 'New Woman,' Whiteness, and Mobile Self-Possession," *Cultural Geographies* 16 (2009), 485–504.

22. Emma Thompson's PSAs are widely available on the Internet. For Thompson's collective portrait of five trafficking victims, go to YouTube (www.youtube.com/watch?v=3-EYIY287LI). Thompson's anti-erotic portrait of Elena/Maria can also be found there (www.youtube.com/watch?v=BdW05BC4emw).

23. There are several PSAs in the Real Men Don't Buy Girls campaign, including spots by Ashton Kutcher, Sean Penn, Justin Timberlake, Bradley Cooper, and others. For Bradley Cooper's spot, see YouTube (www.youtube.com/watch?/v =S7nsB7TFWIs).

24. For Emma Goldman's quote, see Goldman, "The Traffic in Women," in *The Traffic in Women, and Other Essays on Feminism* (New York: Times Change Press, 1970).

Part III

Policymakers' Insights

JAMES B. STEINBERG

10

History, Policymaking, and the Balkans

Lessons Imported and Lessons Learned

The history of ethnic rivalry I detailed reportedly encouraged the President's [Clinton's] pessimism about the region,
and so—it is said—was a factor in his decision not to launch
an overt military response in support of the Bosnian
Moslems. . . . That policymakers, indeed a President, might
rely on such a book in reaching a momentous military
decision would be frightening, if true.
—ROBERT KAPLAN "FOREWORD," IN *BALKAN GHOSTS*

This chapter is a two-part reflection on the role of history in shaping policy, based on my two principal stints in government—first during
the administration of President Bill Clinton and the period of the Balkans
conflict, which featured two military interventions by the United States
(Bosnia and Kosovo), and second, during the administration of President
Barack Obama, when the experience of the Balkans played an important
role in shaping the U.S. response to the most serious humanitarian crisis

---

The views expressed herein are those of the author and do not necessarily reflect
the views of the U.S. government.

of Obama's first term, the conflict in Libya following the outbreak of the Arab Spring.

For each of the two periods I examine three different but interrelated ways in which I believe history shaped the response. First, "deep history"[1]— the ways in which policymakers understood the historical context from which the current conflict arose; second, analogic history, how policymakers sought to draw on other historical experiences to assess the proper policy to pursue in the current case; and third, personal history, how policymakers' own previous experience shaped their approach.[2]

Of course, the three categories are not fully distinct from each other. For many of the policymakers involved, the "deep history" included their own personal experience in dealing with the Balkans and Libya—for example, Lawrence Eagleburger's two tours in Belgrade and Brent Scowcroft's experience in the Balkans during the era of Josip Broz Tito.[3] Similarly, the "analogies" that policymakers drew on were often (but not exclusively) derived from their personal experience—Madeleine Albright's childhood experience of communist Eastern Europe, as well as the entire Clinton administration's contemporary experiences in dealing with Somalia and Rwanda. Nor is history (of the three types discussed here) the only factor that shapes policymakers' decisions. Other factors, including resource constraints and domestic political factors, also play an important role.[4]

The Balkan Wars, 1990–99: Why Did Bush Stay Out and Clinton First Hesitate, Then Plunge In?

There is an enormous literature on the policymaking process in which scholars and practitioners identify a variety of factors that shape how decisionmakers respond to policy challenges. Theories about the nature of the international system (drawn from international relations theory either explicitly or implicitly), definitions of national interest, calculus of the efficacy of means to achieve ends, and domestic and bureaucratic politics all go into shaping decisionmaking. History plays a central role, both because it informs each of the above factors (for example, which international relations theory a policymaker favors will typically be informed by her understanding of history) and because it provides the context in which policymakers debate and incorporate these other dimensions. In the case of the Balkans, the three dimensions of history I identified above (deep history, analogic history, and personal history) shaped policy in significant ways.

Deep History

Few policymakers come into office with rich education in history, especially with respect to parts of the world that are not a mainstream part of the educational curriculum for the typically well-informed nonspecialist. The Balkans certainly fit this category for most of the relevant policymakers—especially American policymakers—for the years 1990–99. Nuggets of the deep history of the region were, of course, well known—Sarajevo instantly evoked the assassination of Archduke Ferdinand and the outbreak of World War I, and there was widespread familiarity with the role of Tito during the Cold War. Some, but probably not the majority, had more than a passing awareness of how Yugoslavia emerged from the Paris Peace Conference following World War I and was later shaped by the bloody fight between the Nazi supporters in Croatia (Ustashe) and the pro-Alliance partisans (as well as the more Serb nationalist "chetniks") in Serbia during World War II. Fewer still had much knowledge of the impact of the Ottoman Empire on the region (including the iconic battle of Kosovo Polje between Serbs and Ottomans, which ultimately led to Ottoman control over what we now know as Kosovo); the place of the Balkans on the borderline between the Christian and Muslim worlds; or the tensions between Orthodox and Catholic Christianity.

little knowledge about Balkans

European counterparts on the whole did have a more sophisticated historical knowledge of the region, which both shaped their thinking and colored their interactions with U.S. officials—whom the Europeans believed were woefully ignorant of the region's history and therefore likely to misunderstand the context of the conflict and pursue ahistorical policies that would not achieve the desired result. This deeper historical knowledge was in part a function of their education, but for many (for example, French president François Mitterrand and German foreign minister Hans-Dietrich Genscher) it came from their personal experience. Similarly, the handful of Americans with experience in the Balkans also came armed with a greater understanding of its deep history and, especially in the administration of President George H. W. Bush, that combination of deep knowledge and personal experience wielded an important influence in shaping policy both in forming their views and—because of the credibility that comes from experience—bolstering their influence over others.

Because the "going-in" knowledge of deep history was thin for most involved, a handful of historical accounts played an oversize role in shaping thinking on the nature of the conflict as well as the likely impact of the

oversized role of little, known info.

various policy options available. Not surprisingly, more popular accounts—which tended to be more accessible to busy policymakers, and which had more "thematic" points of view—had the largest impact in comparison with, for example, more academic histories. In particular, Robert Kaplan's *Balkan Ghosts* shaped the early thinking of many, including (as several journalists and historians have noted) the thinking of President Clinton (to Kaplan's chagrin).[5] In this category, though undoubtedly less well-read, was Rebecca West's *Black Lamb and Grey Falcon*,[6] which was seen as a sympathetic portrait of the Serbs. Recent history also played a role in framing regional impressions—most notably the Sarajevo Olympics, which for many policymakers was the only image they held of Bosnia, as a kind of urbane, multi-ethnic oasis in a more feudal desert.

During the period prior to my own service in the Clinton administration, I was a senior researcher at the RAND Corporation. I joined RAND after spending several years at the International Institute for Strategic Studies in London, working on NATO and transatlantic issues and, since my arrival more or less coincided with the end of the Cold War, my work focused on analyzing the post–Cold War security environment in Europe. I joined a group of scholar-analysts who had spent the majority of their careers studying Central Europe, Eastern Europe, and Russia. As a result, during the four years prior to working in the Clinton administration, I had a significantly greater opportunity than many of my future colleagues to immerse myself in the history of the region and its contemporary developments. These included more scholarly writings on the Balkans (for example, Suzanne Woodward's research that led to the publication of *Balkan Tragedy* in 1995, and Charles and Barbara Jelavich's *History of the Balkans*) as well as a broader range of the "classic" accounts (such as Ivo Andric's *Bridge on the Drina* or Milovan Djilas's account of the Tito era).[7]

However accurate (or superficial), the more widely read deep histories had an important impact in shaping how policymakers perceived the nature of the conflict and the efficacy of intervention. To the extent that the contemporary violence was seen as the latest manifestation of what Kaplan calls "ancient hatreds" that had been temporarily suppressed during the Tito era, policymakers were inclined to see the conflict as a long-standing ethnic/religious dispute in which the United States had little stake, little ability to influence through intervention (especially military intervention), and risked prolonged and costly commitment in blood and treasure. To the extent that policymakers viewed the region (and especially Bosnia) as a uniquely successful and tolerant blending of religion and culture, which was threatened by exploitative ex-communist leaders (for example, Serbia's Slobodan Milosevic and Croatia's Franjo Tudjman) seeking to sustain their grip on power by stirring up ethnic animosity where none had existed for some time, intervention appeared both more compelling and more likely to lead to a stable and successful outcome.

One important dimension where understandings of history divided American policymakers from their European counterparts was in how each viewed the protagonists in the conflict. It seemed clear that for leading European policymakers, their understanding of the respective roles of Croatia, Serbia, and Bosnia (the latter a proxy in many European minds for the Ottoman Empire) shaped their response to the crisis. Thus, German policymakers in particular were inclined to see Croatia through the lens of its identity as a truly "European" state by virtue of its role in the Austro-Hungarian Empire as well as ties between Catholic Bavaria and Croatia, which contributed to an important degree to Germany's push for European recognition of Croatian independence in the early months of the conflict.[8] By contrast, France's sympathy with Serbia was deeply intertwined with the partisan resistance to Adolf Hitler and his ally, the Croatian Ustashe, leading both to skepticism about supporting Tudjman-led Croatia and greater sympathy for Serbian arguments for seeking to preserve some kind of confederated Yugoslavia. Both Russia's and Greece's historic and cultural ties to the Serbian Orthodox Church also inclined them to see the conflict through Serbian eyes. Most Europeans tended to be skeptical about Bosnia, seeing it more as an artificial collection of three distinct nationalities with very disparate histories and traditions rather than a distinctive "Bosniac" history and culture that would support a nation-state—the latter being a view more widely accepted by American policymakers. Thus, even those Europeans who were inclined to support independence for Slovenia and Croatia balked at recognizing Bosnia. (The perspective of former British minister David Owen, who led early efforts to negotiate a political settlement in Yugoslavia, is reflective of this view.)

Over time, the impact of these diverse understandings of deep history dissipated, in part because policymakers became more aware of the competing historical narratives and paradigms, and in part because their own personal exposure to the conflict and interactions with the protagonists allowed them to form their own personal judgments. Most important, the impact dissipated because, as the political stakes grew in the United States and Europe as the conflict deepened, the deep history seemed less relevant than the complex contemporary reality and assessments of the impact of various courses of action on policymakers' perception of national interest—such as the future viability of NATO, the attitude of the Muslim world toward the United States and Europe, and the possible spillover effect on other countries in the region.

Analogies and Paradigms

As many observers have noted, analogies and paradigms play a powerful role in shaping the perspectives of policymakers. Analogies are epistemological—they help policymakers define which aspects of a phenomenon are significant and which should be treated as epiphenomenal. They also serve as a laboratory for causal explanation, relating means and ends, and a test of the efficacy of various policy responses. While policymakers employ a range of methodological sophistication in how they use analogies, and how well they understand the utility and limits of them, in the policy and political debates over the Balkans analogies undoubtedly played a significant role.

Most of the analogies that dominated the U.S. debate were drawn from European experience, and so could also be seen as an element of deep history. But others emerged from prior experiences of U.S. foreign interventions and experience with the use of force to achieve national objectives.

There were two dominant competing paradigms that helped influence Balkan policy in the 1990s. One was drawn from the experience of the late nineteenth and early twentieth centuries (encapsulated in Otto von Bismarck's epigram, "the Balkans were not worth the bones of a Pomeranian grenadier"), which tended to reinforce a view that events in the Balkans were not central to European security but through misguided intervention could lead to wider conflict (a view that was reinforced by Russia's support for Serbia and the danger of spillover to NATO/Russia relations—so vividly illustrated by the Pristina Airport confrontation during the Kosovo War). The second was the Munich/Holocaust analogy, which focused policymakers on both the moral and practical consequences of standing by in the face of aggression and genocide.

Personal History

Some of the key policymakers in both the Bush and Clinton administrations had their own personal histories in the Balkans which shaped their views of the conflict.[9] Both Scowcroft and Eagleburger had served in Belgrade, and though it is hard to say with certainty (and I suspect they would not necessarily agree), their time there had two possible impacts. The first was their familiarity with Serbian history and culture, which led them to be more reluctant to demonize the Serbs as Yugoslavia began to disintegrate. Second, that same familiarity led them to a greater willingness to sympathize with the Serbian narrative—that Serbian actions to prevent the independence of Croatia and Bosnia were motivated by a desire to prevent the persecution of ethnic Serbs that would follow the breakup rather than to preserve Serbia's domination of the region.

This is not to say that this was the sole or even dominant factor influencing the Bush administration's reluctance to intervene—it can be credibly argued that the administration was worried in the immediate aftermath of the reunification of Germany that supporting the dissolution of Yugoslavia would lead to similar developments in the Soviet Union and that this would be highly destabilizing.

In the Clinton administration, two key U.S. policymakers also had personal histories in the region—Madeleine Albright (who served first as U.S. permanent representative to the UN and later as secretary of state) and Richard Holbrooke (Clinton's second assistant secretary of state for Europe and later Albright's successor at the UN). Albright's father had served in Serbia as a Czech diplomat (indeed, she was born in Belgrade). Holbrooke had as a young man traveled in the region—an experience he features in the Prologue of *To End a War*, his autobiographical account of the U.S. role in bringing about the Dayton Accords.[10]

For Albright, as a Czech, personal history also played an important role by virtue of the family's exposure first to the abandonment of Czechoslovakia to the Nazis at the outset of World War II and later, following the war, to the Communists—a history that made her especially sensitive to the powerful Munich and Yalta analogies.[11]

Personal history undoubtedly influenced Joint Chiefs of Staff chairman Colin Powell—though it was not personal history with the Balkans, but instead with Vietnam, that had broadly influenced his view about U.S.

Albright v. Powell ✱

Vietnam legacy

intervention and the use of force. In simplified terms, Powell and like-minded general officers who came of age during the Vietnam War drew on that experience for two lessons: skepticism toward deploying U.S. military forces in the absence of direct threats to U.S. security, and opposition to the limited U.S. of force short of "total victory." Albright characterized the cautious approach of Powell as a product of the Vietnam and Gulf War Syndromes.[12]

Those disparate historic frames dominated the often heated debate between Albright and Powell, so vividly captured in the infamous situation room confrontation where Albright's advocacy for intervention led Powell to his "near aneurysm."[13]

For the Clinton administration, and especially for President Clinton himself, who had little "personal experience" of international relations before becoming president, the personal history was largely the near-contemporary experiences of the first year in office—especially those of Somalia and Rwanda. Clinton's campaign for the presidency was highly critical of the Bush administration's failure to act in the Balkans—a position that some saw as an effort to bolster his credibility as a strong foreign policy leader as well as to provide a contrast with his opponent. But once in office, the decisive tone of the campaign was succeeded by greater uncertainty and division within the administration about what course of action to pursue—a division compounded by the events of the first year.[14] Of course, these experiences cut in opposite directions. The tragic U.S. involvement in Somalia's ethnic and tribal conflicts lent resonance to Kaplan's narrative for the Balkans and reinforced caution. But the experience of Rwanda, and the failure of the United States and the international community to halt the genocide there, lent even greater power to the Holocaust/Munich analogies, especially after Srebenica.

This historical overlay on the way in which the United States should use force also influenced the decisions over the nature of the peacekeeping operation following the Dayton Accords. For the president and many of his civilian advisers in the White House and at the State Department, there was a strong inclination to try to minimize the size, duration, and rules of engagement associated with the NATO-led peacekeeping operation, the Implementation Force; this was driven by concerns about cost and congressional opposition to U.S. involvement in peacekeeping operations fueled by the Vietnam analogy of "quagmire" and the experience of trying to sustain military operations without substantial public support or a clear exit strategy. But the Pentagon, led by officers who had served in Vietnam, drew a different lesson from that war and pushed hard and for a substantial force with robust rules of engagement and no time limit on the deployment. The end result split the difference: a large force with robust rules of engagement, but with an initial one-year time limit.[15]

By the time the United States and Europe began to debate the need to intervene in Kosovo in 1998–99, these considerations of history had receded, but still exercised an influence—particularly over the choice of military strategy. Here the historical understanding of the role and limits of strategic bombing figured into the debate, with civilian advisers largely focused on the danger of a ground war without popular support (as in Vietnam), while the military focused on the difficulty of achieving war termination objectives solely through the use of air power (as in World War II).

Taken together, these three dimensions of history helped frame for policymakers the nature of the stakes (or lack thereof) in the Balkans, helped shape their views of the efficacy of intervention, and helped color their perception of the longer-term consequences of intervention.

The Impact of the Balkan Conflict on the Decision to Intervene in Afghanistan and Libya

It seems only fitting, given the prominent role of history in shaping the debate over U.S. intervention in the Balkans, that this historical experience of the Balkans should shape subsequent debates over U.S. intervention—first in Afghanistan under Bush, and then in Libya under Obama.

For the Bush administration, most of the lessons from history from the Balkans were negative ones. During the 2000 campaign, Bush's key advisers heavily criticized the U.S. decision to intervene in Kosovo—vividly encapsulated in Condoleezza Rice's and Robert Zoellick's respective *Foreign Affairs* articles in 2000 and Rice's opposition to the use of the Eighty-Second Airborne Division "to escort children to school."[16] For them the experience of Kosovo validated their earlier paradigm from the George H. W. Bush administration and led to the early statements of President George W. Bush that criticized nation building.

Kosovo also shaped the thinking of the Bush administration on the application of force. While the Clinton team tended to view the often painstaking coalition efforts to prosecute the war as central to sustaining political cohesion (and thus contributing to the ultimate successful outcome), for Donald Rumsfeld and his advisers, the opposite lesson was drawn: never again should the United States agree to allow the alliance to constrain operational military decisions. This historical lesson profoundly shaped Rumsfeld's approach to the Afghanistan War where, despite NATO's political decision to invoke article 5 of the Washington Treaty, the Bush administration declined to use NATO mechanisms to organize the intervention in Afghanistan. The Bush administration's historically based reservations about peacekeeping and nation building also shaped the approach to the aftermath of the initial interventions in both Afghanistan and Iraq—a focus on the near-term military objective of defeating an enemy regime and a reluctance to plan and execute for a long-term engagement.

If for the Bush team Kosovo was a lesson in what not to do, for the veterans of the Clinton administration who joined the Obama administration Kosovo was an important success. Their version of the lessons of Kosovo contained at least five elements: (1) U.S. soft power and moral legitimacy, damaged by the delayed intervention in Bosnia, was at least partially restored by preventing a genocide in Kosovo; (2) by intervening on behalf of a Muslim population persecuted by a "European" nation, the United States helped quell a perception that America and NATO cared only about protecting Christians, and this would help Washington in working with allies in the Arab and Muslim world; (3) building a broad-based political coalition through NATO helped strengthen the legitimacy of the intervention (particularly in the absence of a UN Security Council resolution); (4) the United States could successfully pursue limited war aims (reversing the ethnic cleansing of Kosovar Albanians) while deferring the "regime change" objective (of unseating Milosevic) to subsequent political and economic tools; and (5) an air campaign, in conjunction with indigenous armed force on the ground, could succeed in achieving military objectives.

As the crisis in Libya began to unfold, the Kosovo (and Bosnia) analogy became increasingly compelling to many in the Obama administration. Muammar Qaddafi's actions and rhetoric vividly recalled the humanitarian catastrophe that unfolded in Kosovo in 1998 and early 1999, and the Obama team thus began to put together the Kosovo playbook, drawing on the five elements discussed above. It led the effort to assemble a broad-based coalition to provide political legitimacy, with NATO at the core for military operations, and adopted a military strategy that rejected the idea of safe havens (the failed pre-Srebenica approach in Bosnia) but also rejected "boots on the ground" intervention. The Obama team took advantage of a de facto alliance with an indigenous force that substituted for the lack of ground operations on the part of the United States and its allies; it articulated war termination goals that focused on ending the humanitarian threat, while deferring the political objective of replacing Qaddafi to nonmilitary means. A political soft power rationale supplemented the humanitarian argument for intervention; in particular, the administration worried about the impact on prodemocracy forces in the wider Arab world if Washington stood by while democracy advocates where crushed by Qaddafi.

Not surprisingly, many of the alumni of the Bush administration joined the critics of the Libya intervention, in part based on their negative conclusions from the Bosnia and Kosovo narrative. They questioned whether America had sufficient strategic interests in Libya to justify even the limited costs in blood and treasure. They doubted the efficacy of an air-only campaign—particularly one run through NATO. They saw in Libya another ethnically/tribally divided artificial state, where the long-term outcome was likely to be sustained civil war. They doubted the democratic/liberal credentials of the forces the United States was supporting (in Libya, the danger being one of Islamic extremists; in Kosovo, the illiberal and corrupt Kosovo Liberation Army). And they worried about sacrificing relations with key international partners (Russia and China) for nonstrategic purposes (recalling the deep impact that the interventions in the Balkans had on souring U.S.-NATO relations with Russia and strengthening nationalist/anti-Western forces, not to mention the impact of the Kosovo bombings on China).

Conclusion: The Balkans and the Uses of History

The experience of the Balkans, both as the object and subject of the use of history in policymaking, illustrates some of the common themes that run through the literature on the use and abuse of history. First, these experiences show the power of historical narratives in how policymakers define the nature of the policy problem as well how they make judgments about the efficacy and consequences of the choice of policy options. Second, they suggest, as Richard Neustadt and Ernest May argue, that some historical analogies are more powerful, influential, and seductive than others, and policymakers try to associate their contemporary arguments with the more "compelling" narratives (Munich rather than Vietnam, for example). Third, these cases suggest that personal experience plays a particularly significant role in choosing which historical experience to apply.[17] Finally, the cases suggest the inherent indeterminacy of reasoning from history, in the sense that policymakers could derive diametrically opposite conclusions from looking at the same historical experiences.

This final conclusion seems deeply unsatisfactory. Can anything be said from these experiences to improve policymaking going forward? If history decides nothing, why bother? Yet this seems too pessimistic. If nothing else, historical experience and analogy help clarify the issues. The debate over which historical analogies to use and what conclusions should be drawn makes more transparent the underlying assumptions and causal logic that inform policy choices. In addition, once assumptions and implied causal chains are clarified by arguments from history, it may be easier to bring quantitative and qualitative research to bear and to adapt and adjust policy as it moves forward.

In fact, the conjunction of these two policy episodes illustrates that constructive historical learning does take place. For example, the Clinton administration's assumptions about the efficacy of coalition warfare and air-only campaigns was put in doubt by Milosevic's resistance to the initial air attacks and the limited capability of the Kosovo Liberation Army to operate on the ground—which undoubtedly helped play a role in the Obama team's greater willingness to support arming the Transitional National Council in Libya and insistence on a wider mandate for the UN-authorized NATO military operation.[18] Although there are risks from learning from failure as well as success, there is a greater likelihood that failure will lead to a more penetrating and nuanced look at the potential contributing factors, whereas there would seem to be a greater danger that success will lead to an unexamined instinct to "run the same play again" without reflecting on whether the conditions that made the play successful the first time around will prevail in the subsequent case.[19]

These episodes also have some bearing on the value of personal (historical) experience. Many analysts have rightly pointed to the dangers of reliance (or at least overreliance) on personal experience. Robert Jervis quotes Bismarck as saying: "Fools learn by experience, wise men learn by others' experience."[20] But I believe that this excessively discounts the value gained from personal experience—particularly the contextually rich knowledge that firsthand participants can bring to understanding all the factors that went into decisionmaking and their potential impact on outcomes. In this respect, personal experience is equivalent to deep history: the participant brings some of the same value that a historian brings via a deep knowledge of a particular era or series of events, though perhaps lacking the "detachment" of the scholar.[21] Although there are risks in learning from experience, it still seems preferable to superficial appeals to historical learning and analogy, or the application of theory without the benefit of context.

Notes

1. This is similar to what Richard E. Neustadt and Ernest R. May call "issue history." See Richard E. Neustadt and Ernest R. May, *Thinking in Time: The Uses of History for Decision Makers* (New York: Free Press, 1988).

2. In *Thinking in Time*, Neustadt and May do not seem to consider this as history; they distinguish history as "vicarious" as opposed to actual experience. But the events that are personally experienced by some in the policy deliberations are vicarious to others. Those who have experienced historical events will bring a distinct perspective, but it is not obviously less a use of history than those whose interpretation is colored by an influential teacher or author.

3. Eagleburger served as second secretary in Belgrade from 1962 to 1965 and ambassador from 1977 to 1981. Scowcroft was assistant air attaché from 1959 to 1961. See Tom Gallagher, *Outcast Europe: The Balkans 1789–1989, from the Ottomans to Milosevic* (New York: Routledge, 2001), 196.

4. To be clear at the outset, this is not a research paper. I have not attempted to interview the participants involved to get their views on the role of history in shaping their ideas, nor consulted either primary sources (for example, oral histories) nor reviewed in detail secondary accounts (biographies and analytic studies). In a few places I have cited secondary material where it was previously familiar to me. For this reason, the observations here are highly impressionistic and subjective—except, of course, with respect to my own thinking (and even there runs the risk of distortion through blurred memory and the impact of hindsight).

5. Robert D. Kaplan, *Balkan Ghosts* (New York: Picador, 2005).

6. Rebecca West, *Black Lamb and Grey Falcon* (New York: Penguin, 1969).

7. Suzanne Woodward, *Balkan Tragedy: Chaos and Dissolution after the Cold War* (Brookings Institution Press, 1995); Barbara Jelavich, *History of the Balkans,* vol. 1: *Eighteenth and Nineteenth Century* (Cambridge University Press, 1983) and Barbara Jelavich, *History of the Balkans,* vol. 2: *Twentieth Century* (Cambridge University Press, 1983); Charles Jelavich and Barbara Jelavich, *The Balkans*

(Englewood Cliffs, N.J.: Prentice Hall, 1965); Ivo Andric, *The Bridge on the Drina*, Phoenix ed. (University of Chicago Press, 1977); Milovan Djilas, *Rise and Fall*, translated by John Fisk Loud (San Diego: Harcourt, Brace Jovanovich, 1986).

8. See Marcus Tanner, *Croatia: A Nation Forged in War*, 3rd ed. (Yale University Press, 2010). Genscher himself attributes the German position to its commitment to freedom and self-determination; see Hans-Dietrich Genscher, *Rebuilding a House Divided* (New York: Broadway Books, 1998); and Sonia Lucarelli, *Europe and the Breakup of Yugoslavia* (Leiden, Netherlands: Nijhoff, 2000), 124–25.

9. For a discussion of the impact of personal experiences, see Robert Jervis, *Perception and Misperception in International Politics* (Princeton University Press, 1976).

10. It is noteworthy that in the prologue to his memoir, Holbrooke characterizes the assassination of Archduke Ferdinand as an "act of extreme nationalism" that "came back to me vividly when Yugoslavia fell apart." Indeed, Holbrooke's account is full of historical allusions—see, for example, his diary note for August 14, 1992: "Such destruction is clearly not the result of fighting, but of a systematic pogrom. . . . This is how it must have been in Central Europe and Russia a century ago." Holbrooke, *To End a War* (New York: Modern Library, 1999), xix, 37.

11. See Michael Dobbs, *Madeleine Albright: A Twentieth-Century Odyssey* (New York: Henry Holt, 1999), 418: "Madeleine's interest in the Balkans was not just academic. It was personal and visceral."

12. Dobbs, *Madeleine Albright*.

13. Ibid., 360. Dobbs suggests that Tony Lake, who also served in Vietnam, shared some of Powell's reservations for the same reason.

14. For a more in-depth discussion on how campaigns shape new administrations' approach to foreign policy in the early years in office, see Kurt Campbell and James Steinberg, *Difficult Transitions* (Brookings Institution Press, 2008).

15. Albright characterized this as the Gulf War Syndrome: "Don't do it unless you can deploy 500,000 Marines." Dobbs, *Madeleine Albright*, 360.

16. Condoleezza Rice, "Campaign 2000: Promoting the National Interest," *Foreign Affairs* 71, no. 1 (2000); Robert B. Zoellick, "Campaign 2000: A Republican Foreign Policy," *Foreign Affairs* 71, no. 1 (2000; www.foreignaffairs.com/articles /2000-01-01/campaign-2000-promoting-national-interest). As with Clinton in 1993, the critique was also colored by the political campaign—as a means of drawing a contrast with the incumbent administration, represented by the Democratic candidate, Vice President Al Gore.

17. Jervis noted this much earlier; see Jervis, *Perception and Misperception*, 215.

18. Although beyond the scope of this paper, it can also be argued that the difficulties encountered by the Obama administration in the aftermath of the Libya intervention—difficulties that suggest that Kosovo might not have been as good an analogy as was first thought, and as critics at the time argued—have in turn led to the administration's caution about intervention in Syria.

19. For a discussion of the different lessons learned (and mislearned) from success and failure, see Jervis, *Perception and Misperception*, 231–33.

20. Jervis, *Perception and Misperception*, 239. Jervis is particularly critical of and cautionary on learning from personal experience.

21. Jervis acknowledges the logic of this argument but dismisses it on the grounds that "a person who knows the details and complexities of the case should be slow to see other situations as being like it and should draw only careful, limited conclusions." He implies that misuse of personal experience leads to worse outcomes than no experience at all. Jervis, *Perception and Misperception*, 247. He is right to caution about the risks, but his argument goes too far. Of course, personal experience should be used judiciously, just as historical learning, not personally experienced, should be used judiciously. But, as I suggest above, for the thoughtful practitioner it is surely preferable to decisionmaking with no empirical underpinning.

11

PETER FEAVER AND WILLIAM INBODEN

Looking Forward through the Past

The Role of History in Bush White House
National Security Policymaking

Reading history gives a long-term perspective. The job of a
president is to look over the horizon to how things might be,
not just how they are at that moment. Looking over the
horizon helps you be optimistic.

—GEORGE W. BUSH, INTERVIEW, JUNE 21, 2011, DALLAS, TEXAS

This quote from President Bush captures some of the complex ways
history has shaped the consequential and controversial efforts of the Bush
administration to respond to the national security challenges of the 9/11
era. A historical sensibility pervaded the thinking of Bush and many senior members of his administration, just as critics of the administration's
foreign policy also often marshaled historical arguments in making their
critiques.

However, for all of the various efforts by the Bush administration to
apply historical insights to the post-9/11 national security environment,
the fact remained that the attacks on September 11, 2001, were themselves
historically unprecedented. This itself functioned as a "lesson of history"
for the Bush administration in that it highlighted just how profoundly new
and alien this new era would be. History demonstrated that never before

253

in the modern era had the American homeland suffered such a catastrophic and costly attack from a foreign enemy. Never before had a foe been able to use such asymmetric and irregular means to wreak such destruction; never before had American civilians been the targets of such a massive strike; and never before had Islamic jihadists wrought such carnage on the United States as part of a global ideological campaign. All of these "never befores" served as their own lessons of history—in this case, searing in the minds of President Bush and his team the resolve that "never before" would also have to mean "never again."

Bush and his national security team believed they were consequential actors in a historical drama that would neither be concluded nor fully understood during his administration, but only over a longer span of time with the unfolding of history. This dynamic plays out on two broadly defined levels.

First and most fundamental is the ideational level. Leaders arrive in office with a worldview profoundly shaped by their own historical experience. They have a theory of how the world works, which helps assign priorities, warn against certain pitfalls, and make particular policy approaches salient and attractive. Some aspects of this ideational influence are implicit, discernible in hindsight through the patterns of response the administration accumulates. Others are quite explicit—for instance, when flagged in contemporaneous invocations of the "lessons of history."

The second level is instrumental, referring to the operational way any White House establishes procedures for policymaking and implementation. The pragmatic choices of staffing, organization, and procedures all have profound implications for the way the historical mind-set will be brought to bear.

In this chapter we trace the ideational and instrumental roles of history in the Bush White House, especially as it pertains to foreign policy. We cover the entire Bush presidency, but focus particularly on the second term, when we observed these dynamics firsthand while serving on the National Security Council staff. Our argument is that the themes present in this edited volume were especially vivid in the Bush presidency. Bush was a leader with a definite historical cast of mind; he served at a time when historical thinking was an especially fertile way of approaching the major policy challenges of the day; and the administration's most consequential choices could often be traced back to specific historical judgments.

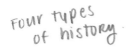

We have specific meanings in mind by our terms *history, historical,* and *historical cast of mind.* We argue, as one of us has previously written, that policymakers use four types of history: experience, memory, tradition, and study. Experience describes the firsthand policy experience that policymakers participated in at previous points in their careers. Memory refers to formative life episodes that leaders lived through personally but did not participate in as policymakers. Tradition describes the historical impressions that exist in the collective mind of a society and are inherited by succeeding generations, although not experienced firsthand. Study is learning of the past through reading books about history.[1] Although all four of these types of history functioned in the minds of Bush administration policymakers—as is the case with any presidential administration—this chapter will contend that experience and study were the two most preponderant types.

Any effort to explore the use of history in the Bush administration soon confronts two paradoxes. First, a president widely reviled as anti-intellectual and supposedly bereft of intelligence was in fact the most avid reader of history among presidents since Harry S. Truman, and possibly since Theodore Roosevelt. Second, an administration that self-consciously tried to draw on historical insights found itself facing what appeared to them to be a historically unprecedented conflict against a foe steeped in its own peculiar history. In short, history was inescapable, yet it was also an uncertain guide.

President Bush often deflected requests for self-assessment and critique with the observation that "I did what I did and ultimately history will be the judge."[2] Such historical judgment is evolving and will continue to evolve. Yet it is not too soon to recognize that this was a president and a presidency profoundly shaped by history—a legacy formed by certain worldviews and by explicit steps taken to translate those historical judgments into far-reaching policies.

Context at the Ideational Level: Worldviews and Historical Legacies

President Bush arrived in office with certain historically informed judgments that collectively added up to a worldview.[3] Some of these judgments were explicit and perhaps even partisan: he believed that President Bill

Clinton had brought dishonor to the presidency because of his promiscuous behavior in the White House, and so Bush arrived determined to restore the dignity and honor the office had enjoyed in earlier times.[4] Likewise, Bush believed that the United States had lost global stature because of what he deemed as Clinton's feckless and arrogant approach to foreign policy. In contrast, Bush stated his determination to restore respect for American power and purpose, and campaigned on the promise of a more "humble" foreign policy.[5] Moreover, the president and his team believed that the authority and power of the presidency had eroded in the decades since the Watergate scandal, and they arrived determined to restore presidential prerogatives that they believed had been wrongly ceded to other branches of government.[6]

These historical judgments, and the concomitant antipathy to policies and practices associated with President Clinton, translated into specific initiatives during the earliest days of the Bush administration. Yet it was a deeper context, more implicit than explicit, that arguably had the most profound effect on foreign policy: the way in which one particular episode, the end of the Cold War, shaped the worldviews of the Bush team.

Key members of Bush's national security team (including Dick Cheney, Condoleezza Rice, Colin Powell, Steve Hadley, Paul Wolfowitz, Robert Zoellick, and Richard Armitage) played pivotal roles in bringing about the successful conclusion of the Cold War. In historian Melvyn Leffler's words, "The decisive experience in the professional lives of Bush's advisers was the U.S. victory over the forces of Soviet-led world communism."[7] Philip Zelikow made a similar observation: "The new group did not have a tragic view of America's history. Their formative years as public leaders had been in the late 1980s and early 1990s—the end of the Cold War. They had personally been very close to some remarkably positive changes in the world. They associated these changes with America's beneficial influence and example."[8] Arguably Zelikow's description here could apply to President Bush himself, who had witnessed firsthand his father's deft management of the Cold War's peaceful and successful end. The optimism of this post–Cold War worldview emerges, among many other places, in the opening sentence of Bush's letter introducing the 2002 National Security Strategy, which states, "The great struggles of the twentieth century between liberty and totalitarianism ended with a decisive victory for the forces of freedom—and a single sustainable model for national success: freedom, democracy, and free enterprise."[9]

Two caveats should be noted here. First, as formative as the end of the Cold War was for many administration principals, they did not all take away the same lessons and paradigmatic insights from the Cold War's denouement. For example, Powell, Armitage, and arguably Rice and Hadley seemed to have been most influenced by the prudent alliance management and restrained use of force that characterized American policy during the George H. W. Bush administration, whereas Cheney, Wolfowitz, and Douglas Feith took away from the same period the lessons, in Leffler's description, "that toughness, determination, and conviction were the values that shaped history. Moral clarity was imperative."[10] Second, a partial exception to the dominance of the end of the Cold War paradigm was Donald Rumsfeld, whose formative policy years had been during the administration of President Gerald R. Ford in the midst of the Cold War, and who did not hold any policy leadership positions in the pivotal 1988–91 window. However, Rumsfeld arrived for his second tour as secretary of defense with his own set of historical lessons in mind. For example, his view of the Cold War shaped his view of the very different post–Cold War security environment. This included the perceived need for a wholesale transformation of the military into a lighter, more flexible, technologically astute force; strong support for a full spectrum of ballistic missile defense capabilities to defend against the possibility of missiles launched by rogue actors; and Rumsfeld's belief that the ongoing U.S. troop presence on an open-ended peacekeeping deployment in the Balkans represented lamentable mission creep and cultivated unhealthy local dependencies on American forces.[11]

While Leffler, Zelikow, and others are essentially correct in highlighting the Cold War victory as the foreign policy experience that was the most formative on most Bush administration principals, the Cold War conflict itself should not be underestimated as an influential factor. Several features of the Cold War conflict—such as maintaining an international balance of power, engaging in a global ideological contest, developing cooperative alliances with unsavory regimes, and marshaling all elements of national power—also shaped the Bush administration's approach to the so-called war on terror. One way to summarize the competing impulses in the Bush administration's national security policy would be the perpetual tension between two historical experiences: the Cold War's conduct in the 1970s and 1980s, and the Cold War triumph of 1989–91.

As dominant as the Cold War paradigms were on the collective minds of Bush administration leaders, other dimensions of history also played a part. For example, Peter Baker describes how Vice President Cheney read classicist Victor Davis Hanson's book *An Autumn of War*, which "made such a powerful impression on him that he invited Hanson for a visit. Cheney was particularly interested in the classically tragic view, from Sophocles to the American Western, that there are not always good and bad choices, but bad and worse choices." In the context of the 2002 debate over Iraq, Baker notes that "for Cheney, leaving Hussein in power was worse than the bad choice of taking him out."[12] This tragic view of history and policy, generally underexplored by scholars and other observers of the Bush administration, played a larger role than has thus far been appreciated in shaping the administration's difficult choices in the post-9/11 era.

Context at the Institutionalist Level: A Team of Historians

The president and his senior national security team had not only well-developed historical worldviews but also an abundance of what might be called the "historical cast of mind." To a remarkable extent, they were formally trained in history, identified mentoring from historians as key formative experiences, or were simply avid readers of history.

Both President Bush and Vice President Cheney were devoted readers of history even before they arrived in office. Condoleezza Rice, the national security adviser, was an academic political scientist, but in the historical-qualitative tradition of such predecessors as Henry Kissinger and Zbigniew Brzezinski. One of her most important academic publications was a richly detailed history of the end of the Cold War and the unification of Germany.[13] Karl Rove, the president's chief political adviser, never finished college but was an especially well-read amateur historian. At first blush, Secretary of Defense Rumsfeld and Secretary of State Powell would not seem to fit the pattern, yet both in their own way had a pronounced sense of history. Rumsfeld came to office with an unusually extensive background in public service and, as noted above, held especially vivid lessons of history relating to the proper use of American power. Powell, as the first African American to serve in several senior posts (national security adviser, chairman of the Joint Chiefs of Staff, and now secretary of state), likewise seemed markedly self-conscious about his role in history.

The pattern was replicated at the senior levels of staff. Deputy National Security Adviser Stephen Hadley often noted how his own intellectual development had been shaped by the influence of renowned Cornell University diplomatic historian Walter LaFeber, and Deputy National Security Adviser Robert Blackwill was a protégé and former faculty colleague at Harvard University's Kennedy School of Ernest May, author of the most influential books yet written on how history shapes statecraft.[14] Other notable national security staff in this category included Drew Erdmann (with a Ph.D. in history, and also a protégé of Ernest May) and Aaron Friedberg (a historically minded political scientist). The speechwriting shop is often a home for history aficionados, and in Bush's White House two speechwriters in particular—Michael Gerson, the head speechwriter and later senior adviser to the president, and Peter Wehner, who went on to head the Office of Strategic Initiatives under Karl Rove—read widely and deeply in history. Together these staffers inaugurated a practice that was expanded in Bush's second term: convening White House "salons" with distinguished intellectuals and scholars to discuss ways of bringing historical insight to bear on pressing policy problems.

The Strategic Context and the 9/11 Shock: Which Lesson of History to Invoke?

Every president thinks he is in a special historical period, a pivotal time of choosing. President Bush arrived in office believing that his key foreign policy strategic choice involved the opportunity to jump a generation in the arms race and thus lock in American pre-eminence for many years to come.[15] He also came into office determined to do big, consequential things. He criticized the Clinton approach as a "small ball" one: additional cops on patrol, midnight basketball leagues, and other poll-tested initiatives that narrowly split the difference between liberals and conservatives.[16] Instead, President Bush was determined to pursue major foreign policy initiatives, such as a fundamental reform of foreign aid, a new approach to China and India, and completing former president Ronald Reagan's vision by deploying a viable missile-defense shield. As it happened, the Bush presidency proved more pivotal than Bush himself expected, and in ways he never anticipated. Far from presiding over a time of strategic pause, Bush became a permanent "wartime president," launched into a difficult and violent struggle with a network of violent terrorists inspired by a perverse form of militant Islamism.

The 9/11 attacks constituted a profound strategic shock, arguably more consequential in terms of concentrating the mind of the president, his cabinet, and key White House staffers than any other external shock since the day of infamy at Pearl Harbor. The trauma was especially vivid because the participants had good reason to believe that they were personally in the crosshairs and, but for some twists of fate or hand of providence, might have been victims themselves of the terrorists' plots.

As detailed in each of the many memoirs produced by Bush administration veterans, the attacks triggered agonizing discussions and intense reflection on their significance and meaning—as well as a persistent climate of anxiety about future attacks.[17] While the team viewed the jihadist threat as novel and to a certain extent unprecedented, the president and his team also quite deliberately looked to history to help them interpret this attack and to identify key parameters of this new age. The first intellectual move of consequence was to identify the most suitable historical parallel or analogy against which to measure, assess, and respond to the terrorist threat.[18] Initial punditry in the media drew the obvious parallel to the other famous sneak attack, Pearl Harbor. But despite its superficial similarities, President Bush and his team soon rejected that analogy as deficient; there would be no mass mobilization military response, and this would not end with a peace treaty signed aboard a battleship.[19] The White House also saw more contrasts than similarities with previous terrorist attacks, including earlier unsuccessful efforts by al Qaeda sympathizers to blow up the World Trade Center and the lone-wolf bombing attack by Timothy McVeigh in Oklahoma City. Those had been seen as crimes requiring a law enforcement response, whereas the Bush team saw 9/11 as unmistakably an act of war requiring a war frame to properly understand it and a war response to confront it properly.

The president and his advisers soon settled on the Cold War as the most insightful historical analogy overall. While they realized that there were certainly dissimilarities between the Cold War and the post-9/11 era, the parallels were seen as compelling. This would be a generational struggle, one that would likely outlast the Bush presidency even if he won a second term. It would have certain pitched battles, but would be fought just as much in the shadows using tools of intelligence, covert action, and other techniques developed during the Cold War. Most profoundly, this was an ideological struggle, pitting the terrorists' perverse aspirations of a dystopian future against the vision offered by free societies. Just as the Cold War had been won when the appeal of democracy and free markets trumped the allure of communism, so too would the war against terror be won when the appeal of ordered liberty would trump the allure of militant Islamism.[20] As Bush later reflected after leaving the White House, "History teaches that ideological struggles take time, and are long-term conflicts . . . as a leader it helped steady your nerves to know that over time terror tactics can be defeated."[21]

The Cold War analogy led administration principals to conceive of themselves at times in Trumanesque terms. As with the earlier architects of the Cold War, President Bush and his advisers saw themselves as laying the foundations and developing the new institutions and tools that future presidents would need to wage the war effectively. The institutional landscape was more cluttered at the start of the war on terror than it had been at the start of the Cold War, so the rate of institutional development and change was slower. Nevertheless, the Bush administration developed new international institutions (e.g., the Proliferation Security Initiative), new military tools/concepts (drone strikes and the fusion of intelligence and special operations forces), and new intelligence and law-enforcement tools (the Terrorist Surveillance Program, and extended detention at Guantanamo Bay), along with new positions and departments, such as director of national intelligence and the Department of Homeland Security. Many of these were continued and, in some cases, expanded by President Barack Obama.

The Bush team also looked to history to warn of possible errors in the American response to a surprise attack. From the outset, the administration was determined not to replicate the egregious mistake of World War II when the Roosevelt administration's war fervor swept up patriotic Japanese Americans en masse and interred them in detention camps. President Bush went to considerable lengths to avoid demonizing Islam and Muslims in general, and in particular called upon Americans to reach out to fellow Americans who were Muslim.

Likewise, the president saw in the 9/11 attacks a particular lesson of history: the danger of letting problems fester in the in-box. He and his team had arrived with a critique of the Clinton approach to terrorism—one that Bush derided in saying, "When I take action, I'm not going to fire a $2 million missile at an empty $10 tent and hit a camel in the butt"—but then had been deliberate in developing a comprehensive alternative approach.[22]

Indeed, a draft of such a comprehensive new strategy was literally on Rice's desk when the attacks hit, proving that the administration did not have the luxury of time that it had assumed. As a consequence, Bush and his advisers were determined to seize the initiative and not to "stand idly by while threats gather." This putative lesson led directly to the preemption doctrine, memorably articulated in the 2002 national security strategy and consequentially implemented in the 2003 invasion of Iraq.

Institutionalizing the Role of History in White House Policymaking: The Second Term

The trends and developments relating to the uses of history that were introduced in Bush's first term became more deeply entrenched in his second term because the strategic horizon was no longer reelection but rather policy consolidation and historical legacy.

Some of the developments involved significant personnel shifts. Historically minded players were given more institutional clout, as Condoleezza Rice moved over to the Department of State and Mike Gerson was elevated to assistant to the president for policy and strategic planning. Likewise the second term brought the ascendance or appointment of senior officials such as Robert Gates (with a Ph.D. in history), Robert Zoellick (an avid reader of history), and Eric Edelman (with a Ph.D. in history), as well as influential senior staff members such as Philip Zelikow (a history professor), Eliot Cohen (a historically minded security studies professor), Michael Doran (a history professor), Thomas Mahnken (a historically minded strategic studies professor), Mary Habeck (a history professor), and Paul Lettow (with a Ph.D. in history). In short, the historical cast of mind demonstrated at the top of the Bush administration was replicated in many ways at staff levels.

Other trends were more superficial but still revealing. For example, President Bush's passion for reading, especially for reading histories and biographies, blossomed into a celebrated reading competition with Karl Rove.[23]

Within the National Security Council (NSC), Stephen Hadley, who took over from Rice, created a new office, Strategic Planning and Institutional Reform (SPIR) and hired the two of us to get the office started.[24] SPIR had a broad portfolio, but one of its distinctive roles was the theme of this edited volume, self-consciously thinking through the use of history in national security policy. Hadley wanted the office to have a more "academic think-tank" flavor than the typical NSC directorate, and the choice of two Ph.D.s

to staff it—one a card-carrying academic and the other a card-carrying diplomatic historian—was deliberate.

SPIR institutionalized the uses of history in at least six different ways:

1. The office provided on-demand historical analyses. From time to time
   the president and other White House principals would ask for a historical analysis of a policy problem or other issue that was prominent
   on the president's agenda. This was in addition to and separate from
   the daily requests for further information that would be sent to the
   intelligence community and elsewhere asking for issue-specific background information. For example, one time during his daily brief in
   the summer of 2005, President Bush got into a debate with his briefers
   about the extent to which the White House directly intervened in
   embassy operations leading up to the 1979 Iranian hostage crisis.
   SPIR was tasked with writing a memo, based on the relevant academic
   literature, clarifying the matter.

2. The office developed self-initiated historical analyses. From time to
   time, SPIR identified issues that were ripe for historical analysis, perhaps because they pointed to an opportunity that the administration
   might otherwise be missing or to a challenge that warranted a different administration response. This was in addition to and separate
   from the myriad policy recommendations and intelligence warnings
   that the interagency system produced on a daily basis. For example,
   in early 2006 the SPIR office produced a memo for President Bush on
   the numerous parallels between his administration and the Truman
   administration in both domestic and international policy and politics. As one of us has described elsewhere in summarizing the
   themes of the memo, these similarities included "a populist diction
   style, low approval ratings, an unpopular localized hot war amidst a
   global ideological conflict, disputes with Congress and the Supreme
   Court over executive authority, efforts to forge new domestic and
   international institutions to address the prevailing security threat,
   and confidence in the eventual vindication of history."[25] The memo
   was intended to provide Bush and other senior administration officials with a sense of how the various national security policy and
   political issues it faced might interact with each other and might
   play out over time. This use of history is what Francis Gavin has described as "horizontal history," wherein history "can expose horizontal

connections over space and in depth" and provide "a more holistic picture of how policymaking actually works, allowing government officials to organize their processes to more effectively consider horizontal linkages in their work."[26] Bush began to make frequent references to the Truman administration in both public and private comments during his second term. For example, he devoted his May 27, 2006, West Point commencement address to parallels between Truman's efforts to build a strategy and institutions for the Cold War and the Bush administration's efforts to do the same in the war against Islamist terrorism.[27] In his memoir, Bush describes reading multiple histories of the Truman administration and drawing ample comparisons with his own presidency.[28]

3. The office identified and lobbied for historical milestones worth replicating. We were directly tasked with looking for opportunities that would allow President Bush to advance his policy agenda by referencing the past. For example, one initiative developed by the SPIR office and directly informed by history was Bush's 2007 visit to the Islamic Center of Washington. Mindful that 2007 marked the fiftieth anniversary of the center's dedication and President Dwight D. Eisenhower's historic visit, we proposed that President Bush make a sequel visit to the mosque on June 27, the same date as Eisenhower's attendance a half century earlier. Our proposal self-consciously drew on the Cold War analogy to serve as a reminder that the war on terror was not a war on Islam but a battle of ideas in which peaceful Muslims had an indispensable role to play. Just as President Eisenhower had used his mosque visit to encourage Muslim communities worldwide to support the West's effort in the Cold War against atheistic communism, we suggested that Bush's visit could show American support for peaceful and reformist Muslims in our shared struggle against violent jihadism. In proposing the presidential visit, we also included an idea developed in tandem with an interagency task force on counterradicalization: to appoint a special envoy to the Organization of the Islamic Conference (OIC). While Bush's visit drew on the historical precedent of Eisenhower's, the OIC appointment was historically unprecedented.[29]

4. The office took the lead in promoting and organizing the "salons" at the White House. SPIR would organize small group meetings for the president and senior staff with academic experts to provide a deeper

examination of a topic of special interest to the president. SPIR drew from a wide range of academic specialties, but the kind of academic that connected best with the president was the historian. In setting up these meetings, the SPIR office often worked closely with the White House Office of Strategic Initiatives, headed by Pete Wehner and overseen by Karl Rove. Historians who participated in such meetings included John Lewis Gaddis, Allen Guelzo, Mary Habeck, Gertrude Himmelfarb, Frederick Kagan, David M. Kennedy, Wilfred McClay, Walter McDougall, Andrew Roberts, Robert Satloff, and Jay Winik. Sometimes an author would be invited to meet after President Bush had read his or her book. For example, at Henry Kissinger's suggestion, President Bush read *A Savage War of Peace* as part of his effort to deepen his understanding of insurgency and counterinsurgency. Bush then invited the author, Sir Alastair Horne, to the White House for a follow-up discussion. Bush noted from the book that deaths in Algeria actually increased after the French withdrawal, an insight that appears to have influenced the president's decision to order the troop surge in Iraq.[30] Ironically, some scholars have regrettably misinterpreted this particular episode, which may serve as an unfortunate example of scholarly confirmation bias. For example, Margaret MacMillan snidely asserts without any citation, "The President does not seem concerned that the French eventually lost their war. . . . Bush found the book interesting but came to the conclusion that the French failed because their bureaucracy was not up to the job."[31]

5. SPIR was an active contributor to the list of recommended readings for the president. The president read voluminously, and encouraged senior staff to recommend books to fill his queue. The books that went over the best tended to be biographies and histories because the president saw them as most useful and instructive to his current circumstances. This was an opportunity to shape the White House policy conversation by bringing to the attention of senior leaders concepts and insights from academic history. For example, during the "revolt of the generals" episode in the spring of 2006, SPIR recommended that President Bush read H. R. McMaster's *Dereliction of Duty*, which described the Lyndon Johnson–Robert McNamara–Joint Chiefs relationship during the Vietnam War.[32] The rationale was not that Bush's relationship echoed Johnson's, but instead that McMaster's

book encapsulated how the U.S. Army "remembered" Vietnam and, in particular, enshrined certain military understandings of how the army should push back against White House policies it did not like. Reading the McMaster book helped Bush understand the norms that were shaping military behavior and dissent in his own time. On a similar theme, Bush also described himself as influenced by the reading of Eliot Cohen's *Supreme Command: Soldiers, Statesmen, and Leadership in Wartime* and its historical argument that civilian leaders need to assert strong leadership in holding their military commanders accountable.[33]

6. SPIR drew directly upon particular interpretations of history to develop policy options that were not organically arising from the interagency process. For example, during the winter of 2005–06, SPIR joined with the Near East and North Africa Directorate in a zero-based review of our Iran policy. President Bush had asked Stephen Hadley for new options, believing that the then extant policy line of negotiations led by the EU-3 was reaching the end of its utility.[34] The NSC staff were particularly interested in opportunities for forging deeper multilateral cooperation among the Gulf States, but in a way that would not automatically trigger the security spiral of containment alliances and encirclement. SPIR drew on the earlier Helsinki Accords process to propose that the administration consider establishing a Helsinki-like process in the Persian Gulf. Of course, the modalities would be different, but the thought was that a properly designed process could function as a "poisoned carrot" for the Iranian regime, just as the original Basket III in the Helsinki Accords had functioned for the Soviet Union. The idea never garnered enough support to come to fruition, but it is an example of a very deliberate review of history in order to broaden the options under consideration by policymakers.

Evaluating Patterns in History and White House Policymaking

Notably, as Jim Steinberg describes in his chapter on the Clinton and Obama administrations, personal history was a very powerful lens that refracted insights and applied them to the current policy problems in distinctive ways.[35] The most obvious example of this is how the national security team's personal experience with the way the last Iraq war ended unsatisfactorily primed the team members to avoid those problems, but perhaps also led them to underestimate the problems that they did encounter. These were, ironically, the problems arising from occupying Iraq—the very problems that they had avoided in the earlier war.

History was the lingua franca in which very disparate policy communities and individuals coming from very different disciplines could communicate. Economists, lawyers, engineers, natural and physical scientists, social scientists, and academic historians found common reference points in history. This cacophony of other voices making historical arguments can sometimes pose a particular challenge for academic historians, who often fall into one of two categories: they either eschew any policy engagement as "presentism," a hopelessly corrupting bastardization of the discipline, and instead argue (usually in vain) that history should not be employed in public policy debates, or they become so consumed by the political passions of the day that they lose a sense of historical perspective and merely become echoes of other partisan commentators.[36]

The Bush case also vividly illustrates how the rhetorical demands of the presidency place a premium on history. With nonstop speechifying, there is always a danger that history can be reduced to a crass instrumentalization as off-the-shelf anecdotes or allusions are exploited for their emotive appeal rather than consulted for their insight. But—these risks notwithstanding—history can and should be a part of statecraft. Among other things, history is indispensable for how leaders attempt to understand their own roles, craft their policies, and communicate with their own citizens as well as international audiences.

President Bush used his own reading of history to identify what he believed were patterns in the American past and to help him gauge the public mood. He would then try to address, and hopefully ameliorate, those concerns in speeches. For example, public disenchantment with international engagement became a particularly acute concern for Bush during his second term, and he warned against it in both private comments to his staff and public remarks to the American people. During his March 14, 2008, appearance at the Economic Club of New York, Bush was asked about diminishing public support for free trade initiatives. In a lengthy extemporaneous answer, he discussed the protectionist and isolationist impulses that he believed had developed in recent years. He noted that "the two run side by side: isolationism and protectionism. I might throw another 'ism,' and that's nativism. And that's what happened throughout our history. And probably the most grim reminder of what can happen to America during periods of isolationism and protectionism is what happened in the late— in the '30s, when we had this 'America first' policy, and Smoot-Hawley. And look where it got us."[37]

In making these remarks Bush used history as both a diagnostic tool to illuminate the prevailing domestic attitudes toward internationalism, and also as a warning—with the invocation of the Great Depression and World War II—against the maladies that can result from such attitudes and their concomitant policies. As the president later recalled, "History teaches that protectionist policies lead to economic deprivation. History teaches that cycles of isolationism, nativism, and protectionism emerge periodically in American history," and American leaders need to recognize and work against those trends.[38]

More controversially, Bush also invoked history in his September 12, 2002, address to the United Nations General Assembly, calling for robust action against Saddam Hussein's Iraq, using a provocative example from past efforts at international organization and collective security: "The founding members resolved that the peace of the world must never again be destroyed by the will and wickedness of any man. We created a United Nations Security Council so that, unlike the League of Nations, our deliberations would be more than talk, our resolutions would be more than wishes."[39] In pulling the League of Nations off the shelf of historical ignominy, Bush intended with just one phrase to remind his audience of the perils of inaction against a perceived threat. Not only could tyranny be strengthened and even greater war result but the international organization itself could destroy its relevance or even place its own continuing existence in peril.

The overall thrust of Bush's General Assembly speech, relying as it did on erroneous intelligence that Saddam possessed weapons of mass destruction, does not read well in hindsight. Yet two points should be borne in mind. First, the basic critique that the UN risked losing legitimacy if multiple UN Security Council resolutions went unenforced still rings true, perhaps all the more so in light of multiple resolutions flouted in subsequent years by the likes of Iran and North Korea. Second, as historian Melvyn

Leffler—certainly no apologist for the Bush administration, and in other ways critical of its foreign policy—points out, when it came to assessing Saddam's intentions, the Bush administration war proponents "actually got it right. Their assessments based on Saddam's history captured his intent. The inspectors who went back after the war and found no weapons of mass destruction nevertheless found ominous signs of a reckless regime in the hands of a ruthless leader whose intentions could not be trusted."[40]

History also played a major role in inspiring and shaping Bush's doctrine of democracy and human rights promotion, commonly known as the "freedom agenda." The president offered one of his most expansive early articulations of this strategy in his November 6, 2003, speech to the National Endowment for Democracy (NED)—a speech pervaded by historical consciousness. Because his remarks came on the occasion of NED's twentieth anniversary, Bush began paying homage to President Reagan's original creation of NED in his landmark 1982 Westminster speech. Noting how the former president's call for liberty in communist nations had been widely derided at the time, Bush contended that Reagan had been vindicated by subsequent events and by history itself. With this reference Bush also used history to preemptively caution contemporary skeptics of his democracy promotion policy. He then described the considerable growth of freedom and free institutions worldwide over the previous three decades and suggested that this represented a unique historical moment that would continue: "As the 20th century ended, there were around 120 democracies in the world—and I can assure you more are on the way. Ronald Reagan would be pleased, and he would not be surprised." From here Bush offered a predictive historical judgment: "Historians in the future will reflect on an extraordinary, undeniable fact: Over time, free nations grow stronger and dictatorships grow weaker."

The most notable and controversial part of the speech came when Bush turned to the "freedom deficit" in the Middle East, a region that had largely resisted the democratizations that had taken place on other continents. While noting the responsibility that Middle Eastern nations held for their own development, the president also offered an unvarnished historical critique of past American policies: "Sixty years of Western nations excusing and accommodating the lack of freedom in the Middle East did nothing to make us safe—because in the long run, stability cannot be purchased at the expense of liberty." This represented another use of history, as a penitential explanation of current challenges, and also a motivation for a new policy direction. Bush concluded by using a different history of American policies to cultivate support for his new democratization policy: "From the Fourteen Points to the Four Freedoms, to the Speech at Westminster, America has put our power at the service of principle. We believe that liberty is the design of nature; we believe that liberty is the direction of history."[41] In offering these contrasting narratives of American history—what he saw as the mistaken support for autocratic regimes against a more inspired tradition of supporting liberty—Bush used an appeal to the past to try to inspire a new policy direction.

Some of these same historical themes pervaded Bush's second inaugural address and its vigorous call for the global advance of freedom. Here Bush also employed history in another way with his assertion that "it is the policy of the United States to seek and support the growth of democratic movements and institutions in every nation and culture, with the ultimate goal of ending tyranny in our world."[42] This formulation represented a self-conscious historical echo of the Truman Doctrine, and in turn was Bush's effort to locate his freedom agenda in a particular tradition of American foreign policy.

An assessment of Bush's use of history would be incomplete without including the category that one of us has identified as "existential succor."[43] This describes leaders who read history—usually biographies of past statesmen—for comfort and perspective amid the acute loneliness of holding office as a chief executive. Terms like *succor* and *comfort* should not be misconstrued as condescending or indulging in psychological pabulum; rather, this use of history can provide a president a sense of perspective on his own situation, and often humility and gratitude. As Bush reflected after leaving office, "it is tempting to think that you've had it worse than anybody who went before, but a leader can't have self-pity. A way to help buoy your spirits is to read history" and understand that you are not the only one who has faced the challenges of office. Reading history is also "a way to understand how other presidents made decisions. Leaders need principles, vision, and implementation—and history gives perspective and usable lessons on leadership."[44] During the darkest days of the Iraq War, and particularly after he announced the controversial "surge" decision, Bush cited reading biographies of Abraham Lincoln as especially helpful. As he commented at the time to some NSC staff, including one of the present authors, "Thinking about what Lincoln went through lends some of that perspective to things. . . . I am no Lincoln, but I am in the same boat."[45]

Of course, the historical impulse did not always lead to policy success. In at least one case, analogizing may have backfired on the administration. In thinking about the postwar reconstruction and democratization project in Iraq, the White House quite explicitly analogized the difficulties Germany and Japan had democratizing after World War II and thereby underestimated the difficulty of doing so in Iraq. However, while the crucial decisionmaking period happened before we were there, so we cannot say for certain, when we looked into the matter we concluded that this was a case where the highest profile and most consequential analogizing came during the post-hoc explanation phase of the policy process rather than during the policymaking phase.[46] In other words, the White House was guilty of the venal sin of rhetorical carelessness in historical analogizing rather than the mortal sin of analytical carelessness in fashioning policy.

This is not to say that historical thinking was entirely absent from the process. Bush was mindful of history's informing other errors to avoid. For example, in explaining why he did not support the installation of an Iraqi exile as the initial post-Saddam ruler, Bush recalled, "I was mindful of the British experience in Iraq in the 1920s. Great Britain had installed a non-Iraqi king, Faisal, who was viewed as illegitimate and whose appointment stoked resentment and instability."[47] The critiques of the massive failures of the Iraq War's phase IV planning and execution have significant merit, yet the roots of the administration trouble do not trace back to a misleading Germany/Japan analogy but instead to systematic failure to think through a "plan B" scenario: "What if the Iraqi state collapses?"[48] Ironically, more reliance on the Germany/Japan analogy earlier in the process might have brought to light more of these issues in precisely the way that the use of the analogy in rhetoric quickly brought them to light.

History also helped shape several aspects of one of Bush's most controversial and consequential decisions, to order the "surge" of additional troops and a new counterinsurgency strategy in Iraq in January 2007. A historical sense informed President Bush's decision to override many of his own advisers, prevailing political sentiments, and public opinion in ordering the surge in Iraq. He believed that, in light of history, the risk of the United States losing the Iraq War substantially outweighed the risks of further escalation. In a pointed exchange with General Peter Schoomaker, who feared that the deployment of additional troops risked "breaking the army," Bush noted that "what's going to break the army is a defeat like we had in Vietnam that broke the army for a generation."[49]

In working on Iraq policy, many members of the Bush national security team, including the present authors, believed that while the nature of the Iraq War itself was quite dissimilar to that of the Vietnam War, some of the domestic political dynamics were disturbingly similar. For example, in considering the domestic political dynamics in 2006 of pressure for troop withdrawals, we recalled Henry Kissinger's famous "salted peanuts" caution about a drawdown of forces in Vietnam. In a 1969 memo to President Richard Nixon, the national security adviser warned that "it will be like salted peanuts to the American public: The more U.S. troops come home, the more will be demanded."[50] In a similar vein, mindful of how Congress had attempted to pass increasingly restrictive measures on U.S. forces in Vietnam, we studied those episodes for insights on how to manage contemporary pressures from Congress to curtail the U.S. mission in Iraq. The past history of other counterinsurgency campaigns also informed the development of the surge policy. This included a study of the duration of past counterinsurgency efforts (including nineteenth-century Indian wars and the Philippines campaign in the early twentieth century) for insights into both the operational timeframe and efforts to maintain domestic political support.

Finally, history played a substantial role in shaping the Bush administration's response to the 2008 economic crisis. From the outset, the overriding historical analogy that obsessed Bush and his team—and that they sought desperately to avoid—was the Great Depression. When Vice President Cheney tried on October 1, 2008, to persuade some reluctant Republican senators to vote in favor of the administration's initial bailout package, he warned them, "If you don't pass this, you're going to make George W. Bush into the Herbert Hoover of the twenty-first century." Two months later, during remarks at the American Enterprise Institute, Bush defended his administration's significant interventions to stabilize financial markets by asserting, "I didn't want to be the president during a depression greater than the Great Depression, or the beginning of a depression greater than the Great Depression. So we moved, and moved hard."[51] For all of the uncertainties and confusion that consumed business and political leaders at the outset of the crisis, at a fundamental level history guided Bush's decision to take extraordinary measures in two ways. First, the analogical precedent of the Great Depression warned him of the possible catastrophic economic straits that could ensue. Second, the historical obloquy that has condemned Herbert Hoover served as a historical caution that Bush sought to avoid.

Conclusion

Only with the perspective that comes from the passage of time and the opening of archives will historians be able to render informed judgments on the Bush administration's foreign policy. In our proximate judgment, with both the biases and benefits of having been participant-observers, overall national security policy in the Bush administration was better than it otherwise would have been because the White House was so engaged with historical thinking.

President Bush's tenure was also consequential in part because he was so self-conscious about the importance of legacy—particularly the legacy he would leave for his successors. For Bush, legacy was also a concept of history, and he was conscious of himself as an actor in the stream of history, with both upstream predecessors and downstream successors.[52] In his words, "History teaches you obligations. I felt obligated to leave tools for future presidents. I felt responsibility to leave strong Article 2 policies for my successors, such as the Patriot Act, military tribunals, and effective surveillance capabilities."[53] In his desire to develop and institutionalize these policies for successive administrations, Bush's historical sensibility reminded him that history's judgments would be wrought not merely on events during his two terms but also—especially—on what happened after he left office.

Our own provisional thoughts for what can be learned from the use of history in the Bush administration include:

- Applying history to statecraft means much more than just selecting past episodes as analogies for contemporary policy choices. In the case of the Bush administration, it also meant looking for patterns in the past to help explain the present; considering how policy choices would be judged by history rather than just the prevailing political environment; distinguishing between events that were historically precedented and those that were unprecedented; and drawing encouragement from the trials that previous leaders had endured.

- In developing the strategic framework for the war on terror, the Bush administration drew perceptively and successfully from a combination of historical paradigms (primarily the Cold War, but also World War II) and a historical appreciation for the unprecedented aspects of the conflict.

- In planning for the Iraq War, the Bush administration rightly used historical judgments to judge Saddam Hussein's malicious intentions yet extrapolated too far in judging his capabilities. The administration also did not adequately draw on historical insights in planning phase IV of the war, or in preparing for contingencies that did not meet the desired optimistic projections.[54]

- For a presidential administration to most fruitfully draw on historical wisdom, it needs to have a critical mass of historically interested senior officials and staff willing to participate in historical dialogue.

- History can shape an administration's temperament as much as its policies. A sense of history can inspire prudential virtues in statecraft such as humility, resilience, perspective, and confidence.

Notes

1. William Inboden, "Statecraft, Decision Making, and the Varieties of Historical Experience: A Taxonomy," *Journal of Strategic Studies* 37, no. 2 (2014), 291–318.

2. George W. Bush, quoted in Peter Baker, *Days of Fire: Bush and Cheney in the White House* (New York: Doubleday, 2013), 647.

3. For a more thorough and thoughtful exploration of the backgrounds and formative experiences of the Bush national security team, see James Mann, *Rise of the Vulcans: The History of Bush's War Cabinet* (New York: Penguin, 2004).

4. The administration took certain symbolic steps to emphasize this point—for instance, implementing a dress code for staff attending weekend meetings in the Oval Office, sharply reducing the number of commissioned officers among White House staff, and requiring punctuality of all staff members. Richard L. Berke, "Bush Is Providing Corporate Model for White House," *New York Times,* March 11, 2001.

5. Condoleezza Rice, "Campaign 2000: Promoting the National Interest," *Foreign Affairs* 71, no. 1 (2000; www.foreignaffairs.com/articles/55630/condoleezza-rice/campaign-2000-promoting-the-national-interest).

6. Baker, *Days of Fire*, 101–02.

7. Melvyn Leffler, "Fear, Power, and the War in Iraq: Historical Sensibilities and Decision-Making," remarks delivered at the University of Texas–Austin on November 2, 2013, quoted with permission of the author.

8. Philip Zelikow, "Histories Personal and Collective—And U.S. Grand Strategy in 2001–2002," unpublished paper delivered at the University of Texas–Austin on November 1, 2013, used by permission of the author. See also Philip Zelikow, "U.S. Strategic Planning in 2001–2002," in *In Uncertain Times: American Foreign Policy after the Berlin Wall and 9/11*, edited by Melvyn P. Leffler and Jeffrey W. Legro (Cornell University Press, 2011).

9. George W. Bush, "2002 National Security Strategy" (http://georgewbush -whitehouse.archives.gov/nsc/nss/2002/nssintro.html).

10. Leffler, "Fear, Power, and the War in Iraq."

11. Donald Rumsfeld, *Known and Unknown* (New York: Penguin, 2011), 286–88, 482, 649.

12. Baker, *Days of Fire*, 210. Note that this description of a "tragic" understanding of history contrasts with Zelikow's argument that Bush administration principals generally did not have a sense of the tragic.

13. Philip Zelikow and Condoleezza Rice, *Germany Unified and Europe Transformed: A Study in Statecraft* (Harvard University Press, 1997).

14. See, for example, Ernest May, *"Lessons" of the Past: The Use and Misuse of History in American Foreign Policy* (Oxford University Press, 1983); and Richard R. Neustadt and Ernest E. May, *Thinking in Time: The Uses of History for Decision Makers* (New York: Free Press, 1988).

15. George W. Bush, "A Period of Consequences," speech presented at the Citadel, Charleston, South Carolina, September 23, 1999 (www.fas.org/spp/starwars /program/news99/92399_defense.htm).

16. Fred Barnes, *Rebel-in-Chief: Inside the Bold and Controversial Presidency* (New York: Crown Forum, 2006), 20.

17. See the rich discussion of this point in Melvyn P. Leffler, "The Foreign Policies of the George W. Bush Administration: Memoirs, History, Legacy," *Diplomatic History* 37, no. 2 (2013), 194.

18. Some might argue that searching for an analogy is itself a sign of dysfunction, but this view betrays a fundamental misunderstanding about how human beings come to understand any new thing. Analogizing is indispensable in learning. The way human beings learn new things is by linking the new thing to something else that is already known—analogizing. This new thing is like something we already know in some respects and different from it in other respects. We learn how to run by analogizing to walking. We learn how to skip by analogizing to running. And so on. What is true for individuals is true for the public as a whole. The public learns and accepts a new thing by linking it to something it already knows and accepts.

19. There were also some substantive similarities with Pearl Harbor, most especially in the realm of strategically destructive surprise attacks that draw the nation into a prolonged global conflict. This dimension is insightfully probed in John Lewis Gaddis, *Surprise, Security, and the American Experience* (Harvard University Press, 2005).

20. These ideas were evident in nascent form in the president's earliest messaging after the 9/11 attacks, especially in the remarks he offered on the very day of the attacks. George W. Bush, "Address to the Nation on the Terrorist Attacks" (http://www.presidency.ucsb.edu/ws/?pid=58057) and the September 14 remarks at the National Cathedral, "Remarks at the National Day of Prayer and Remembrance Service" (http://www.presidency.ucsb.edu/ws/?pid=63645). The ideas were also anticipated more explicitly by some contemporaneous punditry; see Peter Feaver, "Cold War II," *Weekly Standard*, October 1, 2001; and Eliot Cohen, "World War IV," *Wall Street Journal*, November 20, 2001. They then reached their most complete articulation in President Bush's second National Security Strategy, released in March 2006. In full disclosure, the authors of this chapter also served as the primary staff authors of that strategy.

21. George W. Bush, interview with the authors, June 21, 2011, Dallas, Texas.

22. George W. Bush, quoted in Micah Zenko, *Between Threats and War: U.S. Discrete Military Operations in the Post–Cold War World* (Stanford University Press, 2010), 9.

23. Baker, *Days of Fire*, 188.

24. For more on the functioning of this office, see Peter Feaver and William Inboden, "What Was the Point of SPIR? Strategic Planning in National Security at the White House," in *Avoiding Trivia: The Role of Strategic Planning in American Foreign Policy*, edited by Daniel Drezner (Brookings Institution Press, 2009).

25. Inboden, "Statecraft, Decision Making, and the Varieties of Historical Experience."

26. Francis Gavin, "History and Policy," *International Journal* 63, no. 1 (2007–08), 170–72.

27. George W. Bush, Commencement Address at the United States Military Academy at West Point, May 27, 2006, West Point, New York (www.presidency.ucsb.edu/ws/?pid=83). See also Elisabeth Bumiller, "At West Point, Bush Draws Parallels with Truman," *New York Times*, May 28, 2006.

28. George W. Bush, *Decision Points* (New York: Crown, 2010), 156, 174–75.

29. For Bush's remarks on this occasion, see "President Bush Rededicates Islamic Center of Washington," June 27, 2007 (http://georgewbush-whitehouse.archives.gov/news/releases/2007/06/20070627-2.html). This episode also serves as an ironic example of how the policy use of history can actually help revive and preserve history, as the imam at the mosque was not aware of the center's fiftieth anniversary until we told him about it in proposing President Bush's visit.

30. Baker, *Days of Fire*, 518. For more on this, see Gary Kamiya, "Bush's Favorite Historian," *Salon*, May 8, 2007 (www.salon.com/2007/05/08/alistair_horne/).

31. Margaret MacMillan, *The Uses and Abuses of History* (London: Profile Books, 2009), 151–52. MacMillan attributes this to "an aide," but offers no evidence or footnote in support. It is possible that Bush could have made such a pass-

ing comment about French bureaucracy, although we have found no other evidence for it nor was this the understanding among White House staff at the time. Unfortunately, MacMillan's account gives the impression that this was the only insight Bush drew from Horne. There is also no evidence for her assertion of Bush's indifference to the French defeat, which in fact helped elicit Bush's original interest in the book.

32. For more on the revolt of the generals, see Baker, *Days of Fire*, 452–54. See also Thomas E. Ricks, *The Gamble: General David Petraeus and the American Military Adventure in Iraq, 2006–2008* (New York: Penguin, 2009), 38–40.

33. Bush, *Decision Points*, 364.

34. The internal NSC staff review was part of a larger interagency effort to energize U.S. policy toward Iran. The larger policy review is described in David Crist, *The Twilight War* (New York: Penguin, 2012), 488–89, 495–96. See also the review of the evolution of Bush-era policy toward Iran in Stephen J. Hadley, "The George W. Bush Administration," U.S. Institute of Peace, *The Iran Primer* (December 2010; http://iranprimer.usip.org/resource/george-w-bush-administration).

35. See Jim Steinberg, chapter 10, this volume.

36. There are abundant examples of partisanship masquerading as dispassionate academic analysis. See, for example, the polls of academic historians rating Bush against other presidents, such as this one in 2006 by the Siena Research Institute, accessible here: (https://www2.siena.edu/uploadedfiles/home/parents_and _community/community_page/sri/independent_research/Presidents%20Survey _06_may.pdf); and Douglas Brinkley, "Lincoln Wins: Honest Abe Tops New Presidential Survey," CNN.com (www.cnn.com/2009/POLITICS/02/16/presidential .survey/). When such polls include evaluations of a sitting or very recent president, they are problematic from a methodological standpoint in that participating historians act as contemporary pundits rather than scholars employing the historical method and historical perspective.

37. George W. Bush, "President Bush Visits the Economic Club of New York," March 14, 2008 (http://georgewbush-whitehouse.archives.gov/news/releases/2008 /03/20080314-5.html). Note that this has continued to be a concern of Bush's in his postpresidential years. See, for example, "Q&A with Former President George W. Bush" (interview), January 24, 2011 (http://c-spanvideo.org/program /AwithFo).

38. George W. Bush, interview with the authors, June 21, 2011, Dallas, Texas.

39. George W. Bush, "Address to the General Assembly of the United Nations, September 12, 2002," in *Public Papers of the Presidents: George W. Bush* (Government Printing Office, 2003), 1529.

40. Leffler, "Fear, Power, and the War in Iraq."

41. George W. Bush, "Remarks by President George W. Bush at the 20th Anniversary of the National Endowment for Democracy," November 6, 2003 (www

.ned.org/george-w-bush/remarks-by-president-george-w-bush-at-the-20th
-anniversary). For more of Bush's perspective on his "freedom agenda," see Bush,
Decision Points, 395–38. Note that Bush dates his first decision to make democracy
promotion central to his foreign policy to 2002 and his frustration with Palestinian
Yasser Arafat and the need for more accountable Palestinian leadership.

42. George W. Bush, Second Inaugural Address, January 20, 2005 (www.npr
.org/templates/story/story.php?storyId=4460172).

43. Inboden, "Statecraft, Decision Making, and the Varieties of Historical
Experience."

44. George W. Bush, interview with the authors, June 21, 2011, Dallas, Texas.

45. George W. Bush, quoted in Baker, *Days of Fire*, 528–29. Baker also notes
that during his presidency Bush read fourteen different biographies of Lincoln
(479).

46. Internal advocates of going to war against Iraq, such as Douglas Feith,
were aware of the analogy to democracy-building efforts in Germany and Japan
and generally saw the analogy as supporting the case, as Feith makes clear. See
Douglas J. Feith, *War and Decision: Inside the Pentagon at the Dawn of the War on
Terrorism* (New York: Harper, 2008), 127, 234, 236. And the analogy certainly cir-
culated in internal debates; see, for example, Assistant Secretary of Defense Peter
Rodman's August 14, 2002, memorandum, reproduced in Feith's book, which argued that the analogy to the postwar occupation of Japan and Germany might be
misleading and that the occupation of France would be a better analogy. In retrospect, Rodman's memorandum is somewhat ironic, since it criticized the Japan and
Germany analogy because it yielded overly pessimistic predictions about Iraq and
advocated the French analogy, which yielded more optimistic predictions. Nevertheless, the memorandum is proof that the analogy was at least partly shaping policymakers ex ante; see Feith, *War and Decision*, 546–48. Moreover, as is clear from
John Dower's October 2002 op-ed in the *New York Times*, hopeful references to the
Japan analogy were circulating in the popular debate as well; Dower sharply criticizes the analogy and argues that the occupation of Iraq would be far more difficult than the occupation of Japan. See John Dower, "Lessons from Japan about
War's Aftermath," *New York Times*, October 27, 2002. But since building democracy in Iraq was not the central pillar in the case for *initiating* the war that it was
in the case for *sustaining* the war effort afterward, the analogies were more salient
in the ex post setting. If anything, the Japan and Germany analogy was invoked
by skeptics who warned that postwar Iraq might require a costlier and longer
occupation than the Bush administration seemed to envision; see, for example,
Michael O'Hanlon, "The Price of Stability," *New York Times,* October 22, 2002
(www.nytimes.com/2002/10/22/opinion/the-price-of-stability.html). After the
occupation proved so difficult, Japan and Germany were invoked in a more hopeful context; see, for instance, the farewell speech by Ambassador Paul Bremer on

June 28, 2004, discussed in Office of the Special Inspector General for Iraq Reconstruction, *Hard Lessons: The Iraq Reconstruction Period* (Government Printing Office, 2009), 159.

47. Bush, *Decision Points*, 249.

48. For more on phase IV planning, see Joseph Collins, "Planning Lessons from Afghanistan and Iraq," *Joint Force Quarterly Forum* 41 (2006), 10–14.

49. Baker, *Days of Fire*, 520. See also Bush, *Decision Points*, 367.

50. Henry Kissinger, quoted in Robert Dallek, *Nixon and Kissinger: Partners in Power* (New York: Basic Books, 2007), 153–54.

51. Baker, *Days of Fire*, 616, 626. See also Bush, *Decision Points*, 440.

52. This concept of history as a stream in the context of policy was developed by May and Neustadt in *Thinking in Time*.

53. George W. Bush, interview with the authors, June 21, 2011, Dallas, Texas.

54. One thoughtful effort to draw on the insights of history in postconflict stabilization and reconstruction was authored by Andrew Erdmann and Richard Haass of the State Department policy planning staff. See September 26, 2002, memorandum from Haass to Secretary of State Powell, "Reconstruction in Iraq—Lessons of the Past," in Richard Haass, *War of Necessity, War of Choice: A Memoir of Two Iraq Wars* (New York: Simon and Schuster, 2009), 279–93.

PHILIP ZELIKOW

12

The Nature of History's Lessons

No one sees farther into a generalization than his own
knowledge of details extends.

—WILLIAM JAMES, IN *THE LETTERS OF WILLIAM JAMES*

What happened in the past can be very complicated, as is life. One
way to learn from the past is to simplify the record of what happened: distill and distill until, at last, the final essence offers a usable generalization,
a parable.

Another way is to accept how difficult it is to understand the past, that
foreign country. Accept the complexity and try to master some of it: struggle and struggle until, at last, growing comprehension provides the satis-
factions of knowledge.

This essay argues for the second way. Embrace the complexity! It is the
more reliable path to knowledge.

More than two hundred years ago Edmund Burke warned princes not
"to be led into error" by a false use of history. "Not that I derogate from the
use of history," Burke assured his audience. "It is a great improver of the
understanding, by showing both men and affairs in a great variety of views.
From this source much political wisdom may be learned."

But Burke cautioned his listeners as strongly as he could that the wisdom came not from converting history into "precept." Historical study could be "an exercise to strengthen the mind, as furnishing materials to enlarge and enrich it." But there is great danger if it is used as "a repertory of cases and precedents." If history is thus misused, "better would it be that a statesman had never learned to read."[1]

Yet the way of simplification is so much easier. The reader or listener does not need much background information or special training. The simpler the points, the easier they are to explain. And many simple generalizations do have obvious value along with the value of being, well, obvious.

The second way, however, offers greater and more lasting yields. In medicine, for example, there have long been many rewards from studying gross anatomy, examining what anyone could see. It might have seemed simpler not to bother with microscopes. After all, few people had microscopes or could use them. And it may have seemed as if so much could be understood without bothering about the significance of things like germs, genes, or molecules. Hardly anyone could see those things; they were hard to understand.

So, too, in the examination of great human actions. It is tempting to draw inferences from that which everyone can see. The Vietnam War was a great tragedy; everyone could see that. So it is easy to then simplify generalizations, such as, more foreign interventions; no more land wars in Asia; or no more arrogant meddling in faraway places that Americans do not understand.

Unfortunately, these simplicities are not very interesting in real life, because real life usually does not present its issues in such simple forms. The Vietnam tragedy repays microscopic examination precisely because a number of quite intelligent Americans—"the best and the brightest," in David Halberstam's great phrase—made decisions that to us, now, seem so strange. They wrote wise, prescient papers; they had good, prescient discussions. And then, it seems, they sleepwalked off a cliff.

Only closer examinations that welcome complexity can decode such strange doings. Only thus can we prepare ourselves through such vicarious experiences for the ways these challenges actually arise, the kinds of faces they really present. The path of complexity is difficult, but the rewards include more lifelike fitness training for the intellect.

Seen through a historian's microscope the world can be far stranger and more fascinating than anything that can be seen by the unaided eye. I am currently writing a book, working through some puzzles about the ways America has gone to war. Seemingly familiar stories become profoundly strange. Even those close to the choices have trouble reconstructing why wars were waged in the way they were.

One such story is of how America went to war in Iraq in 2003. This story was personal for me. In early 2005, back in government working as a kind of deputy to Secretary of State Condoleezza Rice, I found myself in a position of some responsibility for the U.S. war in Iraq.

The war in Iraq was then in a bad place and about to get worse, descending into another phase of horror. Over the following couple of years I traveled many times around Iraq, talking with hundreds of civilians, soldiers, and Marines. Listening to their frustrations, observing the range of heroism and venality, visiting mangled soldiers in their hospital beds, I had plenty of occasions to wonder how America had gotten into this fix.

How America found itself again at war in Iraq (for the third time, after the wars in 1991 and 1998) was perplexing. But to me it was not the hardest puzzle. Harder to explain was why, having gotten into the war, the powerful nation had gotten into such a deep hole. The standard explanation was simple: the United States was in this hole because a foolish administration—notably, a foolish defense secretary—had just not prepared adequately for the occupation to follow.

Yet closer study soon reveals that the foolish defense secretary had not prepared for the occupation to follow because he did not intend that there should be such an occupation. And his president had placed him in charge of preparing for the postinvasion phase. The defense secretary even feared that if he did prepare for an occupation, why then someone might just be tempted to ask him to lead one!

That insight still does not solve the puzzle of how the powerful United States had then gotten into such a deep hole in Iraq. That realization only sets up why it really is a puzzle. Then the hard work begins.

Yet for those who want lessons, this is where the real education can happen for adults who appreciate the complexities of the real world. It is these explorations that are Burke's "exercise to strengthen the mind, as furnishing materials to enlarge and enrich it."

Life Cycles of Historical Belief

Those who consider the matter for a minute or two realize that historical reasoning is as common in public affairs as oxygen is in water. People catalog past experiences to inform their present choices. Sometimes they do this quickly, intuitively, half consciously. Every so often someone will even try to do this more formally, taking an inventory of or classifying the past experiences in some scheme through which they think they can estimate future probabilities.

These habits are natural for humans. Histories envelop us. Personal, institutional, local, national, tribal: there are so many stories. But history does not automatically convert itself into usable stories.

Lived moments are jumbles of experiences and impressions: Heels clicking on the marble floor of a palace while hastening to the next meeting. Hot, dry air and the smell of smoke blasting through the helicopter amid the thudding roar of the rotors. The startling comment by the defense secretary, punctuating another tedious meeting in a handsome, sterile, windowless White House conference room, while everyone pretends not to notice. The blood-soaked Humvee from which the dead and wounded have just been extracted. Struggles to stay awake, jet-lagged, three days into the latest transcontinental hopscotch. The memo full of concentrated passion, filed unread, and a week later forgotten.

Later, recalled for "history," anecdotes—once the stuff of corridor talk and dinner parties—are reassembled. The detritus of related documents are collected, if they can be found. Composing, simplifying, the mélange is turned into a narrative, and the narrative becomes a tellable, recallable story.

From such stories, further distilled, the usual path is to further simplification. The more universally known the stories, the more they supply common reference points. So distill, distill. Turn the stories into a shorthand for instant communication. Shared narratives about history become tokens of identity. When this work is done, often only a word or a phrase is needed, the invoked narrative becomes the word picture that is worth a thousand other words. One need do no more, in the right context, than pronounce *appeasement, Pearl Harbor, Vietnam, Great Depression, 9/11, American empire,* or *Iraq* and, presto, a whole worldview can instantly be shared.

This progression can be diagrammed:

History, unrefined . . .

Relatable stories . . .

Mass cult shorthand . . .

Flowing into judgment

And the cumulative judgments flow again into history's stream.

This cycle is a human process. Historical beliefs are not inherited in some national DNA. They are transmitted through culture and environment, learned through experience, direct or vicarious. One person's experience is idiosyncrasy. A nation's common trauma is a touchstone.

Back in the mid-1930s a great many educated Americans were very influenced by a set of historical beliefs. Most important, they believed that their country's 1917 intervention on the side of the Allies in World War I had been an awful, bloody mistake. They looked back on the U.S. entry into World War I in the way many Americans now think of the U.S. intervention in Vietnam or the invasion of Iraq—as something that definitely should have been avoided.

In the mid-1930s many Americans had imbibed a powerful, pervasive narrative about why the United States had entered World War I, a narrative about rich bankers and "merchants of death" who had sought war to protect their interests. There were also narratives full of scorn for the quality of the peace settlement, prefigured by John Maynard Keynes's early indictment.[2]

Narratives such as these gained a firm purchase in American politics because they resonated so well with a far older tradition that warned against getting into "entangling" commitments in Europe. That warning had been sonorously repeated as a kind of guiding gospel not only by politicians. Experts said this too; men like the most well-known historian of U.S. diplomacy.[3]

Much about those narratives were wrong. Having sifted the evidence, present-day historians do not now believe that bankers and munitions makers drove the United States into the war. Nor do they now tend to blame foolishly vengeful peacemakers of 1919 for the rise of Adolf Hitler or the monstrous Nazi designs.

But in the mid-1930s just such misleading generalizations were sovereign, even among some leading historians. So law after law tumbled out of the Congress to guarantee that—whatever happened in Europe—the United States would not repeat the supposed mistakes of World War I.

That experience of the 1930s then generated a fresh set of traumas and collective beliefs. On June 25, 1950, President Harry S. Truman was told that North Korea had invaded South Korea. South Korea was a new country, much troubled. Truman and his government had recently and very deliberately decided it would not defend this country if it was attacked from the north.

Yet when such an attack actually happened, Truman's thinking instantly flew back to the 1930s. The start of World War II had become a new narrative. Memories of words like *Munich* and *appeasement* were not distant for someone like Truman. A veteran of World War I, during the late 1930s Truman had been a midwestern senator arguing for preparedness while trying not to anger his quite isolationist constituents. Back then Truman felt someone should have stood up to the dictators.

Such memories were searing, too, for someone like Truman's assistant secretary of state, Dean Rusk, a recent veteran of the Second World War. Back in the 1930s Rusk had been a young academic at a college in California. He bitterly remembered the arguments on his campus against getting involved in war. As he later put it, "In the Thirties, they said Manchuria was too far away to matter and I found myself at war in Burma."[4]

Men like Truman and Rusk had experienced the shocks of aggression as personal traumas that shook up their lives. So, years later, when news poured in of a North Korean invasion in June 1950, no one needed to tell Truman or Rusk what lesson to remember.

Some reigning lessons become so well known, taught and retaught, that they ossify into one of the small number of master scripts that can mold public policies across whole eras. These aging shibboleths can go on for quite a long time until they are overthrown. There is a similar evolution that happens in the life cycle of paradigms in science.[5] When the shibboleths are finally toppled, it may not be because the historians have gotten better or the history readers have become wiser. More often, some new collective trauma—a war, a depression—has displaced them, swept them away with compelling needs for fresh social constructions.

All right, then. Having observed these life cycles at work, there are two benefits. The observations do help explain some otherwise puzzling choices in the past. But looking to the future the observations invite us to ask: Can we do anything else to improve the quality of thought around such beliefs? Can we use a historian's microscope to dispel illusory simplicities?

How to Dissect Choices

Two of my mentors, Ernest May and Richard Neustadt, taught courses at Harvard University for many years musing about these historical cycles and discussing the "uses of history" in public affairs. I took one of their courses in 1983. Soon after, I went into the government. When I joined the Harvard faculty in 1991 I returned to this very course, now as their faculty colleague. I taught it with them through most of the 1990s.[6]

At Harvard, May taught the history of American foreign relations for more than fifty years. But before moving to Cambridge he had earned a doctorate out west and did his military service during the Korean War as a naval officer, closing his tour with a short assignment as a historian for the Joint Chiefs of Staff. He never forgot those days spent near the policy kitchen, seeing how the sausage was made.

So May was always inclined to put policy episodes under a microscope. His consistent objective was to examine more carefully the beliefs that drove the action. Where did these beliefs come from? Through what filters did people see the situation they were in?

Of course, May found that these prisms were usually constructed from historical experiences, personal or vicarious. He analyzed how people use analogies. He studied public opinions, how they arise. He looked harder at the nature of the press and opinion leaders and where they derived their views. Such investigations also led him to a lifelong interest in the way governments prepare and use intelligence assessments.[7]

To dissect sovereign beliefs, the analyst has to cut them up. One hundred and fifty years ago, Alexis de Tocqueville speculated about the course of the February 1848 overthrow of France's monarchy. De Tocqueville had been an important participant in the turmoil and, as he reflected later on the experience, "The Revolution of February, in common with all other great events of this class, sprang from general causes, impregnated, if I am permitted the expression, by accidents."

Regarding "general causes," he nicely summarized, "Antecedent facts, the nature of institutions, the cast of minds and the state of morals." But de Tocqueville was drawn back to those small causes. He had begun by calling them "accidents," but they were more than that.

De Tocqueville despised the "narrow" theories, "false beneath their air of mathematical exactness," that would not grant the disproportionate importance of small events. Vexed with "the writers who have invented these sublime theories in order to feed their vanity and facilitate their work," he insisted that many important historical events could only be explained by accidental circumstances, to the extent that they could be explained at all.

Yet, de Tocqueville added, these accidental circumstances were not, in fact, really accidents at all. "Chance" was really "that tangle of secondary causes which we call chance, for want of the knowledge how to unravel it."[8]

In biology, specimens are cut up for examination under the microscope; they are "fixed" in lifelike condition and sliced, "sectioned." In history, where the specimens are metaphysical, the "sectioning" of the specimens is conceptual. The analyst can try to identify the sequence of distinct choices and the possibilities attendant at each stage.

So as May and I tried to learn how to dissect choices for the historian's microscope, we eventually found it was helpful to cut them up into three sorts of interacting judgments.[9]

1. *Value judgments.* What do they care about?
2. *Reality judgments.* What is going on?
3. *Action judgments.* What can they do?

Each of these kinds of judgments constantly informs and interacts with the others. It is hard to overstate the importance of this point.

For instance, suppose your friend Alex cares about the crisis in Syria because he feels that he, or perhaps his country, can do something about it. This would be a value judgment influenced by an action judgment.

Or suppose Alex pays more attention to what is going on in Syria because he cares about it. This would be a reality judgment influenced by a value judgment. In turn, he might be more likely to act—even the act of voicing an opinion—because he felt he knew more about what was going on. Thus an action judgment is influenced by a reality judgment. There are many possible combinations.

To illustrate how to dissect a choice in this way, we can use a low-power microscope to examine a set of choices that the administration of President George W. Bush made about Iraq in the first half of 2002. This is when the Bush administration decided it had to take major action that would at least resolve uncertainties about Iraq's weapons of mass destruction program. This choice was a compound of distinct judgments about value, reality, and action, interacting in no set sequence. Nested in each such judgment are historical beliefs.

Reality Judgments: *What's Going On in Iraq in Early 2002?*

After the 1991 war with Iraq was halted by an armistice, a kind of truce, UN inspectors learned a lot more about Iraq's nuclear program. U.S. intelligence analysts were then disturbed to find out how much they had underestimated the scale of Iraq's secret work on weapons of mass destruction; they had, in particular, underestimated the scale and scope of Iraq's nuclear weapons program. This turned out to be a scarily elaborate nuclear weapons program, proceeding along multiple parallel tracks, and Saddam Hussein's Iraq had come frighteningly close to being able to build a nuclear weapon. That was in 1991.

Later in the 1990s and throughout 2002 the great lesson from that 1991 experience, then, was not about how to interpret what you knew. It was a lesson in how to interpret what you did *not* know. When they had assessed Iraq's progress in 1990 or earlier, there had been, of course, many gaps in what the analysts could know. When in doubt, they doubted. Probably, they thought, there is nothing there. But after the experience of 1991, the analysts would not make that mistake again. That "lesson of history" was learned. Thus, after UN inspectors were kicked out of Iraq in 1997–98, analysts indeed did not make *that* mistake again.

Action Judgments: *What Can Be Done about Iraq?*

By early 2002 every leading figure of the Bush administration felt a slightly surprised satisfaction with the progress of the post-9/11 war to run al Qaeda and its allies out of Afghanistan. After all, the administration's critics had been the ones summoning the lessons of history. The Washington sage R. W. Apple of the *New York Times* had evoked them on the front page with that surefire historical shorthand: "quagmire." Yet, by early 2002 the United States seemed instead to have achieved military and political success in Afghanistan with astonishing ease and economy of force—no U.S. occupation of the country then seemed needed.

It seemed that such so-called lessons, the prophecies of "quagmire," had been disproved. So by early 2002 a fresh generalization was supplanting "quagmire." It was a new, glowing lesson of possibility—military and political possibility.

The lesson was learned just as American leaders wondered anew just what they should do now about Iraq. The UN inspectors had been kicked out; uncertainties about Iraq's weapons of mass destruction programs had returned. The problem had bedeviled American policymakers for five years. The United States had even launched a small-scale, preventive war against Iraq in December 1998, and it was still flying regular combat missions over Iraq as the situation simmered. What to do?

Value Judgments: *How Much Should We Care about Iraq?*

How much should anyone care about the doings of Iraq's dictator, Saddam Hussein, who back then was generally regarded as perhaps the most vicious tyrant in the world? Some people naturally carried with them deeply ingrained values invoked by their experience with or reading about other evil rulers in history. For many inside and outside of government, the question, "Do you care much whether Saddam Hussein runs a murderous dictatorship?" was answered, in their heads and hearts, with responses conditioned long before.

And then there was another historical experience: 9/11. To all relevant public officials and many citizens who remembered that day, September 11, 2001, seemed to cry out for lesson-drawing. It seemed to be a lesson, above all, about how to think about risks, about what weight America's leaders should now attach to certain kinds of risks.

There they are: three kinds of interacting judgments about Iraq—reality, action, and value. Outsiders could see and second-guess some of these. But these three kinds of judgments are not equally apparent or understandable to outsiders. That was true then and it is true now. Regrettably, though there are some sterling exceptions, in their own studies of weighty choices historians rarely improve much upon the quality of understanding available to outsiders at the time.

Outsiders, both those at the time and those looking back later, will do best at understanding those judgments that are apparent to them and that remain stable over some period of time. They will do least well in grasping—or even being aware of—those judgments that are secretive and more volatile, changing from one month to the next.

A rough matrix can depict the point this way:

	Apparent to Outsiders?	Stable?
Value judgments	High	High
Reality judgments	Medium	Medium
Action judgments	Low	Low

Naturally then, citizens at the time and the historians who come later both tend to focus on the value judgments. They argue mainly about what people care about, or should care about. But since they tend to see only part of the compound, their understanding of choices goes downhill from there. Value judgments may get the most attention, but they may often be the least interesting judgments to track.

On any given issue usually there are many potential values lying dormant, ready to be evoked. For instance, Americans tend to believe their country should be peaceful, but they also tend to believe it should be strong. They may disapprove of tyrants, but they also disapprove of costly interventions overseas. And so on. One or another latent value can be lit up, activated, by the interaction with the news from one day to the next.

People in positions of responsibility are besieged by constant evocations of every value. Rivers of information flow by about the reality around them. Thus, action judgments often are the vital elements that help them sort. Yet action judgments are the hardest to nonspecialists. Such judgments are the hardest ones for outsiders to understand even if outsiders had access to the relevant information about action options—information they almost never have.

Generalizations, Hard and Soft

Inside every judgment there are generalizations. These are the pithy summaries, the relatable stories refined from the raw ore of history.

A hard generalization is the kind that presents a factual statement. This thing happened; that was its cause. For example, someone could say that America suffered a Great Depression that began in 1929. This depression was caused by constrained monetary policies, a pinched supply of money, which in turn was induced by adherence to the gold standard.

A soft generalization is not so direct and it is not so factual. It might be a presumption. It might be an inference. For example, having considered the depression story, someone could say that in a financial crisis, leaders should loosen monetary policies. This loosening will counter the ebb of ordinary credit flows.[10] That is a kind of soft generalization, the kind that attempts to build a bridge, a bridge from the past to the future.

A hard generalization is one that says: "This *is* true, you may rely on it." A soft generalization says, in effect, "This *might* be true."

Historians rarely do enough to harden the first kind of generalization—about what happened and why in a particular case. They can usually do very well, professionally, by suggesting a fresh and sufficiently plausible additional explanation. They can succeed in academia by making what might have already seemed a soft account softer still.

Social scientists, on the other hand, often do too much to harden soft inferences. They can do well in academia by discovering systematic patterns and probabilities.

These two professional tendencies combine in unfortunate ways. The historians are weakening, not shoring up, the factual foundation. The social scientists are eagerly building ever higher towers atop this soft soil.

In my mention of the Great Depression in the paragraphs above, I used two generalizations. The first was about constrained monetary policies as a cause; the second was that in the future less constrained policies are a likely remedy to head off a depression. When the Great Recession arrived in 2007, it turned out that a pivotal figure in U.S. policymaking, Federal Reserve Board chairman Ben Bernanke, used both of them, partly drawing from his own scholarship on the history of the Great Depression.[11]

Yet the first generalization—the Great Depression was caused by constrained monetary policies induced by adherence to a gold standard—turns out to be weak. It goes too far toward a deterministic overemphasis purely on economic structures, like the gold exchange standard. Those were important. But such explanations tend to slight the underlying political issues that inhibited more effective cooperation that could have occurred even within these flawed structures.

The decisive, devastating phase of the Great Depression was from 1931 to 1933. That phase of the crisis arose out of Europe. That phase was driven at least as much by political conflicts like the antagonism and suspicion between France and Germany, the British Empire's withdrawal from free trade, and by the new administration of Franklin Roosevelt's demolition of efforts to reconstruct international economic cooperation. All these ruptures may have had a more damaging effect between 1931 and 1933 than the supposed rigidity of the underlying monetary constraints of the gold exchange standard.[12]

For Bernanke, in 2008–09, the "loosen constraints" generalization seemed to work well, validating its power. But that may have been only part of the story. Again, the political variables were vital. In 2008–09, it turns out that quite a lot of the credit for avoiding a second, catastrophic, stage of the crisis may have been due to the very high level of political cooperation among the key players in the United States and Europe. Too soft a version of the second generalization—now just loosen constraints—could slight or obscure the importance of this close cooperation.

By the way, it took decades for any of these generalizations about what happened during the Great Depression—about either the structural constraints of the gold exchange standard or the breakdown of political cooperation—to gain wide public understanding. The generalization most Americans made at the time, in the 1930s, was more moralistic. They blamed greedy bankers and others who were out for too-easy money.

As we can see in this little illustration about Depression history and anti-Depression prescriptions, the foundational generalizations—what happened and why—are hard to get right, and there may be a long wait before better histories are available. But people want and need to leap to prescriptions. So there is a great temptation to find shortcuts. This trick is usually attempted by using *less* information about what happened before.

So, instead of trying to fathom a deep, detailed account of the Great Depression, another approach would just extract some data about specified outcomes. Then the seer would find other episodes that seem comparable and could be mined for similar-seeming outcome data. Finally the seer offers inferences—predictive generalizations—built up with methods of scientific inference.

Thus it would seem, very temptingly, as if the desired lesson, the bridging generalization to the future, can be derived without so much bother about getting the underlying history right. Just typecast the episode, plug in the relevant data about it, and get the generalization that is needed.

This is the more sophisticated way of returning to history lessons through simplification. It is another way to distill and distill. The problem, however, is that the more superficial the labeling and typecasting of historical experience, the more what actually happened is liable to be fatally misrepresented.

The Representation of Experience

To generalize about how people behaved in a historical episode we need to be able to relate to recognizable experiences of actual people, not relate to choices made by symbols or abstractions. That is the purpose of trying to dissect their choices. One could, for example, classify the Soviet invasion of Afghanistan in 1979 as an example of "power-seeking." And one could also classify the American invasion of Iraq in 2003 as an example of more "power-seeking." But these labels are so detached from an actual description of the interactive judgments in play that they become empty and artificial.

In other words, "If appropriate representations [of reality] come presupplied [by labels], the hard part of the analogy-making task has already been accomplished."[13] The similarity comes from attaching similar labels. Histories are bound to be profoundly misrepresented whenever they are extracted from their original context of place and time.[14] A battery of historians demonstrated the enormity of these distortions, using as their test case a well-known treatment of "neorealism" and "power-seeking" by the political scientist, John Mearsheimer.[15]

The more a writer converts an episode from detailed historical narrative into a typecast or generic event, the more the connection to a description of reality will be lost.[16] What actually happened gets converted into "irreducibly alien terms." Indeed, such high concepts become so far divorced from natural realism that there is a case, the philosopher Willard Van Ormond Quine explained, for barring such terms from our language as meaningless. Quine would consign them to the limbo of "nonsentences" in order to prevent "an encroachment of coherence considerations upon standards of truth."[17]

Iron pyrite glitters, but it is not gold. There is actually quite a bit that is golden in Carmen Reinhart and Kenneth Rogoff's now famous book, *This Time Is Different*, about what happens to countries throughout history that have run up large public debts.[18] Any reader of that book would find a very intensive effort to catalog histories from around the world of all kinds of debt stories—domestic and external. The reader will find lively illustrations of how governments have coped with debt problems. The book canvasses many different possible actions and the kinds of consequences that can ensue.

Yet the authors got into trouble, and it came from their much-publicized attempt to boil their public debt histories down to a master generalization.

They seemed to offer a "scientific" threshold for safe levels of public debt: debt–to–gross domestic product ratios over 90 percent were given as the tipping point.

It was that assertion of a practically law-like generalization that set the authors up for attack, and they got plenty. The 90 percent threshold turned out to be vulnerable to reinterpretation of only a few data points, on which the authors may have made some errors.[19]

But there is a deeper concern. Suppose the correction of a few details in the data set, for instance in tabulating economic results in places like New Zealand in 1951, can disturb a supposed law-like scientific generalization. Then the generalization doesn't seem very law-like. And whatever golden historical knowledge lying underneath might then be overlooked, because what glittered on the surface was only the iron pyrite, the "fool's gold."

In a leading text on research in political science, Gary King, Robert Keohane, and Sidney Verba explain that *"the best way to understand a particular event may be by using the methods of scientific inference also to study systematic patterns in similar parallel events."*[20] In this view of scientific progress, wrote Paul Diesing, "The immature social sciences should move up through economics toward physics, and physics should become more fully axiomatized and its laws should become more general and simpler."[21]

But in the "hard" sciences, including physics, this notion of scientific progress has become increasingly doubtful. More knowledge has revealed greater complexity in the interplay of nature's parts. The laws are not becoming more general and simpler. Indeed "in biology," remarked one participant in a 1994 conference on the limits of scientific knowledge, scientists had learned from experience that "Occam's razor cuts your throat."[22]

Writing about physics, Nancy Cartwright has argued that a search for fundamental, transcendent laws inevitably takes the scientist further from reality. The laws of physics, for example, can be poor predictors of specific events: "If we follow out their consequences, we generally find that the fundamental laws go wrong; they are put right by the judicious corrections of the applied physicist or the research engineer." Thus "there are no rigorous solutions for real life problems. Approximations and adjustments are required whenever theory treats reality."

Generic laws only explain generic situations. There are few of these. "Things are made to look the same only when we fail to examine them too closely."[23]

Meanwhile some social scientists have become more dogmatic in prescribing more novel statistical or scientific methods for their disciplines—though, as I have discussed, these representations of reality are founded on philosophical principles far less secure than those underlying physics or biology.[24]

King, Keohane, and Verba concede that there is a mix of systematic and nonsystematic variables in historical episodes. This produces what they call, quoting Paul Holland, the "fundamental problem of causal inference." To contain this problem, students are taught methods to try and separate, pull out, the variables that are systematic from those that are not.

The philosophical problem, though, as William James once put it, is that "novelty, as empirically found, doesn't arrive by jumps and jolts, it leaks in insensibly." A scholar of political science methodology, Christopher Achen, is scornful of techniques like introducing random variables in statistical estimators in order to simulate the nonsystematic aspect. Indeed, Achen argues that if an event has more than three explanatory variables, social scientists should step back. Such an event just cannot be handled meaningfully with statistical analysis.[25]

Even if the systematic variables could be extracted, a combination of systematic variables can also produce a nonsystematic result. A Nobel Prize-winning physicist, Philip Anderson, articulates this well in his 1972 essay "More Is Different," explaining how each level of reality, each new aggregation, introduces a need for qualitatively different explanations: "At each stage, entirely new laws, concepts and generalizations are necessary, requiring inspiration and creativity to just as great a degree as in the previous one. Psychology is not applied biology, nor is biology applied chemistry."[26]

These philosophical problems may help explain why, in the case of scholarship on international relations, "several decades of empirical research . . . has failed to produce a single meaningful lawlike generalization in international relations research." As prominent scholars of international relations theory John Mearsheimer and Stephen Walt have acknowledged, "None of the existing IR theories has enormous explanatory or predictive power."[27] Or, as Achen put it, "we have had difficulty with the real task of quantitative work—the discovery of reliable empirical generalizations."[28]

Statistical methods *can* produce important inferences about well-structured mass behavior. Take voting in American elections: there are many thousands or millions of data points, and research can validly look for likely patterns among further thousands or millions of such occurrences. In other words, quantitative methods seem useful in analyzing quantitative behavior. But the aggregate behavior of governments, or individual leaders, is not as easily converted into such large and comparable data sets.[29]

Future Generalizations Are Only about Possibilities

At their very best, statistical methods can do no more than suggest probabilities.[30] "Maximum likelihood estimates" is one common term.

Suppose, then, that the scientific generalization can do no more than establish a probability. But the difference in a soft generalization between a 20 percent probability and an 80 percent probability (describing proportions in the historic sample) is not so significant as a lesson for the next case. Why? Because governments do not behave according to a stochastic, random formula.[31]

Suppose a researcher concluded firmly that the probability of war in other international disputes between democracies around the world over the last two hundred years was 20 percent. That does not mean that the next case ($n + 1$) has only a 20 percent chance of war. For $n + 1$ we can rely on little more than a suggestive set of significant possibilities.

To illustrate this we can use an argument made recently by a well-known scholar. Suppose a president of the United States was told that China is a rising power and the United States is an established Great Power. Suppose he was further told that, based on social science analysis, in eleven out of fifteen cases since 1500, rising powers went to war against the established power.[32] Would any thoughtful leader then believe that this meant that this record established that there was a greater than 70 percent chance that in the next few years China would go to war against the United States?

No. No statement of any particular percentage is remotely valid, purely based on the history. Suppose, therefore, the only valid claim is that conflict with a rising power is a possibility. Of course it is. No one would need to canvass all the past histories in this simplified way to prove that. The possibility of conflict is already evident to any casual reader of the newspaper. Such a soft generalization about the future ends up gaining nothing from layering it with a veneer of historical data sifting.

Since the $n + 1$ probability fallacy is so obvious, why bother with all the apparatus to establish probabilities at all? Within the international relations subfield of political science, the scholars might say that they are not answering questions about a specific case. They are not interested in $n+1$. They are just interested in knowledge that may span generations past and future.

But if the supposed "lesson" amounts to no more than a suggestive possibility, then law-like generalizations about national or international behavior may actually be *worse* than useless. This is because their scientific veneer is meant to make them *seem* harder than they are. That is what makes them so seductive, combining the appearance of simplicity and scientific authority.

"The marking off of certain conclusions as alone truly science," John Dewey wrote, "whether mathematical or physical, is an historical incident. It sprang originally from man's desire for a certainty and peace which he could not attain practically in the absence of the arts of management and direction of natural conditions."[33] We are encouraged to rely on those generalizations deemed to be scientific, encouraged to be freer from doubt. In high-stakes policymaking, freedom from doubt is dangerous.

Dewey believed in the application of scientific inquiry to social problems. But he thought a valid theory only revealed more about what was possible, the "resources to be exploited in action." If the situation seemed obscure, Dewey urged analysts to examine the components of the situation at hand and remain "capable of enjoying the doubtful." Only those who "sustain and protract that state of doubt which is the stimulus to thorough inquiry" can "protect the mind against itself." After all, Dewey wrote, "the full and eventual reality of knowledge is carried in the individual case, not in general laws isolated from use in giving an individual case its meaning."[34]

We therefore find ourselves having made our way back to the assertions that opened this chapter. Between the two pathways to learning history's lessons, the path of simplification and the path of complexity, I am arguing for acceptance of complexity as a more reliable source of knowledge.

The challenge is then to make complex stories more legible. That means the use of conceptual tools that help to dissect choices in their historical moment.

If there are no easy shortcuts, the reader of history also returns to the challenge of getting the "harder" generalizations right, the foundational ones about what happened and why. And the foundations are stronger if they are built on more immersion in details of particulars.

History as a Re-enactment of Possibilities

To untangle what did happen, to unpack de Tocqueville's "accidents," the historian needs to consider too what was *not* chosen, what did *not* happen. And why.

Fixing only on what actually did happen in a past experience is what can convert the past episode from a menu of mind-opening options into a mind-closing axiom.[35] These axioms are almost always carried in the vehicle of some historical analogy, relating a present circumstance to some past outcome.[36]

Instead, "history teaches us about human nature and our future best choices by teaching us about *possibilities* rather than *regularities*."[37] We should not try too hard to use the past to build dikes "to contain [the] future's uncertainty," because "the more we trust these 'dikes,' the less they provoke our curiosity."[38]

Naturally people are tempted to boil down their experiences into pat lessons. One former secretary of defense even published a little book of his aphorisms, "Rumsfeld's Rules." They seem like the sort of lessons that Isaiah Berlin once scorned as "a very thin, generalized residue, and one far too unspecific to be of much help in a practical dilemma."[39]

But knowledge, like life, really does not need to be reduced to such precepts in order to communicate it. In fact, such distillations impair real communication of the knowledge by divorcing it even further from the contextual details that enrich the experience with real-life educational nutrients.[40]

Historical literature, like fictional literature, can be a path to understanding human nature and the possibilities that lie within it. What can be learned from any literature at all? People read stories because they are drawn to the depictions of people in situations. What was it like? How did they respond?

British historian and philosopher Robin Collingwood found in history a form of instructive re-enactment. Consider Julius Caesar's decision to take his army "cross the Rubicon" and challenge his Roman Republic. To understand Caesar's choice, to add it to the reservoir of knowledge about human nature and political judgments, Collingwood urged the use of critical judgment to enter Caesar's world with whatever evidence could be found: "This implies envisaging for himself the situation in which Caesar stood, and thinking for himself what Caesar thought about the situation and the possible ways of dealing with it."[41]

The work of the historian in this case is not mere reproduction or description. To offer insight, "this re-enactment is only accomplished . . . so far as the historian brings to bear on the problem all the powers of his own mind and all his knowledge of philosophy and politics. It is not a passive surrender to another's mind; it is a labour of active and therefore critical thinking." Such critical analysis "is not something secondary to tracing the history of it. It is an indispensable condition of the historical knowledge itself."[42]

The method I recommend has only a couple of steps. The first is to break the puzzling decision/outcome into its sequence of successive, different choices.

Then, for each, consider the possibilities attendant at each stage. Not only might this method improve the explanation; it makes the explanation a good deal more interesting for the reader. This is a kind of counterfactual analysis, constrained by contemporary evidence of plausibility. It analyzes roads not taken to see the turns that were.[43]

For instance, consider briefly the Japanese Empire's decision in 1941 to go to war against the United States and the British Empire. On its surface this was a very strange decision. Even in 1941 Japan would seem overmatched by such an assault. With hindsight we know what an utter disaster would ensue for Japan and millions of Japanese.

An initial breakdown of this seemingly strange Japanese choice would notice that there were actually at least three sets of choices.

First, in July 1941 Japan chose to occupy the southern half of French Indochina. This was valuable in itself and better positioned Japan for further expansion in Southeast Asia. Somewhat to Japan's surprise, the United States responded with a cutoff of oil and other commodity exports. These supplies were absolutely vital to Japan's military independence and capacity to continue its war in China.

Second, in September 1941, rather than just attack the mineral-rich British and Dutch possessions and hope the United States would stay out, Japan chose to go to war against the United States, too, *if* a suitable diplomatic understanding could not be worked out. If Japan had not directly attacked the United States, and had only gone after the British and Dutch, it was not 100 percent clear that the U.S. government would—or could—have gone to war with Japan. But the Roosevelt administration and Congress would not end up having to confront that problem.

Third, in November 1941 Japan chose to reject available U.S. terms and decided that a suitable diplomatic understanding was not possible. It proceeded with a war. The greatest sticking point was the U.S. insistence that Japan abandon its ongoing war of imperial expansion in China. This U.S. insistence was controversial in Washington; some top officials did not regard China's future as vital to the United States. And there was an obvious risk that the United States might slide into a war with Japan instead of a war with Germany. That could be disastrous for the United States because America's strategists had judged that Germany was the more important and more dangerous enemy. Again, the United States avoided that awkwardness. After Japan's attack, Germany declared war on the United States. Hitler did something unusual: he kept a promise. This was a secret promise he had made to the Japanese, to join them in the war if they would attack America.

At each of these times, for each of these sets of choices, different kinds of options seemed to come into view on all sides. The situation in the world was not static, either. For instance, look at when Japan made its risky decisions, then look at the military situation, at those moments, in the supreme battle then going on—the German invasion of the Soviet Union. In each case Japan made its decisions at times when the odds of a German victory over the USSR seemed good. Had Japan's decisions been put off, even delayed until December 1941, when a Soviet counteroffensive made it clear that German victory there would not come soon, Japanese leaders then would have had a different kind of evaluation to make.

The dire position of the Soviet Union earlier in 1941 had also been a key factor for the Americans. Some of them were conscious of great risks that might come with the August 1941 choice to impose oil sanctions against Japan. But the Americans were anxious to draw Japanese attention and energy away from a possible attack on the Soviet Union, an attack to help Germany destroy the USSR. The Americans achieved that objective, but found they had grabbed a tiger's tail.

The events leading to the Japanese attack on Pearl Harbor have been examined repeatedly and with care, and this little summary will be familiar to many historians. Yet it is relatively rare to see accounts that employ even this modest amount of complexity, that notice the different kinds of options available at each stage.[44] Though without that extra effort, it is much harder to understand the fateful choices on either side, Japanese or American.

Hindsight is not 20/20. In fact, as the 9/11 Commission report observed, hindsight blinds. It blinds because the path of what happened is so brightly lit that all the other possibilities are cast even more deeply into shadow. History lessons should try to overcome that blindness.

My method does dig a little deeper into a critical set of choices, requiring more of an effort to recover—to "re-enact," in Collingwood's term—the choices as perceived by people at the time. The method will certainly be recognizable to those who study social history, where some of the best scholars have painstakingly reconstructed microhistories to recover the uncertainties and curious little worlds of the past. But the study of a White House in any particular presidency is not so different from the study of a medieval village. Each has its folkways, its routines, and its votaries.

Political judgment, for Isaiah Berlin, was a "gift" that seemed to mean that "above all, a capacity for integrating a vast amalgam of constantly changing, multicolored, evanescent, perpetually overlapping data, too many, too swift, too intermingled to be caught and pinned down and labeled like so many individual butterflies." To Berlin it was this knowledge of the varied capacities inherent in a situation that great statesmen seem to have "in common with the great psychological novelists."[45]

To revisit these strange other worlds in the past, breaking down how some puzzling choices actually happened, does require some imagination. Our senses now sharpened to the "changing, multicolored, evanescent" beliefs that once held sway, we are that much better equipped for the amalgam we encounter every day.

Notes

1. Burke then elaborated that: "This method [turning history into precepts] turns [statesmen's] understanding from the object before them, and from the present exigencies of the world, to comparisons with former times, of which, after all, we can know very little and very imperfectly; and our guides, the historians, who are to give us their true interpretation, are often prejudiced, often ignorant, often fonder of system than of truth." From Burke's remarks on the policy of the Allies with respect to France, begun in October 1793, in *The Writings & Speeches of Edmund Burke*, vol. 4 (Boston: Little, Brown & Company, 1901), 468. I am indebted to Hiroshi Nakanishi of Kyoto University for calling my attention to this address by Burke.

2. See Warren Cohen, *The American Revisionists: The Lessons of Intervention in World War I* (University of Chicago Press, 1967). Cohen pays particular attention

to the influence of Harry Elmer Barnes, Charles Beard, C. Hartley Grattan, Walter Millis, and Charles Tansill.

3. Samuel Flagg Bemis, *A Diplomatic History of the United States* (New York: Henry Holt, 1936), the first of five editions. Shortly after World War II, Bemis decried the influence of historians like the ones studied by Cohen, though before the war few historians had done more than Bemis to preach the wisdom of America's long and splendid isolation from Europe's quarrels.

4. This was a line Rusk would use later in reacting to the protests against the Vietnam War. Dean Rusk, quoted in Thomas Zeiler, *Dean Rusk: Defending the American Mission Abroad* (Wilmington, Del.: Rowman and Littlefield, 2000), 10.

5. See Thomas Kuhn, *The Structure of Scientific Revolutions*, 4th and 50th anniv. ed. (1962; repr. University of Chicago Press, 2012), especially 1–9.

6. May, Neustadt, and I taught a course titled "The Uses of History in Public Affairs," and May and I taught it after Neustadt retired. May and I also regularly taught the course "Assessing Other Governments" in undergraduate classes and executive programs at Harvard that touched on many of the same issues.

7. A seminal essay is Ernest May, "The Nature of Foreign Policy: The Calculated versus the Axiomatic," *Daedalus* 91 (1962), 653–67. This was followed by Ernest R. May, *"Lessons" of the Past: The Use and Misuse of History in American Foreign Policy* (Oxford University Press, 1973). Neustadt and May published illustrations and suggestions for better use of historical reasoning in *Thinking in Time: The Uses of History for Decision Makers* (New York: Free Press, 1986). May's groundbreaking study of public and elite opinion, an aim that was unfortunately veiled by his book's title, is Ernest R. May, *American Imperialism: A Speculative Essay* (Chicago: Imprint, 1991); originally published in 1968, the 1991 edition added a useful introductory essay. Some illustrations of the way May turned his inquiry to the study of intelligence assessments are Ernest R. May, ed., *Knowing One's Enemies: Intelligence Assessment before the Two World Wars* (Princeton University Press, 1986); Ernest R. May and Philip Zelikow, eds., *Dealing with Dictators: Dilemmas of U.S. Diplomacy and Intelligence Analysis, 1945–1990* (Cambridge University Press, 2006); and key aspects of his landmark study of the 1940 fall of France, Ernest R. May, *Strange Victory: Hitler's Conquest of France* (New York: Hill and Wang, 2000).

8. The definitive French text is Alexis de Tocqueville, *Oeuvres Completes*, vol. 12: *Souvenirs*, edited by J. P. Mayer (Paris: Gallimard, 1964); for an English translation, see Alexis de Tocqueville, *Recollections*, edited by J. P. Mayer and translated by Alexander Teixeira de Mattos (Westport, Conn.: Greenwood, 1948), 67–68. Stephen Jay Gould, *Wonderful Life: The Burgess Shale and the Nature of History* (New York: W.W. Norton & Company, 1989), 289–90, makes a rather similar point in its discussion of natural history: "Invariant laws of nature impact the general forms and functions of organisms; they set the channels in which organic design must evolve. But the channels are so broad relative to the details that fascinate us! The

physical channels do not specify arthropods, annelids, mollusks, and vertebrates, but, at most, bilaterally symmetrical organisms based on repeated parts. The boundaries of the channels retreat even further into the distance when we ask the essential questions about our own origin. . . . When we set our focus upon the level of detail that regulates most common questions about the history of life, contingency dominates and the predictability of general form recedes to an irrelevant background."

9. May and I developed this template for our teaching during the 1990s. It is based on a framework persuasively articulated by a British lawyer, philosopher, and occasional public servant named Geoffrey Vickers in his book *The Art of Judgment* (1965; Beverly Hills, Calif.: SAGE Publications, 1995). An early elaboration of this template appears in the introduction May and I wrote for our edited volume, *Dealing with Dictators*, 1–17.

10. For scholars who work on theories of history, this distinction between particular explanations and generalized inference is sometimes described, following Wilhelm Windelband's 1894 formulation, as a contrast between "idiographic" and "nomothetic" sciences. There is a temptation even among historians to slight rigorous explanation of particular episodes as they embed their descriptions in some more universal generalization. See Allan Megill, *Historical Knowledge, Historical Error: A Contemporary Guide to Practice* (University of Chicago Press, 2007), 83–88. Megill is trying to attract more respect for particular descriptions. He also rightly urges historians to use more rigorous methods in explaining these particulars.

11. See Ben S. Bernanke, *Essays on the Great Depression* (Princeton University Press, 2000), viii, for Bernanke as historian: "A striking example of what can be learned by international comparisons is the fact, emphasized by Barry Eichengreen and Jeffrey Sachs, among others, that countries that abandoned the gold standard at an early stage recovered more quickly from the Depression. This robust empirical finding has proven to be the key to a greatly improved understanding of both the Depression itself and the effects of monetary policies and exchange rate systems in general, as I discuss extensively in this book." Bernanke also emphasizes nonmonetary factors in his historical analysis, though by these he means the effects of banking panics and business failures.

12. This is ably summarized in Charles P. Kindleberger, *The World in Depression 1929–1939*, rev. ed. (University of California Press, 1986), 142–29; and Zara Steiner, *The Lights That Failed: European International History 1919–1933* (Oxford University Press, 2005), 635–99. See also Stephen Schuker, "Central Bankers in the Dock," review of Liaquat Ahamed, *Lords of Finance: Bankers Who Broke the World*, H-Diplo, October 24, 2011 (http://h-diplo.org/essays/PDF/Schuker-Ahamed.pdf).

13. David Chalmers, Robert French, and Douglas Hofstadter, "High-Level Perception, Representation, and Analogy," in Douglas Hofstadter and the Fluid

Analogies Research Group, *Fluid Concepts and Creative Analogies: Computer Models of the Fundamental Mechanisms of Thought* (New York: Basic Books, 1995), 182.

14. Drawing from arguments made centuries ago by Immanuel Kant, see Ernest R. May, "History-Theory-Action," *Diplomatic History* 18 (1994), 589–603.

15. See Ernest May, Richard Rosecrance, and Zara Steiner, eds., *History and Neorealism* (Cambridge University Press, 2010).

16. See William James, *Essays in Radical Empiricism*, edited by R. B. Perry (1912; repr. New York: Longmans, Green, and Company, 1938), 40–41. James's principle of "radical empiricism" argues that philosophers should only debate "things definable in terms drawn from experience." See also William James, *The Meaning of Truth: A Sequel to "Pragmatism"* (1909; repr. Cambridge University Press, 1978), 6–7. A corollary principle is one of "natural realism." See Hilary and Ruth Anna Putnam, "What the Spilled Beans Can Spell: The Difficult and Deep Realism of William James," *Times Literary Supplement*, June 21, 1996. The James position is attacked by some as holding that it makes all reality either subjective or instrumental, as suits the observer, but such an attack misunderstands James. For more elaboration, especially on the "interpenetration," not indistinguishability, of fact and value, see Hilary Putnam, *Pragmatism: An Open Question* (Cambridge University Press, 1995), 7–23; see also John Searle, *The Construction of Social Reality* (New York: Free Press, 1995).

17. W. V. Quine, *Pursuit of Truth*, rev. ed. (Cambridge University Press, 1990), 98. The artificiality of the categories is a necessary by-product of the quest to produce scientific generalizations in a manner that emulates the natural sciences. In the natural sciences, the use of sharply defined categories of phenomena is justified because the method is "applied only to carefully chosen subject matter under highly contrived conditions." The social domain also has categories, but their delineations are rarely as sharp as those in which "deductive argument can be applied with reasonable certainty. Without such categories, conventional scientific method is hamstrung." John Ziman, *Reliable Knowledge: An Exploration of the Grounds for Belief in Science* (Cambridge University Press, 1978), 160–62. See also the related argument in the works of Nelson Goodman, especially *Fact, Fiction, and Forecast*, 4th ed. (Cambridge University Press, 1983). Hence the search for measurable choices of a highly repetitive character (in voting, for example, or in consumer purchases) among utility theorists in the social sciences. For a skeptical view of the possibilities, see Ziman, *Reliable Knowledge*, 158–86.

18. Carmen Reinhart and Kenneth Rogoff, *This Time Is Different: Eight Centuries of Financial Folly* (Princeton University Press, 2009).

19. See Thomas Herndon, Michael Ash, and Robert Pollin, "Does High Public Debt Consistently Stifle Economic Growth? A Critique of Reinhart and Rogoff," *Cambridge Journal of Economics* 38, no. 2 (2014), 257–79; Carmen Reinhart and

Kenneth Rogoff, "Debt, Growth, and the Austerity Debate," *New York Times*, April 26, 2013; and Robert Pollin and Michael Ash, "Debt and Growth: A Response to Reinhart and Rogoff," *New York Times*, April 29, 2013.

20. Gary King, Robert O. Keohane, and Sidney Verba, *Designing Social Inquiry: Scientific Inference in Qualitative Research* (Princeton University Press, 1994), 43, emphasis in the original.

21. Paul Diesing, *How Does Social Science Work? Reflections on Practice* (University of Pittsburgh Press, 1991), 25.

22. John Horgan, *The End of Science: Facing the Limits of Knowledge in the Twilight of the Scientific Age* (New York: Perseus Books, 1996), 234.

23. Nancy Cartwright, *How the Laws of Physics Lie* (Oxford University Press, 1983), 13, 11, 19. "Fundamental laws," she adds, "do not govern objects in reality, they govern only objects in models." Ibid., 18, 109. For her discussion of the descriptive weaknesses of one of the strongest law-like generalizations in all of natural science, the law of gravity, see 56–67.

24. See John Lewis Gaddis, "History, Science, and the Study of International Relations," in *Explaining International Relations since 1945*, edited by Ngaire Woods (Oxford University Press, 1996).

25. William James, *A Pluralistic Universe* (1909; repr. New York: Longmans, Green, and Company, 1947), 349–50; Christopher Achen, "Toward a New Political Methodology: Microfoundations and ART," *Annual Review of Political Science* (2002), 423, 424.

26. Philip Anderson, "More Is Different," *Science* (August 4, 1972), 393. For a different road to a similar conclusion, see also Murray Gell-Mann, *The Quark and the Jaguar: Adventures in the Simple and the Complex* (New York: W. H. Freeman & Co., 1994), 76–80, 100–06, 116–19.

27. John Mearsheimer and Stephen Walt, "Leaving Theory Behind: Why Hypothesis Testing Has Become Bad for IR," Faculty Research Working Paper RW13-001 (John F. Kennedy School of Government, 2013).

28. Some, like Achen, think the "democratic peace" hypothesis may have made the cut; see Achen, "Toward a New Political Methodology," 424. Though, in that illustration, other critics of statistical uses have pointed out that the democratic peace hypothesis was more about correlation. There had actually not been good tests for any particular theory about just what the cause might be that explained these correlations. Bear Braumoeller and Anne Sartori, "The Promise and Perils of Statistics in International Relations," in *Models, Numbers, and Cases: Methods for Studying International Relations*, edited by Detlef Sprinz and Yael Wolinsky-Namias (University of Michigan Press, 2004), 134. On the democratic peace hypothesis Achen also acknowledges that it would be helpful if the labelers knew better just "what 'democracy' meant" in the way they typecast different governments across history; Achen, "Toward a New Political Methodology," 442.

29. Philosophically, the compared behaviors must be scientifically homogeneous. This comparability will be greatest in situations that are epistemically objective, so that the facts making up the situation do not depend for their existence on a particular person's attitude toward them, and where the reactions to the situations have a structured, repetitive quality that can be measured in ways that are also epistemically objective; see the discussion of ontological and epistemic objectivity in Searle, *The Construction of Social Reality*, 7–23. This is why, in the natural sciences, there is so much emphasis on physical observations that can be perceived identically by independent observers. Ziman, *Reliable Knowledge*, 42–56; see also Ziman's earlier point (28) that the science of physics actually defines itself as being concerned only with those aspects of reality that are amenable to mathematical analysis. On the problems of using statistical associations to assess more subjective behavior, see, for example, Albert S. Yee, "The Causal Effects of Ideas on Policies," *International Organization* 50 (1996), 69, 71–76.

30. As Max Weber explained early on, "It is customary to designate various sociological generalizations . . . as scientific 'laws.' These are in fact typical probabilities confirmed by observation." Max Weber, "The Methodological Foundations of Sociology," translated by A. M. Henderson and Talcott Parsons, reprinted in Weber, *Sociological Writings*, edited by Wolf Heydebrand (New York: Bloomsbury Academic, 1994), 244. The covering law model of historical explanation usually associated with Carl Hempel actually treats such "laws" as probability statements. For a defense of Hempel's position in these terms, see May Brodbeck, "Methodological Individualisms: Definition and Reduction," in *Philosophical Analysis and History*, edited by William H. Dray (Westport, Conn.: Greenwood, 1966); and Carl G. Hempel, "Reasons and Covering Laws in Historical Explanation," in *The Philosophy of History*, edited by Patrick Gardiner (Oxford University Press, 1974). A much wittier defense of generalizations from history is offered in Edward Hallett Carr, *What Is History?* (New York: Vintage, 1962), 74–143. For a sampling of the best criticisms of the attempt to derive covering laws of historical explanation, see the essays by Isaiah Berlin, Maurice Mandelbaum, and especially William Dray reprinted in the Gardiner collection. For a brief overview, see also William H. Dray, *Philosophy of History* (Englewood Cliffs, N.J.: Prentice-Hall, 1964), 4–11.

31. See the important and very similar argument made in James D. Fearon, "Selection Effects and Deterrence," *International Interactions* 28, no. 1 (2002), 5–29.

32. This particular argument, for instance, was used in Graham Allison, "Thucydides' Trap Has Been Sprung in the Pacific," *Financial Times*, August 21, 2012; and again in Graham Allison, "Obama and Xi Must Think Broadly to Avoid a Classic Trap," *New York Times*, June 6, 2013.

33. John Dewey, *The Quest for Certainty: A Study of the Relation of Knowledge and Action* (New York: Minton Balch and Company, 1929), 220.

34. Alan Ryan, *John Dewey and the High Tide of American Liberalism* (New York: W. W. Norton and Company, 1995), 99; James Campbell, *Understanding John Dewey: Nature and Cooperative Intelligence* (Chicago: Open Court Press, 1995), 52; Dewey, *The Quest for Certainty*, 207–08, see also 228. James made the same point: "*Theories thus become instruments, not answers to enigmas, in which we can rest.*" See William James, *Pragmatism: A New Name for Some Old Ways of Thinking* (1907; Cambridge University Press, 1978), 48, emphasis in the original.

35. See May, "The Nature of Foreign Policy."

36. May, later joined by Richard Neustadt, thus naturally moved from writing about axioms to writing about analogies. He eventually came to a position that comprehensively rejected the use of historical cases to establish structured, predictive models of probable behavior; see May, "History-Theory-Action." On the temptations and dangers of analogical reasoning, see also Yuen Foong Khong, *Analogies at War: Korea, Munich, Dien Bien Phu, and the Vietnam Decisions of 1965* (Princeton University Press, 1992); Robert Jervis, *Perception and Misperception in International Politics* (Princeton University Press, 1976); and Daniel Kahneman, Paul Slovic, and Amos Tversky, *Judgment under Uncertainty: Heuristics and Biases* (Cambridge University Press, 1982).

37. Michael Scriven, "Causes, Connections and Conditions in History," in Dray, ed., *Philosophical Analysis and History*, 250, emphasis in the original. For the sympathetic argument that generalizations about regularities can yield plausible association, but that these produce only a hypothesis of appropriateness, see Rex Martin, *Historical Explanation: Re-enactment and Practical Inference* (Cornell University Press, 1977). Megill, *Historical Knowledge, Historical Error*, 154–55, posits that "the only view of explanation that works for historians is one that focuses on counterfactuality and that allows the regularity criterion to recede into the background." I am not sure that most historians adhere to this view, however.

38. Bertrand de Jouvenel, *The Art of Conjecture*, translated by Nikita Lary (New York: Basic Books, 1967), 47. To similar effect, see Harvey Brooks, "The Typology of Surprises in Technology, Institutions, and Development," in *Sustainable Development of the Biosphere*, edited by W. C. Clark and R. E. Munn (Cambridge University Press, 1986), especially 326, 335–39.

39. Isaiah Berlin, "On Political Judgment," *New York Review of Books* (October 3, 1996), 26, 27.

40. Michael Polanyi, *Personal Knowledge: Towards a Post-Critical Philosophy*, rev. ed. (University of Chicago Press, 1962), 33–37, 49–65, 69–124; see also Max Black, *Models and Metaphors: Studies in Language and Philosophy* (Cornell University Press, 1962), 25–47, 219–43.

41. Robin G. Collingwood, *The Idea of History*, edited by Jan van der Dussen (Cambridge University Press, 1994; essays originally published between 1936 and 1940), 215.

42. Ibid. See also William Dray, *History as Re-enactment: R.G. Collingwood's Idea of History* (Oxford University Press, 1995).

43. As Megill, *Historical Knowledge, Historical Error*, 153, notes, "In imagining how things might have been different, the restrained counterfactualist tries to understand better what actually did happen." Following on work by James Fearon more than twenty years ago, Robert Jervis, "Counterfactuals, Causation, and Complexity," in *Counterfactual Thought Experiments in World Politics*, edited by Philip E. Tetlock and Aaron Belkin (Princeton University Press, 1996), 309–16, notes that there is also growing acceptance in political science that "counterfactuals can alert us to the possible operation of dynamics and pathways that we would otherwise be prone to ignore." Ibid., 308.

44. One especially insightful history of Roosevelt's decisions about war and peace in 1941 does most of its work by reconstructing the world as it presented itself to the president month by month during that year, reconstructing what he seemed to be choosing at any given moment and why one course seemed more appropriate than another at that time. See Waldo Heinrichs, *Threshold of War: Franklin D. Roosevelt and American Entry into World War II* (Oxford University Press, 1988); see also the important work in David Kaiser, *No End Save Victory: How FDR Led the Nation into War* (New York: Basic Books, 2014).

45. Berlin, "On Political Judgment," 27–28.

About the Authors

HAL BRANDS is an associate professor of public policy and history at Duke University and the author of three books, including *What Good Is Grand Strategy? Power and Purpose in American Statecraft from Harry S. Truman to George W. Bush* (2014). For 2015–16, he is a Council on Foreign Relations International Affairs Fellow at the U.S. Department of Defense.

H. W. BRANDS holds the Jack S. Blanton Sr. Chair in History at the University of Texas at Austin. He has written on presidents, politics, and foreign policy; his books include *What America Owes the World: The Struggle for the Soul of Foreign Policy* (1998); *T.R.: The Last Romantic* (on Theodore Roosevelt, 1998); *The Strange Death of American Liberalism* (2001); *Traitor to His Class: The Privileged Life and Radical Presidency of Franklin Delano Roosevelt* (2009); and *Reagan: The Life* (2015).

PETER FEAVER is a professor of political science and public policy at Duke University. For 2005–07 he served as special adviser for strategic planning and institutional reform on the National Security Council.

WILLIAM INBODEN is the executive director of the William P. Clements, Jr. Center for National Security and an associate professor at the Lyndon Baines Johnson School of Public Affairs, both at the University of Texas at Austin. He previously served as senior director for strategic planning on the National Security Council, as a member of the U.S. State Department's policy planning staff, and as a staff member in both the U.S. Senate and House of Representatives.

MARK ATWOOD LAWRENCE is an associate professor of history at the University of Texas at Austin. He is author of *Assuming the Burden: Europe and the American Commitment to War in Vietnam* (2005) and *The Vietnam War: A Concise International History* (2008).

THOMAS G. MAHNKEN is the Jerome E. Levy Chair of Economic Geography and National Security at the U.S. Naval War College and a senior research professor at the Philip Merrill Center for Strategic Studies at the Johns Hopkins University's Paul H. Nitze School of Advanced International Studies. Between 2006 and 2009 he was deputy assistant secretary of defense for policy planning.

JENNIFER M. MILLER is an assistant professor of history at Dartmouth College. Her main research interests are the early Cold War, U.S.-Japanese relations, and the history of the Pacific region. She is currently writing a book titled *Contested Alliance: The United States, Japan, and Democracy in the Cold War.*

MICHAEL COTEY MORGAN is an assistant professor of history at the University of North Carolina at Chapel Hill. He is currently writing a book on the origins of the 1975 Helsinki Final Act.

GUNTHER PECK is an associate professor of history and public policy at Duke University and the author of *Reinventing Free Labor: Padrones and Immigrant Workers in the North American West, 1880–1930* (2000), which won three prizes. His current work focuses on white slavery and anti-human trafficking campaigns.

JAMES B. STEINBERG is dean of the Maxwell School of Citizenship and Public Affairs at Syracuse University. He has served as deputy secretary of state, deputy national security adviser, director of the U.S. State Department's policy planning staff, and deputy assistant secretary of state for analysis at the Department of State's Bureau of Intelligence and Research. His most recent book, coauthored with Michael O'Hanlon, is *Strategic Reassurance and Resolve: U.S.-China Relations in the Twenty-First Century* (2014).

JEREMI SURI is the Mack Brown Distinguished Chair for Leadership in Global Affairs at the University of Texas at Austin, and a professor there in the Department of History and the Lyndon B. Johnson School of Public Affairs. He is the author and editor of six books, including, most recently, *Foreign Policy Breakthroughs: Cases in Successful Diplomacy* (2015).

PHILIP ZELIKOW is the White Burkett Miller Professor of History at the University of Virginia, where he has also served as dean of the Graduate School of Arts and Sciences. He has also held a number of full- and part-time positions in the U.S. government.

Index

CPSIA information can be obtained at www.ICGtesting.com
Printed in the USA
LVOW10s0612151015

458354LV00004B/4/P